Real Estate Markets
An Introduction

MURTAZA HAIDER

DEDICATION

This book is dedicated to Sophia, Mikael and Massem.

CONTENTS

PREFACE

It happens at breakfast tables. It happens at dinner tables. It even happens at restaurants. After gossiping about friends and family, rehashing the scores from last night's game about one's favourite sports franchise, and exchanging tips about the new movie or show on Netflix, the conversation often gravitates to "what's happening with the real estate market?" Not surprisingly, everyone has an opinion about real estate. Except for a few, most believe they have the inside scoop on real estate. With confidence and no hint of self-doubt, friends and family members sharing a meal will make predictions about real estate markets.

For most consumers, housing is their largest investment. After taxes, shelter costs constitute one of the largest components of household expenses. Buying, renting, and selling housing involves almost everyone. The ability to participate in such a large market, be able to borrow huge sums from financial institutions at very lucrative interest rates, making purchases of assets whose value is in multiples of one's annual income makes housing in particular and real estate in general, attractive to most.

During boom times, the conversation is about investments and benefiting from the equity one has in housing. During tough times, concerns about meeting the shelter costs, may that be rent or mortgage payment, becomes a big concern. At the same time, housing accounts for a significant component of the national economy. Outstanding mortgage debt is in trillions of dollars in Canada and much more so in the United States. Before 2007, housing markets were seldom the primary focus of investment banks and governments. The Great Recession in 2007 – 09 changed that. A crisis brought about by subprime mortgages resulted in a contagion that brought economic and financial markets down across the globe. Since then, any sudden or massive movement in housing markets or a change in the status of borrowers attracts immediate scrutiny by financial institutions and government regulators.

Despite the widespread interest in real estate among borrowers, lenders, and regulators, there are hardly any books available that could inform the decision-making of those involved or interested in real estate markets. The specialized knowledge, restricted to academic journals and professional publications, is often beyond the reach of those who need it the most. The academic literature in urban economics is rich in housing and real estate market research, yet the prevalence of jargon and overzealous use of calculus and econometrics restricts the reach of such knowledge and deprives it of a broader readership. Hence, access to specialized knowledge in real estate suffers from scarcity.

This book addresses the accessibility gap to specialized knowledge in real estate markets. The book draws heavily from the academic literature and data and translates the specialized knowledge so that it is accessible to students, real estate practitioners, and public-sector policymakers. Consider that this book does not expect readers to know that "rent-seeking" in economics does not refer to a landlord seeking rents from tenants but refers to an entity that is trying to profit without contributing to productivity.

The other key distinguishing features of this book are that it is topical and issues-oriented. Topics and issues addressed in this book relate to the current challenges facing real estate markets. Furthermore, the book focuses on the ongoing debates in real estate markets and tries to answer the questions being posed to businesses and policymakers. For instance, does rent control improve or worsen the long-term welfare of renters? The coverage of rent control in the popular press often suggests that such measures are necessary to secure shelter for low-income households. However, a preponderance of evidence suggests otherwise. Hence, the narrative in this book is framed around current issues and supported by empirical evidence.

As I write this preface in September 2020, an op-ed in the *Globe and Mail*, one of Canada's national newspapers, argued that the spike in housing prices observed primarily in Toronto and Vancouver in the past few years was a result of "strong demand pressures" and that housing supply scarcity is not the issue.[1] Supply skeptics, my term of affection for those who ignore the fact that housing demand has far exceeded housing supply resulting in pressures on prices, get a special mention in the book in Chapter 6, where I discuss in detail the investment processes behind the development of new real estate. Another indication of the book's currency is a detailed chapter that focusses on how pandemics, especially COVID-19, affect real estate markets.

Another distinguishing feature of this book is that it is unapologetically Canadian. The data, case studies, empirical evidence, and the narrative focuses mostly on Canadian real estate markets. I have studied and taught land development, real estate markets and urban economics for almost 24 years in Canada. I have often struggled to find Canadian examples in academic literature to support my research and teaching. Often, reading lists and textbooks in real estate curricula in Canada are based on research with examples from the US or the UK. Hence, generations of students in Canada in urban planning, business management, geography, and other related disciplines have been trained on real estate facts and research from other countries. A quick look at the book's index will reveal our obvious Canadian bias.

---

[1] Gordon, Josh. 2020. The 'supply crisis' in Canada's housing market isn't backed up by the evidence. *The Globe and Mail.* September 13, 2020.
https://www.theglobeandmail.com/opinion/article-the-supply-crisis-in-canadas-housing-market-isnt-backed-up-by-the/.

This book is written primarily for students and practitioners interested in the functioning of real estate markets. The accessible writing style is free of jargon and attempts to translate knowledge from academic journals and trade publications. Topics in the book are chosen to relate to those studying business, management, geography and urban planning. The choice of topics and the level of complexity in the book is such that it is suitable for an undergraduate course focusing on housing or real estate markets. At the same time, the breadth of topics addressed in the book also makes it suitable for graduate courses in business and urban planning. The book intentionally avoids illustrating technical topics using calculus or econometrics.

Since the book is focused on applied challenges in real estate markets by focusing on topics that concern borrowers, lenders, regulators, and other real to state stakeholders, such as brokers and agents, the book should be of value to those preparing for licensing exams in real estate or are interested in improving their professional credentials.

The book is organized as follows. The opening chapter focuses on how demographics are one of the driving forces behind the functioning of real estate markets. The chapter focuses on key demographics, such as first-time homebuyers, the millennials, seniors, single women, immigrants, and students, among others, to illustrate how housing needs and demand is differentiated.

The second chapter illustrates the workings of housing markets in large and small Canadian cities. It explores the spatial diversity in housing market outcomes across Canada and identifies behavioural responses to policy changes that may push or pull housing transactions from one time period to the other. The chapter discusses fundamental changes in regulatory frameworks, such as the introduction of mortgage stress tests in January 2018, which influenced the housing market outcomes in Canada.

The third chapter discusses how real estate markets reacted to COVID-19. Since the lockdown measures were enforced in mid-March, real estate markets in Canada have been on a roller coaster ride with precipitous declines in March and April followed by stability in May and a resurgence since July 2020. Early government intervention, supported by lenders and financial institutions, resulted in loan forbearance and a freeze on rental evictions. These measures helped maintain stability in housing markets and prevented the bloodbath many expected. At the same time, some businesses suffered the brunt of the economic lockdown, and many are not expected to survive. Hence, real estate in the hospitality, tourism, and restaurant sectors suffered a significant loss in revenue and faced a crisis of survival. The chapter discusses in detail what measures worked in stabilizing the real estate markets and how borrowers, lenders, landlords, and renters collaborated to avoid even deeper losses.

Chapter 4 is focused on housing affordability. The rapid increase in housing prices, which have been out of step with the increase in household incomes over the past few years in Toronto, Vancouver and some other large housing markets, has been a concern for Canadian families. The government response to improve housing affordability was on and off the mark. Chapter 4 discusses some government initiatives, such as shared equity mortgages, and evaluate their efficacy.

Real estate markets, especially housing, are governed by diverse regulations enacted by the three tiers of government. Essentially, local or municipal governments enact laws that govern the use of land. However, senior tiers of government also enable or restrict land and property use. Chapter 5 builds on the dialogue on regulatory issues discussed earlier in Chapter 2 and focuses on government regulations that impact home buying and selling. For instance, mortgage stress tests introduced in January 2018 raised the conditions for obtaining a mortgage by requiring borrowers to qualify for a mortgage at a rate approximately 2% higher than the contracted rate with the lender. The chapter reviews changes in regulations such as the stress test or a land transfer tax imposed on foreign homebuyers and their impact on housing markets.

Chapter 6 focuses on the mechanics and entities necessary for the development of new real estate or to promote and facilitate transactions in real estate markets. Construction of any real estate requires investments and investors. Investors are also risk-takers whose expectations of the future returns, pejoratively called speculation, is necessary for new construction without which the initial mobility capital to advance these construction projects would be missing. Furthermore, this book repeatedly makes a case for additional supply to counter the increase in housing prices resulting from an increase in demand for housing. Hence, investments in new housing construction by investors is seen as a pivotal driver to expand the real estate stock in Canada. Other issues, such as a lack of adequate public infrastructures, such as roads, water supply, or drainage, are discussed to illustrate the prerequisites for land development. A brief discussion of the alarm raised about the use of laundered money in real estate is also presented with the argument that the hue and cry about laundered money being behind the increase in housing prices in British Columbia lacks hard evidence.

Almost one in three Canadians are renters. In big cities, such as Montréal, Toronto, and Vancouver, the share of renter households is much higher. In fact, in Montréal, renters outnumber owners by a large margin. Chapter 7, therefore, focuses on the rental market in Canada. It takes a deep dive into the reasons that stifle the supply of purpose-built rental housing in Canada in the early 70s. It also critically evaluates the oft-cited quick fixes, such as rent control, to illustrate that such restrictive interventions constrain the supply of new rental housing, contribute to the deterioration of the existing rental housing stock, and limit the choices of renters in the long run.

Chapter 8 embraces the new urban realities where the development of real estate has gone beyond the urban core and is now concentrated in the suburbs. The chapter highlights how the search for Amazon's new headquarter found homes in suburban locations though many large urban centres competed to host the planned second headquarter for the retailing giant. The chapter also addresses myths and misconceptions about the enabling interventions for new development. It critically evaluates the limits of Tax Increment Financing in promoting new development. It also addresses the interaction between transportation accessibility and new development. Lastly, it takes a quick look at the emergence of new transportation technologies, such as autonomous vehicles, and their role in redefining the urban landscape in the future.

Real estate transactions are partially a result of the emotional highs and lows individuals experience as they evaluate and decide upon what real estate to buy or rent. At the same time, real estate agents, also humans, also respond to behavioural stimuli and incentives. Chapter 9 briefly discusses the behavioural underpinnings of real estate markets by looking at what motivates real estate agents, homebuyers and sellers. It looks at the thorny issues involving motivations and biases in the real estate industry, income falsification by homebuyers, and behavioural responses of buyers who might be willing to pay more for a property in a particular month of the year.

The final two chapters in this book are forward-looking, with chapter 10 focusing on the emerging trends in new types of real estate offerings and Chapter 11 focusing on the use of technology in real estate, known as *proptech*.

Chapter 10 presents a discussion on how real estate responds and reacts to changes in economic and social norms. Last year, the Canadian government legalized the recreational use of marijuana and, at the same time, permitted individuals to grow a limited amount of marijuana plant for their personal use. Besides, the production of cannabis products by licensed producers and distribution by retail outlets was also legalized. This opened a new use for the warehouse, greenhouse, and retail real estate. Whereas the initial response was one of elation and estimates of *high* returns on investments in real estate focusing on the production and distribution of cannabis products were in plenty, subsequent market performance did not share the exuberance felt earlier by investors and some market watchers. Chapter 10, therefore, presents a critical review of emerging trends, such as the legalization of marijuana, innovations in short-term rentals, such as Airbnb, and innovative ways to assemble land to produce multi-family housing.

The advances in computer and information technology have impacted all sectors of the economy and are now increasingly impacting the real estate industry. Chapter 11 identifies how ubiquitous computing and information technology are providing new ways to bring buyers and sellers together. The real estate brokerage industry is set for a reset with technology ready to redefine the transactional landscape but also providing ways and avenues to expand the scope of businesses possible in the real estate sector. At the same time, upcoming technologies, such as blockchain and artificial intelligence, are also going to influence how real estate is bought and sold. The chapter also discusses the importance of ready availability of real estate transaction data for innovators to create new products and services to benefit the industry and other stakeholders. The reluctance to release data or to limit its use for the benefit of the sector is also discussed. Lastly, the chapter illustrates how building management will change and evolve by embracing technology for sustainable and profitable operations of large and small real estate.

ACKNOWLEDGMENTS

This book and I owe a mountain of debt to colleagues, family, friends, and mentors who have helped me over the years in my academic pursuits. I started researching real estate markets in 1996, when I decided to pursue graduate education. I researched housing prices and developed a housing valuation model (hedonic price model) as the key deliverable for my Master's thesis at the University of Toronto. Later, I developed forecasting models to capture the behavioural underpinnings of homebuilders and land developers. Over the past 24 years, I continued analyzing real estate markets as an academic, researcher, and consultant.

This book benefits from the years of research I have done in housing markets in particular and real estate in general. The book also draws from a series of columns I have been writing for Post Media in collaboration with Stephen Moranis. Many ideas presented in this book originated with Stephen whose family has been in the real estate business for decades. This book would not be possible without his contribution to generating ideas and introducing me to the nuances of the real estate industry, which as an outsider, I would have certainly missed.

Over the past few years, I have been fortunate to collaborate with Liam Donaldson, who is a senior researcher with the Urban Analytics Institute at Ryerson University. Liam and I started collaborating when he was a graduate student in a transportation planning course that I taught. Later, he completed his Masters under my supervision and, since then, has been a research collaborator on several projects with me. He has read, edited, and organized several chapters in this book as it benefits from his extensive edits for which I am truly grateful.

I am also grateful to my editors at Financial Post, especially Joe Hood and Andy Holloway, who have been diligently editing our columns that have appeared over 800 times in the Financial Post and its sister publications since November 2017. I am also thankful to Paul Godfrey and Nicole MacAdam, who championed our column and supported the idea for informed commentary on real estate markets. Thanks are also due to the graphics team at Post Media, who turn data into eye-catching charts, some of which are highlighted in the book.

I am also deeply indebted to my friend, Antoine Haroun, who has been one of the strongest proponents of this book and the one I wrote earlier. Antoine and I have been friends since our days as graduate students at the University of Toronto. Though his focus is on technology, as he serves as the chief information officer for Canada's second-largest school board, he is one of the most informed individuals on housing markets. Our shared interest in housing helped us co-author a paper on the impact of high-voltage power lines on property values. Antoine and his wife, Rita Sawaya, have been generous friends whose support and encouragement have always been available when I needed it.

I am also grateful to my colleagues at Ryerson University. I teach in the School of Real Estate Management, along with a team of highly accomplished academics who are authorities in their own right. I have abundantly drawn from their knowledge and expertise over the years through numerous conversations, which facilitated exchange of ideas and papers.

My research as a graduate student was supported by data provided by the Toronto Regional Real Estate Board (TRREB). Working with a data set comprising half a million transactions, I developed models to predict housing prices and valuations for commercial real estate. Without the generous support from TRREB, I would not have been able to finish my research, nor would I have developed a data-driven understanding of the real estate industry. I have been, and will always be, grateful to TRREB and, by extension, the Canadian Real Estate Association, whose data I use to write columns and produce research.

Real estate research is not possible without data and the tools to manipulate it. In this regard, I have been fortunate to have enjoyed the generous support from Caliper Corporation as they equipped my research labs with software, earlier when I taught at McGill University and now at Ryerson University. Dr. Howard Slavin and Stewart Berry facilitated access to the GIS software, Maptitude and TransCAD, and provided copious amounts of demographic data to help me generate maps and spatial insights. Some maps in the book were produced using Maptitude, which remains my tool of choice for spatial analytics.

Though I started formal research in real estate in the mid-nineties, however, housing has been a topic of conversation at our breakfast table even as I grew up in Pakistan. My younger brothers, Irteza and Mustafa, were and continue to be sounding boards for my ideas as they bring market insights and infrastructure engineering expertise to the conversations.

My family has always been my strength and motivation. My late parents were educators. They instilled in us the love for books and a quest for forthrightness. I strive to live up to the ideals they set for us. My wife, Sophia has been a patient and steadfast supporter of my research. I have benefited not just from her love and encouragement but also from her insights about the functioning of financial markets.

1 DEMOGRAPHICS AND REAL MARKETS

Demographics, according to David Foot, explain two-thirds of everything. Canada's foremost demographer and an academic economist, Professor Foot, is credited with the quote. He alerted the businesses and policymakers to the role demographics play in all aspects of consumer behaviour. In this chapter, we explore the intersection of demographics with housing markets. Some demographic trends have an overwhelming influence on Canada's housing markets. The falling fertility rate below the replacement levels means that Canada must rely on immigration to sustain its population and economic growth.

Demographics have a direct bearing on homeownership decisions. A household's decision to own or rent is determined, albeit partially, by household's demographics. Single-person households are more likely to rent, whereas households with children are more likely to own. There are two exceptions to the preceding statement, yet it holds for most.

In this chapter, we explore how demographics interact with housing markets. We focus on specific cohorts that are relevant to present-day Canada's housing and economic markets. We begin in this chapter with a discussion about the unique demographics of the millennials who are the focus of governments and businesses all over. We determine whether millennials are different from other cohorts, such as the baby boomers or that their consumption behaviour is similar to the cohorts that preceded them. In the same vein, we explore how housing choices of millennials differ, and a striking feature of their unique housing preferences is the greater willingness to continue living with the parents.

From millennials, we shift our attention to immigrants, who are vital to Canada's population and economic growth. We explore the question of what impact immigrants have on housing markets. We also explore how immigrants (by overwhelmingly opting for homeownership) have been able to, over time, reduce the wealth gap with the Canadian born cohorts. From

1

a slight disadvantage starting point, immigrants' dedication to homeownership has helped them increase their wealth rapidly over time as they catch up with the native-born Canadians over time.

We also look at the unique circumstances of single women in Canada and the United States where women have become more active in homebuying than the women in previous generations. This is partly due to the increase in education levels of younger women today who constitute the majority of university graduates in Canada.

Because of the falling fertility rate, Canada's senior population has been growing at a faster rate such that seniors over the age of 65 outnumber, for the first time, children 14 years old or younger. The rapid increase in senior population could pose unique housing demands that may not only affect the housing needs of seniors but also of younger cohorts who would have to wait until the senior-held housing stock is vacated.

We then focus our attention on public housing for low-income households who have been priced out of the housing markets. The rapid escalation of housing prices since 2015 and the subsequent increase in rents implies that a larger segment of working-age population does not earn enough to pay even the minimum market rents. It is incumbent upon governments in the society to provide enough safety nets so that those who have been priced out of the markets are still able to find shelter at affordable costs. We review research from Toronto that shows that an investment in subsidized housing offers significant benefits to the society that go beyond the benefit related to housing markets.

We conclude the chapter with a focus on student housing. Currently, approximately two million students are enrolled in postsecondary institutions in Canada. Given Canada's population of approximately 37 million, post-secondary students present a sizable cohort. Their housing needs in the vicinity of institutions of higher learning are an important consideration for promoting higher education in Canada.

DEMOGRAPHICS GOVERN HOME OWNERSHIP

Demographics explain two-thirds of everything, contends David Foot, Canada's foremost demographer and a bestselling author.[2] Home ownership is no different. At a certain point in their lives, most individuals, responding to demographic triggers, give up renting for owning.

Younger adults under the age of 30 are more likely to rent than to own. But something happens at 30, and the majority of those above that threshold are owners. Understanding the demographic factors that determine housing demand is critical for public policy, and construction and mortgage finance.

---

[2] http://www.footwork.com/bbe.asp

Why is 30 a magic number when it comes to home ownership? A series of life-cycle events and a natural progression in age and income enable drastic changes in how and where we live. Settling down with a spouse or partner, starting a family or starting to think about it, and earning enough to save for a down-payment are discrete developments that influence the home ownership decision.

The relationship between household income and home ownership is quite straightforward. Census data reveals that higher income earners are much more likely to own than rent. Stated differently, homeowners have significantly higher incomes in Canada than those who rent. However, when we mix location with income, differences emerge.

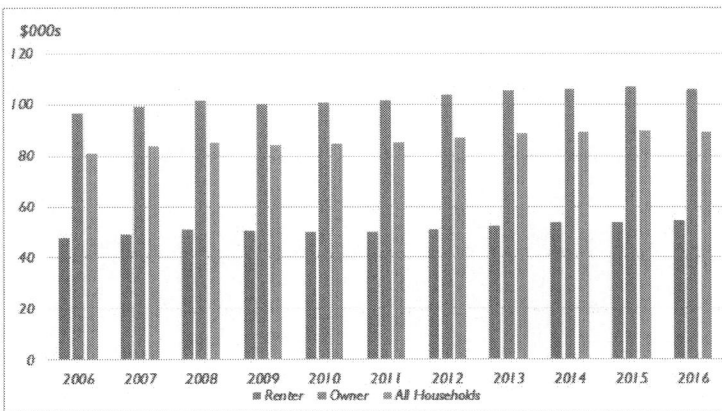

Figure 1.1 – Average before-tax household income (owner and renter), 2016 constant dollars

Source: CMHC, Retrieved on October 26, 2019[3]

Consider that most Canadian households earning under $30,000 are renters. The same is true for Vancouver. However, in Montreal most earning under $60,000 rent, pointing to the unique housing stock and taste preferences where renting is a preferred choice for most households.

At the same time, in cities where housing prices have increased out-of-step with incomes, the transition to home ownership has been delayed by a few years. Statistics Canada figures that break down the owner/renter divide by age cohort show that overall, it is not until the 30-34-year-old cohort that owners begin to outnumber renters.

---

[3] Canada Mortgage and Housing Corporation. (2018, April 13). Homeowners income was about double that of renters in 2016. Retrieved from https://www.cmhc-schl.gc.ca/en/housing-observer-online/2018-housing-observer/homeowners-income-was-about-double-that-of-renters-2016

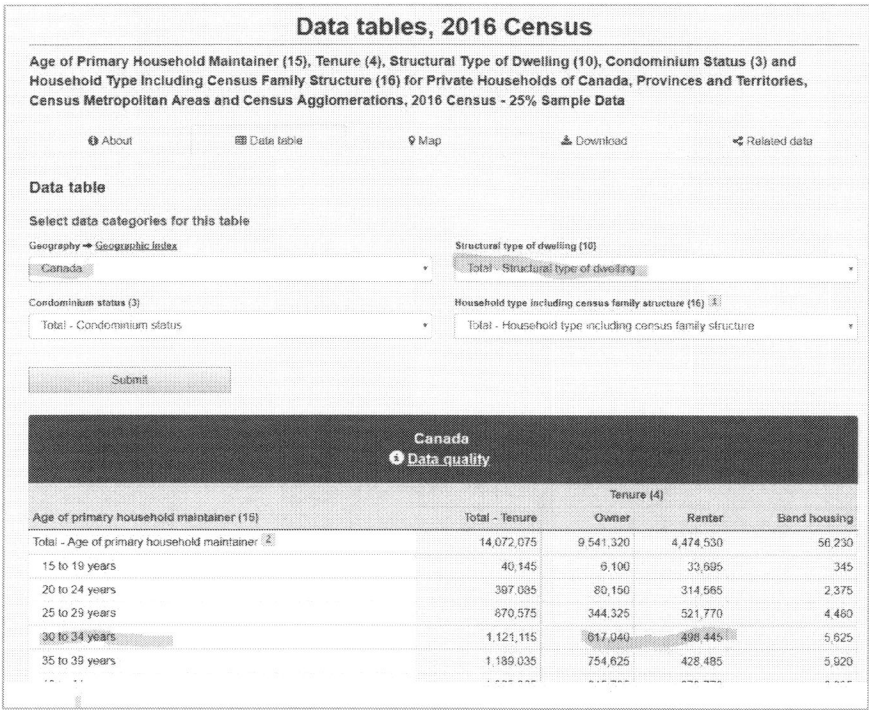

Figure 1.2 – A breakdown by tenure and age of the primary household maintainer

Source: Statistics Canada (2016 Census data)[4]

Statistics Canada reveals that in Montreal, Toronto, and Vancouver, however, that transition does not occur until the age 35-39 cohort. By comparison, in Saskatoon owners begin to outnumber renters even among 25-to 29-year-olds.

Life-cycle events are also key differentiators, even among those at similar income levels. Having children is one such primary trigger. The 2016 Census revealed that couples with children embarked on home ownership sooner than the couples without children. Most couples in the age 25-29 cohort with children are owners, whereas it is not until the 30-34 cohort that the balance tips among couples without children.

For single-parent families the shift comes even later, at 45 years or older. One-person households (those living alone) take the longest to embrace home ownership - it is only among the age 50 or older cohort that owners outnumber renters.

---

[4] Government of Canada, Statistics Canada. (2018, April 26). Data tables, 2016 Census. Retrieved from https://www12.statcan.gc.ca/census-recensement/2016/dp-pd/dt-td/Index-eng.cfm

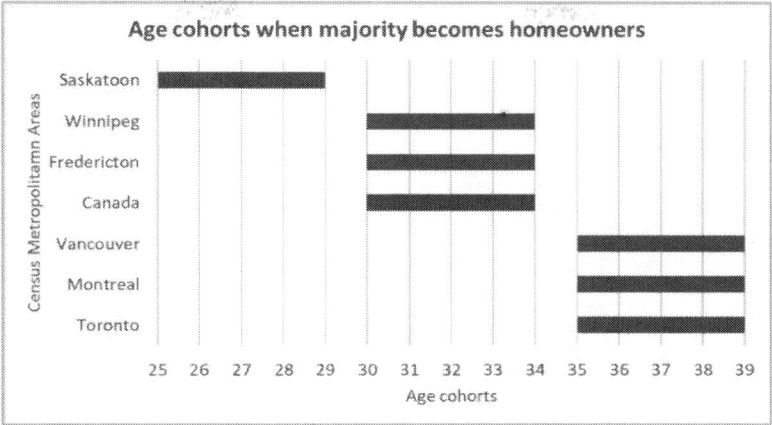

Figure 1.3 – Age at which most households become homeowners.

Source: Statistics Canada (2016 Census)

Personal tastes and predispositions also matter. Most of those preferring high-rise apartment or condominium living remain renters irrespective of their age and are more than twice as likely to rent than own. But the reverse is true for those living in single-detached housing. Even within the 20-24 cohort, the majority are owners, likely in part due to the extremely limited stock of rentable single detached homes. For semi-detached home dwellers the balance shifts to ownership slightly later, in the 25-29 cohort in Toronto and at 30-34 in Vancouver.

Age of primary household maintainer (15)	Total - Tenure	Tenure (4) Owner	Renter
Total - Age of primary household maintainer	1,390,775	416,250	974,465
15 to 19 years	8,805	1,395	7,405
20 to 24 years	72,520	9,145	63,360
25 to 29 years	139,820	28,190	111,625
30 to 34 years	144,295	39,345	104,940
35 to 39 years	113,135	32,115	81,015
40 to 44 years	95,070	28,325	66,740
45 to 49 years	96,065	29,450	66,615
50 to 54 years	103,915	33,095	70,815

Figure 1.4 – A breakdown by tenure and age of the primary household maintainer for apartment dwellers

Source: Statistics Canada (2016 Census data)

5

Geography ➜ Geographic index	Structural type of dwelling (10)
Canada ▾	Single-detached house
Condominium status (3)	Household type including census family structure (16) [i]
Total - Condominium status ▾	Total - Household type including census family struc

Submit

Canada
❶ Data quality

Age of primary household maintainer (15)	Total - Tenure	Tenure (4) Owner	Renter
Total - Age of primary household maintainer [2]	7,541,550	6,858,540	634,945
15 to 19 years	6,665	2,635	3,755
20 to 24 years	83,880	43,675	38,350
25 to 29 years	276,385	204,480	68,420
30 to 34 years	476,740	396,210	75,965

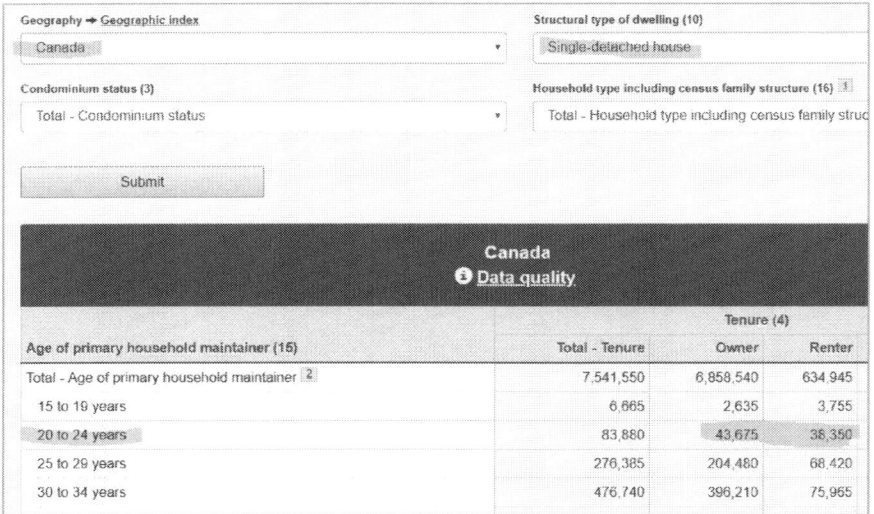

Figure 1.5 – A breakdown by tenure and age of the primary household maintainer for single-detached dwellers

Source: Statistics Canada (2016 Census data)

The statistical portrait of how we live and what we own, as is painted by Statistics Canada's data, suggests that demographics explain two-thirds - or some similar proportion - of home ownership. What is more important is how we put this information to good use.

Urban economists have long argued that the headship rate, a proxy for new household formation, influences the demand for housing. Equally important is where the new households are being formed, what they earn, and what preferences they may have for living arrangements.

Tracking and forecasting demographic trends offer investors, mortgage lenders and governments the opportunity to make wise decisions about housing markets. That demographics are location-specific suggests that overarching national or provincial strategies or policies could miss the mark in local housing markets.

In the next two sections, we will take a closer look at how increased housing prices in many Canadian cities have resulted in millennials living with their parents longer than previous generations and delaying their first home purchases.

ARE MILLENNIALS DIFFERENT FROM OTHER COHORTS?

Millennials have earned a reputation for being slow to leave their parents' basements, but as the generation begins to grow older, things may be about to change.

A report revealed that in the Greater Toronto and Hamilton Area (GTHA), a conurbation of seven million persons, as many as 700,000 millennials could leave their parents' homes in the next 10 years, creating nearly 500,000 new millennial-led households. Without changes to the pace of home construction, the region could as a result be faced with a shortfall of 70,000 low-rise dwelling units.[5]

The report, by Ryerson University's Centre for Urban Research and Land Development, pegged the number of millennials in the region at 1.9 million - meaning they outnumbered the baby boomers and constituted the largest source of housing demand. But are millennials really that different from the generations that preceded them? Research from the U.S., for instance, suggests that millennials are ditching car purchases and instead prefer public transit and ridesharing alternatives.[6,7] Whereas others have argued that alarms about the millennials ditching car ownership are exaggerated.[8]

A closer look at consumption patterns, however, revealed that millennials were not necessarily abandoning car ownership, but were rather delaying it. The same is pretty much true for millennials' homeownership in Canada: They are not necessarily abandoning it, they are simply delaying it.

According to 2016 census data reported by Statistics Canada, 50.2 per cent of those in their 30s owned their homes. In comparison, 55.5 per cent of baby boomers owned a home at age 30. In 1981, 44.4 per cent of the then young baby boomers lived in single detached homes. That share dropped to 35 per cent for the millennials in 2016.[9]

This, however, does not suggest a shift in preferences, but in timing. Consider that the 2016 census reported that whereas 43.6 per cent of 20-to 34-year-olds owned homes, homeownership jumped to 76.3 per cent for 35-

[5] Petramala, D., & Clayton, F. (2018). *Millennials in the Greater Toronto and Hamilton Area: A Generation Stuck in Apartments?* Retrieved from https://www.ryerson.ca/content/dam/cur/pdfs/policycommentaries/CUR_Research_Report_Millennial_Housing_GTHA_May_22.pdf

[6] Eliot, L. (2019, August 4). The Reasons Why Millennials Aren't As Car Crazed As Baby Boomers, And How Self-Driving Cars Fit In. *Forbes Magazine.* Retrieved from https://www.forbes.com/sites/lanceeliot/2019/08/04/the-reasons-why-millennials-arent-as-car-crazed-as-baby-boomers-and-how-self-driving-cars-fit-in/

[7] Quora. (2017, October 16). Why Millennials Are Buying Fewer Cars Than Older Generations. *Forbes Magazine.* Retrieved from https://www.forbes.com/sites/quora/2017/10/16/why-millennials-are-buying-fewer-cars-than-older-generations/

[8] Bershidsky, L. (2019, March 27). Don't Expect Car Ownership to Become Obsolete. *Bloomberg News.* Retrieved from https://www.bloomberg.com/opinion/articles/2019-03-27/millennials-aren-t-making-car-ownership-obsolete

[9] Government of Canada, Statistics Canada. (2017, October 25). The Daily — Housing in Canada: Key results from the 2016 Census. Retrieved from https://www150.statcan.gc.ca/n1/daily-quotidien/171025/dq171025c-eng.htm

to 54-year-olds. Similarly, the Royal Lepage Peak Millennial survey in 2017 revealed that 61 per cent of those aged 25 to 30 (peak millennials) would prefer owning a detached home, though only 36 per cent believed they would be able to afford one.[10]

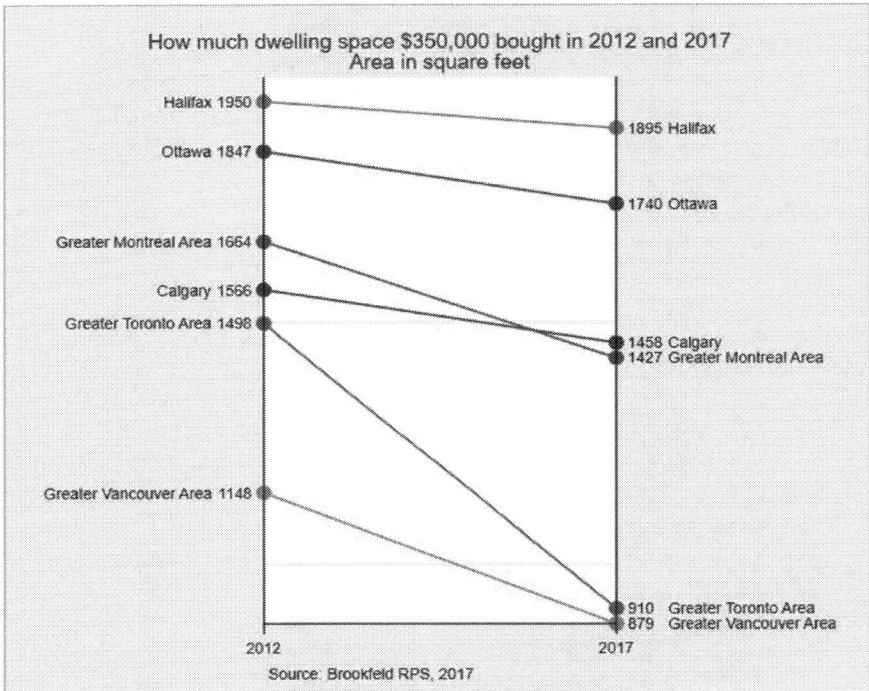

How much dwelling space $350,000 bought in 2012 and 2017
Area in square feet

Halifax 1950 — 1895 Halifax
Ottawa 1847 — 1740 Ottawa
Greater Montreal Area 1664
Calgary 1566
Greater Toronto Area 1498 — 1458 Calgary / 1427 Greater Montreal Area
Greater Vancouver Area 1148
910 Greater Toronto Area
879 Greater Vancouver Area
2012   2017
Source: Brookfield RPS, 2017

Figure 1.6 – Living Area that $350,000 Can Buy in Select Canadian Cities

Source: Data from Brookfield RPS, 2017. Visualization by the author.

Housing affordability remains a formidable challenge for millennials. An analysis of housing markets by Brookfield RPS revealed that even during a relatively short period between 2012 and 2017, the amount of shelter space you could buy for $350,000 declined across all major urban markets in Canada. Toronto and Vancouver reported the steepest decline.

The millennials, though, face additional challenges. In addition to the steep rise in home prices, stagnant wages, precarious employment brought about by the sharing economy, and the expected shifts in labour markets resulting from automation and AI are some of the factors that have

---

[10] Royal LePage. (2017, August 17). Largest Cohort of Millennials Changing Canadian Real Estate, Despite Constraints of Affordability and Mortgage Regulation. Retrieved from https://www.royallepage.ca/en/realestate/news/largest-cohort-of-millennials-changing-canadian-real-estate-despite-constraints-of-affordability-and-mortgage-regulation/

influenced their lifecycle decisions.

At the same time, millennials are the most educated cohort and the largest segment of the labour force. Though they make up only 27 per cent of the population, they represent 37 per cent of the labour force.[11] More than 75 per cent of the young women and 65 per cent of the men have received post-secondary education.[12]

A lack of full-time employment opportunities that pay wages sufficient to save for home ownership is perhaps keeping the millennials longer in the education system. Currently, nearly two million millennials are pursuing post-secondary education in Canada. This is twice as many gen Xers when they were at a similar stage in their development.[13]

The millennials are certainly not without help. Analysis of First Time Home Buyer's finances reported by the Ontario Securities Commission (OSC) revealed that the millennials are indeed a 'gifted' generation as they received large amounts as gifts from family to help them with home purchases. Whereas 31 per cent of the baby boomers and 37 per cent of the Gen Xers received gifts to assist with first home purchase, 45 per cent of millennials received a hand.[14]

Cheap and plentiful mortgage credit also helped. OSC reported that for households under the age of 35, mortgage debt jumped from $141 billion in 2005 to $240 billion in 2012. The nonmortgage debt for the same cohort increased by a mere $10 billion to $60 billion during the same time.

Over time and at a slower rate, the millennials are conforming to lifestyles and preferences of cohorts that preceded them. Millennials are not much different, just delayed.

RENTING, BUYING, OR HOTEL MOM

Should millennials rent, or should they own? To rent or not to rent is not the question. At least, it is not the complete question. When housing prices escalated in the late 2010s, some experts recommended prolonged renting to

---

[11] Mendes, S. (2018, April 2). Understanding the Millennial Workforce. *Restaurants Canada*. Retrieved from https://blog.restaurantscanada.org/index.php/2018/04/02/understanding-the-millennial-workforce/

[12] Heisz, A., & Richards, E. (2019, April 18). Economic Well-being Across Generations of Young Canadians: Are Millennials Better or Worse Off? Retrieved from https://www150.statcan.gc.ca/n1/pub/11-626-x/11-626-x2019006-eng.htm

[13] Government of Canada, Statistics Canada. (2018, November 28). Canadian postsecondary enrolments and graduates, 2016/2017. Retrieved from https://www150.statcan.gc.ca/n1/daily-quotidien/181128/dq181128c-eng.htm

[14] Ontario Securities Commission. (2017). *Missing Out: Millennials and the Markets*. Retrieved from https://www.osc.gov.on.ca/documents/en/Investors/inv_research_20171127_missing-out-report.PDF

those who couldn't afford to own. Some even wondered if Canada would transform into a nation of renters while others dreamed of a "Wealthy Renter."

Despite the recent romanticizing of renting and the hypothetical assertions that millennials have shunned homeownership, renting is unlikely to become a national aspiration. The desire to own a home is likely to continue driving growth in housing markets.

The rapid increase in housing prices in large urban areas has created additional barriers to homeownership for low-income renters. This is increasingly true for millennials whose incomes are not sufficient to accumulate a down payment.

For millennials, though, housing tenure is not necessarily confined to a binary of being a renter or a homeowner. It is more nuanced. Millennials are fortunate to have a third fallback option of continuing to lodge with their parents.

In fact, young adults staying longer with their parents represent a large demographic shift in attitudes and living arrangements. Pew Research Center in the U.S. reported that in 2014, for the first time in 130 years, 32.1 per cent of those aged between 18 to 34 years "were slightly more likely to be living in their parents' home than they were to be living with a spouse or partner in their own household."[15]

Compared to older cohorts, millennials are increasingly comfortable staying longer with parents. Census data crunched by Pew revealed that no fewer than 15 per cent of the 25-to 35-year old millennials were housed in their parents' homes. In comparison, a mere 10 per cent of Generation Xers in 2000 stayed with their parents. A mere eight per cent of the same age cohort in the '60s lived with parents.[16]

---

[15] Fry, R. (2016, May 24). For First Time in Modern Era, Living With Parents Edges Out Other Living Arrangements for 18- to 34-Year-Olds. *Pew Research Center*. Retrieved from https://www.pewsocialtrends.org/2016/05/24/for-first-time-in-modern-era-living-with-parents-edges-out-other-living-arrangements-for-18-to-34-year-olds/

[16] Fry, R. (2017, May 5). More young adults are living at home, and for longer stretches. *Pew Research Center*. Retrieved from https://www.pewresearch.org/fact-tank/2017/05/05/its-becoming-more-common-for-young-adults-to-live-at-home-and-for-longer-stretches/

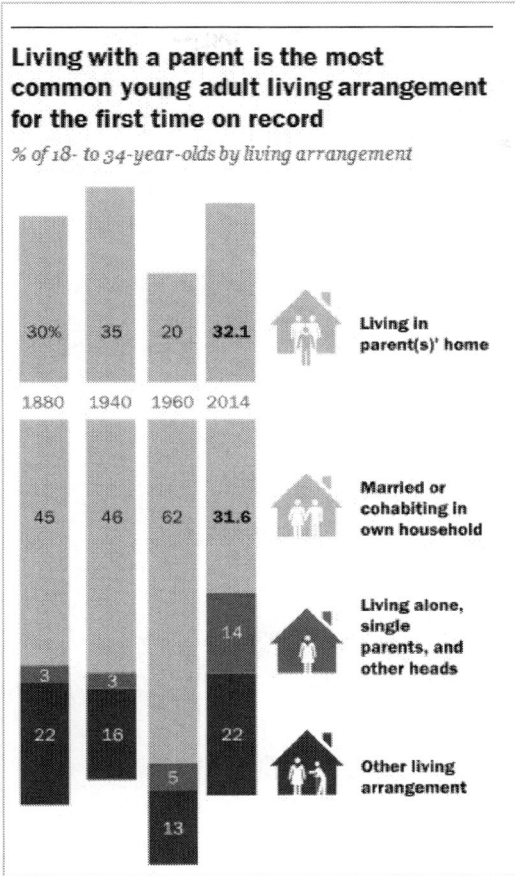

Living with a parent is the most common young adult living arrangement for the first time on record

% of 18- to 34-year-olds by living arrangement

30%	35	20	32.1	Living in parent(s)' home
1880	1940	1960	2014	
45	46	62	31.6	Married or cohabiting in own household
			14	Living alone, single parents, and other heads
3	3			
22	16	5	22	Other living arrangement
		13		

Figure 1.7 – Living Arrangements of Young American Adults

Source: Pew Research Centre (2016)

The situation in Canada is not much different. The 2016 Canadian census revealed similar trends of young adults living with parents. Almost 35 per cent of young Canadian adults, aged between 20 and 34 years, lived with their parents in 2016. This number was up from 31 per cent in 2001.[17]

Many believe that shifts in the labour market with the gig economy delivering more part-time jobs than full-time ones are the reason behind millennials not being able to earn living wages and starting their own households. The U.S. labour force data, however, suggests otherwise. Pew

---

[17] Government of Canada, Statistics Canada. (2017, August 2). Census in Brief: Young adults living with their parents in Canada in 2016. Retrieved from https://www12.statcan.gc.ca/census-recensement/2016/as-sa/98-200-x/2016008/98-200-x2016008-eng.cfm

reported that in 2016 only 5.1 per cent of young adults were unemployed, which was half of the rate in 2010.

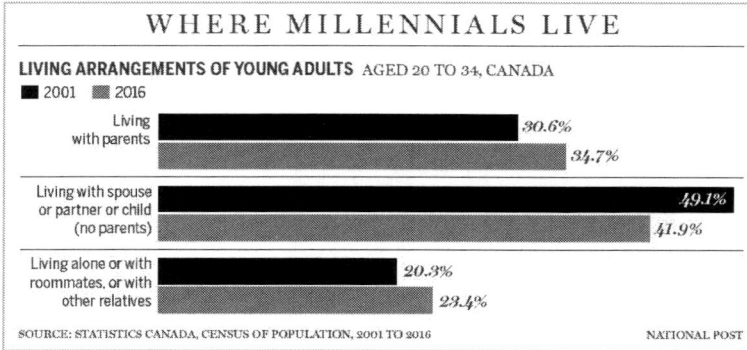

WHERE MILLENNIALS LIVE

LIVING ARRANGEMENTS OF YOUNG ADULTS AGED 20 TO 34, CANADA

■ 2001 ▨ 2016

Living with parents	
2001	30.6%
2016	34.7%

Living with spouse or partner or child (no parents)	
2001	49.1%
2016	41.9%

Living alone or with roommates, or with other relatives	
2001	20.3%
2016	23.4%

SOURCE: STATISTICS CANADA, CENSUS OF POPULATION, 2001 TO 2016   NATIONAL POST

Figure 1.8 – Living Arrangements of Young Canadian Adults

The prolonged stay at the parents' home by millennials has a profound impact on housing markets. It affects the rate of new household formation (the headship rate), which is a key driver of housing demand. Concomitantly, the same trend prevents parents from listing their larger homes for sale and downsize. One can't be an empty nester if millennials refuse to spread their wings and fly on their own.

Staying with the parents allows millennials to save on rent and expediently save for a down payment. And while millennials might feel the urge to leapfrog from parents' home to homeownership, they might want to consider renting from a career perspective.

Renters, unlike owners, are relatively more mobile since they can readily relocate to take advantage of better career opportunities elsewhere. The large transaction costs (transfer taxes, brokerage fees, legal costs, etc.) faced by young homeowners at times deter them from exploring career opportunities elsewhere.

However, renting for too long is also not advisable. In parts of urban Canada where population pressures are expected to increase, housing prices are likely to rise in the long run. This helps homeowners build equity that they can draw upon in old age or transfer housing wealth to their children.

The good news for millennials is that they will have more housing choices in the future than the previous cohorts because millennials are a much smaller cohort. This implies that the supply of existing homes is likely to be larger than the housing demand millennials will generate in the future. Until then they may continue to lodge at the Parents Inn.

IMMIGRATION'S IMPACT ON HOME PRICES

Recent immigrants are another cohort that influence housing and rental markets in Canada, particularly in Toronto, Montreal, and Vancouver. However, research suggests that even though immigrants are the biggest factor driving population growth in Canada, their impact on home prices is still relatively modest.

Housing markets respond to demand generated by households. An increase in population or the purchasing power of buyers is likely to exert upward pressure on housing prices and rents. But how much of that pressure is generated by immigration, the biggest factor driving Canada's population growth? The interest in that question has increased since housing affordability become a significant concern in large cities in Canada.

Rapid price escalation in Toronto and Vancouver during 2016-17 raised concerns about the impact of foreign money, something provincial governments addressed by implementing measures including a foreign homebuyers' tax. But those concerns, and the resulting tax measures, primarily involved the influence of non-resident speculators, not immigrants looking to build lives here.

In the past, research focused primarily on the shelter needs of recent immigrants who struggled to find adequate employment in Canada. New immigrants usually found housing in low-income and predominantly rental neighbourhoods. Over time, as they assimilated, immigrants transitioned from rental to owner-occupied housing.

Immigrants to Canada may not necessarily be low-income. For instance, investor-class immigrants are usually wealthier than the native-born population, and could have a more substantial effect on housing prices.

Immigration is also responsible for the net increase in the Canadian population. With an aging workforce, the influx of younger and highly educated immigrants is even more critical for the Canadian economy. Thus, between 2019 and 2021, Canada plans to bring in over one million immigrants, of which most will be economic migrants.

Most economic immigrants continue to settle in the three most populous city regions in Canada, namely Montreal, Toronto, and Vancouver. However, the big three are attracting a smaller share of immigrants now than before. For instance, 72 per cent of the economic principal applicants initially settled in the big three in 2004. By 2014, their share had declined to 51 per cent.

However, the lure of big cities is more pronounced for business class immigrants and skilled workers. In 2014, the three populous city regions attracted 85 per cent of the business class immigrants and 70 per cent of the skilled workers.

Immigrants usually flock to larger cities because of the abundance of employment opportunities there. When housing prices are falling, immigrants generate the additional demand for housing needed to stabilize the markets. However, when housing prices are escalating, especially in supply-constrained urban markets, new immigrants might contribute to the growing demand for housing.

Ather Akbari and Yigit Aydede of Saint Mary's University estimated the effects of immigration on house prices in Canada. Writing in the journal *Applied Economics,* they determined that immigration contributed to no more than 0.1 per cent to 0.12 per cent increase in housing prices. But it was immigrants who had arrived in Canada at least 10 years earlier who were contributing to the rise, the study found, not recent arrivals.[18]

The authors believed the small effect of immigration was because out-migration of the native-born from the neighbourhoods where new immigrants usually settle softened the impact on housing markets. Furthermore, an increase in new housing construction in response to higher demand also moderated the effect of immigration.

While Akbari and Aydede's findings suggest that immigration is unlikely to be a driving force in the rapid escalation of housing prices in Canada, recent research suggests that wealthy immigrants can be responsible for price escalation in choice neighbourhoods. Writing in the journal *Real Estate Economics,* Andrey Pavlov of Simon Fraser University and Tsur Somerville of the University of British Columbia found that the unexpected closure of an investor immigration program "had a negative impact on house prices of 1.7 - 2.6 per cent in the neighbourhoods and market segments most favoured by the investor immigrants."[19]

Immigrants are responsible for the lion's share of population increase in the Vancouver Metropolitan Area. Also, British Columbia has been the choice destination for investor immigrants. The investor immigration program, which has been running since 1986, was suddenly suspended in 2012 and eventually closed in 2014.

The program's closure allowed the researchers to determine whether housing prices in Vancouver neighbourhoods favoured by wealthy immigrants declined as a result. The authors found that high levels of wealthy immigrants in select Vancouver communities contributed "to higher relative neighbourhood house prices."

The effect of immigration is also extended to rental markets. A paper in the journal *Economic Issues* by Ehsan Latif of Thompson Rivers University found that an increase in immigration relative to the size of the province's population had a small impact on housing rents. The author believed that out-migration of the native-born from areas where immigrants settle could

---

[18] Akbari, A. H., & Aydede, Y. (2012). Effects of immigration on house prices in Canada. *Applied Economics, 44*(13), 1645–1658. https://doi.org/10.1080/00036846.2010.548788

[19] Pavlov, A., & Somerville, T. (2018). Immigration, Capital Flows and Housing Prices. *Real Estate Economics, 41*, 221. https://doi.org/10.1111/1540-6229.12267

be the reason for a minor increase in rents from immigration.[20]

Research in Canada has shown that the overall impact of immigration on housing markets is modest at best in most cases. The effect could be substantial in the case of wealthier immigrants destined to select neighbourhoods. The more important realization is that an absence of immigration would result in a declining population and aging of the workforce, which could have a much larger negative impact on Canadian housing markets.

The next section will discuss how rising home prices and the resulting increases in housing equity has played a larger role in growing wealth for immigrant families compared to Canadian-born families.

IMMIGRANT FAMILIES CLOSE THE WEALTH GAP WITH HOUSING

The early 2019 slump in real estate sales and prices in Canada led some to question whether housing remains a good investment. For immigrant families in Canada, the stakes may be particularly high. That's because research from Statistics Canada shows that investment in housing by immigrant families has been a major factor in helping them plug the wealth gap that exists between them and their Canadian-born compatriots.

Whereas the study found wealth growth for Canadian-born families has in recent years been driven both by increases in housing and registered pension plan assets, for immigrant families, housing alone has been the primary driver of wealth growth.

René Morissette, a senior economist with Statistics Canada, in a report released in April 2019 used data from several waves of the Survey of Financial Security to compare the wealth growth of immigrant and Canadian-born families.[21] The designation of a family being immigrant or otherwise was based on the immigration status of the major income earner.

The report generated synthetic cohorts in order to compare similarly structured immigrant and Canadian-born families over time. The benchmark cohort comprised recent immigrant families whose primary income earner in 1999 was 25 to 44 years old and had been in Canada for fewer than 10 years. The other cohort comprised established immigrant families whose primary income earner in 2016 was 42 to 61 years old (on average 17 years older relative to 1999) and had been in Canada for 18 to 26 years. The comparable Canadian-born cohorts were of the same relative age groups.

---

[20] Latif, E. (2015). Immigration and Housing Rents in Canada: A Panel Data Analysis. *Economic Issues, 20*(1).

[21] Morissette, R. (2019, April 16). The Wealth of Immigrant Families in Canada. Retrieved from https://www150.statcan.gc.ca/n1/pub/11f0019m/11f0019m2019010-eng.htm

Interestingly, while immigrant families started at lower rates of home ownership in 1999, by 2016 the homeownership rates between comparable immigrant and Canadian-born families converged.

On average, 31 per cent of the benchmark cohort of recent immigrant families in 1999 owned a principal residence compared to 56 per cent of comparable Canadian-born families. By 2016, established immigrant families led by a primary earner of 42 to 61 years of age reported a homeownership rate of 78.7 per cent compared to 74 per cent for their Canadian-born counterparts.

A key finding of the report is how the immigrant families caught up to their Canadian-born counterparts in growing wealth over time. In 1999, the median wealth of Canadian-born families with the major income earner aged 25 to 44 years old was 3.25 times higher than that of comparable recent immigrant families. However, when the two synthetic cohorts were compared 17 years later, the difference in median wealth between the immigrant and Canadian-born families almost disappeared.

Canadian-born and immigrant families relied on different asset classes for wealth growth. The wealth composition of families in 2016 revealed that housing equity explained about one-third of the average wealth of Canadian-born families. By comparison, housing equity was responsible for a much larger share of immigrant families' wealth, accounting for anywhere between one-half to two-thirds.

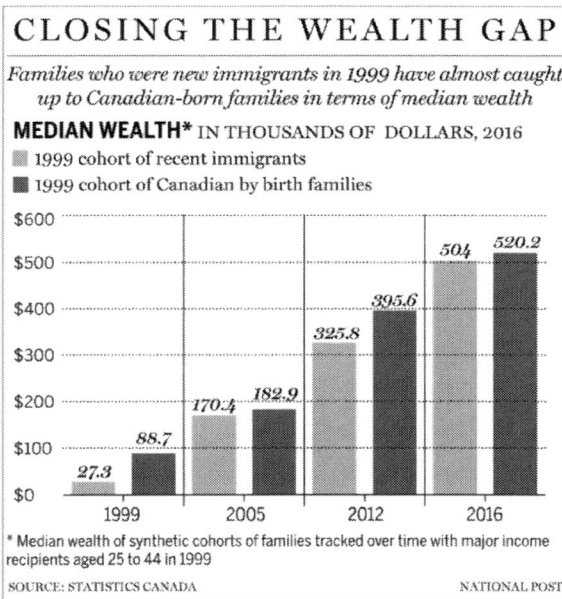

CLOSING THE WEALTH GAP

Families who were new immigrants in 1999 have almost caught up to Canadian-born families in terms of median wealth

MEDIAN WEALTH* IN THOUSANDS OF DOLLARS, 2016

▨ 1999 cohort of recent immigrants
▧ 1999 cohort of Canadian by birth families

	1999	2005	2012	2016
recent immigrants	27.3	170.4	325.8	504
Canadian by birth	88.7	182.9	395.6	520.2

* Median wealth of synthetic cohorts of families tracked over time with major income recipients aged 25 to 44 in 1999

SOURCE: STATISTICS CANADA   NATIONAL POST

Figure 1.9 – Median Wealth of Recent Immigrant and Canadian Born Families (1999-2016)

The wealth growth observed for immigrant families has a side story of high indebtedness. The report found that in 2016, immigrant families, in general, had "markedly higher debt-to-income ratios than their Canadian-born counterparts."

Immigrant families often, but not always, are larger in size. This is partly because immigrants are more likely to live in multi-generational households or to have siblings and their respective families occupy the same dwelling.

The unit of analysis in Statistics Canada's report is economic family, which "consists of a group of two or more people who live in the same dwelling and are related to each other by blood, marriage, common law or adoption." An economic family may comprise of more than one census family.

The expected differences in family size and structure between immigrants and Canadian-born families could have influenced some findings in the report. For example, the family wealth held in housing by immigrant families might lose its significance when wealth growth is compared at a per capita basis.

Housing is more than just an asset class. Homeownership provides shelter and the opportunity to grow equity over time. Canadian data show that rising home prices over the past two decades has helped immigrants bridge the wealth gap even when the gap between the average incomes of immigrants and Canadian-born has persisted.

Homeownership also provides immigrant families an opportunity for multi-generational living, where at least three generations of a family live under one roof. Such arrangements are more common amongst immigrant families than Canadian-born families, particularly in the suburbs of large metropolitan areas where single-detached housing is cheaper.

'MULTI-GENERATIONAL LIVING' MAY BE THE NEW OLD SOLUTION

Given the uniqueness of their location, no two houses are alike. Similarly, given the differences in households' demographic makeup, no two households are alike.

Multi-generational households, the ones where at least three generations of a family are living under the same roof, are even more distinct. Whereas such households represented a mere 2.9 per cent of all Canadian households in 2016, they represent a much larger segment of the population near large urban centres.[22]

When housing prices were escalating rapidly, multi-generational

---

[22] Government of Canada, Statistics Canada. (2017, August 2). The Daily — Families, households and marital status: Key results from the 2016 Census. Retrieved from https://www.150.statcan.gc.ca/n1/daily-quotidien/170802/dq170802a-eng.htm

households provided a buffer by first reducing the demand for housing and at the same time providing housing for seniors, who are among the fastest growing cohorts in Canada.

In 2017, Statistics Canada reported that 6.3 per cent of Canadians living in private households, almost 2.2 million people, lived in a multigenerational household. Such households have increased in numbers significantly over the years because of immigration from countries where similar living arrangements are the norm. The share of multi-generational households was the highest in Nunavut at 12.2 per cent. Ontario with 3.9 per cent and British Columbia with 3.6 per cent, were next.

What is hidden in provincial aggregations are pockets of spatial concentrations where such households are far more prevalent. The spatial diversity, for instance, is more pronounced at the Census Metropolitan Area (CMA) level with 5.8 per cent of households in Toronto, 4.8 per cent in Vancouver, and only 1.8 per cent in Montreal being multi-generational households.

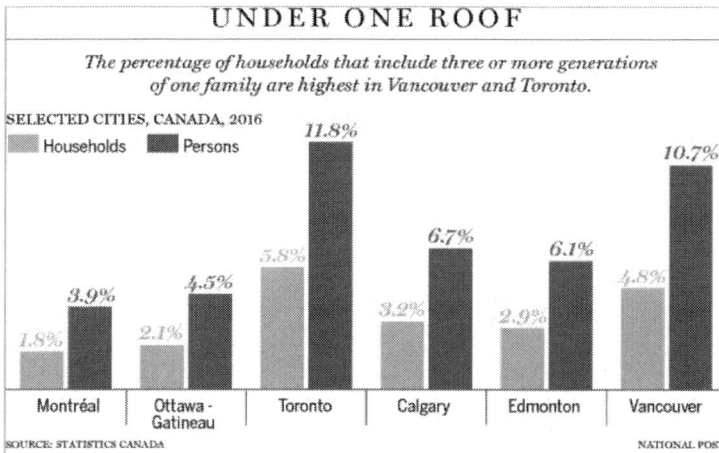

UNDER ONE ROOF

The percentage of households that include three or more generations of one family are highest in Vancouver and Toronto.

SELECTED CITIES, CANADA, 2016

Households   Persons

City	Households	Persons
Montréal	1.8%	3.9%
Ottawa - Gatineau	2.1%	4.5%
Toronto	5.8%	11.8%
Calgary	3.2%	6.7%
Edmonton	2.9%	6.1%
Vancouver	4.8%	10.7%

SOURCE: STATISTICS CANADA   NATIONAL POST

Figure 1.10 – Percentage of Multi-Generational Households in Canadian Cities

Given that multi-generational households are, by default, larger in size than other household types, a better comparison is to report the share of the population living in such households. The results are strikingly more pronounced. Whereas multi-generational households account for 5.8 per cent of all households in the Toronto CMA, for example, they are home to almost 12 per cent of the Toronto CMA's population. Similarly, almost seven per cent of those living in Calgary CMA and six per cent in Edmonton CMA live in multi-generational households. While these numbers are large, they are still aggregates of many urban and suburban municipalities.

Digging deeper with the help of data from Statistics Canada, we computed the share of multi-generational households at the municipal level in Toronto and Vancouver. The results were even more dramatic. In Brampton, a large municipality of 600,000 people in the northwest of the city of Toronto, one in four persons lives in a multi-generational household. In Markham, another large municipality to the north of Toronto, 18 per cent of the population lives in a multi-generational household. On the west coast in Surrey, British Columbia, almost one in five persons live in a multi-generational household.

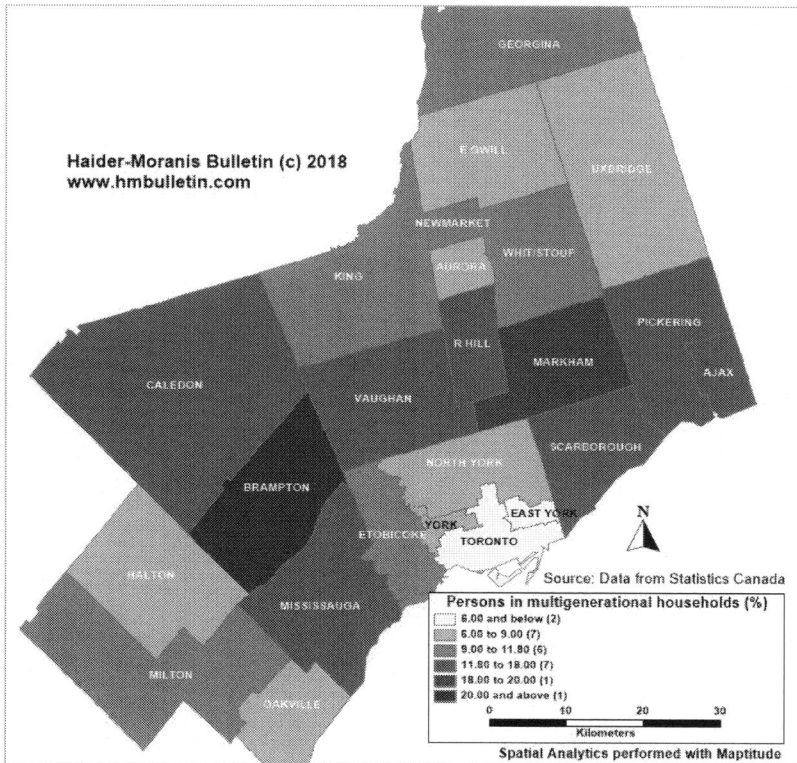

Figure 1.11 – Spatial distribution of Multi-Generational Households in Toronto CMA

The diversity doesn't end at the municipal level. Within the City of Toronto, 14 per cent of the residents in the former municipality of Scarborough live in a multigenerational household. In Toronto's downtown core and other central neighbourhoods, the proportion of such households is much smaller. This has much to do with the structure of the housing.

Multi-generational households are larger in size and therefore require more shelter space. Large suburban homes with four to five bedrooms are more compatible with such lifestyles than condominiums or small-sized homes that are more pronounced in the urban core.

In addition to the obvious advantages of multi-generational households, where grandparents substitute for childcare or where grown-up children can look after their frail parents without having to travel, multi-generational households help ease pressure on housing demand while utilizing the available shelter space more efficiently.

Most statistics on housing affordability report price per dwelling unit, which assumes that the household size does not vary in the population. But it does. Thus, if we were to compute shelter costs as the price per person living in the dwelling unit, the affordability dimension of multigenerational living becomes obvious. Consider that a $750,000 suburban home inhabited by six persons in a multigenerational household pays $125,000 per person compared to a couple paying $375,00 per person for a $750,000 condominium.

Multi-generational living is not for everyone. Such lifestyles are more pronounced among immigrants from cultures where such arrangements have been a norm. However, escalating housing prices have forced changes in lifestyles even among those households where such living arrangements have not been prevalent in the past. In Toronto, almost one in two young adults between the ages of 20 and 34 still resides with their parents. Going forward, if housing prices refuse to adjust to what buyers can afford, buyers may have to adjust their lifestyles to housing prices.

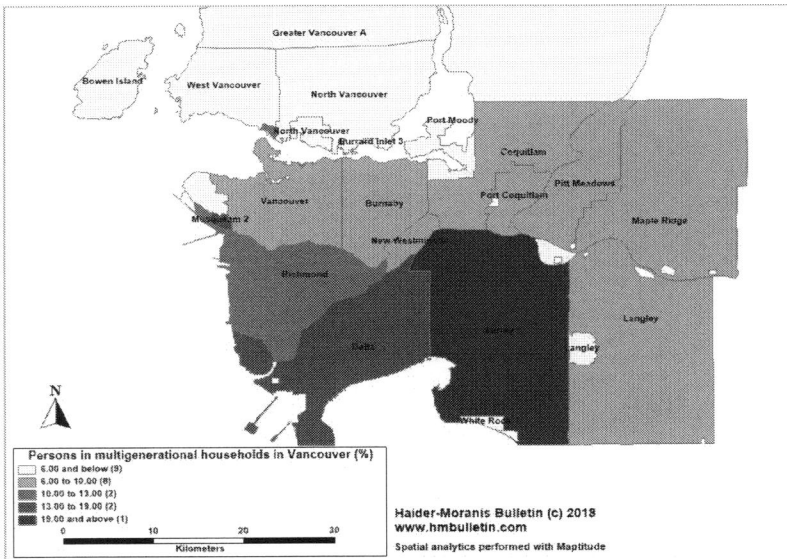

Figure 1.12 – Spatial distribution of Multi-Generational Households in Vancouver CMA

While multi-generational households accounted for roughly three per cent of all Canadian households in 2016, around the same time in the U.S., single women became the second largest cohort of home buyers after married couples.

SINGLE WOMEN LEAD THE CHARGE AS DEMOGRAPHICS SHIFT

Women are redefining how homes are bought and sold. In the U.S., single women have grown to become the second-largest cohort, after married couples, of home purchasers.

A report by the U.S. National Association of Realtors (NAR) revealed that single women are more active in buying homes and condos than single males. Single women bought 18 per cent of the homes sold in 2017. Single men, by comparison, accounted for just seven per cent of the home purchases.[23]

The change in homebuying demographics has also alerted the builders who responded by customizing the new dwellings to conform to the evolving taste preferences. In North Carolina, for instance, more than half of the homes in one new development were bought by single women.

Why are single women more inclined to buy than single men? Experts cite differences in priorities where women see purchasing a home as an investment while men are concerned with the need to relocate for employment and believe owning a home might prove onerous for relocating. The Canadian data on homebuyers is not readily available to determine the share of homes purchased by single men and women. Yet, some similarities between homebuyers in Canada and the U.S. do exist.

The NAR report revealed that first-time homebuyers comprised 35 per cent of all homebuyers in the U.S. Among the Millennial and Gen Y cohorts (those aged 36 years or younger) who purchased homes, 66 per cent were first-time homebuyers. At the same time, the Millennials and Gen Yers together accounted for the largest age group of homebuyers.[24]

The Canadian stats are similar. Of the 625,000 homes sold between 2013 and the first quarter of 2015, almost 45 per cent of the homes were purchased by first-time homebuyers. The Canadian Millennials and Gen Yers (aged between 18 and 34 years) constituted the largest age group as they acquired

---

[23] Harney, K.R. (2018, May 8). Single women account for more real estate purchases than single men. *The Washington Post*. Retrieved from https://www.washingtonpost.com/realestate/single-women-account-for-more-real-estate-purchases-than-single-men/2018/05/08/0f3cee66-521e-11e8-a551-5b648abe29ef_story.html

[24] National Association of Realtors. (n.d.). *Home Buyer and Seller Generational Trends Report 2017*. Retrieved from https://www.nar.realtor/sites/default/files/reports/2017/2017-home-buyer-and-seller-generational-trends-03-07-2017.pdf

41 per cent of the homes sold.[25]

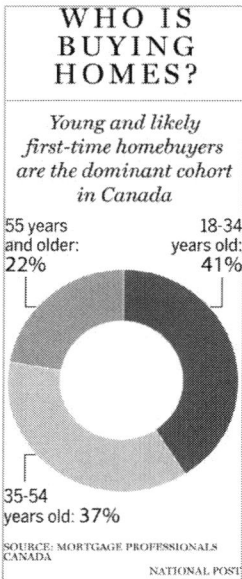

WHO IS
BUYING
HOMES?

*Young and likely
first-time homebuyers
are the dominant cohort
in Canada*

55 years
and older:
22%

18-34
years old:
41%

35-54
years old: **37%**

SOURCE: MORTGAGE PROFESSIONALS
CANADA

NATIONAL POST

Figure 1.13 – Canadian Home Buyers by Age Group

The breakdown for Canadian data revealed that women accounted for 49 per cent of all home purchases. The Canadian data is based on a smaller survey of 800 respondents by Bond Brand Loyalty Inc. and does not drill down to comparisons between single females and males. Yet, other data on searching for homes suggests women are more actively browsing for homes than are men.

Using six million online searches by potential homebuyers in Canada, Point2Homes - a real estate market intelligence firm - estimated that women constituted the majority of those searching for homes in Canada. They analyzed online searches over a three-month period in 2016.[26]

An age-wise distribution revealed that Millennials were the most active in online searches for homes priced between $300,000 and $400,000, which was significantly below the average home price in 2016.

The changing demographics in Canada suggest that gender differences in homebuying are likely to increase in the future as the proportion of young

---

[25] Mortgage Professionals Canada. (n.d.). *A Profile of Home Buying in Canada*. Retrieved from https://mortgageproscan.ca/docs/default-source/default-document-library/infographic2.pdf?sfvrsn=ab289ea_0

[26] Baiceanu, R. (2016, September 12). The Profile of the Canadian Home Buyer. Retrieved from https://www.point2homes.com/news/canada-real-estate/profile-of-canadian-home-buyer.html

women graduating from university has been increasing over time. Already, 41 per cent of the women in Canada between the ages of 25 and 34 years had a bachelor's degree in 2016. In 2006, a little under 33 per cent of the women in the same age group possessed a university degree.[27]

In fact, since the early nineties, the proportion of young women with a bachelor's degree has been higher than the comparable proportion for men. For the first time in 2016, women accounted for a slight majority of young Canadians with an earned doctorate.

As an increasing proportion of young women earn university credentials, their earning potential improves as well. Women with a bachelor's degree earned 40 per cent more than women with a college diploma and 60 per cent more than those with a high school diploma.

Going forward, as their incomes grow, Canadian women are expected to continue to invest even more in housing, as data in the U.S. already suggests. The housing industry must be cognizant of the demographic shifts in housing demand and be prepared to cater to a market where woman homebuyers will be the dominant segment.

While more single women are buying homes, fewer seniors are selling. The decision to age-in-place is an important one for many younger seniors under the age of 75 that influences housing stock and home prices as a result.

THE SENIOR BOOM WILL RESHAPE THE WAY WE LIVE

Canada is aging rapidly. A Statistics Canada brief revealed that in 2018, there were 106 seniors aged 65 and older for every 100 children under the age of 15. Comparatively speaking, the population of children was twice that of seniors in 1986.[28]

The two driving forces are increased life expectancy and fertility rates that are below replacement level. It's a demographic shift that is likely to have a significant effect on housing markets - but just what that effect will be is not entirely clear.

On the one hand, the increasing number of seniors could generate new demand for senior-focused housing. At the same time, many seniors are finding aging in place attractive, as it enables them to continue living in the same dwelling in familiar neighbourhoods. Such preferences might mitigate the demand for retirement homes or assisted living in the short run.

---

[27] Government of Canada, Statistics Canada. (2017, November 29). The Daily — Education in Canada: Key results from the 2016 Census. Retrieved from
https://www.www150.statcan.gc.ca/n1/daily-quotidien/171129/dq171129a-eng.htm
[28] Government of Canada, Statistics Canada. (2019, January 25). The Daily — Canada's population estimates: Age and sex, July 1, 2018. Retrieved from
https://www.www150.statcan.gc.ca/n1/daily-quotidien/190125/dq190125a-eng.htm

One of the key unknowns is how younger seniors - those under 75 years of age - will differ in their housing and other choices from the previous cohorts of similar age. Seniors today are healthier and wealthier than their older counterparts. Many seniors are asset-rich and wonder whether they should continue to own or switch to renting.

With retirement, baby boomers no longer will be tied to the nine-to-five routine. Retirement affords new possibilities to relocate within the same town or to a different province, spend winters in moderate climates, and take on new hobbies and projects.

Better health also has led to longevity, which means seniors will have more time to live independently. During this period, they also may have to continue to support their children.

Changes in the economy, cultural shifts and spikes in housing markets all have contributed to millennials staying with their parents longer than similar-aged cohorts in the past.

Seniors with financially dependent children thus will have a constrained choice set as they might have to choose living arrangements that are optimal not just for them but also for their adult dependent offspring. For instance, seniors might dispose of large properties and rent smaller dwellings and use part of the proceeds to assist their children with home-buying.

The choice between renting and owning is not trivial for young seniors who now are approaching retirement age. They are likely to spend a decade or two before they may feel the need for assisted living. The choices they make now are likely to impact them for decades.

Statistics Canada's General Social Survey from 2007 revealed that 80-plus per cent of those between the ages of 55 and 74 owned their homes. For those who were 75 years and over, three out of four lived in owned dwellings. Furthermore, almost 80 per cent of those over the age of 55 lived in the same house for more than five years. At least 62 per cent had lived in the same dwelling for over 10 years.[29]

The Statistics Canada survey revealed that young and old seniors were more likely to age in place. Only one in five respondents in the survey indicated that they would consider downsizing or purchasing a retirement home.

In the U.S., the number of homeowners who were at least 55 years old has increased by 9.6 million since 2006. At the same time, the number of younger homeowners under the age of 45 has declined by 4.3 million.[30]

---

[29] The General Social Survey: New Data Overview. (2008). Retrieved from
https://www150.statcan.gc.ca/n1/pub/89-631-x/89-631-x2008001-eng.htm
[30] Sen, C. (2019, April 25). Young People Can't Buy Homes Until Older Owners ... Move On. *Bloomberg News*. Retrieved from https://www.bnnbloomberg.ca/young-people-can-t-buy-homes-until-older-owners-move-on-1.1249312

Housing choices by age cohorts

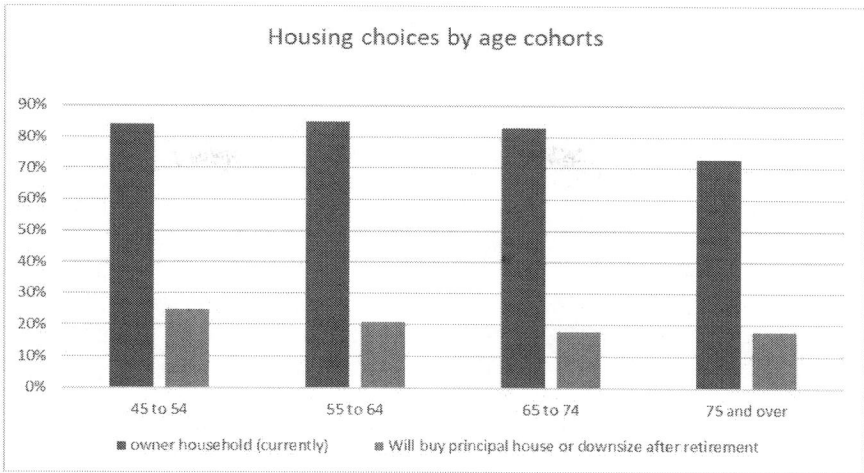

Figure 1.14 – Housing choices for adults and seniors

Source: Statistics Canada, 2007 General Social Survey

Older households in the U.S. are holding on to a large inventory of dwellings that is not available for purchase by younger cohorts. Eventually, American baby boomers will vacate their current homes to live in assisted housing. However, this may still be a decade or so away. Canadian demographics show similar trends.

In the meantime, if seniors age in place in large numbers, it could reduce the demand for senior residences. If the construction of senior residences is maintained at an average pace, the vacancy rates and hence the rents for senior housing would be expected to remain stable.

Seniors are likely to cause shifts in housing supply and demand in the early 2030s when they may face challenges with aging in place. As they will then vacate the larger homes they have occupied for decades, the rise in inventory is likely to moderate housing prices of single-family dwellings, which will benefit older millennials raising young families.

Seniors, while greatly influencing housing markets, are also more at-risk compared to younger populations of living in housing that is not structurally sound, spacious or affordable. Often housing exhibiting these characteristics can pose health risks to seniors as evidenced by the July 2018 heat wave in Quebec that caused 70 deaths.

HEAT WAVE DEATHS LINKED TO HOUSING

The July 2018 heat wave in Quebec is reported to have caused 70 deaths, with Montreal alone recording 34 of them.[31] While many in Canada are alarmed by the numbers, the fact remains that the heat wave-related deaths in Quebec pale in comparison with the August 2003 death toll in France, where a spike in temperatures that lasted for weeks caused 15,000 excess deaths.[32]

The subsequent analysis of at-risk populations in France revealed that the elderly, women and those living alone faced much higher odds of dying in a heat wave. Furthermore, those without air-conditioned dwellings also faced higher risks of mortality.[33]

The lessons learned from the 2003 heat wave in France suggest that living arrangements and dwelling conditions are two important determinants of vulnerability to heat waves. Seniors living alone in inadequate housing are more likely to experience the adverse impact of a sudden heat wave than others. Any plans to safeguard against future heat waves must, therefore, include improving dwelling conditions and real-time health monitoring of seniors living alone.

The link between dwelling conditions of seniors and vulnerability to heat waves has already been suggested in Quebec. Dr. David Kaiser of Montreal's Regional Public Health Department revealed that many heat wave victims in Montreal were more than 50 years old, male, and lived alone in non-air-conditioned dwellings.

---

[31] Cullinane, S. (2018, July 10). Up to 70 people dead after Quebec heat wave. *CNN*. Retrieved from https://www.cnn.com/2018/07/10/americas/quebec-heat-wave-deaths-wxc/index.html

[32] France-Presse, A. (2019, September 8). Summer heatwaves in France killed 1,500, says health minister. *The Guardian*. Retrieved from http://www.theguardian.com/world/2019/sep/09/summer-heatwaves-in-france-killed-1500-says-health-minister

[33] Peltier, E. (2019, July 26). As Extreme Heat Becomes New Normal in Europe, Governments Scramble to Respond. *The New York Times*. Retrieved from https://www.nytimes.com/2019/07/26/world/europe/france-europe-extreme-heat.html

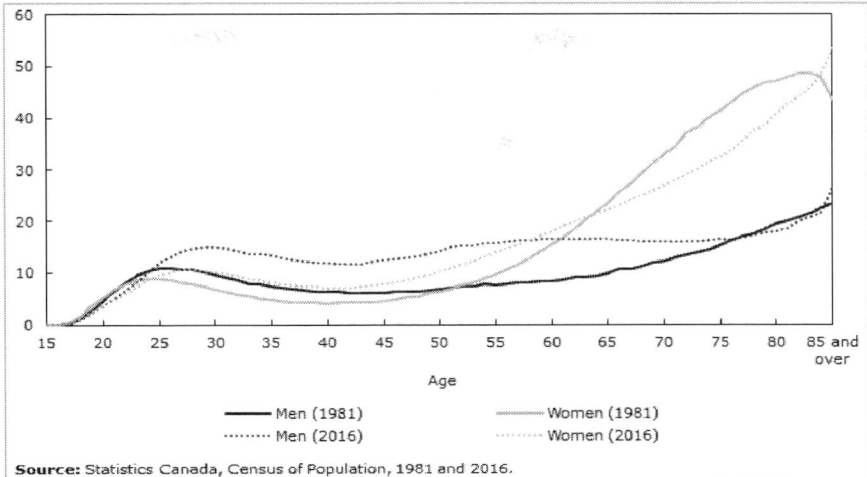

Figure 1.15 – Proportion of population living alone

Source: https://www150.statcan.gc.ca/n1/pub/75-006-x/2019001/article/00003-eng.htm

A review of Census data can help us identify the likely size of vulnerable populations in Canada. For the first time in 2016 since Confederation, seniors over the age of 65 outnumbered children. The 2016 Census recorded 5.9 million seniors (over the age of 65 and 5.8 million children, 14-year-old or younger.[34] More than one in four seniors lived alone.[35]

Statistics Canada and the CMHC have jointly developed three indicators of housing appropriateness. Adequacy refers to housing being structurally sound for a living. Suitability refers to having enough space (i.e., bedrooms) for those living in the dwelling. Lastly, affordability refers to households spending 30 per cent or more of their total income on shelter costs. A senior household who does not meet any one or more of the three criteria is considered living in inappropriate housing.

---

[34] Grenier, É. (2017, May 7). Seniors now outnumber children in Canada, census figures show. *CBC News*. Retrieved from https://www.cbc.ca/news/politics/2016-census-age-gender-1.4095360
[35] Galbraith, N., Truong, J., & Tang, J. (2019, March 6). Living alone in Canada. Retrieved from https://www150.statcan.gc.ca/n1/pub/75-006-x/2019001/article/00003-eng.htm

Seniors living in inappropriate housing (%)

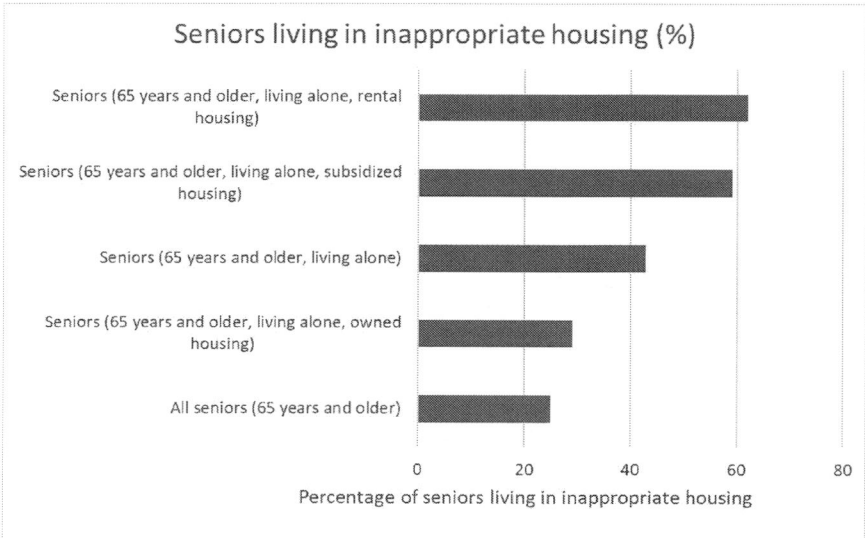

Figure 1.16 – Proportion of population living alone

Based on the above standards and calculations by the author using the Census 2016 data from Statistics Canada, one in four seniors lives in inappropriate housing in Canada. Affordability is the single largest component that defines why a senior's dwelling might be inappropriate. Dwelling inappropriateness worsens with age. Whereas one in four seniors (65 years or older) fit the criteria, that number rose to almost one in three for seniors over the age of 84.

Living arrangements, however, are even more relevant to dwelling appropriateness. Almost 43 per cent of seniors who live alone - the cohort most vulnerable to heat waves - reside in housing deemed inappropriate. By contrast, senior couples whose children no longer live with them are most likely to live in dwelling conditions deemed appropriate.

Household income remains a key underlying variable in explaining the appropriateness of a dwelling. Senior households with larger incomes should be able to live in structurally sound housing, without crowding and with enough funds on hand after paying for shelter.

Seniors living in subsidized housing are, therefore, more vulnerable with 56 per cent of them residing in inappropriate dwellings. One-person senior households in subsidized housing are only marginally worse off at 59 per cent indicating that housing vulnerability is high for seniors in subsidized housing, irrespective of their living arrangements.

Seniors who rent are particularly vulnerable. No fewer than 62 per cent of Canadian seniors living alone in rental units meet the inappropriate housing criteria. In comparison, only 29 per cent of one-person senior households who own live in inappropriate dwellings.

A greater proportion of seniors living alone in urban areas reside in inappropriate dwellings. In Toronto, almost three-out-of-four seniors living alone in rental units reside in inappropriate housing.

It is important to boost the health system's resilience to cope with catastrophic outcomes caused by extreme weather conditions. A preferred approach will be to improve the structural condition of dwellings and increase the supply of affordable housing for the most vulnerable seniors who often live alone.

While low-income seniors are particularly vulnerable in hot weather due to poor housing conditions, wealthier seniors often seek out warmer weather in the winter months by purchasing real estate in the U.S. In fact, Canadians rank second behind China for foreign home purchases.

CANADIANS RANK SECOND AS FOREIGN PURCHASERS IN THE U.S

The Canadian saga with foreign homebuyers continues. In February 2018, the NDP-led government in British Columbia unveiled a budget that included even stricter regulations targeting foreign homebuyers, who were subjected to a 20 per cent transfer tax and additional surcharges for maintaining unoccupied properties.[36]

But while Canadians tighten the squeeze on foreign homebuyers at home, we continue to be among the largest purchasers of real estate south of the border. A report by the National Association of Realtors (NAR) revealed that in 2016-2017, Canadians were the second most active group of foreigners buying residential real estate in the U.S. Buyers from China topped the list.[37]

From April 2016 to March 2017, foreign buyers in the U.S. acquired 284,455 residential properties, representing 10 per cent of all sales by dollar amount or five per cent of all existing dwelling sales. In addition to China and Canada, other dominant buyers of American residential real estate included buyers from the U.K., Mexico and India.

The trends in foreign home buying in the U.S. and Canada are eerily similar. The average price of homes purchased by foreign buyers ($536,852) was 12 per cent higher than the average price of all existing home sales.

Similarly, foreign buyers were more likely to make cash purchases, rather

---

[36] McCarthy Tétrault LLP. (2018, March 8). 2018 B.C. Budget: What It Means for B.C. Real Estate. Retrieved from https://www.mccarthy.ca/en/insights/blogs/lay-land/2018-bc-budget-what-it-means-bc-real-estate

[37] National Association of Realtors. (2017). *2017-Profile-of-International-Activity-in-US-Residential-Real-Estate.pdf*. Retrieved from https://www.nar.realtor/sites/default/files/documents/2017-Profile-of-International-Activity-in-US-Residential-Real-Estate.pdf

than securing mortgage financing. Almost 44 per cent of the foreign home purchases were cash transactions compared to 25 per cent of all existing sales.

Some interesting differences between Canadian and American markets emerge when one distinguishes between homes purchased by non-resident foreigners - who are essentially non-U.S. citizens living abroad - and resident foreigners, who are recent immigrants (not citizens) with fewer than two years in the U.S. or are temporary visa holders. Most of the buyers from China, India and Mexico are resident foreigners reflecting their status as recent immigrants, students, or temporary workers. In comparison, the bulk of the buyers from Canada and the U.K. are non-resident foreigners who mostly purchased vacation homes.

Canadian purchase of U.S. residences has steadily declined from 69,000 units in 2010 to a little under 34,000 in 2017. In contrast, the same period witnessed a dramatic increase in the number of dwellings purchased by Chinese buyers, rising from 27,000 units in 2010 to 40,500 units in 2017. The heightened Canadian interest in 2010 was perhaps a result of the collapse in housing markets in the U.S. that made residences in Florida and Arizona significantly cheaper for Canadian buyers.

Since 2015, one can spot a considerable decline in the share of purchases by nonresident foreigners from Canada, China and the U.K. Increasing employment opportunities in the U.S., higher home prices in Canada, and Brexit in the U.K. are likely to have caused a decline in the share of nonresident foreigners.

The U.S. sunbelt has been the preferred location for most homebuyers. In fact, 54 per cent of the purchases by foreign homebuyers in 2016-2017 were concentrated in just five states. Florida, with 22 per cent of the sales, topped the list. Texas and California each accounted for 12 per cent of the sales, followed by New Jersey and Arizona, each accounting for four per cent of the sales.

The average price of U.S. homes purchased by the Chinese has always been much higher than those purchased by Canadians. The difference is a result of locational preferences and the intended use of the dwellings. Whereas Chinese buyers, predominantly resident foreigners, were concentrated in the more expensive housing markets in California, the Canadian snowbirds landed in the more affordable housing markets in Florida and Arizona, representing 37 per cent and 17 per cent of all Canadian purchases respectively.

Even though foreign homebuyer purchases account for approximately five per cent of the residential units sold in both Canada and the U.S., the opposition to foreign homebuyers is much stronger in Canada. The reason behind it is not likely the concentration of foreign homebuyers, but the difference in the pace at which home prices have recently escalated in the two countries.

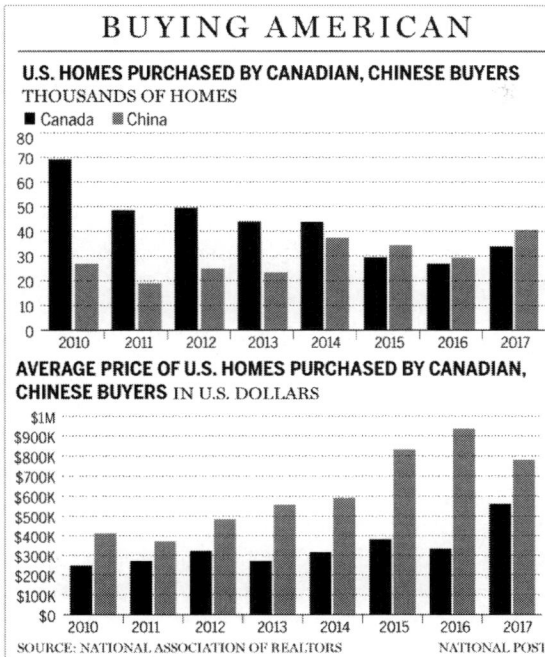

Figure 1.17 – U.S. Homes Purchased by Canadian and Chinese Buyers (2010-2017)

The IMF Global Housing Watch revealed that the real home prices in 2017 increased by 11.3 per cent in Canada compared to 4.3 per cent in the U.S.[38] The house price escalation was even more dramatic in Toronto and Vancouver.

Whereas additional taxes on foreign homebuyers in Canada will temporarily stop housing prices from escalating, an adequate response to a sustained global interest in Canadian real estate is a systematic increase in housing supply. One strategy to increase adequate housing supply is to improve deteriorating social housing stock by investing in community housing.

COMMUNITY HOUSING PAYS DIVIDENDS

In April 2019, the Trudeau government in Canada pledged $1.3 billion to improve the dilapidated social housing stock maintained by the Toronto Community Housing Corporation, Canada's largest public-sector landlord.

---

[38] International Monetary Fund. (2020, April 8). Latest Global Housing Watch Data. Retrieved from https://www.imf.org/external/research/housing/

The billion-dollar-plus commitment in loans and investments over 10 years is much needed: Toronto's social housing has needed major repairs for decades.[39]

But is throwing money at social housing really an efficient use of government funds? The answer seems to be a resounding yes. From a cost-benefit perspective, investing in social housing is one of the best investments governments can make to ensure the socio-economic health and prosperity of growing cities.

Research by the Canadian Centre for Economic Analysis (CANCEA) reveals "that investment in affordable housing not only provides shelter to those who cannot afford market rents but also offers billions of dollars in socio-economic benefits."[40]

The funding announced in April 2019 couldn't have come sooner. For years, the Toronto Community Housing Corp. (TCHC) has been advocating desperately for the money needed to bring its social housing stock into a state of good repair. The City of Toronto has led the investment drive for years yet it could not get either the province or the feds to partner in refurbishing the 2,100 buildings the agency oversees.

In the past, adequate shelter was considered an "elemental human need" in Canada. The former Liberal government of prime minister Pierre Trudeau introduced several reforms to the National Housing Act in 1973. However, over the years, the federal and provincial roles in social housing have declined, leaving many municipalities to struggle to maintain the programs.

TCHC's challenges are large and complex owing to the size of its operations. Over 110,000 residents are housed in TCHC-supported housing. Of those, 38 per cent of residents are children and youth and 25 per cent are seniors. Furthermore, 28 per cent of the households are single-parent families, and 23 per cent of residents face mental health challenges.

The deteriorating social housing conditions create an image of blight that deters, at times, even the necessary service providers from visiting the premises. In summer 2009, paramedics near downtown Toronto waited outside a high-rise building for the police to arrive while a man bled to death inside. The paramedics were "concerned for their own safety."[41]

---

[39] Mathieu, E., & Rider, D. (2019, April 5). Ottawa pledges $1.3 billion for Toronto Community Housing repairs. *The Toronto Star*. Retrieved from https://thestar.com/news/city_hall/2019/04/05/ottawa-pledges-13-billion-for-toronto-community-housing-repairs.html

[40] Canadian Centre for Economic Analysis. (2015). *Socio-Economic Analysis: Value of Toronto Community Housing's 10-Year Capital Investment Plan and Revitalization*. Retrieved from https://www.torontohousing.ca/capital-initiatives/Documents/Third-party%20economic%20impact%20study.pdf

[41] EMS delay caused by safety concerns, chief says. (2009, July 14). *The Globe and Mail*. Retrieved from https://www.theglobeandmail.com/news/national/ems-delay-caused-by-safety-concerns-chief-says/article4213179/

The Liberal government's commitment of $1.3 billion is part loan ($810 million) and part investment ($530 million). The money will be invested in restoring the 58,000 units maintained by TCHC. The recent announcement is part of the $13.2-billion National Co-Investment Fund.

The economic and social benefits of investing in affordable housing are manifold and go well beyond affording shelter to those who can't afford market rents.

In a comprehensive simulation-based economic analysis, CANCEA estimated that an almost $6-billion investment in social housing in Toronto over 30 years would contribute $14.3 billion to the economy while creating 158,000 person-years of employment.

CANCEA went beyond estimating the usual economic benefits and explored health and safety benefits. Safe and affordable living environments promote healthy living because the inhabitants are less likely to fall ill due to inadequate housing. Their analysis estimated that the investment in social housing over 30 years will result in 2.1 million fewer visits to health care facilities that would amount to $3.8 billion in health care savings. CANCEA even estimated that crime would be 15-percent lower in TCHC projects as a result of improved living conditions.

The reduction in crime and improved social housing stock will also have spatial spillover effects: they would improve valuation of the neighbouring properties, CANCEA found, contributing another $13.6 billion to the area's wealth over 30 years. The refurbished units are likely to be equipped with energy-saving appliances and retrofitted with efficient windows resulting in less energy consumption and reduced utility bills.

The case for improved living conditions for the most vulnerable in society must be made on moral grounds. We are reminded that adequate housing is an elemental human need. Still, a dollar-and-cents evaluation of bringing the social housing stock to a state of good repair offers strong evidence that the money will be well-spent.

Prosperity Metrics		Summary of Impacts of Investment: Reward Scenario	
Economic Impacts	Investment evaluated	$5B Revitalization and $2.6B capital repair	TCHC, development partners, and City of Toronto invest $5.9B and Ontario and Federal governments invest $1.73B collectively
	GDP contribution	$18.5B more for Canada	68 per cent occurs within first 10 years. $12.6B of the increased GDP is in the GTHA, of which $8.3B is in the City of Toronto. 2014 real terms.
	Employment years	220,000 more for Canada and Ontario	108,000 for GTHA of which 40,000 are in the city of Toronto. 64 per cent occur within the first 10 years.
	Private capital investment	$5B more for Canada and Ontario	91 per cent located in GTHA with 88 per cent occurring within first 10 years. 62 per cent benefiting industries other than construction. 2014 real terms.
	Ontario and Federal taxation revenues	$4.5B more	$2.3B Ontario government (44 per cent income taxes, 56% consumption/production taxes); $2.2B Federal government (73 per cent income taxes; 27% consumption/production taxes). 2014 real terms.
Community, Health, and Energy Impacts	Condition of TCHC dwellings	28,151 closures avoided. 76 per cent of units in good and fair condition.	Impact upon 109,000 TCH residents of which 30,000 include children and youth.
	TCHC resident illness	544,000 less cases	Annual average of 18,100 fewer cases over 30 years. 48 per cent due to respiratory and mental health conditions.
	Healthcare utilization	2,100,000 less health care cases	82 per cent general practitioner visits
	Healthcare costs	$3.8B less	94 per cent due to fewer hospitalizations
	Greenhouse gas emissions	9 per cent lower	Yearly GHG emissions fall by over 390 kg per unit on average
	Social Assistance	Up to $6.8B less	Up to approximately $756M saved in the first 10 years
	Neighbourhood crime	15 per cent lower	An annual average of 127 crimes avoided per year over 30 years
	Neighbourhood rental income	$4.27B more	Indicating strengthened neighbourhood profitability

Figure 1.18 – CANCEA estimates for rewards of investment in capital repair and revitalization

From senior housing and the need to maintain subsidized housing in a state of good repair, we move our attention to housing for students also face additional barriers in finding affordable housing in tight markets.

STUDENT HOUSING BENEFITS FROM INVESTMENTS

As enrolment at Canada's universities and colleges continues to grow, the space for lecture halls, labs and academic offices is becoming scarcer. The same goes for on-and off-campus student housing.

More than two million fulltime students are currently enrolled in Canadian universities and colleges.[42] They collectively generate a huge demand for rental housing and, in large urban centres where rents are high in particular, present a predictable source of demand for rental units. But these days, students aren't the only ones with an interest in student housing. The previously ignored sector has become a niche opportunity for investors as well, lured by yields that U.K.-based real estate services provider Savills notes are "currently higher than in many sectors."[43]

In 2018, the Canada Pension Plan Investment Board (CPPIB) announced that their joint venture, Scion Student Communities, acquired a student housing portfolio worth US$1.1 billion.[44] The portfolio comprises 13,666 beds in 20 university campus markets across the U.S. A report in The Economist revealed that student housing attracted US$16 billion worldwide investment in 2016, as sovereign wealth funds have increasingly targeted the sector.

Opportunity exists in Canada, as well. The growth in the number of post-secondary students here has not been met with a commensurate increase in student-centric housing. The need is most acute in places like Toronto, where a collaborative initiative, StudentDwellTO - sponsored by the presidents of the four Toronto universities - aims to find solutions for student housing challenges.[45]

While universities may be tempted to secure a larger piece of the student housing pie by getting more involved themselves, that would be a mistake. Universities are in the business of education and not running rental accommodation. They should encourage and facilitate the private sector, which has the experience and the resources to help the hitherto nascent student housing market reach maturity in Canada.

---

[42] Government of Canada, Statistics Canada. (2018, November 28). Canadian postsecondary enrolments and graduates, 2016/2017. Retrieved from
https://www.w150.statcan.gc.ca/n1/daily-quotidien/181128/dq181128c-eng.htm
[43] Savills UK. (2017, October 6). Global Student Housing Investment Breaks Records. Retrieved from https://www.savills.co.uk/insight-and-opinion/savills-news/156478-1
[44] The Economist. (2018, May 10). Big investors are giving university digs an upgrade. Retrieved from https://www.economist.com/finance-and-economics/2018/05/10/big-investors-are-giving-university-digs-an-upgrade
[45] Student Dwell Toronto. (2019). About. Retrieved from https://studentdwellto.ca/About-Main

Brokerage (SVN) specializes in student housing finance.[46] They estimate the unmet (residual) demand for student housing in Canada is over 416,000 beds. This should hardly come as a surprise since even with millions enrolled in Canadian universities, the total number of on-campus beds is just 121,164. SVN estimates the current number of purpose-built off-campus beds across Canada is 39,178, almost half of which are in the Kitchener-Waterloo area.

The unmet demand for such housing is estimated to be huge, with 51,000 off-campus beds needed in Montreal, 32,000 in Toronto and 21,500 in Ottawa. From an investment point of view, the numbers favour student housing over other residential rental projects. For instance, a purpose-built rental with 140,000 square feet of rental space can house approximately 220 people in 140 units. The same space will accommodate 450 students and can generate 30 per cent more rent, explained Derek Lobo, who heads SVN.

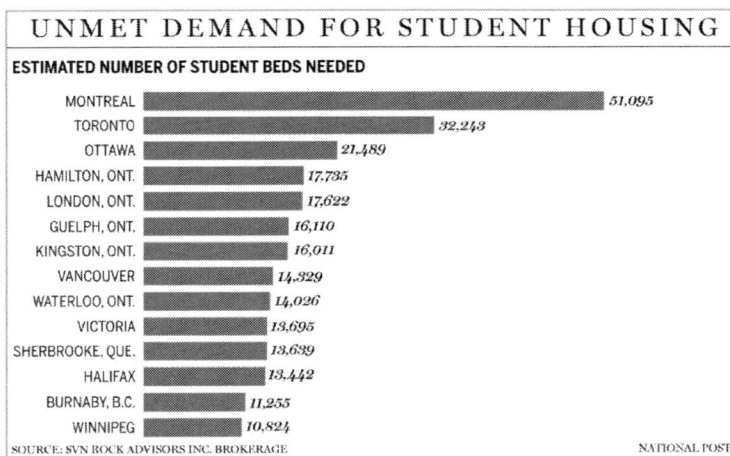

UNMET DEMAND FOR STUDENT HOUSING

ESTIMATED NUMBER OF STUDENT BEDS NEEDED

MONTREAL	51,095
TORONTO	32,243
OTTAWA	21,489
HAMILTON, ONT.	17,735
LONDON, ONT.	17,622
GUELPH, ONT.	16,110
KINGSTON, ONT.	16,011
VANCOUVER	14,329
WATERLOO, ONT.	14,026
VICTORIA	13,695
SHERBROOKE, QUE.	13,639
HALIFAX	13,442
BURNABY, B.C.	11,255
WINNIPEG	10,824

SOURCE: SVN ROCK ADVISORS INC. BROKERAGE   NATIONAL POST

Figure 1.19 – Estimated Number of Student Beds Needed in Canadian Cities

And the demand for student housing in Canada is only expected to rise. The demographic realities of most regions of Canada and the increased appetite for education around the world mean that international students will comprise a larger proportion of university enrolments.

During 2011-12 and 2015-16, the number of full-time Canadian students enrolled in bachelor's or equivalent programs increased by only 2 per cent. In comparison, the number of international students studying in Canada increased by a whopping 52 per cent. In Manitoba and British Columbia, the comparable international student population grew by 88 per cent and 74 per

---

[46] SVN Rock Advisors Inc. (n.d.). Canadian Purpose Built Student Accommodation Advisors. Retrieved from https://svnrock.ca/national-student-housing-group/

cent respectively.[47]

As Canadian universities compete globally to attract international students, they must recognize that "residence life" is very much a part of the educational experience. Universities should collaborate with private sector investors and property managers to provide quality housing services.

The days of aging, rundown student housing are over. Students and their parents expect and demand quality housing. Given a stable source of demand and the willingness to pay, the private sector can develop student housing into a mature class of real estate investments.

SUMMARY

In this chapter, we have demonstrated how demographics impact housing markets. Whereas demographics impact housing markets differently for varying age groups, the interdependence between different age groups also creates interdependencies in housing markets. We learnt that as seniors age, they vacate larger homes that subsequently become available to younger cohorts involving in raising children. Any delay in the availability of the housing stock held by seniors implies that, in the absence of sufficient new housing construction, there will be a shortage of enough housing for younger cohorts raising families. Thus, these interdependencies create challenges and opportunities. We also learnt that economies with low fertility rates must rely on immigration to maintain population and economic growth rates. Immigrant housing, like senior housing, provides unique opportunities and challenges.

In summary, housing markets, like most other markets, are impacted by demographics. Hence, smart managers of real estate markets must have an improved understanding of demographics.

---

[47] Government of Canada, Statistics Canada. (2020, September 9). Postsecondary enrolments, by registration status, institution type, status of student in Canada and gender. Retrieved from https://www150.statcan.gc.ca/t1/tbl1/en/tv.action?pid=3710001801

2 HOUSING MARKETS, POLICIES, AND STRATEGIES

For some, the real estate market is "out of its slump." For others it is simply "stabilizing." Others still see "no signs of cooling." The varying pronouncements about Canada's housing markets in mid-July 2018 suggest that there isn't per se a single housing market, but instead a collection of local markets where prices and sale volumes adjust to local variations in housing demand and supply, sometimes in response to institutional interventions.

The latest release of the monthly housing statistics by the Canadian Real Estate Association (CREA) suggests that a "national" Canada-wide lens on housing markets shows a picture that is necessarily not reflective of any local housing market.[48] Whereas the national housing market is the sum of its parts, it's the parts that matter because consumers do not see or experience the national averages. Housing prices and sales volumes are inherently relevant only at local levels.

Whereas month-over-month comparisons are interesting, given the cyclical nature of housing markets, year-over-year comparisons are more meaningful. Hence, the CREA reported 4.1-per-cent increase in sales volume observed in June 2018 over May 2018 might suggest an upswing in national housing markets. Yet, it is obfuscating the larger underlying market dynamic: A comparison with June 2017 reveals a decline of 6.6 per cent in national housing sales.

But the preceding is just a version of the reality as these numbers are seasonally adjusted to present a picture of housing markets after controlling for the ever-present seasonal variations. The raw sales numbers - CREA calls

---

[48] Canadian Real Estate Association. (n.d.) Housing Market Stats. Retrieved from https://www.crea.ca/housing-market-stats/

them the "actual activity" - show that the national housing sale volumes were down 12 per cent in June 2018 relative to the same month last year. Housing sales in June were also 6.3-per-cent lower than they were in May 2018.

Right there, even at the national level, two contrasting pictures emerge of sales, one suggesting that the sales were up (seasonally adjusted) and the other suggesting sales were down (actual sales) from May to June of 2018.

So, here's the housing version of the glass-half-full riddle: were the markets up or down in June? Barb Sukkau, CREA's president, believes in the seasonally adjusted numbers as she reflected on the impact of stress tests, which increased the mortgage qualification threshold in January 2018, on housing markets. "The increase in June (sales) suggest that its impact may be starting to lift," Ms. Sukkau said.

But when it comes to actual housing prices, signs of a recovery were not visible at the national level where the actual average housing price in June 2018 at $496,000 was 1.3-per-cent lower than the average price a year ago. And this decline is before the prices are adjusted for inflation. Compared to May 2018, average housing prices barely rose by 0.3 per cent. Hardly a hot market, at least at the national level.

THINK LOCAL

How housing prices have changed in different Canadian cities over the past 12 months

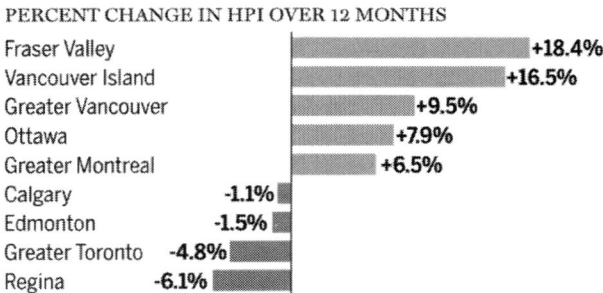

PERCENT CHANGE IN HPI OVER 12 MONTHS

City	Percent Change
Fraser Valley	+18.4%
Vancouver Island	+16.5%
Greater Vancouver	+9.5%
Ottawa	+7.9%
Greater Montreal	+6.5%
Calgary	-1.1%
Edmonton	-1.5%
Greater Toronto	-4.8%
Regina	-6.1%

SOURCE: HOUSING PRICE INDEX, CANADIAN REAL ESTATE ASSOCIATION

NATIONAL POST

Figure 2.1 – Percent Change in HPI from 2017 to 2018 for Canadian Cities

CREA also publishes a home price index (HPI) that accounts for seasonal changes over time. Also, it accounts for the difference in housing types and sizes that may be active at one point in time but not the other. CREA's HPI thus presents the change in housing prices of similar or identical housing stock over time. The HPI for June 2018 also presents a conflicting picture where the index was modestly up by 0.9 per cent since June 2017 but down by 0.13 per cent relative to May 2018.

While the returns in housing markets in mid-2018 were not stellar, a long-term view would suggest housing markets in Canada have performed well where the HPI has been up 46 per cent since June 2013.

Hiding under the national averages are the peaks and troughs of local housing markets. Urban markets in B.C. reported strong gains in prices year-over-year whereas markets in Saskatchewan and the Greater Toronto Area reported declines. The HPI in greater Vancouver increased by 9.5 per cent from 2017 to 2018. The strongest gains though came in the Fraser Valley, with an 18.4-per-cent increase. Prices in Vancouver Island followed with a 16.5-per-cent increase. Meanwhile, the index was down by 4.8 per cent in Toronto, Canada's largest housing market. Contrasting the extremes are the restrained markets in Montreal and Ottawa where the HPI increased by 6.5 and 7.9 per cent respectively.

So, is the glass half full or half empty? It depends. Housing markets across Canada continuously adjust to local dynamics and nation-wide regulatory changes to mortgage finance. While the short-term monthly dynamics might be a bit jittery, the long-term view of housing markets reveals their resilience and suggests the regulatory blues will eventually be shaken off, and the upward stride will continue.

HPIs have unquestioned utility in evaluating real estate markets at the municipal level. However, there is a case to be made that HPIs can and should be employed at the neighbourhood level to gain an even better understanding of housing price trends.

LOCAL PRICES MAY BE THE ONLY ONES THAT MATTER

Real estate markets are inherently local in nature. The value of a property is informed by the sale of similar nearby properties in the recent past. Thus, house price changes in one city may have no relevance to prices in another.

Recent research reinforces the notion that for housing markets, the extent of local may be restricted to the neighbourhood level. Housing values in a mid-income neighbourhood will not necessarily respond to fluctuations in prices in a ritzy part of the town. Whereas homebuyers and sellers, and real estate agents already work with markets at the neighbourhood level, some segments of the industry see housing only at the national or, at best, regional level.

In a world awash with data, cheap data storage, ubiquitous computing and advanced analytics, providing housing insights at the neighbourhood level should no longer be an insurmountable challenge. In fact, researchers at the U.S. Federal Housing Finance Agency have demonstrated how house price indexes can be generated at the postal code level.

Writing in the journal *Real Estate Economics* in 2019, Alexander Bogin and co-authors showcase new series of house price indexes for 914 cities, 2,716 counties, 18,053 five-digit postal codes and 54,901 census tracts. For each local housing market, they developed an annual time series of indexes covering transactions over four decades.[49]

The authors have gone beyond what most indexes were able to do in the past. Consider Canada, where the oft-cited price indexes include the Teranet-National Bank (TNB) House Price Index and the Canadian Real Estate Association's (CREA) MLS Home Price Index. These indexes come in two flavours. The national index is a composite of a subset of urban housing markets. The local indexes are based on the transactions recorded in large urban housing markets.

The city-wide index is a useful metric to know about the trends in broader regional housing market. It will identify times where the housing market was up or down, thus helping the buyers and sellers in their decision-making. However, as the cities have become larger over time and have amalgamated other towns to become city regions, a single index may not suffice. Both MLS and TNB indexes report an index for Toronto, which has a regional population of more than six million. Housing and land prices vary considerably in Toronto. For instance, research by Murtaza Haider and Eric Miller in 1999 showed how housing prices for near-identical units were higher near downtown Toronto and declined with distance from downtown.[50]

A neighbourhood level index will be of higher value to buyers and sellers because buyers search for a specific type of housing and their spatial search is usually confined to a select few neighbourhoods and not the entire city. Thus, house price fluctuations in neighbourhoods of interest matter more to buyers than what the price trends are in other parts of the city or in other cities.

The local price indexes developed by Bogin and his co-authors generated insights that remained hidden from other aggregate indexes. The authors found that house price appreciation in neighbourhoods near downtowns in large American cities was considerably higher than in places that were 10 miles (16 kilometres) away from the city centre.

Insights about the difference in house price appreciation are valuable to all, but more so for investors who would like to know what parts of the city offer higher rates of return on housing investments.

---

[49] Bogin, A., Doerner, W., & Larson, W. (2019). Local House Price Dynamics: New Indices and Stylized Facts. *Real Estate Economics*, *47*(2), 365–398. https://doi.org/10.1111/1540-6229.12233

[50] Haider, M., & Miller, E. (2000). Effects of Transportation Infrastructure and Location on Residential Real Estate Values: Application of Spatial Autoregressive Techniques. *Transportation Research Record: Journal of the Transportation Research Board*, *1722*, 1–8. https://doi.org/10.3141/1722-01

Local house price indexes suggest that an increase in housing demand in areas with highly elastic housing supply, implying that new housing can be built readily in response to higher demand, will result initially in higher prices. However, over time and with new supply, prices return to their long-term trends.

The same is not valid for supply-constrained places. Because of development restrictions, restrictive regulations, or expensive land prices, housing supply will not respond commensurately to shocks in housing demand. Bogin and co-authors point to places near downtowns, "where buildable sites are less available and regulation is presumably more onerous, a permanent demand shock can outpace supply responses, leading to price increases."

Housing transaction data is available with municipal governments and local real estate boards. Statistics Canada has also been working on developing a housing transaction database. The markets would be served better if the existing data were put to good use leading to insights for informed decision-making. Local house price indexes will be one such intelligent use of data as they would further highlight the different cycles experienced by municipal level housing markets across Canada.

LOCAL HOUSING MARKETS ARE NOT ON THE SAME CYCLE

A surprise jump in housing sales in greater Toronto in April 2019 was interpreted in some quarters as a sign of a spring recovery in the housing market. But market movements in other parts of the country were much more nuanced, making any broad statement about a sustainable recovery impossible at this point.

The April 2019 sales figures (reported by CREA) were dominated by a spike in Toronto where sales increased from 7,159 units in March to 9,042 units. The average (nominal) housing price there also increased to $820,148. The last time the average price crossed the $800,000 mark was in October 2018. While the improved conditions were welcomed by most, the question of why sales and prices jumped - and whether those gains will continue - is still in need of an answer.

By contrast, sales continued to struggle in B.C. and prices in the urban housing markets in Alberta and Saskatchewan were lower than five years prior. Housing markets in B.C. were moderating from stringent regulations imposed by the provincial and federal governments. Year-over-year sales in Vancouver were down by almost 30 per cent in April 2019. Residential sales in the Fraser Valley and Victoria, the other large housing markets in the province, were down by 19 and 10 per cent respectively.

Housing sales in markets immediately east of B.C. were higher. Calgary and Edmonton reported modest year-over-year increases whereas sales jumped by 28 and 18 per cent in Regina and Saskatoon respectively. However, the smaller size of the Prairie market means that it would only take a few hundred additional sales to significantly move the needle.

Despite the increase in sales, prices declined in Alberta and Saskatchewan. Though the magnitude of the decline in prices was lower in comparison to the ones observed in B.C., the falling housing prices lasted much longer in the Prairies than elsewhere.

Consider that housing prices in B.C., despite the declines, were still 60-to 80-per-cent higher in 2019 than they were in 2014. It's not the same for the markets in Alberta and Saskatchewan where prices in April 2019 were lower than prices five years prior.

NOT ALL HOUSING PRICES CREATED EQUAL

*Housing price change over
one and five year periods.*

HOUSE PRICE CHANGE
IN PER CENT

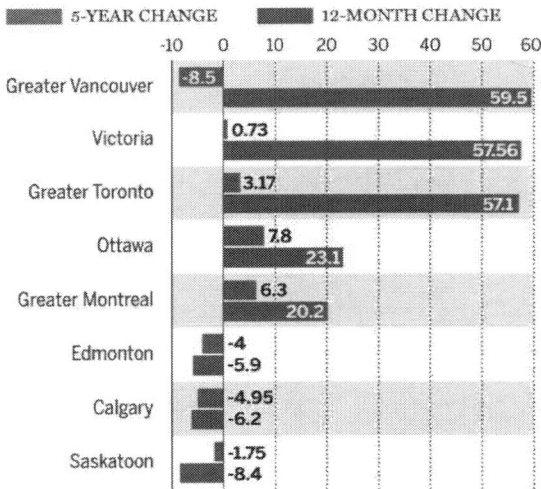

5-YEAR CHANGE   12-MONTH CHANGE

City	5-Year Change	12-Month Change
Greater Vancouver	-8.5	59.5
Victoria	0.73	57.56
Greater Toronto	3.17	57.1
Ottawa	7.8	23.1
Greater Montreal	6.3	20.2
Edmonton	-4	-5.9
Calgary	-4.95	-6.2
Saskatoon	-1.75	-8.4

SOURCE: CANADIAN REAL ESTATE ASSOCIATION   BRICE HALL / NATIONAL POST

Figure 2.2 – Housing Price Change over One- and Five-Year Periods from 2018 for Canadian Cities

Housing markets in Ottawa and Montreal are distinct from other large cities. Not only did they report modest year-over-year increases in April 2019 - 7.7 per cent and 6.3 per cent in Ottawa and greater Montreal respectively - prices increased moderately over the five-year horizon. The HPI in April 2019 was 23-and 20-per-cent higher over five years in the two cities.

Compared to the markets in Toronto and Vancouver, Ottawa and Montreal avoided rapid price inflations that raised alarms about housing affordability. A substantial cohort of renters, which dominates the housing market in Montreal, likely contributed to a modest increase in demand for owner-occupied housing resulting in a moderate increase in housing prices.

By comparison, Ottawa likely benefited from the large number of federal government employees who constitute a big part of the regional labour force and whose numbers and incomes are more stable, which prevents rapid demand shocks.

Across Canada, housing sales, reported by CREA, in April 2019 were up by 4.2 per cent year-over-year. The national HPI though faltered slightly by 0.3 per cent. Higher sales in April 2019 relative to the same month in 2018 were encouraging but come off a relatively low reference point: sales in April 2018 were the lowest for an April in the previous seven years.

The diverse spectrum of housing outcomes in large cities indicates that local housing markets are not on the same cycle. While some markets might have started to recover, others still must experience additional moderation in sales and prices.

While it is tempting to have a one-size-fits-all policy response to housing market challenges, one runs the risk of compounding the problems for markets needing a custom response. Tailoring regulatory interventions to address local market needs would be a better approach. Housing markets in Canada's largest cities vary drastically as evidenced by housing sales in Toronto and Vancouver between March 2018 and March 2019.

VANCOUVER'S HOUSING CHILL

When it comes to housing markets, Vancouver and Toronto are poles apart. The March 2019 update on housing sales by CREA suggested signs of some stability in Toronto's market, where almost the same number of units were sold in March 2019 as in March 2018.

Vancouver presented a different and more dismal picture. The number of sale transactions in greater Vancouver in March 2019 was down 31 per cent from the tally recorded in March 2018. Vancouver had not seen such a lacklustre March since 1986. Housing advocates and some industry observers had suggested that a decline in housing prices would be a boon for those who had previously been priced out of the market. It was argued that declining prices would bring in a rush of buyers who had waited on the sidelines for years for an opportunity to own a home. The evidence for such a narrative was lacking in Vancouver.

Ashley Smith, president of the Real Estate Board of Greater Vancouver, was of the view that housing "demand today isn't aligning with our growing economy and low unemployment rates."[51] She held regulatory changes responsible for the declining market trends in the greater Vancouver area. Smith was of the view that the host of government interventions that introduced new transfer taxes and stringent lending regulations have effectively sidelined "potential homebuyers in the short term."

Garry Bhaura, president of the Toronto Real Estate Board, echoes Smith's concerns. Bhaura also believed the OSFI-mandated stress test, which requires borrowers to qualify for a higher rate than the contracted mortgage rate, and other regulations impacted "homebuyers' ability to qualify for a mortgage."[52]

According to CREA, the MLS Home Price Index composite benchmark price for Vancouver, which compared prices of similar homes over time, was down by 7.7 per cent year-over-year (YoY) in March 2019. The benchmark price for detached homes at $1.43 million was down by 10.5 per cent (YoY). Prices of condominiums and attached homes were also down.

While prices were dropping in Vancouver, buyers also had a richer set of choices. Compared to March 2018, the number of houses listed for sale was 52-percent higher in March 2019. The sales-to-listing ratio was 13.5 per cent for all property types and 9.4 per cent for detached homes.

More choice and lower prices should have attracted more buyers. But that's not what usually happens in real estate markets. When prices fall, potential buyers stay on the sidelines in the hope that prices will drop even further. This reduces demand and puts additional downward pressure on prices resulting in even fewer sales. Remember, sales in March were down 31.4 per cent (YoY) in Vancouver.

Buyers in Vancouver could also have been looking at the long-term trends in housing prices. Despite the declines, the benchmark prices in Vancouver were up by 61 per cent over five years and 102.5 per cent over 10 years. If housing prices in Vancouver had risen rapidly in the previous 10 years, buyers might be expecting the prices to regress further toward the long-term average.

Toronto's housing market was not posting declines in prices, yet the gains were, at best, modest. Composite benchmark prices in Toronto were up by 2.6 per cent in March 2019 (YoY). At the same time, new and active listings were down (YoY) in Toronto.

---

[51] Smith, C. (2019, April 2). Real Estate Board of Greater Vancouver reports brutally slow sales in March. *The Georgia Straight*. Retrieved from https://www.straight.com/news/1222321/real-estate-board-greater-vancouver-reports-brutally-slow-sales-march

[52] Newinhomes.com. (2019, April 4). Greater Toronto Area resale housing market remains steady through first quarter of 2019. Retrieved from https://www.newinhomes.com/blog/greater-toronto-area-resale-housing-market-remains-steady-through-first-quarter-of-2019

Toronto's sales in March 2019 also revealed the urban-suburban divide. Save for a small number of townhouses, sales in Toronto proper were down for detached, semi-detached, and condominiums. In comparison, the surrounding 905 suburbs showed resilience as sales were up for all housing types. Also, the average housing prices in Toronto's suburbs were up for all housing types except detached homes, which were down by 1.2 per cent (YoY).

Interestingly, March 2019 sales of homes under $400,000 represented a mere 7.5 per cent of the residential transactions in Toronto, which suggests that the regulatory changes that made lending tighter have been followed by a reduction and not an expansion in the sale of low-priced homes.

The housing forecasts for Canada suggest a march toward recovery in 2019. However, local markets may experience different outcomes, as is seen from a comparison of Toronto and Vancouver. The urban-suburban divide in large urban markets suggests that buyers should focus on local and not national-level trends in their decision-making. While home sales remained stable in Toronto and declined in Vancouver in 2018, Quebec saw both home sales and prices increase over the same period.

FOR HOUSING, 2018 WAS THE YEAR OF QUEBEC

For residential real estate, 2018 was the year of Quebec. While housing markets lost steam in other parts of the country, Quebec's market remained poised as sales and prices grew.

That was one of the takeaways from data released the Canadian Real Estate Association (CREA), which presented a broad picture of real estate markets across Canada. The data also raised some interesting questions: For instance, in a year in which prices and sales declined in many regions, was it the average price that dropped or the price of the average house? Also, how has Quebec been able to avoid the declining trends? Housing is a heterogeneous good. That means the size and type of houses sold in one year can differ from those sold a year earlier. A decline in housing prices, therefore, could mean that smaller or otherwise cheaper homes sold in 2018 than before. Let's look at the housing markets in the Greater Toronto Area to understand this better.

CREA data showed that the nominal average housing price in greater Toronto in December 2018 was up by 2.1 per cent from the year before. However, CREA's Benchmark Home Price Index, which compares prices of similarly structured homes, revealed that the benchmark price in December 2018 was up by three per cent. That suggests that a greater share of lower-priced homes were sold in 2018. The same index revealed that the prices in greater Vancouver declined by 2.7 per cent but rose by six per cent in greater Montreal in December 2018.

The Montreal housing market is structurally different from the rest of the country. Low-rise multiplexes are the dominant housing type, and renters far outnumber owners in Montreal. The demand for townhouses and row housing is therefore greater in Montreal, which is reflected in a nine-per-cent increase in their prices.

Compared to the prices in other large urban markets, housing prices in Montreal, Canada's second-largest housing market, are significantly lower and have room for further appreciation. The average nominal house price in December 2018 was $394,000 in the Montreal Census Metropolitan Area compared to $750,000 in the Greater Toronto Area.

The primary reasons cited for the decline in transactions are the rising interest rates and the stress test, which, as of January 2018, required residential mortgage applications to federally regulated lenders to qualify at a higher interest rate than the actual contracted mortgage rate. Effectively, the stress test raised the interest rate for residential real estate without having to raise the interest rate for the rest of the economy.

The stress test affected housing markets in three ways. First, a rational response to an impending new tax was to have some households advance their housing purchase to 2017. Thus, some sales that would have been realized in 2018 were advanced to 2017.

Second, some would not have qualified for any mortgage amount under the new regulation, resulting in foregone housing sales. The third impact does not affect the number of transactions, but the transaction price. The higher qualifying interest rate under the stress test lowered the loan amount, pushing demand toward relatively cheaper housing.

Thus, the combined impact of the stress tests is fewer transactions and lower average prices in 2018.

The 2018 sales data reveal that housing sales in Canada declined by 11 per cent. The decline was led mostly by urban housing markets in British Columbia and Ontario. Sales in 2018 were down by 24.5 per cent in B.C. and by 13.7 per cent in Ontario. The two provinces started 2018 weaker than before as they had already experienced other restrictive regulations including higher transfer taxes on nonresident (foreign or out-of-province) buyers and stricter rental controls.

The decline in average sale price and transactions consequently result in a decline of the total dollar volume aggregated over all sales. Whereas the buyers might appreciate the decline in prices, the same may not be true for local and provincial governments, which subsequently experience a decline in tax revenue from the land transfer taxes.

In Ontario, the total dollar volume of all residential sales in 2018 declined by 16 per cent to $108 billion - something that prompted the municipal authorities in Toronto, which levies a land transfer tax in addition to the one imposed by the province, to raise the alarm about an impending revenue shortfall expected to be $99 million.

And since the real estate industry works on commission, a 15-per-cent decline in total dollar volume and an 11-per-cent decline in transactions across Canada means a significant revenue loss for the real estate brokerage industry. Lower prices and fewer transactions also impact mortgage lenders who would have experienced a decline in the growth of their real estate portfolios.

The next section will discuss the phenomenon known as the 'forward buy' that occurred as a reaction to the stress test.

DON'T GET FOOLED BY THE 'FORWARD BUY'

In 2009, as part of a series of fiscal stimulus measures following the financial crisis, the U.S. federal government initiated a US$2.85-billion program aimed at lifting consumption and giving struggling automakers a boost. Known as Cash for Clunkers, the program paid automobile dealers anywhere between $3,500 and $4,500 when a customer traded in an older vehicle for a new fuel-efficient one. Dealers passed on the rebates to customers to incentivize the purchase of new automobiles.

When American economists Atif Mian and Amir Sufi - authors of the bestseller *House of Debt* - analyzed the impact in 957 cities across the U.S., they found the program had indeed induced the purchase of 360,000 automobiles between July and August of 2009.[53] But a deeper dive into sales data revealed that the effect of the program was not all that it seemed. Soon after the program ended, Professors Mian and Sufi, noted, automobile sales declined sharply. "The effect of the program on auto purchases (was) almost completely reversed ... only seven months after the program ended," they observed.

Rather than creating new demand, the program had essentially brought sales that were already probably going to happen forward by a few months. The phenomenon, sometimes known as "forward buy" or "forward purchase," can be seen in Canada's real estate market right now.

Implemented in January 2018, stringent mortgage regulations required borrowers to qualify at a much higher interest rate than the contracted rate with the lender. As a result, home purchases that might have otherwise transacted in 2018 or later were moved forward to November and December of 2017.

The homebuyers' response to the stress tests is completely rational. By advancing home purchases, buyers were eligible for larger loans than they

---

[53] Mian, A., & Sufi, A. (2012). The Effects of Fiscal Stimulus: Evidence from the 2009 Cash for Clunkers Program*. *The Quarterly Journal of Economics*, *127*(3), 1107–1142. https://doi.org/10.1093/qje/qjs024

would when required to qualify for an interest rate 200 basis points higher than the contracted interest rate. This kind of "forward buy" in response to a policy change can create distortions in housing statistics, and lead to an erroneous prognosis of the state of the market. For instance, sales volumes in January 2018 were lower because of those purchases having been pulled forward ahead of the new regulations.

A 2017 report by Mortgage Professionals Canada, a trade group representing mortgage brokers, claims that each year across Canada the stress test could affect 100,000 potential homebuyers who may not qualify for the desired loan amount.[54] Of those, 40,000 to 50,000 may not be eligible for any amount. The report further suggests the stress test might be accompanied with a decline in housing prices between 2.5 per cent and 12.5 per cent or more. Hence, not only are sales volumes forecasted to be lower because of the stress test, but prices are also expected to slip. Furthermore, the report projects the impact to be substantive with prolonged consequences.

GETTING AHEAD OF THE GAME

Toronto real estate sales jumped in 2007 ahead of a new land transfer tax that came into effect the following year

YEAR OVER YEAR CHANGE
IN SALES, IN PER CENT

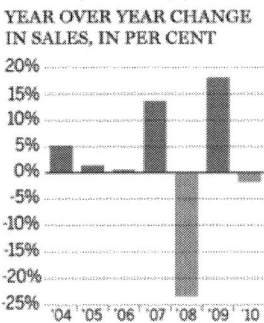

SOURCE: TORONTO REAL
ESTATE BOARD, CALCULATIONS
BY THE AUTHORS
NATIONAL POST

Figure 2.3 – Land Transfer Tax: Annual change in real estate sales in Toronto (2004-2010)

Other reports also painted a gloomy picture for housing markets. We will caution, however, against putting too much faith in forecasts of the impending housing market slowdown. Changes in regulations and housing

---

[54] Dunning, W. (2017). *Annual State of the Residential Mortgage Market in Canada*. Mortgage Professionals Canada.

market activity in the 2010s suggest a tremendous capacity for resilience.

Recall the predictions of a doomsday scenario when a new municipal land transfer tax was introduced in Toronto in 2008. Despite the forecasts of a drastic impact[55] and the lingering effects of the Great Recession, housing markets rebounded quickly.[56]

We witnessed similar resilience in Vancouver in 2017-18 where the housing markets stabilized after a series of tightening regulations, including a 15-per-cent tax on foreign homebuyers that was increased later to 20%.

Housing is a durable good and hence lasts for a long time. Therefore, the demand for housing should also be seen over a longer horizon. Policy changes can shift some sales from one year to another resulting in distortions. However, a healthy economy and a growing demographic, thanks to immigration, is likely to generate a sustained demand for housing in the long run.

The next section discusses how the stress test introduced on January 1, 2018 resulted in fewer housing sales across Canada in the first four months of 2018 compared to previous years.

SEASONAL MOOD SHIFTS IN MARKETS

Housing markets in April 2018 across Canada struggled to ward off the stresses induced by tightening regulations by federal and provincial authorities. The spring thaw many had expected in housing markets didn't realize.

April usually marks the beginning of intense housing activity in Canada. As the temperatures climb and snow melts away, homebuyers emerge from the winter slumber in search of deals. Another reason for the intense sales activity in April is because unlike other products, searching for a house takes much longer. Often, families spend two to five months searching for a home, arranging finances, and finalizing the move. Furthermore, families with children are further constrained as they would rather relocate when schools are closed for summer vacations.

For families to relocate in July or August requires them to make a purchase in April or May giving them enough time to manage the logistics, which often includes the sale of the existing home. Thus, housing markets are usually up in April and May, registering a greater share of sales and experiencing modest to high increases in housing prices.

However, housing market statistics reported by Canadian Real Estate

---

[55] Dachis, B., Duranton, G., & Turner, M. A. (2012). The effects of land transfer taxes on real estate markets: evidence from a natural experiment in Toronto. *Journal of Economic Geography*, *12*(2), 327–354. https://doi.org/10.1093/jeg/lbr007

[56] Ibid

Association (CREA) for April 2018 were devoid of such exuberance. Across Canada, housing prices were down 11.3 per cent when compared with April 2017. At the same time, housing transactions were also down by 13.9 per cent. Even when one excludes housing market activity in the greater Toronto and Vancouver areas, where housing price fluctuations have been more extreme, housing markets in other parts of the country still reported a four per cent decline.

Some would argue that April 2017 may not be a good benchmark given the rapid escalation of housing prices in the Greater Toronto Area. Thus, a comparison with sales and prices in March 2018 maybe more suitable. A month-over-month comparison also reveals that housing markets struggled across Canada as CREA reported a 3 per cent decline in sales from March to April of 2018.

Whereas aggregate housing prices experienced a decline, the same is not true for condominiums, which continued to register an increase in prices. CREA reported that apartments experienced a 14.7-per-cent increase in prices while single-family housing experienced a decline.

The resilience observed in condominium prices might be surprising to those who had warned against an oversupply of high-rise dwellings, especially in Toronto and Vancouver. It appeared that changes in mortgage regulations benefitted condominium sales because households under new regulations could qualify for lower prices that were more commonly found for condominiums.

Industry insiders hold the stress test, which required borrowers to qualify for a higher mortgage rate than the contractual rate, and provincial taxes to discourage foreign homebuyers, responsible for the uncertainty and decline in housing markets. The stress test became effective on January 1, 2018 and was expanded to cover uninsured mortgages issued by lenders regulated by the Office of the Superintendent of Financial Institutions (OSFI).

Industry observers were of the view that some mortgage business might flow to lenders not regulated by OSFI, such as provincially regulated credit unions and alternative lenders including Home Capital. Initial response to the stress test suggests that not much lending has transferred to the others. The stock market performance and valuation of alternative lenders is indicative of a lack of heightened market activity.

Listings present another riddle in housing markets. CREA data revealed that while sales were down in almost 60 per cent of the local markets in April 2018, so were listings. Some argue that the homeowners are unwilling to list homes when prices are down from their historic highs. This might be true. But what is equally interesting is that listings were also low in 2016 and early 2017 when housing markets recorded steep price escalations.

It was then argued that homeowners were waiting for the market to peak and hence hesitated to list their homes. The constrained supply, as a result, in the resale market further fuelled housing price escalation. And when the markets peaked in April 2017, especially in the Greater Toronto Area, homeowners responded, albeit a little too late, a month later by listing homes in large numbers. It appears that when it comes to market timing, many owners are out of step.

A decision facing many prospective homeowners is whether to buy now or wait until later. The stress test incentivized many Canadians to purchase homes in the months before more stringent mortgage regulations took effect in January 2018. But the stress test was just one of many factors influencing the home purchasing decisions of Canadians.

BUY A HOME NOW OR WAIT AND BUY LATER?

Uncertainty arises in markets when their future direction is unknown. Families across Canada, for example, are wondering whether the housing markets will continue to lose steam or reverse their course.

We know many readers are wondering the same thing, because the concern informs a common question: Should I buy now, or wait until later? Before we address that question, we recall a caveat from George Box, a renowned British statistician. Box warned that "all models (forecasts) are wrong; the practical question is how wrong do they have to be to not be useful."[57]

While we will try to share what we see in our "crystal ball," we are always mindful not to confuse a forecast - which is just one possible manifestation of the future out of many - with what will actually come to pass. First, let's address the question of uncertainty in housing markets. When housing prices and sales steadily rise, buyers and sellers feel confident about their decisions because they believe market outcomes are in line with their expectations. But the confidence in markets is shaken when prices or sales fall or rise rapidly.

In Canada's most populous cities, especially Toronto and Vancouver, housing prices started to accelerate in 2014-15. When the provincial and federal governments reacted with measures to instill market discipline, sales and prices declined, starting first with British Columbia in 2016, Ontario in 2017, and across the country in 2018.

Buyers and sellers want to know if the market has hit bottom or if it will decline further, with prospective buyers being particularly interested in the question of when they should jump in. While it is tempting to "time" the market by buying low and selling high, it is increasingly difficult to do it with housing.

That's because search and transaction costs, logistics and other

---

[57] Wikipedia. (2020, September 8). All models are wrong. Retrieved from https://en.wikipedia.org/wiki/All_models_are_wrong

considerations make housing transactions much more complex to structure than those involving other asset classes. Also, buyers can have different motivations: they may be transitioning from renting, switching homes or looking for an investment property. Diversity of family structure in terms of size and composition also plays a factor. Some families will have school-age children, others may have pets or both. The same applies to sellers, complicating further the potential to make a match.

The right decision for a buyer or a seller depends upon their circumstances. Families with children buy earlier in the year so that when the actual move takes places later in summer, they are settled at the new location in time for the start of the school year. This is partially the reason why sales are higher in the spring than in other seasons.

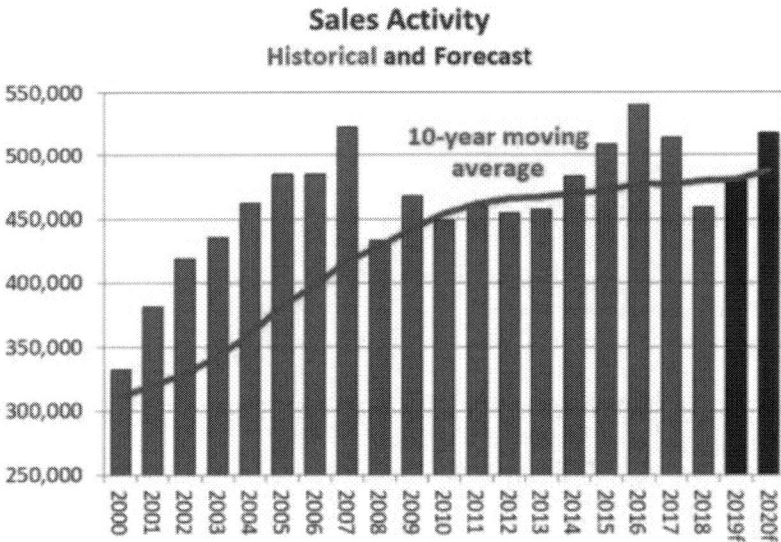

Figure 2.4 – CREA annual housing sales statistics

A buyer may want to hold on to see whether prices will drop further over the summer. For those whose decisions are not constrained by time, that can be an effective strategy. For others, especially parents of young children, a move during the school year could have additional logistical constraints.

At the same time, prospective sellers in general want to wait for prices to rise, or at least stop falling, before they list their properties. This implies that the choice of housing available during downturns might not be as diverse when markets are stable. Thus, buyers might want to wait for the dust to settle.

Housing markets are inherently local in nature. Whereas housing sales and prices declined considerably in Toronto and Vancouver, housing in Montreal presented quite a different picture. Buyers and sellers in Alberta, Quebec and elsewhere must base their decisions on local market conditions rather than on what is transpiring in Toronto or Vancouver.

Those interested in buying investment properties will have additional considerations. If the purchase involves a mortgage, the OSFI-mandated stress test will impact the maximum amount one can borrow.

Research showed that some investors who bought under-construction condominiums in Toronto wound up underwater because rent did not cover mortgage payments, maintenance fees and property taxes. This was true even though rental vacancy rates were as low as one per cent and rents have been steadily climbing in the city.[58]

MONTHLY HOUSING SALES IN TORONTO

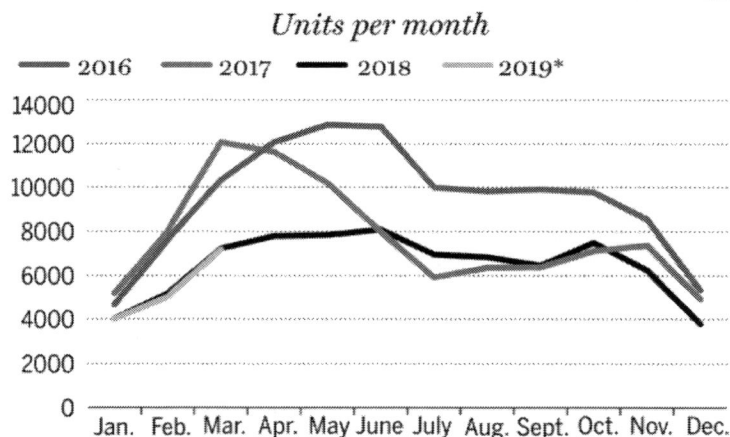

Units per month

SOURCE: CANADIAN REAL ESTATE ASSOCIATION   NATIONAL POST

Figure 2.5 – Toronto Monthly Housing Sales (2016-2019)

The resurgence in purpose-built rental construction, as is evidenced by the spike in the residential building permits in early 2019, suggested the increase in the supply of rental housing will relieve pressure on ultra-low vacancy rates and rents might also moderate as a result.

Thus, making long-term investment decisions based solely on current market conditions might not be wise. A prudent approach might be to base

---

[58] Hilderbrand, S., & Tal, B. (2018, April 6). A Window Into the World of Condo Investors. *Urbanation*. Retrieved from https://www.urbanation.ca/sites/default/files/Urbanation-CIBC%20Condo%20Investor%20Report.pdf

one's decision on a variety of scenarios, in order to ensure you are prepared for a variety of potential future market outcomes.

The future will never be known with certainty. Yet choices must be made now, which makes risks and uncertainty the channels for wealth creation. Thus, readers will be well-served if their decisions are informed by facts, reflective of their circumstances, and are influenced by their understanding of what the future may hold.

The following section will consider how decreased housing sales, brought on in part by the stress test, affected the Canadian economy in the first quarter of 2018.

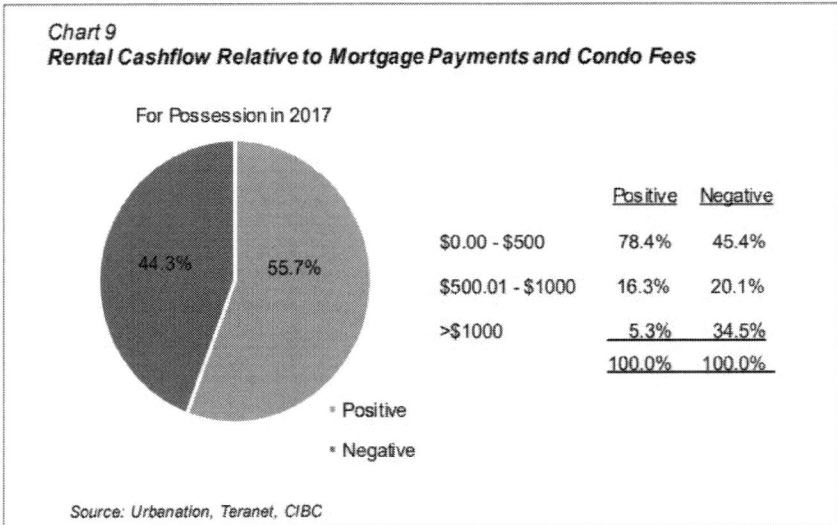

Figure 2.6 – Estimates by Urbanation for rental cashflows

HOUSING TAKES THE LUSTRE OFF THE ENTIRE ECONOMY

Did a slowdown in the housing markets take some shine off the Canadian economy in the first quarter of 2018? The answer is yes if you were to ask Stephen Poloz, governor of the Bank of Canada. Addressing the House of Commons Standing Committee on Finance in March 2018, Mr. Poloz identified two main contributors to a "slower-than-expected" economic growth in the first quarter of 2018: a slowdown in housing markets and weaker exports.[59]

---

[59] Poloz, S. S. (2018, April 23). Opening Statement before the House of Commons Standing

The forecast for the second quarter, however, was essentially positive. "So, after a lacklustre start to 2018, we project a strong rebound in the second quarter," Mr. Poloz predicted. The governor also expected the housing markets to begin recovery in the second quarter of 2018. In his statement, Poloz identified that because of the regulatory changes, including a tightening of mortgage rules in January, households pulled forward their housing purchases to the fourth quarter of 2017, resulting in a slowdown in the first quarter of 2018.

The Haider-Moranis Bulletin in December 2017 also alerted the markets to such consumer responses and explained a slowdown in housing sales in January 2018 would not "necessarily be a sign of weakening housing market, but rather a consequence of those purchases having been pulled forward ahead of the new regulations."[60]

While Poloz projected strong growth in the second quarter of 2018, he expected the growth to shift from household spending to business investment and exports. Why? An expected increase in interest rates and higher mortgage payments might put brakes on household spending on consumer goods.

However, it is not just the expected increase in debt payments that may constrain household spending. A decline in housing markets could affect household spending and, as a result, the entire economy in more ways than one.

Housing prices are tied to a household's overall wealth. Atif Mian and others, writing in the *Quarterly Journal of Economics*, identified the reasons behind a decline in household spending because of changes in housing wealth.[61] They explained that in addition to financial wealth, proxied by stocks, bonds, and other investments, a household's net worth also includes the equity it builds over time when housing values increase relative to the outstanding mortgage debt.

The equity in housing is often used as collateral for credit to finance other purchases of big-ticket items, for example, automobiles. When housing values decline, access to credit becomes difficult and, as a result, household spending declines. When housing prices collapse, the spending doesn't just decline for big-ticket items. Discretionary spending on restaurants and leisure also falls. As a result, local employment in non-tradable sectors shrinks, and

Committee on Finance. Retrieved from https://www.bankofcanada.ca/2018/04/opening-statement-april-23-2018/

[60] Haider, M., & Moranis, S. (2017, December 7). Don't get fooled by the "forward buy" in real estate data. *Financial Post.* Retrieved from https://business.financialpost.com/real-estate/the-haider-moranis-bulletin-dont-get-fooled-by-the-forward-buy-in-real-estate-data

[61] Mian, A., Rao, K., & Sufi, A. (2013). Household balance sheets, consumption, and the economic slump. *The Quarterly Journal of Economics, 128*(4), 1687–1726. Retrieved from https://academic.oup.com/qje/article-abstract/128/4/1687/1849337

the cycle repeats, perpetuating slow growth, or even a decline in economic output.

The public purse is also not immune from a decline in housing prices. A 2018 report by Toronto's city manager also raised alarms about a potential $1.4-billion gap in local revenues in the early 2020s.[62]

One of the culprits for the revenue gap is the Municipal Land Transfer Tax (LTT), implemented in February 2008 in Toronto. Since its implementation, the tax revenue has been growing gradually in step with the increasing housing prices and represented almost nine per cent of the $9 billion the City raised from taxes and user fees.

LTT revenue is expected to be lower given the sudden decline in housing prices after the province imposed new regulations to curtail foreign home buying and the stringent regulations for rental housing. A decline in housing prices affects the overall economy through a decline in property-related public sector revenues, either from a decline in property or land transfer taxes or from indirect channels through lower income and sales taxes.

Thus, a single-purpose policy of slowing housing markets could slow the overall economy. The statement by the Bank of Canada governor also concurs.

The impact of tighter mortgage regulations was longer than anticipated. While the decline in Canadian housing sales in January 2018 was expected, the decline in January 2019 was both unforeseen and disconcerting.

HOW CAN WE HEAT UP THE FROZEN HOUSING MARKET?

A retrospective view of the housing markets raises significant concerns. The impact of stringent mortgage regulations appears to be longer lasting than was initially expected.

In January 2018, housing sales declined after stricter mortgage regulations, including a stress test, were enacted. The January 2019 numbers are the first piece of evidence suggesting that housing market slowdown is deeper rooted than a direct and immediate reaction to policy interventions.

The sustained slowdown in housing markets presents at least two alternatives to the government. The first alternative is to maintain the status quo and do nothing. The second alternative is to rethink the policy interventions made in the recent past and see if there is any new evidence that warrants a change in policy.

The decline in housing sales in January 2018 was expected. A whole host

---

[62] Pagliaro, J. (2018, March 12). Toronto facing a massive $1.42-billion budget gap in five years. *The Toronto Star*. Retrieved from https://thestar.com/news/gta/2018/03/12/toronto-facing-a-massive-142-billion-budget-gap-in-five-years.html

of new regulations designed to tighten mortgage lending became effective on the first day of January 2018. Sales in December 2017 were higher than usual as households rushed to close deals to avoid being subject to stricter mortgage regulations a month later.

When January 2018 housing sales in Canada were 14.5-per-cent lower than the month before, there was no surprise, and the decline was attributed to the new stress test. Similarly, year-over-year sales were down 2.4 per cent from January 2017.

The January 2019 sales figures are more disturbing. Compared to the year before, sales in January 2019 were down by four per cent. In fact, the Canadian Real Estate Association (CREA) revealed that sales in January 2019 were the weakest since 2015. In addition to sales, housing prices also softened. The average house price across Canada was $455,000 in January 2019, 5.5-per-cent lower than the same time the previous year.

The January 2019 statistics offered the first opportunity to compare the annual change in housing market dynamics after the stress test came into effect. The decline in January 2019 above and beyond what was observed a year prior is indicative of the fact that the markets are not merely reacting to new regulations, but the markets have embraced a more systematic response that is characterized by fewer transactions and lower prices.

The weakness in housing markets also affects mortgage lending, a business the Big Five banks continue to dominate in Canada. The continued slowdown in housing sales may have influenced banks' mortgage portfolios - the first signs of such an effect could be seen when the banks release their updated earnings reports in the coming days.

Early 2019 witnessed diverse voices both questioning and supporting the efficacy of the more stringent mortgage regulations. Some believed that stress tests were working fine. Phil Soper, CEO of Royal Lepage, believed that the stress tests were needed "for the longer-term health of the economy."[63]

Others believe that the stress tests have adversely impacted homebuyers who are either unable to buy at all or are forced to accept less adequate shelter space than they would have afforded in the absence of stress tests.

After reviewing the sustained decline in housing sales, Dave Wilkes, president and CEO of the Building Industry and Land Development Association (BILD), concluded that the stress test "has overshot its target." BILD advanced two proposals for the feds to contemplate. First, to consider lowering the stress test threshold that requires borrowers to qualify at 200 basis points above the contracted rate. As the interest rates have been revised upward since the stress test was implemented, there is merit in reviewing the

---

[63] Harapyn, L. (2019, February 8). Overheating housing market was 'terrifying.' Why Royal LePage's CEO is OK with the mortgage stress test. *Financial Post*. Retrieved from https://business.financialpost.com/real-estate/overheating-housing-market-was-terrifying-why-royal-lepages-ceo-is-ok-with-the-mortgage-stress-test

threshold. Housing trade groups are also advocating to reintroduce the 30-year amortization for CMHC-insured mortgages, which was available until July 2012.

First-time homebuyers are likely to benefit more from these changes. The ability to stretch the amortization period to 30 years lowers the monthly payment and allows many to participate in home buying who would otherwise be forced to rent at a time when rental vacancy rates are at historic lows in large urban housing markets.

Critics of the 30-year mortgage point out its two obvious shortcomings. First, borrowers end up paying considerably more in interest. Second, longer amortization periods contribute to house price inflation.

Good public policy should be responsive and rooted in evidence. 2019 housing market data indicates that the impact of tighter mortgage regulations was longer lasting than what most housing experts expected. However, those who are questioning buying a home during a real estate downturn should keep in mind that housing prices generally increase substantially over longer periods.

POLICY AND INTEREST RATES ARE KEY TO THE REAL ESTATE REBOUND

Households, governments and industry watchers alike were concerned about the direction real estate markets took in 2018. Even though sales and, in some places, prices were lower than before, housing affordability did not necessarily improve.

Many wondered if it was the right time to buy or sell. Others wondered whether real estate markets were going to decline even further, or if the markets would turn around in 2019.

The answer to these questions was: It depends. It depends upon interest rates, job growth, wage increases, demand for housing, government interventions and more. While one can speculate about the future, it is always beneficial to first understand what has transpired in the past.

The greater Toronto housing market, the largest in Canada, recorded fewer sales in 2018 than it did in any of the previous 10 years. In fact, the last time Toronto's real estate market recorded fewer than 80,000 sales was in 2008.

That year was exceptional for two reasons. First, the Canadian economy was showing signs of weakness as it and most others around the world entered the Great Recession. Second, the City of Toronto imposed a new land transfer tax that made some buyers advance their home purchases to 2007, resulting in fewer sales in 2008. But even in 2008, nominal housing prices did not fall relative to 2007. That means 2018 is unique because the average nominal housing price actually declined by 4.3 per cent.

Vancouver's housing market, in which 24,619 sales were recorded in 2018, was no better. The Real Estate Board of Greater Vancouver noted sales in 2018 hit "the lowest annual total in the region since 2000." The composite benchmark price in December 2018 declined by 2.7 per cent from a year earlier.

Despite declining prices, many believed housing affordability was unlikely to improve. A report by Royal Bank of Canada observed that homeownership costs relative to median incomes will continue to rise in Canada. The RBC report said that by the end of 2019, "owning a home will take up 79 per cent of the median household income" in Toronto.[64] In Vancouver, homeownership costs claim 88 per cent of the median household income. RBC expects homeownership costs to rise in Calgary, Edmonton, Ottawa and Montreal.

The high levels of household debt in expensive housing markets is another source of concern. CMHC reported that the debt-to-income ratio was 208 per cent for the residents of Toronto. For Vancouverites, it was even worse at 242 per cent.[65]

PAST THE PEAK?

The average price of a home sold in Greater Toronto declined in 2018, after more than doubling over the previous decade

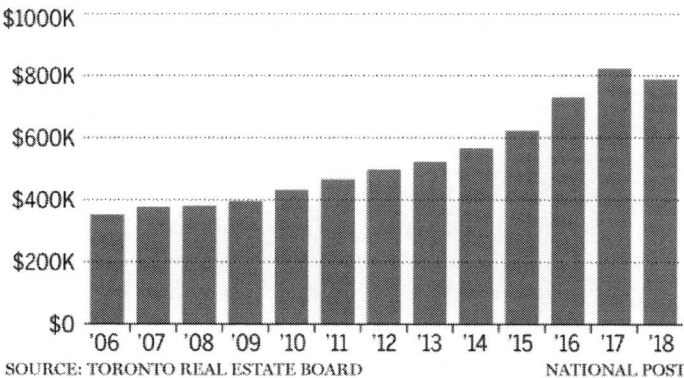

SOURCE: TORONTO REAL ESTATE BOARD   NATIONAL POST

Figure 2.7 – Average Sale Price for Homes in the Greater Toronto Area (2006-2018)

---

[64] Naidu-Ghelani, R. (2019, January 5). Home ownership costs to rise in 2019 even as housing market cools: RBC. *CBC News*. Retrieved from https://www.cbc.ca/news/business/house-prices-affordability-income-1.4966211
[65] Canada Mortgage and Housing Corporation. (2018, December 13). Household Debt-to-Income Ratio Near Record High. Retrieved from https://www.cmhc-schl.gc.ca/en/housing-observer-online/2018-housing-observer/household-debt-income-ratio-near-record-high

Most of the household debt comprises mortgage debt, which is sensitive to changes in interest rates. The Bank of Canada raised interest rates multiple times in the late 2010s. The Bank's decision in January 2019 not to raise rates any further suggests that the Bank is mindful of the slowdown in the global economy that has been worsened by the trade tussle between the U.S. and China.

While consensus is lacking about the future of interest rates in Canada, many believe that the fundamentals are missing to justify significant interest hikes in Canada in 2019. This will be good news for homeownership.

Housing markets have withstood a series of policy interventions by provincial and federal governments that include additional transactional taxes on foreign homebuyers, stringent mortgage regulations, stress tests, rising interest rates and more. The slowdown in housing markets, one must realize, is the expected and intended response to a series of regulatory changes and hence must not be viewed solely as a sign of market weakness.

At the same time, one should also consider a long-term view of the property markets. Housing is a durable good that provides shelter and other amenities while growing in value as an asset class. The average home price in greater Vancouver and Toronto increased by 100 per cent from 2009 to 2019. The increase in average housing prices over the long run should, therefore, provide perspective to those who own or are considering buying a house.

Building equity through home ownership is a goal for many Canadians. However, increased mortgage rates can result in higher mortgage payments and greater home ownership costs which decreases housing affordability and prices some prospective home buyers out of home ownership altogether.

HOUSING CHALLENGES AND HIGH MORTGAGE PAYMENTS

A report by RBC Economic Research warned that housing affordability continues to worsen in Canada. The ownership costs for a home bought in the second quarter of 2018 consumed 53.9 per cent of a typical household's income.[66]

The RBC report claims that housing affordability had not been that bad in Canada since the early '90s. In metropolitan areas that saw a rapid acceleration in housing prices, such as Vancouver and Toronto, housing carrying costs could claim upward of 75 per cent of a typical household's income.

What is driving the latest housing affordability "crisis" is not necessarily a

---

[66] RBC Economic Research. (2018). *Housing trends and affordability*. Retrieved from http://www.rbc.com/economics/economic-reports/pdf/canadian-housing/house-sep2018.pdf

sustained increase in housing prices, but instead an increase in mortgage rates that require a larger share of a typical household's pretax income to cover the payments.

The RBC report reveals that the increase in housing prices was not commensurate with an increase in household incomes. So how did Canadians continue to afford homes as prices increased, but their incomes didn't? The answer is cheap credit and mortgage regulations that promoted binge household borrowing.

Mortgage rates are a double-edged sword. When low, they fuel price inflation and worsen housing affordability. When prices are eventually higher, an increase in mortgage rates further worsens affordability because carrying costs are highly sensitive to lending rates.

Record low mortgage rates, the sustained increase in the size of mortgage loans, and the ability to stretch one's mortgage to 40 years and beyond meant that households could afford to purchase even more expensive homes despite their stagnating nominal incomes and, in many cases, declining real incomes.

CANADA'S GROWING MORTGAGE DEBT

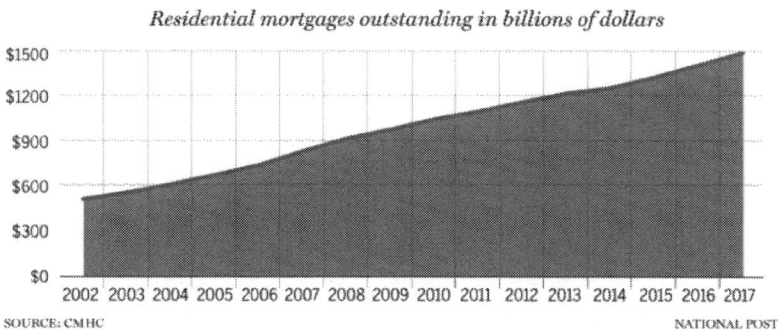

Residential mortgages outstanding in billions of dollars

SOURCE: CMHC   NATIONAL POST

Figure 2.6 – Total Canadian Mortgage Debt (2002-2017)

The usual drivers of an increase in housing prices are higher housing demand resulting from an increase in population or income levels. The increase in the Canadian population is mostly driven by immigration. The increase in urban populations is even more dependent upon immigration levels. The population-based increase in demand is, therefore, a matter of public policy that determines the number of immigrants being allowed in the country.

On the other hand, the increase in household incomes is not necessarily determined by public policy. A growing, innovation-driven economy will induce higher incomes. That's not true for large cities in Canada where a growing segment of recent expansion in jobs is in part-time employment, which is hardly a driver of wage growth needed to support either an increase in consumption or the prices of consumer durables.

The usual suspects for housing price inflation have neither been an excessive out-of-control demographic pressure or higher wages. Hence, when ownership costs are pegged against typical household incomes, one could see the erosion of housing affordability over the past decade.

Household consumption in Canada has essentially been supported by an increase in household debt, which broke through the $2-trillion threshold in 2018.[67] Most of the household debt is tied up in the mortgage markets.

The increase in Canadian housing prices was largely driven by the increase in prices in Toronto and Vancouver. The respective provincial governments in 2016 and 2017 took measures to decelerate the growth in housing prices. Furthermore, the stress tests imposed on lenders regulated by OSFI further moderated the rate at which house prices were rising.

Hence, the worsening of housing affordability in 2018 is not because of the rapid increase in housing prices. What eroded housing affordability is the increase in mortgage payments resulting from higher mortgage rates for housing prices that stood at historically high levels.

The age of cheap credit appears to be over where mortgage rates are likely to increase in the future pushing the carrying costs even higher. The true effects of the tightening mortgage markets will be felt later when borrowers return to renew their mortgages at higher rates.

The last time housing affordability was as bad in Canada was in the early '90s when mortgage rates were in double digits. The ensuing recession contributed to a lost decade for housing when prices either stayed flat or declined. Though mortgage rates inched upward in 2018, they remained at historically low levels unable to trigger a major correction in housing markets.

The next section will consider whether interest rates for the stress test were set too high and led to unintended economic consequences such as pricing out too many first-time homebuyers and subsequently placing increased pressure on rental markets.

ARE MORTGAGE STRESS TESTS MISSING THE MARK?

A series of regulatory changes, which included interest-rate hikes, taxes on foreign homebuyers and stress tests, contributed to a slowdown in housing markets in Canada in 2018.

---

[67] Poloz, S. S. (2018, May 1). Canada's Economy and Household Debt: How Big Is the Problem? Retrieved from https://www.bankofcanada.ca/2018/05/canada-economy-household-debt-how-big-the-problem/

That's the conclusion of a report from the Mortgage Professionals Canada (MPC) that questioned whether government interventions in the mortgage market were too intrusive and could lead to further unintended economic outcomes. Specifically, MPC, an industry group that represents mortgage and service providers, contends that the stress tests have relied on "the wrong interest rate," thereby exacerbating the slowdown.[68]

The report questions the fundamental premise of the stress tests, which were intended to determine the debt worthiness of borrowers in case interest rates were to rise in the future. Mortgage defaults, the MPC argues, are influenced more by increases in job losses and not necessarily by changes in interest rates. Housing sales in 2018 declined by 11 per cent, but the amount of outstanding mortgage credit at the end of 2018 was estimated to be a staggering $1.55 trillion.

NO JOB, NO MORTGAGE PAYMENT

When the unemployment rate rises, Canadians have more trouble keeping up with their mortgage payments

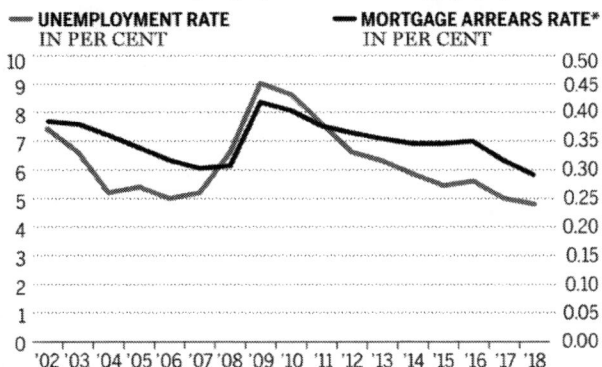

— UNEMPLOYMENT RATE IN PER CENT   — MORTGAGE ARREARS RATE* IN PER CENT

* Data for 2018 includes only January.

SOURCE: CMHC, FEDERAL RESERVE BANK OF ST. LOUIS   NATIONAL POST

Figure 2.8 – Canadian Unemployment and Mortgage Arrears Rate (2002-2018)

While the decline in sales adversely impacted mortgage brokerages and lenders, the MPC report suggests that the effect on the larger economy could include many unintended consequences. The stress tests require borrowers, both first-time homebuyers and those applying for in-transfer of existing mortgages, to qualify at a rate two percentage points higher than the

---

[68] Dunning, W. (2018). *Report on the Housing and Mortgage Market in Canada*. Retrieved from https://mortgageproscan.ca/docs/default-source/consumer-reports/housing-and-mortgage-market-report_july2018.pdf

contracted rate. However, the report argued that the threshold is unduly high and ignored the fact that in five years, a borrower's income would be higher and they would have paid a significant amount toward the principal.

If the average wage increase in Canada is about two per cent, in five years a typical borrower's income would be more than 10-percent higher. Furthermore, in five years, the borrowers would have made a "substantial amount of principal repayment," as much as 13 to 14 per cent.

The stress test should account for higher incomes and reduced principal amount five years down the road. Thus, if one needed to test whether a borrower could service the debt if interest rates were to rise by two percentage points five years later, "a rate that is 0.75 points higher than the initial contracted rate" should have sufficed today.

The MPC report believed that many first-time homebuyers were either prevented from qualifying for the home they desire or were shut out of the market altogether. Those who cannot buy are forced to rent, which increased pressure on the already tight rental markets where rents appreciated by 3.4 per cent in 2018.

The justification for the stress tests is that an increase in interest rates will increase the debt servicing costs that might force some or many homeowners into foreclosures. The MPC report though challenges this assumption and argued that mortgage default rates were not sensitive to changes in interest rates. Instead, they are more sensitive to job losses, and thus the stress tests might not be much of a safeguard. In fact, 2018 estimates of mortgage arrears in Canada were historically low at 0.24 per cent (1 in 424 borrowers) and had been falling since 2009.

Canada's mortgage industry and consumer borrowing are fast evolving. Of the nine-plus million homeowner households, more than six million own with a mortgage. Household debt in Canada has expanded from $349 billion in 1990 to $2.19 trillion in 2018, such that mortgages now account for 65 per cent of household debt.

And then there are informal lenders or *gifters* in the form of the Bank of Mom and Dad. Almost 20 per cent of recent first-time homebuyers acknowledged that gifts and loans from family helped them with the down payment.

The consequences of a slowdown in housing markets affect the entire economy, including jobs in real estate and construction as well as the revenue generated by land-transfer and other related taxes. The unintended consequences, such as the increase in the demand for rental housing, are also numerous.

Stability in labour markets is the key to stability in housing markets. If regulators agree that the ability to service debt is affected more by job losses than the interest rates and that incomes grow and the principal amount owed declines over time, then there is merit in reviewing the stress test thresholds.

Though real estate markets across Canada were down in 2018, statistics showed that the outlook for 2019 was more positive, with prices and sales predicted to grow slightly.

THERE ARE REASONS TO BE OPTIMISTIC ABOUT REAL ESTATE

For housing markets in Canada, 2018 was a year of restraint. The mortgage stress test was perhaps the most influential policy change that affected homebuyers in 2018. Under the rules, which came into effect in January 2018, most homebuyers were required to qualify for a mortgage at a higher rate than the contracted mortgage rate. This was done to determine the borrower's ability to service the mortgage debt in case the interest rates suddenly increased.

To avoid qualifying for a mortgage under stringent regulations, many buyers advanced their housing purchases to 2017. Seasonally adjusted data from the Canadian Real Estate Association (CREA) shows that over 46,000 homes transacted across Canada in December 2017. With stress test in place, housing transactions in January 2018 declined by 14 per cent from the month before.

Regional housing markets were also affected by changes in mortgage regulations. Housing sales in Greater Toronto were slower in 2018 than the in 2017 or 2016.

Across Canada, inflation-adjusted housing prices remained rather flat between the second quarter of 2017 and the fourth quarter of 2018. These trends were essentially driven by the slowdown in Ontario after the province imposed new taxes on foreign homebuyers in April 2017. Given a lacklustre 2018 and in the absence of a major economic shock, housing markets were likely to maintain the status quo or experience a slight growth in prices and sales in 2019.

Canada Mortgage and Housing Corporation (CMHC) expected housing prices to move in step with economic fundamentals. Thus, if incomes, jobs, and population growth evolve stably, housing markets are expected to respond accordingly.[69] CMHC believes sales transacting through the Multiple Listing Service (MLS) to be less than 500,000 in 2019. This number is in line with the slower sales in 2017, but lower than the sales activity observed earlier in 2016.

---

[69] Canada Mortgage and Housing Corporation. (2018, November 6). *Housing Market Activity to Moderate in 2019 and 2020: CMHC Report.* Retrieved from https://www.cmhc-schl.gc.ca/en/media-newsroom/news-releases/2018/housing-market-activity-moderate-2019-2020-cmhc-report

CMHC expects the average Canadian housing price in 2019 to be under $525,000. However, the regional sales and price forecasts differ significantly. Urban housing markets in Ontario were expected to recover from the "dampened activity in 2018" because of expected strong job growth and in-migration.

CMHC expected housing markets in British Columbia to moderate even further given the expected economic and demographic slowdown. Housing prices (measured as a composite index) in Vancouver, B.C.'s largest housing market, were growing at a slower rate since 2016 when British Columbia imposed new transaction taxes on foreign homebuyers. The RBC Economic Research also reported that the housing transactions in Vancouver in October 2018 were 35 per cent less than the sales in October 2017.

RBC data shows that resales in Calgary were down by nine per cent in October 2018 from a year prior. The composite housing price index for Calgary was also down by 2.6 per cent year-over-year in October 2018. No other large housing market reported a decline in composite housing price index in October 2018.

Montreal is likely to benefit from growing interest by foreign-based buyers in 2019. Unlike Toronto and Vancouver, Montreal has not imposed a tax on foreign homebuyers. Some transactions that would have landed in Toronto and Vancouver might end up in Montreal because of the tax advantage. Also, CMHC expected a decline in rental vacancy rates in Montreal resulting from higher demand because of in-migration and favourable economic conditions.

CMHC anticipated housing sales and prices of existing homes in Nova Scotia to appreciate in 2019. The rest of Atlantic Canada, especially the urban housing markets, will continue to face challenges from a lack of sustained demographic growth.

At the same time, there were concerns about the housing markets in the U.S. Writing in The New York Times, Robert Shiller, a Nobel Laureate in Economics, warns that there is a "limit on how much the prices of existing homes can increase." He observed that the rapidly accelerating "prices of single-family homes may fall soon" in the U.S.

Canadian housing markets avoided the fallout from the late 2000s housing market crash in the U.S. In a post-NAFTA world in which Canada is less reliant on the U.S. for trade, it is likely that a future slowdown in the American housing market would be even less of a concern for Canadian housing markets.

The next section will consider the effect of home staging on prospective buyers' opinions and sales prices. As one study found, buyers had a better impression of staged homes but did not necessarily pay higher prices.

REAL ESTATE STAGING IS ON THE RISE BUT DOES IT REALLY WORK?

Most people who have bought or sold a home are familiar with the concept of staging, in which a seller brings in new, sometimes expensive furniture and decor on a temporary basis in order to cast their home in the best possible light. But does home staging really work? Does it help a home sell more quickly or at a higher price? If you ask the real estate industry, most believe it does. However, independent research on the subject is hard to find, and the available evidence is somewhat inconclusive.

While they are not necessarily "staged," almost all homes are prepared to some extent before being sold. Most real estate agents will advise clients to make cosmetic changes to a house before it is listed. Those can include everything from removing clutter to hiding excess furniture to replacing personal artifacts and can even extend to repainting the walls. A full staging, however, usually involves replacing the owners' furniture with rented items while the home is listed, with the living room, kitchen and master bedroom the most likely to be upgraded.

Staging can last from a minimum of two months up to six months or longer for expensive homes, with costs ranging from $2,000 to $10,000 per month depending on how extensive the changes are. And it's a practice that continues to evolve.

Heaps Estrin Real Estate, a Toronto-based real estate firm, struck a partnership with BMW Canada to place high-end luxury vehicles in the driveways of "exceptional properties." As part of an initial pilot project, the real estate firm placed high-end BMW models in select homes listed between $2.9 million to $5.9 million. The vehicles could be used in online listings for the properties as well.[70]

Whereas the real estate industry believes that home staging works, hard evidence to support these claims is harder to find. On a psychological level, there are some obvious benefits. David Nickerson, a professor in the School of Real Estate Management at Ryerson University, noted that a cluttered space is not only unattractive, but "could be interpreted as a signal of inattention to house maintenance on the part of the owner - hence a signal about adverse selection." Put simply, Nickerson believes that "buyers are attracted to neatness."

But does the attraction translate into a higher price? Mark Lane and co-authors writing in the *Journal of Housing Research* studied the merits of staging homes. They found that despite widely held beliefs within the real estate

---

[70] Heaps Estrin. (2019, July 30). BMW Canada and The Heaps Estrin Real Estate Team launch luxury real estate initiative. Retrieved from https://heapsestrin.com/bmw-canada-and-the-heaps-estrin-real-estate-team-launch-luxury-real-estate-initiative/

industry, "furniture quality and colour choices do not appear to have a significant effect on the actual revealed market value of the property."[71] Though the research showed no impact on the willingness to pay a higher price, the researchers found a "strong impact on the perceived livability and overall impression of the home." Specifically, respondents had a lower overall impression of units with unattractive wall colours and/or furniture. Similarly, the respondents also ranked the same homes lower for livability.

Lane and his co-authors, however, did not analyze real home sales data. They created 3-D virtual home tours where they changed the staging attributes (wall colour or type of furniture) one at a time and sought responses from prospective buyers. This raises the question of whether real homebuyers discriminate between staged and un-staged homes.

The National Association of Realtors (NAR) in the U.S. did a review of home staging in 2017.[72] NAR compiled feedback from 1,894 realtors who have worked with clients as sellers' or buyers' agents. The NAR survey revealed that almost half of the buyers' agents believed that home staging affected "most buyers' view of the home." Nearly two in five sellers' agents revealed that they staged all homes before listing.

One in three buyers' agents and 29 per cent of sellers' agents believed that staging a home increased the dollar value of a dwelling, relative to un-staged comparables, by one to five per cent. Another 21 per cent of the sellers' agents thought that the increase in value was between six and 10 per cent. Almost two-in-five sellers' agents also believed that staged homes sold faster than un-staged comparables. As for who pays the staging costs, NAR survey revealed that in 29 per cent of the cases, the seller paid while in 43 per cent of the cases, the realtor personally staged the dwelling unit or offered to hire a staging service.

A review of the literature suggests that staging homes works, at least in the minds of those with a vested interest in selling properties. Real estate agents believe that staged homes influence buyers' opinions and impact their willingness to pay. Prospective buyers also consider the staged homes to be more livable and having a better overall impression. Whether those buyers pay more is a subject that requires further study.

Another strategy used by homeowners to sell their houses faster and for higher prices is open houses. However, municipalities must find a balance between better market outcomes and concerns for safety and aesthetics.

---

[71] Lane, M. A., Seiler, M. J., & Seiler, V. L. (2015). The Impact of Staging Conditions on Residential Real Estate Demand. *Journal of Housing Research*. Retrieved from http://aresjournals.org/doi/abs/10.5555/1052-7001.24.1.21

[72] National Association of Realtors Research Department. (2017). *2017 profile of home staging*. Retrieved from https://www.nar.realtor/sites/default/files/migration_files/reports/2017/2017-profile-of-home-staging-07-06-2017.pdf

OPEN HOUSES HELP SELL HOMES

The real estate sector relies on marketing for success. Despite the innovations in digital technology, traditional marketing strategies of placing "for sale" signs on front yards and directional "open house" signs placed near intersections have survived the digital age.

Most municipalities, with some restrictions, allow realtors to post their temporary signs on public and private properties. However, the proliferation of signs has led some to impose new restrictions to limit visual pollution or possible interference with road and sidewalk use. Stricter regulations on real estate marketing could adversely impact housing sales when markets are struggling. However, in the age of ubiquitous social media, posted signs on lawn fronts could be economically redundant.

Municipal bylaws regulate signage. The bylaws define when and where signs can be placed so that the signage does not interfere with vehicular and pedestrian movements. Signs are also monitored for size and the length of time they are displayed. Some municipalities impose additional restrictions by prohibiting electronic, blinking, or changeable signs. The Toronto Real Estate Board (TREB) in 2019 instructed its members to be mindful of the municipal bylaws about the installation of temporary signs and the Board's professional standards department investigates complaints of bylaw violations.

Richmond Hill, a suburb of Toronto, amended its bylaws in July 2019 to permit signs for open houses as part of a six-month pilot. Previously, the town did not allow such signage. Though the change was likely welcomed by the real estate industry, it came with additional restrictions: The bylaw restricted brokers from displaying their contact information on the sign.

TREB believed the identity restriction conflicts with the Real Estate and Business Brokers Act in Ontario, which required realtors to include identification information on their advertisements. The move also likely increased enforcement costs because bylaw enforcers had to search the particulars of the violating party.

But do open houses deliver better outcomes for sellers? Many home sellers believe that open houses attract prospective buyers resulting in a higher sale price and probably less time on market. Realtors, however, have not always been as sure. A 1998 study of realtors found that "that 77 per cent of brokers surveyed who hold a public open house do so merely to appease the seller and only 41 per cent of the brokers surveyed believe the technique helps sell the house."[73]

Research by Marcus T. Allen and co-authors in the *Journal of Real Estate Research* explored the perceived benefits of several marketing strategies,

---

[73] Harris, J. C. (1998). Survey Slams Door on Open Houses. *Tierra Grande.*

including the staging of open houses for the public and exclusively for other brokers.[74] Working with a large database of 67,295 of single-family home sales in Dallas County, Texas, the researchers found that public open houses did indeed contribute to higher prices with estimates varying between 1.7 per cent to 2.1 per cent. Exclusive open houses for brokers had even more significant price effects ranging from 3.3 per cent to 3.6 per cent. The researchers, therefore, concluded that "public open houses are worthwhile for the seller even if brokers, in general, do not believe they are that beneficial." Open houses, though, did not necessarily help sell the properties faster. The same research found that public and broker open houses were associated with longer time-on-market ranging between one to 25 days.

Online marketing of real estate also delivers desirable outcomes for sellers. A 2018 paper in the *Journal Real Estate Finance and Economics* showed that an "increase in the average daily number of views of a house's listing" on the MLS increased the probability of sale and sale price, and reduced marketing time.[75]

Research has shown that open houses result in a higher sale price. This implies higher land transfer taxes for municipalities. The challenge for municipalities is, therefore, to find the balance between better market outcomes and the concerns for safety and esthetics.

SUMMARY

This chapter has illustrated the workings of housing markets in large and small Canadian cities. It explored the spatial diversity in housing market outcomes across Canada and identified behavioural responses to policy changes that may push or pull housing transactions from one period to the other, a phenomenon known as forward buy. The chapter highlighted the role housing plays in the larger economy. In addition, the chapter discussed fundamental changes in regulatory frameworks, such as the introduction of mortgage stress tests in January 2018, which influenced the housing market outcomes in Canada. Finally, the chapter reviewed marketing strategies in housing markets to determine which selling strategies deliver higher prices or faster sales.

---

[74] Allen, M. T., Cadena, A., Rutherford, J., & Rutherford, R. C. (2015). Effects of real estate brokers' marketing strategies: Public open houses, broker open houses, MLS virtual tours, and MLS photographs. *Journal of Real Estate Research, 37*(3), 343–369. Retrieved from http://aresjournals.org/doi/abs/10.5555/0896-5803.37.3.343

[75] Allen, M. T., Dare, W. H., & Li, L. (2018). MLS Information Sharing Intensity and Housing Market Outcomes. *Journal of Real Estate Finance and Economics, 57*(2), 297–313. https://doi.org/10.1007/s11146-017-9612-5

3 COVID-19'S IMPACT ON PROPERTY MARKETS

In the first quarter of 2020, businesses all over the world became increasingly concerned about the coronavirus's impact on various markets as the death count and the number of affected individuals mounted.

Could the coronavirus adversely impact property markets in China and beyond, many wondered. The answer mostly depended on how quickly the virus was prevented from spreading within China and elsewhere. In the meantime, the uncertainty about the potential for contagion kept chief risk officers awake at night.

The 2020 COVID-19 outbreak was caused by a new strain in the family of viruses characterized as coronavirus. A similar epidemic in 2003 caused by Severe Acute Respiratory Syndrome (SARS) impacted Hong Kong and many other countries, including Canada.

In 2003, Toronto was one of the first places in Canada to experience SARS-related emergencies. Health officials implemented strict protocols to prevent the virus from spreading. Even handshakes were discouraged.

During the 2003 convocation ceremonies at the University of Toronto, the traditional handshake with the school's president was replaced with a gentle head bow. Earlier precautionary measures to contain the virus discouraged discretionary travel and face-to-face interactions.

Generally, a slowdown in market activity is likely when consumers avoid grocery stores, hair salons and/or restaurants, but is it significant enough to cause a decline in economic output, including property markets? Despite the challenges resulting from SARS, the Canadian economy did not necessarily experience a slowdown in 2003. COVID-19 in 2020, however, proved to be a different story altogether.

Even with SARS, Canadian GDP grew to $892 billion in 2003 from $758 billion in 2002, and it ultimately crossed the trillion-dollar threshold in 2004. Hong Kong, the epicentre of the 2003 SARS epidemic, experienced a slight slowdown, with GDP declining to US$161 billion in 2003 from US$166 billion a year earlier. The Hong Kong economy, though, had not been growing since 1997 when GDP reached US$177 billion. Hence, the slowdown in 2003, even if meaningful, could not be entirely attributed to SARS. Even neighbouring China's economy grew, to US$1.6 trillion in 2003 from US$1.3 trillion in 2002. Chinese economic growth, however, took off in 2006, with record year-over-year GDP growth that has lasted for more than a decade.

As for property markets, recall that Toronto bore the brunt of SARS in Canada. If anyone was expecting a slowdown in housing sales or moderation in housing prices, they might look at a city where handshakes were almost forbidden.

Interestingly, housing sales data from 2003 in Toronto show no apparent signs of suffering. Sales increased to 78,898 units in 2003 from 74,759 units in 2002. Similarly, the average sale price increased by around $18,000 during the same time. Essentially, the growth in sales and prices in 2003 was in-line with long-term trends.

The numbers above raise two related questions: Did SARS, despite the enormous death toll and the cost of the resources mobilized to contain the threat, had a limited economic impact elsewhere as well? And can one draw any inferences from SARS for what property markets may experience from COVID-19? The housing market dynamics in 2003 in Hong Kong offer some context.

The SARS epidemic claimed the lives of 300 Hong Kong residents, representing a third of all SARS-related deaths worldwide. Grace Wong Bucchianeri, a former professor at Wharton, reported in the *Journal of Urban Economics* in 2008 that housing prices in Hong Kong fell by eight per cent, equivalent to a total value of US$28 billion.[76]

This raises the question of whether the decline in Hong Kong housing prices in 2003 resulted entirely from SARS or was it an acceleration of the lingering "pre-SARS downward trend." Controlling for the "already frail Hong Kong housing market," Bucchianeri observed a moderate average price decline of 2.6 per cent that could be attributed to SARS.

Coronavirus claimed many more lives than SARS did in 2003. The uncertainty about how long the threat will last and how quickly it can be contained will weigh heavily on the markets. Since the epicentre of the breakout is far from Canada, it would be unwise to assume that the adverse impacts on Canadian markets will be moderate at worst.

---

[76] Wong, G. (2008). Has SARS infected the property market? Evidence from Hong Kong. *Journal of Urban Economics*, 63(1), 74–95. https://doi.org/10.1016/j.jue.2006.12.007

COVID-19, THE EARLY DAYS

The novel coronavirus (COVID-19) may have started as a health scare in China, it quickly spread to more than 100 countries. The contagion sent global stock markets into panic mode. Before the lockdown in mid-March (2020), housing markets in Canada and Australia, appeared undeterred by the jitters. In fact, the markets were strengthened by the interest rate cuts implemented to combat the pandemic.

At the same time, home-refinance applications in the U.S. have surged by 79 per cent, as per the U.S. Mortgage Bankers Association's refinance index. But is real estate truly immune from the impact of the COVID-19, which was officially deemed a pandemic by the World Health Organization in early March 2020?

Some real estate sectors are more vulnerable than others. The surge in cancellations for tourist travel, soon after the pandemic declaration, not only affected airlines but also hotels and others in the lodging industry. By September of 2020, travel and hospitality industry remained in the red facing huge losses.

March is usually one of the busiest travel seasons of the year as families travel during the March break. Because of COVID-19, cancellations were at an all-time high, something that put formidable stress on the hotel industry.

Some investors, meanwhile, expected REITs to do well in times of uncertainty because, with long-term leases, landlords were likely to enjoy more stable cash flows than manufacturers and others who are more sensitive to short-term declines in the demand. In addition to office and large retail real estate, where tenants usually have longer leases, investors were reportedly favouring purpose-built rental housing and self-storage real estate.

On the flip side, growing restrictions on large public gatherings hurt sports arenas and movie theatres. Similarly, emerging disrupters who provide short-term rental space, such as Airbnb and WeWork, were also more susceptible to cancellations and a decline in new business because of shorter leases.

While preparing for possible disruptions to the academic calendar, many universities shifted to digital delivery of classes while shutting down their campuses in a hurry. Harvard University in Cambridge, Mass., for example, emptying university residences and shifted all classes online in March and April of 2020.

If online learning, which has struggled to gain mainstream acceptance, becomes a reasonable substitute for in-class learning, universities might lower future spending on campus expansions in cities with expensive land markets.

If a small-town university were to do the same, the owners of student rental housing might not feel the pinch immediately, given the signed leases, but could eventually find that demand would plummet.

Following the U.S. lead, the Bank of Canada also lowered the key lending rate by 50 basis points in early March. Stephen Poloz, Bank of Canada's governor, believed that the rate cut was more likely to have a stabilizing effect in a downturn "rather than contribute to froth."

Doug Porter, Bank of Montreal's chief economist, disagreed and argued that the rate cut was likely to "put (Canadian) housing on steroids." A 50-basis point rate cut in Australia prompted a similar warning by the International Monetary Fund (IMF). Laxed financial conditions "could re-accelerate house price inflation," urged the IMF. The annual increase in housing prices in Melbourne and Sydney has crossed double digits. Not to mention, the household debt-to-income ratio in Australia was approaching 200 per cent.

The diversity of real estate implies that the impact of the novel coronavirus has not been uniform. Owner-occupied housing has benefitted from the rate cuts and pent up demand, which we discuss later in the chapter.

RESPONDING TO COVID-19 WITH STIMULUS AND FORBERANCE

Governments and businesses all over adapted fast to the restrictions imposed to cope with COVID-19. The ensuing economic slowdown affected cashflows of workers whose jobs were interrupted. By late March 2020, the Canadian government responded with a sizable initial stimulus plan of $82 billion, including $27 billion in direct support and the rest in tax deferrals. The government announced plans to purchase up to $50 billion of insured mortgage pools, a move to provide liquidity to the banks. Also, the big six Canadian banks stepped up with plans for mortgage payment deferrals for up to six months to help homeowners who may experience sudden job loss or are furloughed for an indefinite period.

But were these steps enough? For instance, renters, comprising almost 33 per cent of Canadian households, received no comparable relief in the early stimulus and relief announcements. To support the real estate sector, it is likely that a range of interventions will be needed with mortgage-loan forbearance, a moratorium on rental evictions and a tax holiday from property taxes being among the options. The response should also be broad and include renter households and others, such as small businesses, who may face additional hardships with rent or refinancing of their commercial mortgages.

Recent examples from the U.S. could inform strategies to cope with the unexpected slowdown. In 2011, for instance, the Obama administration adjusted the Federal Housing Administration (FHA) conditions to compel mortgage servicers to extend the forbearance duration from three months to 12 months.

The change in regulation was devised to help homeowners stay in their homes as they search for new employment. Former secretary of U.S. Housing and Urban Development, Shaun Donovan, revealed in 2011 that 45 per cent of unemployed Americans had been out of work for more than six months. Hence, the need for a longer-duration mortgage relief. The forbearance program for unemployed American homeowners was set to expire in August 2013. However, the FHA extended the program indefinitely in July of the same year.

Forbearance on its own might not be a sufficient response. The U.S. government in 2010 had announced a US$7.6-billion Hardest Hit Fund and a US$1-billion Emergency Homeowner Loan Program in addition to the loan forbearance requirements that were announced a year later. Also, the Home Affordable Modification Program (HAMP), launched in 2009, reduced the monthly payments of struggling borrowers to 31 per cent of the borrower's monthly income.

Research by Sumit Agarwal of the National University of Singapore and others found that HAMP "prevented a substantial number of foreclosures." It was also associated with a lower rate of "consumer debt delinquencies, house price declines, and an increase in durable spending."[77]

The authors, though, observed that the program reached only one-third of the targeted households. The extensive screening of qualifying borrowers slowed the pace of the program. The authors recommended that for future implementation, the trade-off between stringent scrutiny and the ability to provide quick relief to many distressed borrowers be viewed with care.

Extending forbearance duration comes at a cost. Whereas the delayed mortgage payments and forgone interest can be added to the owed principal, there are other financial costs to consider. For instance, qualifying the deserving borrowers and monitoring their legitimate attempts for re-employment will impose additional implementation costs on lenders who would then need support from the government to bear additional costs.

The mortgage payment relief should not be restricted to the homeowners' primary residence in case they have rental investment properties. If a renter becomes unemployed and stops paying the rent, private landlords will face hardship servicing the mortgage for investment properties. Hence, qualifying for mortgage payment relief must be tied to the employment status of the resident of a dwelling and not necessarily its owner.

At the same time, the relief must be extended to renters whose finances are often more fragile than homeowners, who, in time of need, can borrow from home equity. A moratorium on renter evictions for 12 months or more

---

[77] Agarwal, S., Amromin, G., Ben-David, I., Chomsisengphet, S., Piskorski, T., & Seru, A. (2017). Policy Intervention in Debt Renegotiation: Evidence from the Home Affordable Modification Program. *The Journal of Political Economy*, *125*(3), 654–712. https://doi.org/10.1086/691701

is needed to provide shelter security to the vulnerable renter households.

Small businesses, such as restaurants or private gyms, are likely to bear the brunt of social distancing. Business owners will experience immediate declines in cash flow, limiting their ability to pay rent or mortgage on their commercial properties. Extending mortgage payment or rent relief to small businesses is equally important.

The federal government in Canada stepped up with a sizable financial package to help Canadians cope with COVID-19. By September, the size of the stimulus exceeded a few hundred billion dollars. Still, additional legislation may be needed to stay all collections, evictions, and protecting the credit history of those who may default as a result.

For financial institutions, the choice is between foreclosures and forbearance. The American experience suggests that housing foreclosures impose larger costs on banks, borrowers, and the broader economy than the costs associated with loan forbearance, which allows homeowners the prolonged security of shelter as they search for gainful employment. By choosing forbearance over foreclosures, Canadian Banks made the right choice. Extending the grace period to 12 months or more, if needed, will also be a prudent response to COVID-19.

CAN AN ACT OF GOD SAVE ONE FROM THE PANDEMIC'S FALLOUT?

Real estate transactions, even at the best of times, are complicated and stressful for buyers and sellers. For the thousands of people who made or received firm offers before the coronavirus outbreak changed everything - and who were left wondering whether their deals would close in the weeks or months to follow - the anxiety level was even greater.

Some have wondered whether a pandemic is considered *force majeure* (unforeseeable circumstances or "acts of God"), which could free them of their obligations in case housing prices were to plummet in the next few weeks. Others may be facing other liquidity issues.

Data from the Canadian Real Estate Association (CREA) indicates that 65,494 homes were sold across Canada in the first two months of 2020, meaning that as many as 130,000 families may be in limbo, waiting for their transactions to close.

Residential sales often involve a few weeks or months between a firm offer is accepted, and the deal is "closed." When a transaction is booked, buyers transfer a deposit that is held in escrow by the seller's lawyers. At closing, buyers transfer the remaining amount to the sellers.

In uncertain times, much can change between a sale and its closing. When prices fall before closing, buyer's remorse sets in, and purchasers may feel they have overpaid. Even those who would like to follow through on the transaction may face challenges. Valuation metrics might change by the closing time such that declining prices could increase the loan-to-value (LTV) ratio, leading lenders to require that buyers put up additional funds.

In a highly unlikely scenario of severe liquidity constraints, financial markets might not extend credit, thus preventing sales from closing. If firm sales fail to close, even sellers will be at risk. Also, many buyers are simultaneously trying to sell their current residences; a failure to sell may limit their ability to buy. Another concern is the trillions of dollars lost in investments since the onset of the pandemic. Some buyers had planned to cash in on investments to make their down payments. As portfolios bleed across the board, real estate transactions contingent on healthy investment returns could be in jeopardy.

So what kind of recourse do buyers have in this situation? We consulted lawyers specializing in real estate transactions and contract law and the unanimous advice we received was that in at least Ontario, B.C. and Quebec, standard residential real estate transactions do not include *force majeure* provisions. Hence, in Ontario, buyers and sellers are bound by their obligations under the Ontario Real Estate Association's (OREA) Agreement of Purchase and Sale.

Mark Weisleder, a partner with the law firm Real Estate Lawyers.ca LLP, told clients in a note that the "only way a deal cannot close is if the government registration system closes down or lenders cannot fund loans, which is not the case right now."

Real estate businesses have been deemed an essential service in Ontario. Thus, real estate brokerages and law firms are allowed to function but with new guidelines to observe social distancing. At the same time, financial institutions are working and extending mortgage credit. While buyers' remorse is real, it is no ground to back out of the deal, warned Mr. Weisleder. During and after the Great Recession in 2008-09 and when the foreign homebuyers' tax was imposed first in British Columbia in 2016 and later in Ontario in 2017, many buyers tried to avoid closings after housing prices declined.

Courts, though, have found in favour of sellers in cases where buyers reneged on a signed deal. An Ontario couple who reneged on a firm offer to buy was ordered by the court to pay $470,000 to make up for the difference in the price they agreed to pay and the subsequent sale price paid by a different buyer. Rosa Lupo, a partner with the law firm Gowling WLG (Canada) LLP, advised that whereas *force majeure* is not covered in OREA's Agreement of Purchase and Sale, parties can include additional clauses in Schedule A of the Agreement. However, such terms must be entered at the execution of the agreement and not after the fact.

In some circumstances, parties may invoke frustration of contract when unforeseen circumstances make it impossible to perform their obligations under a contract. However, the bar to prove the frustration of contract is very high. If a deal hits a snag, the best way forward is to work it out collegially, advised Andrea Sanche, a partner at the law firm Ricketts Harris LLP. Instead of trying to nullify a contract, the parties could agree to a postponement until such time that the transaction can be completed. It is up to the parties to demonstrate that they have made reasonable, good faith efforts to fulfil their obligations, advises Ms. Sanche.

Given COVID-19 and severe weather interruptions like flooding, which can cause severe damage to a property, it might be time to review standard buyer and seller agreements, which are province-specific. Much can transpire during a sale and its closing. Introducing new standard clauses to protect both sides while providing opportunities for insurers to price risk will offer greater stability in uncertain times.

SAVING SMALL BUSINESSES

Whereas residential mortgagors and tenants were promised loan forbearance and a moratorium on evictions, commercial tenants, especially small businesses, were caught in the middle. They were asking for rent relief to survive the next few months while they struggled with diminished or no revenue.

Unlike their larger counterparts, small businesses have limited resources to withstand economic shocks. Without targeted help from government, many small businesses, especially retail and restaurants, may not reopen once the dust settles on the coronavirus pandemic.

Restaurants Canada, a group representing the food services industry, estimated the coronavirus cost the industry 800,000 jobs Canada wide. By April 2020, 10 per cent of restaurants had shut their doors permanently, and many more may follow if an economic recovery is not around the corner.

The International Monetary Fund (IMF) called the virus-infected recession the *Great Lockdown*.[78] Restrictions on commerce and mobility are likely to result in the "worst economic downturn since the Great Depression," the IMF noted while estimating global losses due to the pandemic to the tune of $9 trillion.

Unlike large corporations with substantial lobbying and marketing muscle, small businesses remain overly vulnerable to unexpected market volatility. Their atomized structure makes it harder to lobby for adequate government support to survive market downturns. Hence, the big companies, some of whom are "too big to fail," find ways to be rescued or

---

[78] Gopinath, G. (2020, April 14). The Great Lockdown: Worst Economic Downturn Since the Great Depression. Retrieved from https://blogs.imf.org/2020/04/14/the-great-lockdown-worst-economic-downturn-since-the-great-depression/

bailed out, while small businesses keep struggling for an equitable treatment during the time of financial hardship.

Individually, small businesses might not carry much weight. But collectively, they cast a long shadow. Innovation, Science and Economic Development Canada reported that in 2017, 98 per cent of the 1.18 million employer businesses in Canada were small businesses that employed fewer than 100 workers. No fewer than 8.3 million workers were employed by small businesses representing almost 70 per cent of Canada's labour force. In comparison, large businesses with more than 500 employees provided jobs to only 10.4 per cent of the private labour force.

Businesses falling under small and medium-sized enterprises () experience more volatility than big business. On average, 95,000 SMEs were created annually during 2010 and 2015. At the same time, 85,000 SMEs disappeared every year.

Why then, do governments tend to pay more attention to large businesses? Though large businesses represent a mere 0.2 per cent of the employer businesses in Canada, they account for roughly 47.5 per cent of Canadian GDP.

Very small businesses, employing fewer than 10 employees, comprise 73.4 per cent of businesses. While being numerous, they are also the most vulnerable by virtue of their size. Any disruption to their revenue stream could lead to permanent closure. Remember, 85,000 SMEs shut down each year on average.

A newly formed advocacy group, Save Small Business (SSB), asked recently for immediate rent relief program for small business. The group was critical of the government's emergency loan program, the Canada Emergency Business Account (CEBA). Jon Shell, the group's co-founder, told CBC that "It's unfair to close down local businesses and ask them to take out a loan in order to pay all their expenses."[79] SSB estimates that by the beginning of May, and in the absence of additional government support, 70 per cent of small businesses would default on their commercial rents. SSB recognized that the government was guaranteeing interest-free loans of up to $40,000, but they believed small businesses cannot bear additional debt while they were forced shut. SSB is essentially asked for a commercial rent waiver of up to $10,000 for three months. It further asked for the deferral of debt obligations for commercial tenants and their landlords.

In May 2020, Prime Minister Justin Trudeau announced changes to the CEBA, and lowered the qualifying minimum payroll down to $20,000 from $50,000 to improve inclusion of small businesses in the program. The government also said it was developing a program to help SMEs cover their

---

[79] SaveSmallBusiness.ca. (n.d.) Debt won't save our small businesses. Retrieved from https://savesmallbusiness.ca/

rent. Mr. Shell, though, was not impressed with the new announcements. The lower threshold for payroll "continues to exclude family-run small businesses and others who pay subcontractors," he told the *Financial Post*. His group wants the minimum payroll limit to be dropped to zero dollars.

SSB argues that Canada should consider the example of other countries where governments are offering grants rather than loans to small businesses. Since landlords must first reduce rents and then apply to the government for loans, and because the provinces had not partnered with the feds on this initiative, SSB was concerned that the structure of CEBA initiatives might not be attractive enough for the landlords to participate. The low uptake of the program months later confirmed these concerns.

In the U.S., commercial landlords and tenants have adopted flexible models to help prevent vulnerable tenants from defaulting. The "blend and extend" model modifies the lease terms so that the rent is waived for a period, say six months, and is amortized over the remaining life of the lease. In some circumstances, the leasing period is extended to help the tenant.

Commercial landlords are motivated to accept such terms because defaulting tenants may not readily be replaced in a time when most non-essential businesses are forced to remain shut. Furthermore, landlords save the additional costs associated with finding a new commercial tenant.

If many small businesses default, they will have a humongous impact on job losses in Canada. Helping them stay afloat with rent waivers and loan abatement will keep Canadians employed. The choice for the government is to either support workers through unemployment insurance or help small businesses survive COVID-19. Keeping Canadians working preserves not only their jobs but also their dignity.

HOUSING TRANSACTIONS UNDER LOCKDOWN

Sales and listings in some of Canada's biggest housing markets slowed dramatically in March and April as social distancing measures to combat the spread of COVID-19 took hold, putting an end to any hopes of a strong spring real estate season. In Toronto, for example, sales dropped from 759 in the first week of March to just 299 in the fourth week of the month, according to data compiled by Konfidis Brokerage. While many would-be buyers and sellers were waiting for the storm to blow over, those who need to start or complete a real estate transaction were relieved to know that realtors were declared essential workers and that the land registry offices continued to function. That said, many of the normal steps in the homebuying process were disrupted.

Buyers, for instance, had a difficult time visiting a listed dwelling in person. Open houses were discouraged initially and forbidden later. In their place, digital workarounds gained traction. Virtual home tours have been around for years, but their use has not been widespread, and research has found weak evidence that such marketing methods contributed to higher prices or lower time on the market. But that was before social distancing, which has launched virtual tours from good-to-have to must-have features of a listing.

The option to make or accept an offer digitally has been in place for years. It may not be the same as signing the forms on your breakfast table with the realtor on your side, but digital signatures make the process more efficient. Applying for, qualifying, and securing financing has also long been available digitally. Lenders have even introduced smartphone apps to facilitate that process.

One hitherto digitally unmitigated risk for buyers is the home inspection. For condominiums, physical examinations are not a significant concern because buyers rely on the condominium's status certificate, which speaks to the building's physical and financial health.

For the rest, the home inspection is critical to protect buyers from major repairs of undisclosed structural shortcomings that may not be obvious in virtual or physical tours. Home inspectors were functioning, although the number of inspections was down by 50 to 70 per cent in April 2020, according Enio Ferri of Key Home Inspections.

The new normal in home inspections was that, prior to the visit, inspectors collected information about the health and recent travel records of the residents of the dwelling they are about visit to plan accordingly. On site, the inspectors wore a haz-mat suit and latex gloves with full respirators and not just a mask. Post inspection communication with the clients was done electronically.

The logistics involved in closing a deal are more intricate as they involve other entities, including real estate lawyers who oversee the exchange of funds and house keys. Until only last month, lawyers would often courier cheques to the other party. This practice is going digital in a big way. Real estate law firms are often set up as a "bill payee" with the banks. Buyers and sellers can instruct their banks to e-transfer funds to their lawyers' escrow accounts. Lawyers can also transfer funds electronically to their counterparts. Therefore, an important consideration for buyers and sellers in selecting a law firm is to ensure they are set up to process funds electronically. Similarly, the brokerages must also be equipped to receive commissions digitally.

Transferring keys to buyers, a closing day tradition, was also disrupted as some were reluctant to involve couriers in the process. Instead, some real estate firms were providing lockboxes to sellers so that buyers can directly obtain the keys on the premises.

The sale of tenanted dwellings posed an additional layer of uncertainty. With a freeze on evictions, a tenant in a for-sale dwelling might not agree to leave - or even pay the rent if facing hardship. The buyer could, as a result, be denied occupancy even though the buyer and seller may have met all conditions.

For buyers and sellers, it would be prudent to insist on including clauses that indemnify them if a deal failed to close. Additional clauses must make provisions for the digital signing of documents and the electronic transfer of funds. Furthermore, new terms should specify the circumstances (e.g., temporary closing of the land registry or the financial institutions) under which the closing date can be automatically extended.

A failed transaction can set off a chain-reaction forcing other transactions to collapse even when buyers and sellers involved have fulfilled all obligations. Such unexpected lastminute developments will require contingency planning for all involved.

Making the biggest purchase of your life under these circumstances may not work for everyone, but thanks to modern technology it is still possible.

THE FUTURE OF CITIES WITH PANDEMICS

Man is by nature, a social animal, proclaimed Aristotle.

The desire to interact with other humans was the driving force behind the establishment of large and small communities. Before cities, human settlements were small and spread out. Modern cities pack people into clusters, facilitating planned and chance encounters. COVID-19, at least temporarily, has changed all that. With social distancing being practised by billions across the world, an experiment of unprecedented scale is unfolding. Against their instinct to congregate and socialize, people are being told to stay indoors and limit their interactions with others.

Economic theory recognizes the benefits of density as agglomeration or urbanization economies. Essentially, the external economies of scale through input-sharing, labour-market pooling and knowledge spillovers enable higher productivity for the entire region or industry. But there are diminishing returns to density. Too much of it could lead to overcrowding, where the costs outweigh the benefits. Being stuck in traffic or at a transit platform is one example. Affordability, or the lack of it, is the other. Remember, high-density neighbourhoods are often the ones with high housing prices and rents. Now we are being reminded that pandemics can be another downside to density.

Transforming advances in information and communication technologies, however, are helping to reduce pressures on central places. Emails, cloud-based storage and computing, software as a service, and video communications can help substitute, at least partially, for the interactions in shared physical space with online communications.

When colleges, schools and universities resumed in January 2020, most student-instructor interactions were designed to take place in physical proximity. That model lasted, as it had over several millennia, until early March. By the third week of March, almost two million students enrolled in higher education in Canada had transitioned to online learning. Lectures, tutorials, seminars, meetings and even dissertation defences continued on schedule, but online.

The disruptions resulting from the coronavirus are impacting human settlements and behaviours across the globe. The new restrictions on movement and interaction are not confined to work or school. Indoor activities at gyms, malls and movie theatres are forbidden, as are some outdoor activities. Paris, for instance, banned outdoor exercise during the day. A city known for its magnificent architecture and boulevards restricted where and how people could congregate in or outdoors.

The raison d'être for most if not all cities is commerce. Cities are necessarily exchanges where people have traded goods and services. What may have started as bazaars in the Orient or country fairs in the 18th-century in Europe evolved into specialized auction houses and stock exchanges. The modern-day Chicago Mercantile Exchange (CME), the global marketplace for derivatives, has its origins as the Chicago Butter and Egg Board. The spectacle of traders dressed in brightly coloured jackets executing trades by open outcry or hand signals required the concerned parties to congregate under one roof. This has been the norm for decades. But not anymore. Electronic trading floors have displaced the outcry exchanges. Though coronavirus forced the iconic New York Stock Exchange to shut its doors in March, the move was symbolic since only 18 per cent of trading took place on the floor.

As tens of millions of white-collar workers in North America have started working from home, employees and employers are wondering what it means for their long-term relationships. Could work from home become more frequent, thus mitigating the demand for travel during peak hours? Will it reduce the need for more structures in the urban core? Do workers have enough space at home to work productively? Not all employers will be interested in the remote work model. Marissa Mayer, former CEO of Yahoo!, was not a fan of working from home. In 2013, the tech giant ordered an end to working remotely. Workers were ordered to report at the offices for "a new era of collaboration." But when pandemics strike, employers have no option but to assist workers to work remotely.

Social distancing provides an opportunity to think about the shape and size of cities. Over 450,000 workers congregated in downtown Toronto before COVID-19 restrictions were implemented. From March to at least September, most of the offices were far below their designed occupancy.

When restrictions on congregations are relaxed or removed, we will have the opportunity to reflect on our collective experiences and entertain new questions. Can we, for instance, design cities to cope better with congestion and housing affordability? Can suburbs with larger dwellings, which are conducive for working remotely, be retrofitted with diverse land uses to allow people to walk or bike for groceries and leisure? Can we be social while being physically distanced?

While the short-term effects of COVID-19 are drastic and noticeable, the long-term impacts are uncertain. Much depends upon how much we are willing to embrace new models and channels of being productive. Our relationship with space and real estate may be up for a reset.

THE FUTURE OF WORK AND DOWNTOWNS

Almost 10 million trips are made by public transit in New York City every day, as workers flock in to Manhattan's office towers from the surrounding boroughs. Efficient mass transit is a critical enabling factor for the success of such a vibrant metropolitan downtown - without it, the offices and other skyscrapers that have come to define major cities would face substantial financial challenges.

Cities and property owners are getting a preview of such a scenario thanks to the COVID-19 pandemic, which has put a halt to the ritualistic twice-daily commutes of millions, leaving them to work from home instead.

Commercial real estate clusters in urban cores represent tens of billions of dollars in investments. Being a tenant downtown in a high rise and the assumed economic benefits of being centrally located come at exorbitant rents, which businesses have paid for decades. The underlying assumption has been that the physical location of a firm's offices is instrumental to its success.

COVID-19 has changed that. Given the circumstances, it is likely that businesses are reviewing their operating cost structures to determine whether the productivity benefits of downtown locations justify the occupancy costs.

Over the past few decades, cities such as Toronto have seen a further intensification of knowledge-based employment in and around the downtown core. A 2018 report by the Neptis Foundation on the structure of employment in the Toronto region and nearby cities observed that a "more balanced pattern of urban and suburban employment growth has given way to the hyper-concentration of knowledge-based activities in and around downtown Toronto."[80]

The report noted that downtown Toronto saw an increase of 85,600 total jobs between 2006 and 2016. Meanwhile, the job growth slowed outside of the downtown core. "The hyper-concentration of job growth raises critical issues about planning for a core under intense growth pressure, and an

---

[80] Blais, P. (2018). Planning the Next GGH. Retrieved from https://www.neptis.org/publications/planning-next-ggh

increasingly dominant single centre for the GGH." The hyper-concentration of near 450,000 jobs in downtown Toronto requires a highly functional public transit system to transport the bulk of workers from their suburban residences to the downtown core. Any interruptions and breakdowns of the transit system imply workers may not get to their downtown offices efficiently.

COVID-19 is likely to affect the throughput capacities of public transit infrastructure until immunity levels improve substantially. Transit vehicles are being modified with signage to keep passengers at safe distances that will reduce the number of passengers carried during peak periods.

With a noticeable decline in public transit carrying capacities, downtown-based employment clusters, which are increasingly dependent on public transportation, would experience a drop in commuting. Consequently, offices and buildings will be underutilized. Workers will continue to work from home, making telework more acceptable for large knowledge economy firms.

Working from home or telework is not new. Advances in information and communication technologies (ICT) have influenced the way offices are designed, built, and located. Whereas telework is one manifestation of the changes in working conditions, other subtle changes over time have already modified existing and new office space.

Consider that ICT advances and other developments have contributed to a significant decline in space provided per worker. In a report titled The Shrinking Office Footprint, REIS observed that in the early 2000s, "the typical employee was associated with about 125 square feet of additional space." This was down from 175 square feet of additional space per employee in the late 1990s.[81] The latest numbers suggest that each additional employee "has been associated with only about 50 square feet of additional office space."

The nexus between public transit usage and the profitability of downtown real estate clusters become explicitly apparent during COVID-19. Transit ridership was down by 80 to 90 per cent in cities such as Toronto and New York. Ever busy and bustling downtown streets were eerily silent and deprived of activity.

If COVID-19 related restrictions are withdrawn soon, the decline in work commutes and the emergence of telework may end up being a short-term trend. However, if transit system capacities are constrained over a more extended period, telework will remain widespread for a longer period, thus affecting the bottom line of tenants who occupy, but are not currently using, the expensive real estate in the urban core.

---

[81] Calanog, V., & Denham, B.B. (2017, February 15). The Shrinking Office Footprint. Retrieved from https://www.reis.com/the-shrinking-office-footprint/

With hundreds of billions in commercial real estate assets concentrated in the urban core, mass adoption of telework poses a significant challenge to the financial viability of office real estate and the transit systems that serve them. At the same time, returning to the previous normal will also be a return to congested mobility, crowded spaces, and unaffordable housing.

The future of work must find a balance between the conflicting objectives of sustaining the downtown core while not exacerbating congestion and affordability.

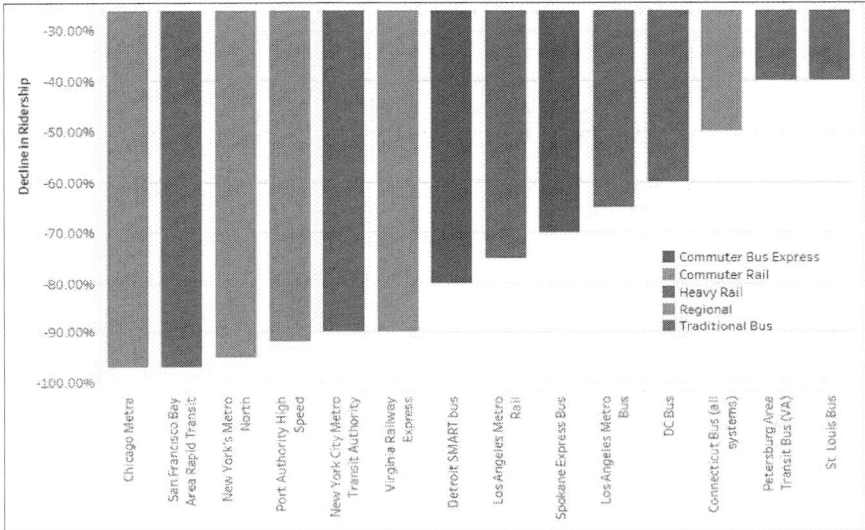

Figure 3.1 – Decline in public transit ridership

Source: https://usa.streetsblog.org/2020/04/30/covid-19-hasnt-impacted-bus-ridership-which-creates-a-huge-post-crisis-challenge/

OFFICE REAL ESTATE DURING AND AFTER THE PANDEMIC

With tens of millions of employees working from home or laid off, the future of the workplace is now a primary concern for commercial landlords and tenants. A report by Cushman & Wakefield (C&W) found that 73 per cent of workers would like their employers to adopt "some level of working from home."[82] Also, 90 per cent of employees believed their employers trusted them to work remotely.

---

[82] Haider, M., & Moranis, S. (2020, June 4). Why office real estate landlords aren't panicking just yet. *Financial Post*. https://financialpost.com/real-estate/property-post/why-office-real-estate-landlords-arent-panicking-just-yet

But do these developments mean the end of "the office" as we know it? Not really. The report describes a new normal that will involve a "total workplace ecosystem" comprising more than a single destination and including a combination of virtual and physical places.

Critics of telework often argue that collaboration weakens when workers are confined to remote silos, but the C&W report suggests otherwise. It found collaborative work increased by 10 per cent with telework over the pre-COVID-19 period, with technological advances being credited for the big shift.

Roelof van Dijk of the CoStar Group saw two opposite forces simultaneously pushing and pulling on the demand for office real estate. On the one hand are the pandemic-related social distancing regulations that are behind the surge in working from home. As the number of workers, especially in the knowledge economy sector, continue to telework on most days, the demand for office space is likely to decline.

At the same time, social distancing regulations will require more space to be maintained between workers. The same floor space in the future will, therefore, hold fewer workers if they are spaced farther apart. Hence, even if a segment of employees continues to telework, spatial distancing measures requiring more space per employee should counteract the decline in demand.

In the short-term, landlords are unlikely to reduce rents drastically if the demand for office space decreases. It is also unlikely that office tenants will seek additional space if social distancing measures mandate more space per employee. Instead, tenants are likely to stagger schedules by having workers come in on alternating days or at different times, allowing tenants to maintain the same amount of space until their leases are up for renewal.

Office real estate markets present a mixed picture for demand. According to data provided by CoStar Group in May 2020, vacancy rates were exceptionally low in some parts of Canada, where the demand for office space was high, and the supply had not kept pace. While in other places, ominous signs of growing weakness were apparent.

CoStar data showed that office vacancy rates in Vancouver averaged 2.9 per cent in the first quarter of 2020, down from 3.3 per cent a year ago. While Vancouver's office real estate market was tightening, Calgary's showed increasing signs of weakness. Already, Calgary''s vacancy rate in the first quarter of 2019 at 14.4 per cent was more than four times that of Vancouver. That vacancy rate increased to 15.6 per cent in the second quarter. By comparison, Toronto's office vacancy rate was around 4.4 per cent in Q1, down slightly from 4.7 per cent the same period last year.

What may happen in the future depends on local market conditions. For Canadian office markets as an aggregate, CoStar forecasted an increase in vacancy rates from 6.2 per cent to 7.1 per cent in the second quarter of 2021. Local office markets present a mixed picture. Vacancy rates are expected to remain mostly unchanged in Vancouver and Edmonton but are expected to climb in Calgary and Toronto.

Commercial leases, unlike their residential counterparts, are of longer duration, often ranging from five to 10 years. It may take up to a few years for most leases to go through renewal. A lot, therefore, depends upon the state of the economy in the near future. If local economies can shake off the pandemic blues sooner, one would expect growth in economic activity, an increase in hiring and a resulting increase in the demand for space, which may still be moderated by a higher prevalence of telework. If local labour markets fail to recover, and job losses become permanent, office markets are expected to struggle with or without telework.

Unlike landlords who hold retail real estate, office real estate owners are likely to fare better with rent collection. With malls closed during the pandemic, their tenants face massive cash-flow challenges, which compromises their ability to pay rents. The good news is that online retail sales are up for some retailers. The bad news for retail landlords is that a shift from brick-and-mortar retail to e-commerce would further lower the demand for retail real estate.

Whereas offices are also closed to employees except for essential workers, office work continued from home, thanks to telework. The business models of office-based firms are thus disrupted, but not discontinued. Hence, many office-based firms can conduct their business remotely and can meet their rent obligations.

A shift in demand for more modern and better-quality office space might also occur. Higher-end office real estate equipped with, for example, advanced HVAC systems and fast elevators, are more likely to adopt readily to social distancing requirements. In comparison, older B Class real estate may find it hard or prohibitively expensive to comply with regulations for improved ventilation and greater distancing between employees.

Telework may not be for everyone. The C&W report revealed that while younger cohorts, i.e., Millennials and Gen Z workers, expressed the strongest desire for flex-work options, they found telework more challenging than older cohorts. Shared living arrangements, smaller dwellings, and a lack of dedicated space to work from home could be the reason for younger workers' struggle with telework.

Real estate markets are in flux, and nothing about the future is known with certainty. Contingency planning based on probable future outcomes will allow smart landlords to cope with the changes heading their way. Waiting for a return to the old normal may not be a wise strategy.

THE ELEVATOR PITCH

Elevators are the unsung heroes of modern urbanism, without which tall and slender buildings would not have been built. So critical are elevators to a building's height that the weight of the elevator cables constrains the height of super-tall buildings. Elevators also deliver bragging rights or prestige to a skyscraper's builders, owners and residents, but they may emerge as bottlenecks during the COVID-19 era, limiting how many people can be transported vertically in a reasonable amount of time.

Physical distancing requirements to keep individuals two metres apart clearly limit the number of people who can share an elevator. Elevator systems are designed to operate at 80-per-cent capacity during periods of high demand, but the throughput capacity could be much lower with COVID-19-mandated restrictions, thus slowing access to and from mid-and high rise floors during the morning, noon and early evening rushes.

Office building managers are concerned about future regulations and the public health implications of sharing small closed spaces. Assuming a return to full occupancy, it could take several hours to populate a building in the morning if elevators are limited to 10 to 30 per cent of capacity, and long queues will form at street level. Restricting operations could also mean that once workers reach their designated floor, they might not be allowed to use the elevators again until they leave for the day. At that point, it might again take hours to depopulate the building. Workers could be restricted to time windows to use the elevators to enter and leave the building.

The regimented use of building amenities might take some shine off the glamour of being on the higher floors. It could also encourage workers to work from home, rather than queuing up to wait their turn to board the elevators. The lack of viable alternatives for vertical transportation - staircases are no better - that comply with physical distancing restrictions and offer adequate throughput capacities will be a challenge. It may also impact the financial viability of buildings in the long run.

Stephen Graham, a professor of Cities and Society at Newcastle University in the United Kingdom, writing in the *Theory, Culture, and Society* journal, noted that so much is written about horizontal mobility on roads and transit networks, yet researchers have "almost completely neglected the cultural geographies and politics of vertical transportation."[83] In vertical cities such as Hong Kong, he pointed out, residents "travel almost as far vertically using elevators as they do horizontally by foot, bus or subway."

There are an estimated one million elevators in the United States and Canada, and another 10 million elsewhere. In the U.S. alone, elevators

---

[83] Graham, S. (2014). Super-tall and Ultra-deep: The Cultural Politics of the Elevator. *Theory, Culture & Society, 31*(7-8), 239–265. https://doi.org/10.1177/0263276414554044

facilitate 18 billion passenger trips in a normal year. They are also the safest mode of personal transportation.

Graham also described the quest for higher elevator speeds needed to construct even taller buildings. Just like the Bullet Train, Japanese engineers are at the forefront of designing super-fast elevators, some reaching a speed of 60 km/h. In suburban Fuchu in Japan, a 213-metre tall building, known as G1 Tower, is one of the highest elevator research tower, which is operated by Hitachi Corp. Kone Corp. uses 350-metre research elevators that are not "elevated" but dug in the ground at an unused mine in Helsinki.

Elevators have a stellar safety record, but they are not much help in times of crisis. Their use is even forbidden during fires and earthquakes, forcing occupants to use the stairs. But during COVID-19, clustering people in narrow staircases, even for fire drills, might pose additional challenges. Erica Kuligowski, a social research scientist in the U.S., and others simulated the evacuation times for the World Trade Center under different occupancy scenarios on Sept. 11, 2001. Their results, published in *Fire Technology*, revealed it would have taken between 92 and 142 minutes to evacuate a tower. They also found that approximately 14,000 occupants would not have been able to evacuate in time from the two towers assuming full occupancy.[84]

Elevators are more than a mode of transportation. They convey images of esteem and opulence in super-tall buildings used by high-income cohorts. Elevators have also become part of the social and business lexicon. Business students are taught to perfect their "elevator pitch," and elevator music is a genre in itself, intended to be part of the ambience but not to attract attention. COVID-19 has stripped elevators of their relative obscurity. Building managers, landlords, residents and tenants will be squarely focused on how to safely use elevators that are transporting hundreds of millions to their chosen destinations multiple times each day.

The economic feasibility of tall buildings is now tied, at least partially, to throughput capacities of elevators, a hitherto unremarked mode of transportation.

FAULTY TOWERS

For those who work in office towers, small or tall, a safe return to work is the joint responsibility of landlords, building managers, employers and workers. Since provincial laws regulate workers' safety and health, regulations will differ across Canada. Here's a look at some of the issues that are front and centre when it comes to reopening office towers across Canada.

---

[84] Kuligowski, E. D., Peacock, R. D., & Averill, J. D. (2013). Modeling the Evacuation of the World Trade Center Towers on September 11, 2001. In *Fire Technology* (Vol. 49, Issue 1, pp. 65–81). https://doi.org/10.1007/s10694-011-0240-y

The first question on the minds of many office workers is whether they can be called back to work at all. Jesse Elders, a lawyer specializing in labour, employment and human rights law at Kastner Lam LLP, advised that an employer in Ontario can indeed ask their employees to come back to work. However, workers have the right to refuse unsafe conditions. The Occupational Health and Safety Act in Ontario stipulates mechanisms for workers and employers to address matters of workplace safety.

Elders pointed out that the Act requires the employers "to take every precaution reasonable in the circumstances for the protection of a worker."

Steve Ichelson, a vice-president with Avison Young, a global commercial real estate brokerage, says his firm advised owners and tenants on what to expect and how to act as they return to work amidst COVID-19. Avison Young prepared a back-to-work guide for occupants, covering a broad range of topics, starting with new and improved conventions for communication to inform all stakeholders of the changes in operating protocols even before employees return.

New signage in and around buildings will also provide an obvious reminder to returning employees that things have changed. The new signage could be extended beyond lobbies to sidewalks outside to keep the returning employees at safe distances while they wait for their turn to board the elevators.

Avison Young did not plan to take the temperature of those entering their buildings - without new regulations, building managers may not be able to enforce mandatory temperature checks. However, they may still ask a standard set of questions to all returning employees to gauge their possible exposure to COVID-19. Many building managers planned to increase the number of security professionals in their lobbies to direct pedestrian flow and prevent crowding.

As noted earlier, elevators in tall buildings are a bottleneck that will play a big role in determining whether employees will be able to get to and from their floors in a reasonable amount of time. The suggested capacity is now four people per car, down from nine to 12 in the past. Asking some elevator riders to face the wall is one option that some buildings are considering to squeeze more riders onto each car.

The estimate for the time it will take to populate a tall building to full occupancy with limited elevator capacity ranges between 90 minutes to four hours. Many returning employees might receive a scheduled boarding time for their ride up and down the elevator. That could leave lobbies looking like the long queues at theme parks, as visitors wait for their favourite rides. Limiting the number of elevator rides each employee takes in a day is also an option. Employees might be limited to use the elevator at lunchtime or for coffee breaks. Smokers would have to use stairs to get to the street level and back.

Improving and maintaining air quality is another concern that building managers will have to grapple with. Avison Young is upgrading air filters to MERV-13 to protect airborne pathogens from travelling through ventilation. Subsequent upgrades will include UV filtration and dehumidification to keep air dry.

Open office spaces are also being reconfigured to keep workers at a distance from each other. An area that accommodated 72 workers might now hold 28, Ichelson said. The same goes for small-to medium-sized meeting rooms: those that might have held 15 to 20 people in the past will now be reduced to half or one third capacity.

A key question to ponder is whether working from the office will be as attractive, or more important, as productive, as it was before the pandemic. Long waits for the elevator, the need to wear a mask while riding public transit or in the office, and staggered seating arrangements are all examples of how work culture will be circumscribed in the age of COVID-19.

Improved communications, sanitation and ventilation will get buildings ready to welcome workers again. However, the more regimented environment and elevated risks that come with commuting may keep many white-collar employees working from home for some time. For the economy to regain its momentum, both buildings and workers must be ready to be back to work.

PRICES HOLD, BUT SALES COLLAPSE

April sales data from some of Canada's large markets confirmed fears that housing sales were continuing to dramatically decline, but while volumes plummeted, prices were more stable or even rising in some sub-markets.

The dichotomy in sales volumes and prices revealed an inherent characteristic of housing prices: they are sticky. Like wages, which do not decline as much during a recession as employment numbers do, housing prices have a way of sustaining themselves in short-lasting economic crises. However, all bets are off if a crisis lasts for a more extended period and has sustained job losses.

A detailed look at various sub-markets suggests that housing prices and sales in the central parts of cities might experience more significant declines. The reason could be that centrally located areas, praised for their accessibility and high walk scores, are frothier when prices are rising faster than the rest of the local housing market.

Housing sales data for the Toronto region in April reported a 67 per cent decline in year-over-year sales, and new listings were down 64 per cent. But the average price was essentially unchanged, with a slight upward tick of 0.1 per cent. Remember, average prices do not account for the differences in structural type and size of housing over time. For example, average prices dropped for detached housing and condominiums in Toronto, but not for semi-detached units and townhouses.

A comparison between Toronto and its 905 suburbs is even more revealing. Average year-over-year prices dropped by only 0.8 per cent for detached housing in the suburbs, but prices were slightly higher for other suburban housing types. Within the city, average prices dropped by 9.4 per cent in the central, more expensive parts, but increased in the eastern and western neighbourhoods. Indeed, prices rose by 8.8 per cent in the eastern parts.

Keep in mind that extraordinarily high and low values skew unadjusted average prices. Median prices, to some extent, adjust for those extremes. Median prices in most districts comprising the City of Toronto were higher in April than a year earlier. Even in the central areas, median prices were slightly up by 0.86 per cent.

The Toronto Real Estate Board publishes indexed benchmarked prices to adjust for the quality and size of housing, which facilitate a comparison of similar units in size over time. Benchmarked year-over-year prices in the Toronto region (including all sub-markets and all types of housing) were up 10.2 per cent.

A nuanced picture of the real estate markets emerges when we put all these numbers together. Unadjusted average prices suggest that housing in the city's core is experiencing a slight decline. But when adjusted for size and quality, the average price rose in April compared to a year ago.

This leads to two critical questions. First, why are housing prices climbing when sales are down so drastically? Second, will prices rise or decline in the future? Skylar Olsen, senior principal economist at Zillow Group, has an explanation for the gravity-defying housing prices. He said that even though housing demand had collapsed, so did the supply, which helps sustain prices at their current levels. Also, many sellers are not motivated yet to cut prices. They believe that once the lockdown-related restrictions are over, buyers will be out in droves to chase housing sales that, because of the decline in listings, will be in short supply.

The question about future housing prices is harder to answer. Some believe pent-up demand will likely push prices upwards when markets resume regular activity. For example, the Federal National Mortgage Association, better known as Fannie Mae, a U.S. government-sponsored enterprise specializing in mortgage securitization, expects median housing prices to be slightly higher in 2020 than last year.

But CIBC Capital Markets economists in a note forecasted a decline in average prices of five to 10 per cent in Canada from 2019 levels. The weakness in labour markets is cited as one reason for the decline, "with high cost units in the high-rise segment of the market seeing the most notable price declines." And Canada Mortgage and Housing Corp. predicts housing prices will not return to pre-COVID-19 levels until late 2022.

Yogi Berra once proclaimed that "it's tough to make predictions, especially about the future." Housing market forecasts are no different. They are driven by assumptions made by forecasters. If governments and businesses join hands to relaunch the economy sooner to prevent layoffs from becoming permanent, housing markets will rebound sooner. Both national and lower levels of governments in North America and Europe are hinting at opening retail, schools and more. An economic relaunch in the presence of the pandemic is a likely scenario and one that may also hold some promise for housing markets. This may allow for a resurgence in sales and housing prices to moderately appreciate.

WILL PRICES COLLAPSE LIKE THE SALES DID?

The economic uncertainty surrounding COVID-19 has contributed to contradictory estimates of future housing prices and sales. Leading the bears is Canada Mortgage Housing Corp. (CMHC), projecting average housing prices to fall by nine to 18 per cent.

Others, including economists at the Canadian Real Estate Association (CREA), are not convinced prices will fall as steeply as CMHC projects. Many homebuyers and sellers have been left perplexed by these conflicting forecasts - much can go wrong if they rely on the wrong estimates in their buy and sell decisions.

Regardless of the sophistication of algorithms, forecasts are necessarily a by-product of the assumptions forecasters make and the data they use. Assumptions, inherently, are neither right nor wrong. They are informed guesses about future outcomes. When reviewing a forecast based on modelling, always remember the advice from the famed statistician, George Box: "All models are wrong, but some are useful."

CMHC forecasts were generated using "a specific set of assumptions for the market conditions and underlying economic fundamentals," CMHC noted in the report's appendix.

But how precise are they? CMHC estimates average Canadian housing prices in 2020 will be anywhere between $493,200 and $518,400, representing a nine-to 18-per-cent decline from pre-COVID-19 levels. The number of sales transacting through the Multiple Listing Service is expected to be between 416,000 and 450,500.

The above forecasts are for the average price in Canada. Local market forecasts could be much different. CMHC reported provincial estimates for prices, sales and housing starts, with all provinces seeing the same trend of falling metrics through 2020 and a rebound starting later in 2021.

The lowest average price forecast for British Columbia at $609,515 is still more than double that for Alberta at $288,522. Both numbers are for the second quarter of 2022. The lower-bound forecast for Ontario at $531,715 is slated for the second quarter of 2021, which suggests CM-HC expects housing markets to recover sooner in Ontario.

CMHC's report does not disclose the methods or data used to generate forecasts. The report mentions that CMHC forecasts deploy the "full range of quantitative and qualitative tools currently available."

The report claims that the forecast's "range provides a relatively precise guidance to readers on the outlook while recognizing the small random components of the relationship between the housing market and its drivers." However, the wide range of forecast for prices and sales is indicative of the "high degree of forecast uncertainty" partly due to the "unprecedented nature of the COVID-19 pandemic." To us, therefore, the claim for precision may be a stretch.

Homebuyers and sellers need to be able to understand what forecasts mean for their decision-making processes. Economists prepare estimates with care. However, when predictions differ from the real outcomes, economists readily revise their projections. Homebuyers and sellers, once they have transacted, cannot "revise" their transactions. Hence the stakes are higher for the ones active in the market.

Another way of thinking about future housing prices is to think about the willingness of sellers to accept lower bids for their listings. If one is of the view that sellers will be, on average, willing to accept bids 18-per-cent or more below what they could have received before March 2020, a significant decrease in housing prices could be inevitable. However, this seems to be an unlikely scenario.

If prices start to decline significantly, sellers can slow or even freeze the market by not listing their properties, withdrawing them from consideration, or refusing a lower bid. Sellers' unwillingness to sell dwellings at lower-than-expected prices can protect against a free-fall in housing prices. Also, when less inventory is available for purchase, buyers may have to compete, which could put upward pressure on prices.

Lastly, the average decline in the average price does not imply that an individual dwelling will experience an average drop in valuation. Why? Because the average price forecasts ignore the differences in sizes and quality of housing or the fact that when economic conditions worsen, higher-priced homes stop transacting, and lower-valued homes dominate the sales. The shift in the structural composition of housing gives a false impression that housing prices are falling. Thus, CREA's estimates of constant quality homes are not as severe as CMHC's.

Homebuyers and sellers should have a look at the market forecasts. But they should base their decisions on their circumstances and local housing market conditions. Remember, forecasts are useful, but not necessarily accurate.

THE GREEN SHOOTS EMERGE

Housing markets in Canada showed considerable strength in May when home sales jumped 56.9 per cent higher from sales in April and new listings rose even higher, confirming an increase in both demand and supply.

Though the green shoots of a real estate recovery were appearing, numerous hurdles and uncertainties must still be overcome for a sustained improvement in housing markets.

For one thing, new regulations starting in July will likely limit some borrowers' ability to qualify for a mortgage.

Markets supported by stimulus spending and forbearance programs could also take a turn for the worse if consumption and production fail to quickly march back to pre-COVID-19 levels.

Data released by the Canadian Real Estate Association (CREA) showed that the month-over-month change in sales in May carried some good news, but year-over-year sales were still down by almost 40 per cent. Looking farther back reveals that sales in May were the lowest recorded for the month in more than two decades.

Housing markets have been struggling with the pandemic blues since mid-March. But not all markets are beating at the same pulse, as 2.5 months of data show. Let's take a look specifically at three metrics: sales (an indicator of housing demand), new listings (a sign of supply) and prices, which emerge at the intersection of demand and supply.

In Montreal, the housing market reported a stellar 92.3 per cent increase in May sales compared to April, and surges were also observed in Calgary (68.7 per cent), Edmonton (46.5 per cent) and Winnipeg (45.6 per cent).

Toronto, Canada's largest housing market, reported a 53 per cent increase during the same period. But nearby Hamilton and Burlington reported a more substantial increase of 69.4 per cent. A similar trend was observed in Greater Vancouver, where sales in May increased by just 20.5 per cent (the lowest rate among the large housing markets), while neighbouring Fraser Valley was up 68.7 per cent.

At the same time, listings have recovered at a faster rate than sales, suggesting that sellers are bullish about the real estate market. It could also be a result of the impending change in mortgage regulations that will become effective July 1.

Canada Mortgage and Housing Corp. has announced it is tightening regulations to qualify for a CMHC-insured mortgage, which include increasing the minimum credit score, lowering the debt-service ratio and disallowing non-traditional sources of funds for the down payment "as equity for insurance purposes." The changes will likely reduce the qualifying loan amount for future homebuyers. However, sales in May and June will continue to be insured under the existing rules. Hence, sellers are motivated to list now to sell their homes under the relatively permissive regulations.

New listings across Canada were up by 69 per cent in May compared to April, but 38 per cent lower year over year. Like sales, the noticeable increase in new listings relative to April is indicative of housing markets recovering from the lockdown's initial shock, which brought markets to their knees in the latter half of March and most of April. Similar to sales, new listings in Montréal for May were up 204.7 per cent from April. Even more significant increases in listings were observed in smaller housing markets in Québec. New listings were up just 35.8 per cent in the Greater Toronto Area, but rose 91.6 per cent in Calgary and 86.5 per cent in Edmonton.

CREA reports a quality-adjusted home price index to account for the diversity in size and type of housing being sold over time, making it a better indicator than average housing prices. Its data showed that despite the alarm about the impending collapse of housing prices, national aggregate benchmarked prices in May were down by a mere 0.08 per cent from the month before and up 0.34 per cent from three months earlier. Similar small fluctuations were noted in the Montreal region (up 0.56 per cent) and the Toronto regional markets (down 0.11 per cent).

The significant increases in listings and sales along with housing prices holding firm in May must not be confused with the beginning of a sustained long-term recovery in the real estate markets. Such optimism would be premature. It is also too early to speak of a post-COVID-19 recovery. The pandemic is still out there, and it's targeting places that were earlier deemed safe and free of the disease.

The trillions of dollars spent on stimulus funding globally, including hundreds of billions of dollars (counting loan, mortgage and rent forbearance) in Canada, are temporary fixes to boost consumption. Implicit in stimulus funding is the hope that markets will pick up before the funds run out. If the economic engines do not ramp-up fast, real estate markets could face severe challenges if demand dries up as job losses start to spread across industries. But in the meantime, one cannot help but be in awe of the resilience of Canadian housing markets.

TORONTO EMERGES FROM THE PANDEMIC

The economic uncertainty induced by COVID-19 and its impact on job security continued to loom large, but housing markets in Canada developed an immunity to the pandemic by June 2020.

For example, the housing markets in Toronto no longer showed any signs of weakness. Indeed, housing sales and prices in Canada's most populous city during June either matched or surpassed their levels from a year earlier.

This resurgence was a welcome sign since it hinted at economic resilience.

But the larger questions are whether housing markets would continue to outperform the rest of the economy and for how long. Some experts believed housing markets might not have fully digested the increase in employment uncertainties that are expected shortly.

That said, let's use housing sales and prices in the Greater Toronto Area to check whether that market is outperforming the underlying economy.

The region recorded 8,701 sales in June 2020, an 89 per cent increase from the number of transactions in the month before. Compared to June 2019, June 2020 sales were a tad bit lower, suggesting the markets were still recovering from the sudden slowdown that accompanied the lockdown.

But the aggregate numbers hide a story: the triumph of the suburbs and the lure of large homes. Sales of single-family detached housing in Toronto's surrounding 905 suburbs increased by 10.4 per cent year-over-year in June, whereas such sales in the City of Toronto declined by 10 per cent. Suburban townhouse transactions increased by 7.8 per cent in the same period compared to a 2.5 per cent increase in the city.

Housing markets during COVID-19 suggested a shift in preferences to larger ground-oriented units with balconies or backyards from smaller dwellings in high rises. Condominium sales, which usually dominate housing transactions in the City of Toronto, were down by 13.6 per cent in June 2020 from the year before. Condominium sales also declined in the suburbs.

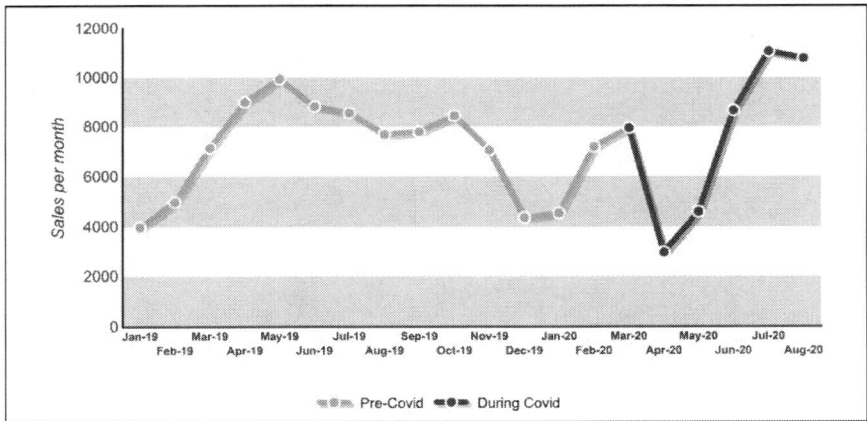

Figure 3.2 – Housing sales in the Greater Toronto Area

The increasing preference for low-rise housing is also reflected in the change in average housing prices. In the City of Toronto, detached housing prices in June increased by 14.3 per cent year-over-year compared to just 5.6 per cent for condominiums. Similarly, detached housing in the suburbs recorded a 10.8 per cent increase in average prices compared to seven per cent for condominiums.

Toronto's regional real estate board also reported quality-and size-adjusted housing prices to allow comparison of similar properties over time. The quality-adjusted Housing Price Index in June indicated a housing recovery, with the index up 8.2 per cent from the year before.

Another sign of a hot market, which is favourable to sellers, was reflected in the average time it takes to sell a property. Compared to 2019, the average days a home was on the market declined by 14 per cent in June 2020. In the eastern parts of the City of Toronto, it took an average of just 17 days for a dwelling to sell.

A lack of supply is the primary driver behind the increase in housing sales during the pandemic. Buyers were out in full force, but many sellers remained on the sidelines. Active listings in June 2020 were down 28.8 per cent from the year before. New listings in June actually increased by 2.1 per cent from June 2019, but it would take a sustained increase in new listings for the number of active listings to match the increase in demand. Until such time, prices are expected to continue climbing if demand holds.

David Rosenberg, president, chief economist, and strategist of Rosenberg Research & Associates Inc. believed recent housing prices were exaggerated. He listed tight housing supply and ultra low-interest rates as the reasons behind the increase in demand.

Rosenberg noted the bedrock of Toronto's regional employment base was finance, tourism, and the public sector. COVID-19 caused a significant decline in travel and tourism jobs, while the financial and public sectors were holding in June 2020.

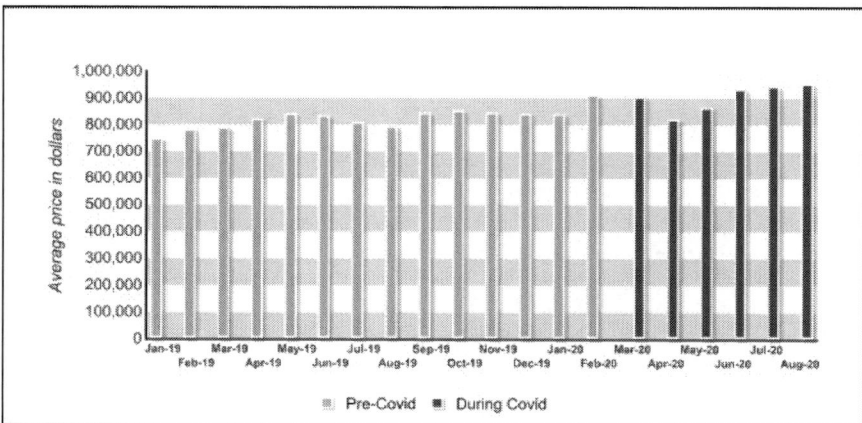

Figure 3.3 – Housing prices in the Greater Toronto Area

The governments were expected to shift their focus from stimulus spending to battling deficits by the fourth quarter of 2020. Banks might also tighten the availability of credit. Furthermore, COVID-19 disrupted immigration flows. Canadian demographics, housing and labour markets have relied on immigration for stability and growth. A considerable decline in immigrant flows would contribute to a reduction in aggregate housing demand in the future. The combined effect of all these forces could increase job losses and decrease job security. Even the low interest rates, which were underpinning the housing markets in June 2020, may not compensate for a lack of job security, Rosenberg warned.

For those with job security and decent incomes, the world is their oyster, Rosenberg said. But without job security, think twice before staking a claim in this economy.

THE PENTUP DEMAND

July 2020 sales data for large cities across Canada showed unprecedented resilience in housing markets. While the economy struggled with the pandemic-induced slowdown and with the unemployment rate still twice what it was just months ago, housing markets in Toronto and Vancouver posted much higher sales than those recorded in July of 2019.

In Toronto, Canada's largest housing market, 11,081 dwellings were sold, a 29.5 per cent increase in sales over July 2019. Sales (not seasonally adjusted) were up by almost 28 per cent from June 2020. Average housing prices in July climbed by over 17 per cent year-over-year.

In Vancouver, July housing sales were up by 22.3 per cent from the year before and up 28 per cent over June 2020. It was the best July in terms of overall sales in the past 10 years and came with a noticeable increase in prices.

The July 2020 surge in prices and sales was somewhat unexpected. The Canada Mortgage and Housing Corporation (CMHC) and some other experts were projecting declining sales and prices. Two key trends would determine the future of housing for the rest of 2020. The first is pent-up demand, which we believe is partially responsible for the recent strength in housing markets. Once that extra demand is exhausted, markets are likely to regress to the long-term average trends.

These are more readily apparent when analyzing year-to-date sales. Despite the strong July 2020 sales, the year-to-date sales in Toronto sales in July 2020 lagged about 10 per cent behind the 52,417 recorded in the first seven months of 2019.

That leads one to conclude that the driving force behind the stronger sales in July was likely the forgone sales in April and May of 2020. Compared to almost 19,000 sales in April and May of 2019, fewer than 7,600 transactions were recorded in the greater Toronto for the corresponding months in 2020.

Buyers entered the market this summer when lockdown restrictions were eased, resulting in an uncharacteristic jump in demand in July. The pent-up demand, however, was not matched with a commensurate increase in listings, which contributed to the rise in prices where buyers competed for a smaller inventory. However, an economic slowdown later in the year, and the job losses that might come with it, could adversely impact housing markets. Hence cautious optimism should guide the way.

The second noticeable trend is the flight to the suburbs. COVID-19 has contributed to a spike in demand for larger homes with backyards and balconies that are more readily available in the suburbs than in the urban core. Housing transactions in Toronto's 905 suburbs increased from 64 per cent of the total in July 2019 to 68 per cent this year. While the increase did not suggest a pivotal shift, the preference for suburbs in Toronto should be considered a bellwether for other large housing markets in Canada.

Larger units were also in greater demand in July 2020. Compared to 2019, when detached units constituted 46 per cent of the transactions in greater Toronto, their share increased to 51 per cent in July 2020. At the same time, the percentage of condominium sales declined by 18 per cent compared to July 2019.

Contributing to the suburban appeal is the widening gap in housing prices between the suburbs and the core municipality in Toronto. Consider that in July 2019, the average price of detached dwellings in the City of Toronto was 32 per cent higher than the same in the 905 suburbs. However, in July 2020, detached housing in the City of Toronto, on average, cost 45 per cent more than suburban dwellings.

COVID-19 and related restrictions shifted consumer demand in time and space. Homebuyers and sellers can plan better by knowing that pent-up demand won't last forever and that the higher prices of low-rise housing units in the urban core are likely to continue pushing homebuyers out to the suburbs.

NOT ALL HOUSING MARKETS ARE CREATED EQUAL

A cross-country comparison of housing markets in July revealed housing markets were showing remarkable resilience except in Alberta and Saskatchewan. Data released by the Canadian Real Estate Association (CREA) showed that national residential real estate sales were accelerating faster than new listings, and prices were up in most places except the Prairies. Housing prices were also up from five years ago in large housing markets in the east and west, but were lower in markets in Alberta and Saskatchewan.

Residential sales across Canada increased by 26 per cent in July 2020 over June, and 30.5 per cent higher than in July 2019. But as sales accelerated, indicating a higher-than-usual demand, the supply side lagged, with month-over-month new listings increasing by just 7.6 per cent.

The mismatch between demand and supply, with sales outpacing new listings, exerted pricing pressure such that the average housing price in Canada increased by 14.3 per cent in July from the same month a year ago.

Canada's three largest housing markets led the charge, mostly because of the pent-up demand from forgone sales in March and April. Seasonally adjusted July 2020 sales were up by 49.5 per cent in the Greater Toronto Area, 43.9 per cent in Greater Vancouver and 39.1 per cent in Montreal over the previous month.

Sales volume was higher in July 2020 in the Prairies relative to last year, but the pace of growth was much slower than the more populous cities. Seasonally adjusted July sales were up by 15.7 per cent in Calgary, 9.7 per cent in Edmonton, 8.2 per cent in Regina and 5.6 per cent in Saskatoon over the previous month.

The slower growth in housing sales in the Prairies masks the broader economic struggles in Alberta and Saskatchewan resulting from the decline in crude prices. A comparative analysis of indexed benchmark prices, which allows for a comparison of structurally similar dwellings, showed that prices over the past five years in large markets were up except in Alberta and Saskatchewan. Benchmarked prices in July were down 10.2 per cent in Calgary, nine per cent in Edmonton, 9.6 per cent in Regina, and 8.3 per cent in Saskatoon over five years. By comparison, prices were up 55 per cent in the Greater Toronto Area, 47 per cent in Greater Vancouver and 34 per cent in the Montreal Census Metropolitan Area (CMA).

Another sign of trouble was recently revealed by Canada Mortgage and Housing Corp. (CMHC), which reported higher mortgage deferral rates in resource-extraction economies. Deferral rates were 21 per cent in Alberta, and 14.8 per cent in both Saskatchewan and Newfoundland, compared to 10.1 per cent in Ontario and 5.6 per cent in Quebec.

The largest price increases over five years were recorded in smaller towns within the commuter shed of more populous markets. For example, benchmarked five-year prices in July increased by 88.5 per cent in the Niagara Region and 66 per cent in the Hamilton-Burlington area near Toronto. Similarly, prices were up by 75 per cent in Fraser Valley near Greater Vancouver. The accelerated price increases in the satellite towns near large urban centres suggest that smaller towns are narrowing the price gap with their larger neighbours. Consider that prices in the Greater Toronto Area five years ago were 226 per cent higher than those in the Niagara Region, but that gap was reduced to 186 per cent by July 2020. Affordable small towns within the commuter shed of larger, more expensive towns might experience greater demand during COVID-19 as homebuyers expressed renewed interest in larger dwellings, which are more affordable in the remote suburbs.

Housing markets in Montreal and further east also showed strength, with sales and prices mostly higher over the past 12 months. The Quebec City CMA, the second-largest market in Quebec, reported a 43 per cent increase in July sales from five years ago. Surprisingly, benchmarked prices were up by just 4.4 per cent over the same period. A strong post-pandemic economic recovery might push prices higher in places such as Quebec City that have not experienced a large increase in prices over the past five years.

Housing markets are being held together by mortgage forbearance and income support measures implemented by lenders and governments to limit COVID-19's adverse impact on the economy and consumption. The preliminary numbers for August sales and prices hinted at the continuation of increasing sales and rising prices, at least partly supported by income support measures, which might be extended into 2021.

At the same time, recent gains in employment suggest an economic recovery, as do reports suggesting that mortgage deferrals are in decline - some borrowers apparently opted to defer as an early precautionary measure - even though CMHC is reporting that almost 14 per cent of the mortgages were in deferral.

AVOIDING THE MORTGAGE DEFERRAL CLIFF

Housing markets in Canada were on the mend in August 2020. Sales data from the Greater Toronto Area showed considerable increases in sales and prices in August. With the mortgage deferral programs set to expire in September and October of 2020, housing market recovery might lose steam or even face significant challenges.

Earlier in March, the uncertainty about the resumption of economic activity and the public health impacts of COVID-19 was high. Many borrowers, who were uncertain about their jobs, opted for mortgage deferral as a precaution. By mid-April, 600,000 borrowers had applied for mortgage deferrals. At its peak, over 700,000 mortgages had been in some form of a deferral representing 16 per cent of borrowers.

Evan Siddall, President and CEO of the Canada Mortgage and Housing Corporation (CMHC), alerted that by October, the financial system might approach the debt-deferral cliff, when loan forbearance programs end and borrowers must start making payments again. Canada's housing future need not be so bleak as heading to a cliff. Already, federal institutions were taking steps to allow deferrals to last until December.

The Office of the Superintendent of Financial Institutions (OSFI), a federal government agency that regulates the banking sector, advised the financial institutions that unlike the six-month deferrals granted until the end of August, those given in September 2020 would be entitled to special treatment for up to three months. The regulator will not treat the deferred loans as past-due and hence not subject lenders to stringent capital requirements.

COVID-19 has hurt the economic fortunes of renters more so than homeowners. Economic data revealed that job losses were more pronounced for part-time workers than those working full-time jobs. As the economic engine was reigniting in the Fall of 2020, most fulltime workers, who are more likely to be homeowners, were expected to be able to meet their financial obligations, including meeting housing and shelter costs. Hence, the majority of those who opted for mortgage deferral as a precaution are expected to exit the program without going into arrears.

A fast economic recovery, therefore, can prevent mortgage markets from approaching the deferral cliff. Also, continued support from the government and lenders can help expedite the economic recovery. For instance, anticipating a slower recovery, Australian authorities announced in July 2020 that mortgage deferrals could last for up to 10 months. In the U.S., the Federal Housing Finance Agency (FHFA) announced an extension of the moratorium on some foreclosures and evictions till December 2020.

The quasi-government housing agencies in the U.S., Freddie Mac and Fannie Mae, instructed the lenders to continue offering relief to borrowers for up to 12 months that may include forbearance and waiving late fee penalties.

In Canada, those borrowers who would need more than six months to resume making mortgage payments could still have the option to defer payments by an additional four months. Canada Guaranty Mortgage Insurance Co., one of the three mortgage-default insurers, advised in March 2020 that the six-month mortgage deferral did not "remove the existing ability to defer up to four months throughout the life of the mortgage."

Mortgage deferrals and Canada Emergency Response Benefit (CERB) have helped Canadian housing markets to avoid huge spikes in mortgage arrears. Analysis by economists at Bank of Canada and Ryerson University showed that without mortgage deferrals, mortgage arrears would have reached an all-time high of 1.3 per cent in the fourth quarter of 2020, up from the pre-pandemic rate of 0.25 per cent.[85] Research showed that mortgage deferrals and other support measures flattened the arrears curve. If the deferrals are not extended, the economists forecasted the arrears to reach 0.53 per cent in the second quarter of 2021, which will be twice the pre-pandemic rate and higher than the arrears rate during the Great Recession in 2009.

The six-month deferral deadline was set in March 2020 with considerable uncertainty about how long the recovery would take. Realizing now that the labour market recovery will take slightly longer, a prudent approach would be to try matching the expiry of deferrals and emergency benefits with the labour market recovery.

---

[85] Bilyk, O., Ho, A.T.Y., Khan, M., & Vallée, G. (2020). Household indebtedness risks in the wake of COVID-19. Retrieved from https://www.bankofcanada.ca/2020/06/staff-analytical-note-2020-8/

SUMMARY

This chapter was prepared in the Fall of 2020 when economies and societies were struggling to recover from COVID-19. Governments across the world reacted to the pandemic by implementing lockdowns by the middle of March 2020. All economic activity froze. Housing transactions also met the same fate. Residential sales collapsed in April and May. Surprisingly, with the easing of restrictions on movement and assembly, housing markets demonstrated great resilience such that sales in June, July, and August surpassed expectations. Housing sales and prices in the summer of 2020 were higher than for the same months in previous years.

At the same time, one could see societies reacting to the new realities of life under a pandemic. Preference for larger homes, often located in the suburbs, increased during the pandemic as many knowledge economy workers started to work from home resulting in a huge spike in teleworking. Bigger homes are more suited for working from home and hence the demand for such dwellings increased considerably. One also observed a reluctance to return to employment hubs located in downtowns. Office work locations located in the heart of the city is often served more efficiently by public transportation. Workers continue to resist the temptation to travel by public transportation such that transit riderships in megacities, which initially declined by 80% to 90%, continued to struggle by the Fall of 2020. Downtown office real estate, which relies on efficient public transportation, as a result suffered. Also, restrictions on the use of elevators posed another challenge to repopulate office towers.

This chapter serves as a running commentary about a pandemic that is far from over. A vaccine is expected to be available by the middle of 2021. During this period, the economic uncertainty will continue to loom large as the trillion-dollar stimuli that supported the workers and consumption globally are now coming to an end along with the accommodations for mortgage forbearance and restrictions on rental evictions.

It is quite likely that the resilience observed in housing markets will overcome the economic challenges expected in the last quarter of 2020 and the early part of 2021. However, much depends upon the pace and scale of the economic recovery that is expected and highly desired.

4 HOUSING AFFORDABILITY

HOUSING AFFORDABILITY IS GETTING WORSE EVEN THOUGH PRICES ARE FALLING

C onventional wisdom states that falling prices should improve housing affordability. Though the logic is appealing, Canadian housing markets paint quite a different picture, with housing affordability worsening even though average housing prices have fallen.

Unlike many other assets classes, housing markets are complex and heterogeneous, with no two homes (or buyers) being identical. As a result, the housing market does not necessarily follow the typical wisdom of markets.

2018 housing market data and research revealed that affordability eroded in Canada even as prices tumbled. The reason for this anomaly is that housing affordability only partially depends on prices. Regulatory changes also play a large role in determining housing affordability.

A report by RBC Economic Research reviewed housing affordability in the third quarter of 2018 and concluded that it was "getting less affordable to own a home in Canada."[86] The report tracks the income required to cover the cost of owning an average home with a 25 per cent down payment. When compared with the third quarter of 2015, the qualifying income had increased significantly by the third quarter of 2018.

---

[86] RBC Economic Research. (2018). *Housing trends and affordability*. Retrieved from http://www.rbc.com/economics/economic-reports/pdf/canadian-housing/house-sep2018.pdf

In Vancouver, for instance, the income required to cover ownership of an average home was $211,000 in 2018, up from $127,000 three years prior. The qualifying income in Toronto was $187,000 in 2018 compared to $103,000 in 2015. In fact, the qualifying income had increased in all large and small housing markets across Canada.

One big reason for the higher qualifying income required in 2018 was the increase in housing prices since 2015, a rise that was most pronounced in Greater Vancouver and Toronto. Qualifying incomes, therefore, increased by $34,000 in Vancouver and $27,000 in Toronto since 2015 as a result of higher prices, the RBC report estimated.

But rising prices were not the only factor. Even without their impact, the qualifying income would have climbed considerably because of the stress test that required the borrowers to qualify at a higher interest rate than the contracted rate as of January 2018. The RBC report estimated that the increase in qualifying income due to the stress test was almost the same as the one resulting from the increase in housing prices. The stress test raised the qualifying income threshold by $36,000 in Vancouver and $27,000 in Toronto. It also didn't help that mortgage rates also increased over the same period further raising the bar to qualify for home ownership.

The RBC Economics Report illustrates the peculiarities of housing markets where price alone does not determine the affordability of an asset. Certainly, the increase in housing prices eroded affordability. However, equally instrumental were the regulatory changes (stress test and mortgage rates) that also erected huge affordability barriers.

HOMES SOLD UNDER $400,000

TORONTO MARKET AS A SHARE OF TOTAL HOMES SOLD

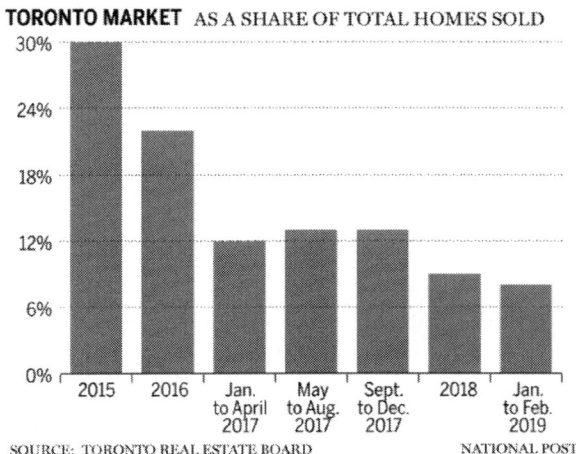

SOURCE: TORONTO REAL ESTATE BOARD   NATIONAL POST

Figure 4.1 – Percentage of Homes Sold in Toronto for Under $400,000 (2015-2019)

The impact of the stress test is further illustrated with data from Toronto where housing prices rose sharply from 2015 to the first quarter of 2017. Toronto's housing market experienced two regulatory shocks. The first shock came in April 2017 when the Ontario government imposed new taxes on foreign homebuyers. The immediate impact was a decline in sales and prices. The second shock came in January 2018 when the stress test was imposed.

Toronto's sales data revealed that the share of the market taken up by the least expensive homes (those sold for less than $400,000) declined as housing prices increased. For instance, 30 per cent of the homes sold in 2015 transacted for less than $400,000. By the first quarter of 2017, when housing prices peaked, the share of low-priced homes accounted for a mere 12 per cent of the transactions.

As the housing prices slid in Toronto as of May 2017, the share of homes that transacted for less than $400,000 increased slightly and represented 13 per cent of the total transactions for the rest of 2017. However, the share of low-priced homes in 2018 declined from 13 to 9 per cent (a 31 per cent drop), which took place even when the nominal average home price in Toronto declined from $822,681 in 2017 to $787,300 in 2018, and $766,197 in February 2019.

Again, the conventional wisdom would have dictated an increase rather than a decline in the share of low-priced homes that attract low-to moderate-income households. But that didn't happen.

The stress test and the increase in mortgage rates increasingly affected the affordability of low-income households and priced them out of the market even when house prices were declining. Housing affordability will improve with a decline in home ownership costs, which will require regulatory changes in the short run and greater housing supply in the long run.

Though many Canadians are unable to purchase homes in major cities like Toronto and Vancouver, those looking to build equity through homeownership should consider more affordable housing markets with lower average house price to income ratios and high livability.

LIVABILITY AND AFFORDABILITY DON'T HAVE TO BE TRADE-OFFS

From 2017 to 2019, the rapid escalation of housing prices in a small number of Canada's largest cities has dominated the discourse when it comes to real estate. But there is more to Canada than unaffordable cities. Mid-to small-sized cities offer good quality of life, similar opportunities for health and education services and - though it may be hard for some to believe - affordable housing markets.

The desirability of a place or a product determines its value. Cities have limited supply of land, and over time as the city is built out, the developable land becomes scarcer. As cities continue to grow, the value of the remaining developable land starts to appreciate at a faster rate. Research from Ryerson University's Centre for Urban Research and Land Development revealed that the City of Toronto led in population growth among a sample of North American cities. Toronto's population grew by 77,435 in the 12 months ended July 1, 2018. Phoenix, Arizona. with an increase of 25,288 followed Toronto. For the same time period, New York City experienced a decline in population.[87]

Housing prices are also influenced by interest rates. Prices appreciate faster when interest rates are at record lows and reached a 30-per-cent year-over-year increase in august 2016 in large housing markets in British Columbia.

But there are choices beyond unaffordable cities, including smaller towns at the urban fringe - where commuting by transit is available while housing is significantly cheaper than in neighbouring large cities - or even more affordable neighbourhoods within otherwise expensive cities.

The 2019 Canada Livability Report by Re/Max attempted to identify affordable places that are also desirable for high livability. Accessibility to shopping, dining and green spaces topped the livability criteria for six in 10 respondents in the survey.[88] Almost 36 per cent of respondents identified proximity to public transit as a desirable neighbourhood attribute. accessibility to work and good schools were also highly ranked.

The Re/Max report also polled brokers to rate their respective cities on 11 indicators of livability including: access to bike lanes, walking paths, green spaces, healthcare, shopping, dining, work, and public transit; housing supply and affordability; economic development; population growth; and high-quality public schools. Re/Max brokers ranked Calgary high in seven out of the 11 categories indicating a high score for livability. Edmonton was also deemed highly livable. The report noted that Calgary and Edmonton "continue to develop as livable cities" despite the talk of an economic slowdown in Alberta.

Not surprisingly, Toronto ranked high for accessibility to retail, but not as much for green spaces. Toronto neighbourhoods with high accessibility to green spaces were also the most expensive in the city. The report identified Scarborough and East York for affordability in Toronto. By comparison, Vancouver was ranked medium for retail, population growth and housing supply. At the same time, it ranked high for accessibility to public transit and green spaces, top-rated schools, and walkability in places like Yaletown. The

[87] Clayton, F., & Shi, H. Y. (2019). *WOW! Toronto Was the Second Fastest Growing Metropolitan Area and the Top Growing City in All of the United States and Canada* (No. Blog Entry 35). Retrieved from https://www.ryerson.ca/cur/Blog/blogentry35/

[88] McNutt, L. (2019, May 2). Best Places to Live: Canada Liveability Report. Retrieved from https://blog.remax.ca/canada-liveability-report/

report identified Main, West End and Kerrisdale as "the top three all-around livable neighbourhoods in Vancouver while Mount Pleasant, Downtown and Renfrew-Collingwood" were the most affordable.

Mid-sized cities such as Halifax, Ottawa and Windsor do not usually make the headlines for housing. However, relative to large cities, housing prices in these cities are more in line with their respective average household incomes. The house price to average income ratio, an indicator of housing affordability, was 4.1 in Ottawa. By comparison, the same ratio was 10.5 in Vancouver and 7.2 in Toronto, Canada's two most expensive housing cities. In addition to high livability, Calgary and Edmonton also rank high for affordability. The same ratio checks in at 2.6 for Edmonton and 2.9 for Calgary.

AFFORDABILITY BY CITY

Housing price-to-income ratios for various Canadian cities

City	Ratio
Moncton	2.4
Regina	2.5
Edmonton	2.6
Saskatoon	2.8
Calgary	2.9
Ottawa	4.1
Montreal	4.4
Niagara Region	4.9
Guelph	5.4
Toronto	7.2
Victoria	7.7
Vancouver	10.5

SOURCE: STATISTICS CANADA, CREA   NATIONAL POST

Figure 4.2 – Housing Price-to-Income Ratios for Canadian Cities

Small-sized towns are even more affordable. Moncton and Saint John in New Brunswick, Saguenay and Trois-Rivières in Quebec, and Charlottetown are smaller towns that are rich in charm and remain very affordable.

Young Canadians would be well-served to think broadly about their career and housing choices. For those looking to build equity, escaping expensive housing markets for affordable ones - even if it means a lower relative income - may be worth considering.

The next section will discuss how erecting barriers to new development often results in land parcels not reaching their true potential, which in turn adversely affects economies.

REAL ESTATE GRIDLOCK IS BAD FOR ALL

When a resource is owned by many, the rights-holders often prevent others from developing the resource, causing its value to deplete. Michael Heller, a professor of real estate law at Columbia University, has dubbed such a situation "the tragedy of the anticommons."[89]

The paradox applies increasingly to real estate markets where not just the real assets are often held simultaneously by many, but other non-property assets, such as data archived on the Multiple Listing Service (MLS), could have numerous rights-holders.

Unlike the tragedy of the commons, which results in overuse of a jointly held asset resulting in its depletion or destruction, the tragedy of the anticommons results in underuse or underdevelopment. This is a familiar theme in property markets, where Nimbys, Nimtos, and Banana Republics often make development difficult or impossible.

Most readers of this column are familiar with Nimbys, whose mantra is Not In My Backyard. Nimbys resist any construction in their neighbourhood - they are not against development per se, they just don't want it near them.

The residents of Marpole neighbourhood in Vancouver, who opposed the plan to build a homeless shelter near them, can be considered Nimbys.[90] They resisted the planned shelter because they believed it would result in higher crime and drug use. Marpole residents were not against the shelter, they just didn't want it near them.

The citizens of Banana Republics have one big goal: Build Absolutely Nothing Anywhere Near Anyone. They are the poster children for preserving the status quo. Land parcels that fall within their zones of influence stand little chance of ever being developed.

Nimtos are the politicians who might see the value in a proposed development but are likely to stand against it fearing backlash by constituent Nimbys and Banana Republics. (The acronym stands for 'Not In My Term in Office'.)

The Nimbys, Nimtos, and Banana Republics either individually or collectively erect barriers against new developments. Thus, undeveloped or underdeveloped land fails to reach its true potential.

The naysayers to development are amazingly effective as they often can influence development outcomes on land parcels they don't even own. To them, the entire neighbourhood is their easement.

Changes in planning regulations can help empower like-minded owners to develop a real asset at a higher intensity. In Vancouver, owners of contiguous lots in a predominantly single-family detached neighbourhood can sell their "assembled" units to a builder who would then develop the site at a higher density. In the absence of such enabling regulations, other

[89] Heller, M. (n.d.). *The Tragedy of the Anticommons | The Wealth of the Commons*. Retrieved from http://wealthofthecommons.org/essay/tragedy-anticommons
[90] Brown, S. (2017, November 6). Daily Poll: Is opposition to Marpole homeless shelter just NIMBYism? *Vancouver Sun*. Retrieved from https://vancouversun.com/news/local-news/daily-poll-is-opposition-to-marpole-homeless-shelter-just-nimbyism

homeowners in the neighbourhood could thwart attempts to densify citing an increase in noise, traffic, parking, and demand for public services, such as schools.

Real estate data is a valuable resource whose ownership is highly atomized. Millions of dwellings are listed each year on MLS in Canada. The data are collected from individual homeowners by listing brokers who archive it on the MLS. The MLS data is an example where one would need a consensus among many stakeholders to decide upon the scope of its use. The Toronto Real Estate Board (TREB), for instance, prohibits real estate agents, brokers, and others from analyzing (mining) data or using it to sell "derivative products or marketing reports."

For innovation to take root in real estate, data must be analyzed using advanced analytics, including deep learning algorithms. But such a socially desirable outcome is unlikely if those who "own" real estate data continue to restrict its innovative use.

One response to real estate gridlock is the use of eminent domain that allows governments to seize property for public use. *The New York Times* building in Manhattan, completed in 2007, became possible because of eminent domain. Otherwise, numerous owners of the assembled parcels would not have voluntarily sold their properties.

A consensus-seeking process in which rights-holders are educated on the benefits of a better use of real assets or data is better than forcing people into compliance. The Nimbys, Nimtos, and Banana Republics should know that gridlocked economies are bad for all in the long run.

While restricting new development often results in less than desirable economic outcomes for municipalities, promoting housing affordability through government policies aimed at decreasing housing prices can have adverse economic effects as well.

MUNICIPALITIES SHOULD BE CAREFUL WHAT THEY WISH FOR

Do falling housing prices eventually impact local and provincial revenue? While governments in Canada are focused on arresting the growth in housing prices to promote affordability, the unintended consequences of steeper-than envisioned declines also merit consideration.

Municipal and provincial revenues are tied to property taxes, and as housing values decline, property-related tax revenues decline as well. The costs of delivering municipal services, however, continue to increase, often at a rate higher than the rate of inflation. Such divergence in costs and revenues at the local government level creates a funding gap that is often plugged by the higher tiers of government. However, a steep and sustained decline in housing prices will impact revenues of higher tiers of governments as well, limiting their abilities to offer adequate support to local governments.

Howard Chernick and coauthors presented a paper at the Urban Institute in 2017 where they examined the adverse impact of declining housing values on local government revenues.[91] Their analysis of 91 cities in the United States revealed that since the Great Recession, which was marked by a collapse of housing markets, "inflation-adjusted per capita revenues and spending remaine(d) below their prerecession levels" in many of those cities.

And even when local tax revenues rose, cuts in federal funding to local governments worsened the fiscal challenges faced at the municipal level. In 2019, the B.C. government proposed even higher transfer tax rates on foreign homebuyers and new annual levies on homeowners who were not residents of British Columbia. These additional surcharges were announced within weeks of the tightening of mortgage regulations that required federally regulated lenders to subject all borrowers to a stress test that includes qualifying at a mortgage rate significantly higher than the contracted rate.

The cumulative effect of tighter mortgage regulation and "speculation" taxes was a softening of the housing market in Vancouver and Toronto where prices and sales declined significantly. However, declining housing values did not immediately impact municipal revenues in Vancouver.

The reason for the municipal revenue resilience was the lag between assessed property values and market values. Often the assessed values lag market values by a few years. Even when market values are falling, assessed housing values may continue to rise.

Consider Vancouver, where housing prices in 2017 declined compared to housing prices in 2016. However, the assessed residential property values increased by 32 per cent in 2017 resulting in a moderate increase in property tax revenue.

When property values continue to decline, assessed values eventually catch up, and a decline in property tax revenue ensues. A countermeasure could be an increase in the property tax rate or greater transfer of funds from higher tiers of government.

Carole James, the B.C. Finance Minister, explained that the goal of placing restrictions on housing markets was to affect a decline in housing prices. Just how steep that decline will be is an important question especially when the tightening of regulations might force many borrowers underwater where their mortgage loans would be larger than the fallen housing values. The minister acknowledged that the Finance Ministry had not modelled the scale and scope of the impacts of the new regulations. "We're taking some very bold

---

[91] Chernick, H., Reschovsky, A., & Newman, S. (2016). *Effect of the Housing Crisis on the Finances of Central Cities*. Retrieved from https://www.urban.org/sites/default/files/the_effect_of_the_housing_crisis_on_the_finances_of_central_cities.pdf

steps.... There are firsts here," the minister said.[92]

Declining housing prices impact other sources of revenue. First comes the decline in land-transfer tax revenue, which is based on sold prices and not assessed values. Next is the decline in sales tax revenue, because of depleting housing equity. And finally, a sustained drop in property values contribute to lower assessed values resulting in a drop in property tax revenue.

The balancing act for the government is to determine whether the additional revenue from new speculation taxes, which could be sizable, will be large enough to counter the eventual decline in property tax revenue resulting from a sustained drop in housing prices.

But the real caveat applies to the unintended consequences when housing markets experience a steeper decline than was envisioned. The experiences in Toronto and Vancouver suggest that the uncertainty accompanying any change in regulations can spook even those who were not targeted by the new regulations.

Municipal governments must, therefore, build reserves while housing prices are rising. Why? Because, if there indeed are housing bubbles, they will be followed by busts. Saving for bad times is equally important as spending in good times for smart local governments.

Another policy initiative aimed at increasing housing affordability, and indirectly encouraging housing supply, is shared equity mortgages which have been used with varying degrees of success in Australia, the U.K. and the U.S.

SHARED EQUITY MORTGAGES ARE NO PANACEA

In 2019, an election year, the federal Liberals were eager to share - albeit partially - the housing pains of low-to mid-income households who have been priced out of the housing market.

Budget 2019 announced a new First-Time Home Buyers Initiative (FTHBI) to assist new homebuyers and indirectly encourage the supply of new housing. At the heart of the initiative are new shared equity mortgages that will help to lower monthly mortgage payments for an expected 100,000 first-time home buyers over the next three years.[93]

Though new to Canada, shared equity mortgages (SEM) have been tried in the past in Australia, the U.K, and the U.S. Though research on the

---

[92] Hunter, J. (2018, February 21). New B.C. housing measures are "bold steps," minister says. *The Globe and Mail*. Retrieved from https://www.theglobeandmail.com/news/british-columbia/canadians-with-bc-vacation-homes-to-be-hit-with-new-tax/article38061049/

[93] Department of Finance Canada. (n.d.). An Affordable Place to Call Home - Backgrounder. Retrieved from https://www.budget.gc.ca/2019/docs/themes/housing-logement-en.pdf

effectiveness of SEMs and their variants is not readily available, they have usually been introduced by governments faced with housing affordability challenges.

The details of the Canadian plan are not yet known. The government has entrusted the Canada Mortgage and Housing Corporation (CMHC), which will partner with homebuyers for the mortgages, to release the terms and conditions later.

While CMHC is busy delineating the contours of the FTHBI, we will take this opportunity to offer a perspective on SEMs. In a typical SEM, a lender takes an equity stake in the property being purchased. Whereas the ownership remains with the buyer, shared equity implies that the lender will claim a part of capital gains or bear losses.

Consider the following example. A first-time homebuyer is interested in purchasing a newly constructed house for $400,000. The buyer comes up with a five per cent ($20,000) down payment for a CMHC insured mortgage. CMHC will provide up to 10 per cent of the purchase price as an SEM ($40,000).

SEM effectively reduces the mortgaged amount from $380,000 to $340,000, which the government believes results in a $228 reduction in monthly mortgage payments. For many struggling households, $228 in monthly savings will be helpful. Also, the reduced loan amount will help partially address the raised bar for mortgage qualification resulting from the stress test, which requires the borrowers to qualify at a rate 200 basis points higher than the contracted rate.

The budget also suggests the government understands that buyers are only part of the equation when it comes to tight housing markets. The question of supply is also paramount: a budget backgrounder rightly recognized that the "most effective way to address affordability in the long run" is to "increase the supply." Thus, the SEMs proposed in the budget involve a 10 per cent equity stake in a newly built home and only a five per cent stake in an existing home. The differential is designed to increase the demand for new housing, which should in turn increase housing supply.

While SEMs could be moderately effective in increasing housing supply if combined with other initiatives, they are likely to do little to address supply challenges in expensive housing markets. That is because in order to participate in the FTHBI, a household's income must be under $120,000, and the mortgage and incentive amount together cannot be greater than four times the household income. Finding adequate shelter priced under $500,000 for growing households will be a formidable challenge in places like Toronto and Vancouver where housing affordability is already acute. At the same time, FTHBI will pit qualifying households, who will only pay 90 per cent or 95 per cent of the eventual price, against families who do not qualify and will be forced to pay full price.

While homebuyers might find the initiative helps them buy a home, there will be a downside when they sell and must share the capital gains with the CMHC. (In the U.S., private investors at times claimed 50 per cent or more of the price appreciation, depending on the terms of the arrangement, for as little as a 10 per cent stake. There is no indication the CMHC will be so harsh.) Also, participating households might have to incur additional costs (interest payment on equity loan) over time.

Over three years, 100,000 beneficiaries of the FTHBI will represent fewer than 10 per cent of the homebuyers in Canada. Though the number of affected households is small, still the recipients will likely push the price of low-priced homes upward, which could inadvertently worsen affordability for the same buyers the government is trying to help.

In the late seventies, shared equity and shared appreciation mortgages were tested by private lenders in the U.S. However, such mortgages failed to take off because private lenders were not keen on waiting for undetermined years to claim their share of the capital gains. The lack of private interest is perhaps the reason that the Liberal government has asked CMHC, a crown corporation, to extend credit for the initiative.

SEMs are not without investor risk, especially markets where housing prices are falling and economic outlooks are increasingly recessionary. CMHC may end up sharing more capital losses than gains if average housing prices continue to fall.

Housing affordability has worsened for a very large segment of the Canadian population, especially in large cities. Even if SEMs were to improve affordability for 100,000 first-time home buyers over three years, is the initiative an adequate response or just "a snowflake on an iceberg"? Only time will tell.

We continue our discussion of shared equity mortgages by considering the effectiveness of SEMs in the U.K. where homeowners used them primarily to buy bigger houses, not take on less debt.

UK BUYERS USED SHARED EQUITY MORTGAGES TO BUY MORE HOUSE

Whether or not the Liberal budget proposal to implement shared equity mortgages (SEMs) will improve housing affordability for first-time homebuyers was the subject of some debate when the 2019 budget was released. The full details of the SEM program have not yet been disclosed by the Canada Mortgage and Housing Corp. (CMHC), which has been entrusted with managing the $1.25 billion program over three years, but the basic outline would see the agency offer to take either a five-or 10-per-cent stake when qualifying first-time homebuyers purchase a home, depending on whether it is an existing or new-build home.[94] The Liberal government hopes to assist 100,000 first-time buyers with the incentive.

While government subsidized SEMs are new to Canada, other jurisdictions have tried them with varying levels of success. A similar initiative by the U.K. government invested 10 billion pounds in the first five years after its launch in 2013.

A research paper released in March 2019 by Matteo Benetton, a professor with the Haas School of Business at the University of California, and co-authors, presents a detailed review of SEM in the U.K. They concluded that the households used SEM "to buy more-expensive properties, and not to reduce their mortgage debt and house price risk exposure."[95]

There are several lessons to be drawn from the U.K. experience. The U.K. government launched the Help-to-Buy Equity Loan scheme in April 2013. The SEMs provided up to 20 per cent of the home purchase price "in exchange for the same share in its future value." Since houses are significantly more expensive in London, the scheme increased the equity threshold in February 2016 when it began to contribute up to 40 per cent of the purchase price for homes bought in London.

The scheme came with some restrictions. Only newly built homes sold for 600,000 pounds or less were eligible. Borrowers were required to put up a minimum down payment of five per cent. Both first-time homebuyers and people moving between homes were eligible. However, the scheme did not support the purchase of second homes or investment properties. Also, the buyers were required to satisfy affordability requirements, one of which was a British version of the stress test.

For the first five years, the government charged a symbolic one pound per year in interest fees for the equity it provided. Afterward, the government charged 1.75 per cent in interest fees that increased each year by inflation plus one per cent. The households, therefore, enjoyed an interest-free loan for the first five years and only later were charged interest fees on the balance they owed the government. While the SEM maturity was set at 25 years, it could be terminated earlier by the sale of the house, prepayment, or default. If the borrower defaulted, the government had the right to foreclose.

Professor Benetton and co-authors compared 99,571 home purchases between April 2013 and March 2017 that benefitted from SEMs with 157,620 additional purchases that were eligible for the scheme, but in which the buyers chose not to participate. They observed that the SEM borrowers were

---

[94] Canada Mortgage and Housing Corporation. (2019, June 17). Federal Government Makes it Easier for Middle Class Canadians to Buy their First Home. Retrieved from https://www.cmhc-schl.gc.ca/en/media-newsroom/news-releases/2019/federal-government-makes-easier-for-middle-class-canadians-buy-first-home-toronto

[95] Benetton, M., Bracke, P., Cocco, J. F., & Garbarino, N. (2019). *Housing Consumption and Investment: Evidence from Shared Equity Mortgages.* https://doi.org/10.2139/ssrn.3374421

younger, more likely to be first-time homebuyers, had lower incomes and, on average, purchased properties that were seven-per-cent less expensive than those bought by the non-SEM borrowers who would have qualified regardless. The SEM borrowers were more leveraged than their comparables such that the loan-to-value ratio was 91 per cent for SEM borrowers compared to 65 per cent for the comparables. Similarly, SEM purchasers borrowed larger amounts relative to their incomes and their mortgage maturity periods were also considerably longer.

The experience in London revealed that when SEM contribution was increased from 20 to 40 per cent, qualifying homebuyers used the facility to purchase even more expensive units rather than reducing the mortgage amount. Also, after the equity contribution was increased for London, borrowers bought even larger homes than before.

The question to ask is the following: What would SEM borrowers have done in the absence of the shared equity programs? The researchers found that without SEM, the households would have either bought smaller, less-expensive homes or they would have opted to rent.

Another interesting finding was that most of the eligible borrowers in the U.K. (61 per cent) did not take advantage of the SEM. The authors believe that the borrowers were mindful of the future house price appreciation and were reluctant to share the expected capital gains with the government. The other less-plausible explanation was that borrowers were not aware of the SEM scheme.

In the U.K., SEM contributed to higher prices and facilitated the purchase of even bigger homes by first-time homebuyers. At the same time, the majority of those who could benefit from the scheme decided not to.

Improving affordability in Canada's most expensive housing markets will take more than SEMs. What's needed are aggressive plans that incentivize homebuilders and developers to produce more housing of diverse types to offset the increase in housing demand. Such changes will require cutting the red tape that delays approvals and streamlining levies and development charges to help build vibrant and sustainable communities.

SUMMARY

The focus of this chapter was on housing affordability. The rapid increase in housing prices, which have been out of step with the increase in household incomes over the past few years in Toronto, Vancouver and some other large housing markets, has been a concern for Canadian families. The government response to improve housing affordability was on and off the mark. The chapter reviewed the potential of select government initiatives, such as shared equity mortgages, and evaluated their efficacy.

5 PUBLIC POLICY AND HOUSING

Mortgage brokers and lenders have argued that the tightening of mortgage regulations in January 2018 adversely impacted the growth of mortgage lending in Canada. A report released in July 2019 by the Canada Mortgage and Housing Corporation confirmed this assertion, finding that 2018 saw the slowest growth rate of outstanding mortgages in a quarter-century.[96] Interestingly, the intervention-driven slowdown in the mortgage growth rate in 2018 was more severe than the housing market slowdown sparked by the Great Recession in 2008.

The CMHC's inaugural Residential Mortgage Industry Report exposed the extent of the impact of regulatory changes, especially the tightening of the underwriting criteria, which affected the number of housing transactions (down by 11 per cent in 2018) and housing prices (down by four per cent). The cumulative impact of the changes resulted in a decline of 19 per cent in the demand for mortgages for the purchase of property.

The report also highlighted distortions introduced by the revised stress test implemented in January 2018, which required borrowers to qualify for a higher rate than the contracted mortgage rate. Consider, for instance, that while refinancings with the same lender were down by 12 per cent in 2018, renewals with the same lender were up by 16 per cent. The report noted that the renewals were "not specifically subject to the new stress test and are more likely to meet current lender criteria."

The overall impact of these regulations meant a constrained choice set for borrowers who could not shop around at renewal and were constrained to negotiate with the same lender. This implies that the homeowners were more

---

[96] Canada Mortgage and Housing Corporation. (2019). *Residential Mortgage Industry Report*. Retrieved from https://assets.cmhc-schl.gc.ca/sf/project/cmhc/pubsandreports/residential-mortgage-industry-report/residential-mortgage-industry-report-69589-2019-en.pdf?rev=b3a87353-b29f-4926-a460-572ef239dd41

likely to stick to the same lender to avoid being subject to the stress test irrespective of their credit history or credit worthiness.

Another large impact of the regulatory changes is the 16-percentage-point decline in the share of insured mortgages, which fell from 57 per cent in the first quarter of 2015 to 41 per cent in 2019. The report suggested that the 2016 stress test for high-ratio mortgages was behind the shift to uninsured mortgages.

DIFFERENT DIRECTIONS

Year-over-year change in 2018 for different types of mortgage financings

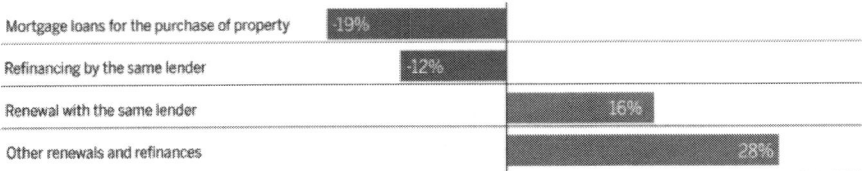

Mortgage loans for the purchase of property	-19%
Refinancing by the same lender	-12%
Renewal with the same lender	16%
Other renewals and refinances	28%

SOURCE: CMHC, RESIDENTIAL MORTGAGE INDUSTRY REPORT, 2019   NATIONAL POST

Figure 5.1 – Year-Over-Year Change in Different Types of Mortgage Financing (2018)

The CMHC report describes the four primary types of mortgage providers and their operating characteristics. In 2018, the chartered banks held the largest market share of mortgages accounting for no less than 75 per cent of the residential mortgage market share. The interest rates charged by the banks ranged from 3.3 to 5.4 per cent. Credit unions and caisses populaires accounted for 14 per cent of the residential mortgage market share. The report did not disclose the interest rates charged by credit unions. Mortgage finance companies (MFCs), often not federally regulated, held a six per cent market share. Lastly, Mortgage Investment Corporations (MICs) and private lenders were estimated to have a market share of just one per cent.

Compared to the banks, MICs charged much higher interest rates that ranged between 7 and 15 per cent. At the same time, the mortgage delinquency rate for the MIC borrowers at 1.93 per cent was higher than that for those who borrowed from the banks or MFCs.

The much higher default rate for those borrowing from private lenders and MICs suggest that high-risk borrowers were pushed to lenders who offer high-price mortgage solutions, as is evidenced by the significantly higher interest rates, to account for the weak creditworthiness of their clients. At the same time, the excessively high cost of borrowing could also trigger higher than expected default rates. The average loan size was the largest for the banks at $220,650 and the lowest for credit unions at $150,995. Private lenders and MICs issued loans with an average amount of $194,760.

The CMHC report explicitly demonstrates that regulatory changes could have a large impact on housing markets. At times, the regulation-driven impacts might be larger in magnitude than the ones resulting from an economic recession.

Changes in regulations could be successful in achieving the intended goals, such as imposing market discipline by limiting high-risk lending. A slowdown in housing sales and price appreciation could also be part of the intended outcomes, yet their larger impact on the overall economy might help stimulate the very undesirable market conditions the regulators intended to safeguard against.

In the following section, we will continue our discussion of the stress test by considering some of its intended and possibly unintended consequences.

WHAT ARE STRESS TESTS SUPPOSED TO DO AGAIN?

Housing sales data for February 2019 in Toronto and Vancouver revealed even fewer sales than February 2018, when sales had already declined because of stricter mortgage regulations.

The real estate industry held the mortgage stress test responsible for the slowdown. The test requires borrowers to qualify for an interest rate that is 200 basis points higher than the contracted rate. The proponents of the stress test believe it is working as intended and credit it for improving housing affordability resulting from the falling housing prices.

But here lies the problem. Unlike the proponents, the regulator which instituted the tests - the Office of the Superintendent of Financial Institutions Canada (OSFI) - says they were never intended to address rising housing prices in Canada.

So, are falling housing sales and prices an intended or an unintended consequence of the stress test? There is little doubt that housing markets have weakened since January 2018, when the stress test first came into effect across Canada. In greater Toronto, housing sales in February 2019 were 2.4 per cent lower than a year ago. But sales in February 2018 had already declined 35 per cent from those recorded in February 2017. Housing sales in greater Vancouver were even weaker, with February 2019 sales 33 per cent lower than the same month in 2018. In fact, February 2019 sales are 43 per cent lower than the 10-year average for sales in February.

Housing prices also depict similar trends in Vancouver. A quality-controlled index of housing prices revealed that prices in February 2019 were down by six per cent year-over-year. The same metric for housing prices in Toronto was up by 2.4 per cent.

Evan Siddall , who heads the Canada Mortgage and Housing Corporation (CMHC), believes that the stress test is bitter medicine that is working fine. He thinks the critics are "short-sighted" and "aren't thinking beyond the next commission cheque." Siddall credits the stress test for lowering housing prices. "Houses are something like $40,000 (5.3 per cent) cheaper in Toronto because of the stress test," he recently noted. "So, while the medicine may taste awful, it's working well," he concluded.[97]

Based on Siddall's comments, one might assume the tests were designed to make housing cheaper, but Carolyn Rogers, the Assistant Superintendent at OSFI, dispelled this misconception in a recent speech to the Economic Club of Canada. Addressing the criticism of the stress test, she clarified that while some assumed it was "designed to target escalating home prices" that was not the case. Rather, she explained, the stress test "was designed to target mortgage underwriting standards."[98] In her words, the test was intended to provide a safety buffer so that borrowers do not "stretch their borrowing capacity to its maximum."

THE DISAPPEARING HIGH-RISK MORTGAGE

The percentage of new mortgages that have a loan-to-income (LTI) ratio of more than 450 per cent is on the decline, especially since the stress tests.

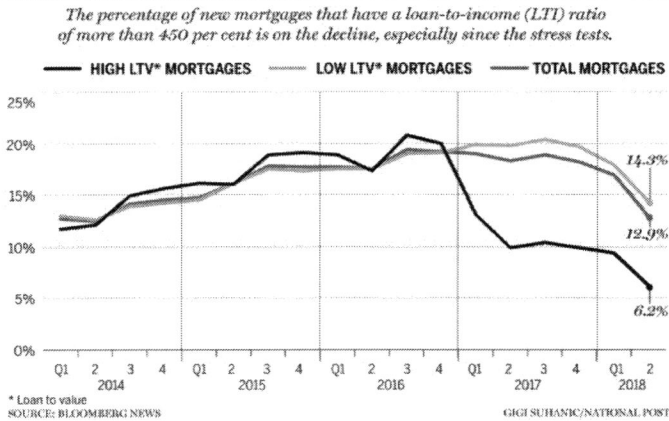

* Loan to value
SOURCE: BLOOMBERG NEWS   GIGI SUHANIC/NATIONAL POST

Figure 5.2 – Percentage of High and Low Loan to Value Mortgages (2014-2018)

As such, the stress test has been successful in lowering the prevalence of high-risk lending. A report by the Bank of Canada revealed that the "number of new highly indebted borrowers has fallen" and the quality of credit has improved while the quantity of credit being offered has declined significantly.[99]

The first phase of the stress test in 2016 addressed high-ratio mortgages

[97] Siddall, E. (2019, March 5). Are current mortgage rules too strict? No. *The Toronto Star.* Retrieved from https://thestar.com/opinion/contributors/thebigdebate/2019/03/05/are-current-mortgage-rules-too-strict-no.html

[98] Bains, J. (2019, February 5). Watchdog stands by controversial mortgage stress test. Retrieved from https://ca.finance.yahoo.com/news/watchdog-stands-controversial-mortgage-stress-test-191901661.html

[99] Bilyk, O., & teNyenhuis, M. (2018). *The Impact of Recent Policy Changes on the Canadian Mortgage Market* (No. 2018-35). Retrieved from https://www.bankofcanada.ca/2018/11/staff-analytical-note-2018-35/

where the loan-to-value ratios exceeded 80 per cent. In particular, the test targeted highly indebted borrowers whose loans were more than 4.5 times their annual income. In January 2018, the stress test was expanded to include low ratio mortgages (loan-to-value ratios under 80 per cent). Whereas the first iteration of the stress test in 2016 dramatically reduced the share of new high-ratio mortgages involving highly-indebted borrowers, it did not reduce as much the share of total mortgages extended to highly-indebted borrowers. However, when low-ratio mortgages became subject to the stress test in January 2018, a decline in the share of total mortgages extended to highly-indebted borrowers realized.

In summary, the stress test made progress in achieving its intended target of reducing the share of highly indebted borrowers. Declining housing sales and prices came along for the ride (whether they were truly an intended or unintended consequence, we will leave to readers to decide).

But what about other unintended consequences, such as driving those who do not qualify for a mortgage under the new regulations to lenders that are not regulated by OSFI and who might charge significantly higher interest rates? Remember, the stress test is only enforced on federally regulated lenders. Those governed by provincial authorities or otherwise are not affected.

OSFI is correct in ensuring that a "margin of safety" is maintained at a time when the interest rates are historically low and consumer debt levels are high. However, economic conditions are seldom stagnant, and policies must adapt to market conditions. If OSFI independently finds that the market conditions have changed sufficiently in the past 14 months, a review of the margin of safety might be a good thing.

Next, we will discuss how the narrative that places much of the blame of rising home prices in Toronto and Vancouver on foreign investors divides the real estate market into 'us and them' and does not fully explain all the forces at play.

MORE TO RISE IN REAL ESTATE THAN FOREIGN BUYERS

When it comes to housing, it's not just about us and them. Many believe that the rise in housing prices in Canada in 2017-18 was fuelled, to a large extent, by foreign homebuyers (them) and not by Canadian residents (us). However, such divisive binaries do not explain all the forces at play.

An analysis of mortgage issuance by the CMHC revealed that the participants in housing markets in Canada involve not just us and them, but also two additional cross-over cohorts. In addition to permanent residents, the CMHC broke out data for non-resident owners (NROs), a broader category than just foreign buyers which also includes Canadian nationals who have settled abroad, and nonpermanent residents (NPRs), which comprises international students and temporary workers who live in Canada and thus contribute to our economy and society. A breakdown of NPRs revealed that in 2015 almost 52 per cent were students and 46 per cent were temporary workers, with the number of the former having doubled to 353,355 between 2006 and 2015.

NPRs are increasingly responsible for population growth in urban Canada. From 2004 to 2015, NPRs accounted for 20 per cent of the population growth in Vancouver and 11 per cent in Edmonton. Their contribution to population growth in Montreal and Toronto was slightly lower at 8.5 per cent.[100]

The NPR contribution to population growth is even more pronounced among younger cohorts. For the period 2004-2015, NPRs accounted for 46 per cent of the growth in the 18-44-yearold demographic in Vancouver. Their share in the growth of younger cohorts stood at 42 per cent in Montreal and 28 per cent in Toronto.

With such a profound influence on the demographic makeup of large cities, NPRs are bound to have an impact on urban housing markets, and were the focus of a CMHC report on the influence of foreign funds in Canadian housing markets. According to the report, the NPR share of mortgages issued in large urban housing markets has been increasing over the past 10 years. Nearly four per cent of the mortgages issued in 2016 in Vancouver were held by NPRs, which was significantly higher than the share of mortgages held by non-resident owners (2.6 per cent). NPRs accounted for approximately three per cent of the mortgages issued in Edmonton in 2016 and 2.7 per cent in Toronto.

[100] Canada Mortgage and Housing Corporation. (2018, February 6). Non-permanent residents: increasing influence on housing. Retrieved from https://www.cmhc-schl.gc.ca/en/housing-observer-online/2018-housing-observer/non-permanent-residents-increasing-influence-housing#:~:text=Because%20of%20the%20way%20their,overall%20population%20numbers%20would%20suggest

NON-PERMANENT RESIDENTS PAYING UP

In 2016, NPRs paid more for housing than permanent residents

AVERAGE SINGLE-DETACHED DWELLING VALUE

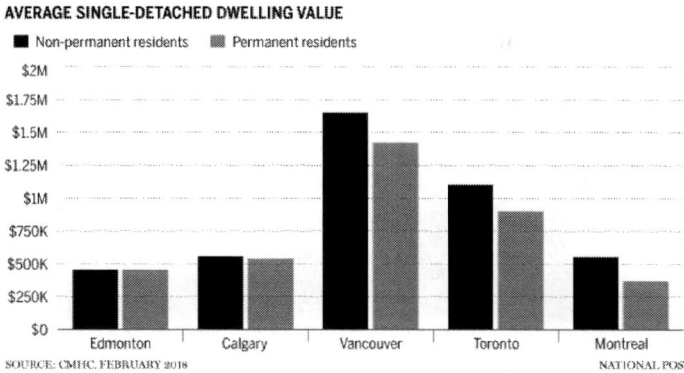

Figure 5.3 – Average Single-Detached Dwelling Value for Permanent and Non-Permanent Residents in Canadian Cities

Compared to permanent residents (PR), NPRs purchased significantly more expensive housing in 2016. For example, on average NPRs paid $1,088,477 for single detached dwellings compared to $901,938 paid by PRs. In Vancouver, NPRs paid $230,000 more for single-family units than did PRs. In Montreal, NPRs paid 50-per-cent more for single-detached dwellings than PRs.

The role of NPR homebuyers is even more pronounced among those under 25 years old, who are more likely to be students in Canada than temporary workers. NPRs accounted for 10 per cent of all mortgages issued in 2016 to those under 25 in Vancouver and Toronto.

2017 witnessed a sudden and significant increase in the number of international students applying to Canadian universities and colleges. The University of Alberta, for instance, has experienced an 82-per-cent increase in applications from international graduate students. Many experts believe this to be a response to the tightening of immigration regulations in the U.S. and a reaction to the rise of ultra right-wing movements in Europe that has made Canada more attractive to international students.

In the late 2010s, provincial governments in British Columbia and Ontario moved to combat rapidly escalating housing prices by targeting punitive taxes at foreign homebuyers. A further tightening of mortgage regulations also occurred at the same time, thus slowing house price escalation and reducing the number of transactions.

While foreign homebuyer taxes target non-residents, NPRs are essentially exempted since they can ask for a rebate later after satisfying residency requirements. And while most NPRs rent, a large number do purchase housing. The mortgage data from the Big Five banks reported by the CMHC suggests that NPRs account for a larger share of mortgages than do NROs.

A knee-jerk response to the CMHC report might be to consider eliminating exemptions for NPRs from taxes on foreign home buyers. That would be a mistake. Anything that dissuades international students from coming to Canada - and staying after they graduate - could have a significant knock-on effect on the economy.

Those students, after all, are helping to staff the science and engineering labs that are driving innovation at Canada's universities and in the technology sector, and are a big part of the appeal of Canada to tech giants such as Google and potentially Amazon. Reducing things to "us and them" could be costly indeed.

We continue our treatment of NROs in the housing market by considering how non-residents are often falsely equated with foreigners in real estate discussions and how breaking down housing sales by citizenship status is urgently needed to evaluate the effectiveness of foreign homebuyer taxes.

NON-RESIDENT DOES NOT EQUAL FOREIGNER

Statistics Canada has answered questions about housing markets that no one asked. In a 2017 release, Canada's national statistics agency revealed that nonresidents owned only a small percentage of homes in Toronto and Vancouver. Also, the data showed, nonresidents were more likely to own condominiums than any other type of housing.

As housing prices escalated rapidly in Toronto and Vancouver, many suspected that foreign homebuyers were responsible for price escalation. However, without robust data, the extent of home buying by foreigners was not known for certain.

A $40-million federal government initiative, Canadian Housing Statistics Program (CHSP), was supposed to fill the information gap in housing markets. The initial release of CHSP data and analysis has done little to fill the information gap on who has been buying residential real estate as of late. Instead, it describes who owns housing in Canada.

In this case, homebuyers and homeowners are not necessarily the same. At any given point in time, only a subset of existing homes is bought and sold. Similarly, only a fraction of the population is busy buying and selling. The information gap in housing markets is about homes being bought (a flow variable) and not the entire housing stock; and about those active in buying and selling and not necessarily about passive owners.

Furthermore, Statistics Canada has concentrated on non-residents instead of foreign buyers. Again, they are not necessarily the same. For instance, a Canadian citizen living abroad is a nonresident. At the same time, a non-Canadian citizen could be a permanent resident.

What markets really wanted to know is the share of the residential real estate being purchased by foreigners with no real connection to Canada, i.e., those who are neither Canadian citizens nor permanent residents. Instead, we got a breakdown of home ownership (not necessarily home buying) by residency status, irrespective of citizenship.

Why we insist on differentiating between buyers and owners matters. In relative terms, non-resident homeowners might constitute a much smaller fraction of all homeowners than foreign homebuyers as a percentage of recent homebuyers. By focusing on home ownership, Statistics Canada's figures did little to clear up our understanding of home buying by foreign individuals.

Even with these caveats, we find interesting differences in home ownership between residents and non-residents. First, nonresidents owned only 3.4 per cent of all residential properties in Toronto Census Metropolitan Area (CMA) and 4.8 per cent of properties in Vancouver CMA. The average assessed value of residential properties owned by non-residents in Vancouver was $80,500 higher than that of residents. The same was not true for Toronto, where the assessed value of properties owned by non-residents was on average $83,200 less than that of residents.

THE MEDIAN
TELLS THE STORY

RESIDENT AND NON-RESIDENT OWNERSHIP OF RESIDENTIAL PROPERTIES, TORONTO VS. VANCOUVER, MEDIAN ASSESSED VALUES, 2017

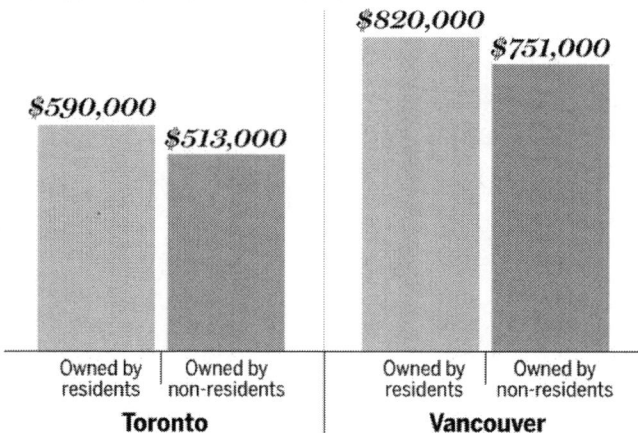

	Owned by residents	Owned by non-residents	Owned by residents	Owned by non-residents
	$590,000	$513,000	$820,000	$751,000
	Toronto		**Vancouver**	

SOURCE: STATISTICS CANADA   NATIONAL POST

Figure 5.4 – Median Assessed Values for Homes Owned by Residents and Non-Residents in Toronto and Vancouver (2017)

StatsCan explained that the assessed value of homes owned by non-residents in Toronto was lower because they owned proportionately more condominiums, which are usually cheaper than low-rise housing.

A smaller number of very expensive housing units owned by non-residents might have skewed the averages in Vancouver. Therefore, instead of comparing averages, we may want to compare the difference in median values, which are less affected by outliers.

This time we get a different picture where the median assessed value of homes owned by non-residents was lower even in Vancouver. The same applied to Toronto.

Non-residents are indeed a distinct cohort from the rest in their housing preferences since they prefer condominiums over other types of housing. In Vancouver, for instance, two-thirds of the properties owned by non-residents were condominiums. Almost half of the properties owned by nonresidents in Toronto were also condominiums. A breakdown of housing sales by citizenship status is urgently needed to evaluate the efficacy of foreign homebuyer taxes imposed in Toronto and Vancouver.

The Ontario government filled in part of that picture in December 2017, when it reported that, in Toronto, the percentage of sales to buyers who were neither citizens nor residents declined from 5.6 per cent in the May-to-July 2017 period to 3.8 per cent in the subsequent three months, suggesting that government efforts were indeed having some effect.

At the same time, it will be helpful to know who resides in properties owned by nonresidents. Are these units being kept empty and therefore contributing to a shortage of available dwellings or are these units being rented out and thus providing a useful service? While we are grateful to Statistics Canada for shining more light on housing markets, we hope that in future releases, the agency will cast further light on segments of the housing market that need illumination.

The following section will discuss why most Canadian homeowners have not opted for fixed-rate long term mortgages of more than five years.

MORTGAGE REFORM MAY HAVE TO WAIT FOR LEGISLATION

If it ain't broke, don't fix it, so the saying goes. It's something to keep in mind when considering suggestions that Bank of Canada Governor Stephen Poloz floated for the Canadian mortgage market in a May 2019 speech.

Among Poloz's suggestions was that lenders and borrowers consider mortgages with durations of more than five years. While long-term mortgage options are currently available, only two per cent of fixed-rate mortgages issued last year were for more than five-year renewal terms. Poloz believes longer-term mortgages would help improve financial stability, allowing borrowers to lock in interest rates and avoid frequent renewals.[101]

But if fixed long-term mortgages are such a good thing for borrowers and the economy, why have homebuyers not opted for them in the past? Most homebuyers, after all, do extensive due diligence on mortgage terms and conditions. Some options are obvious: borrowers would like to qualify for the lowest interest rate possible, and in uncertain times, they would like to lock in those terms for longer periods. When interest rates are expected to decline, borrowers usually prefer adjustable-rate mortgages to negotiate lower interest rates in the future.

There are several other considerations. For fixed-rate mortgages, lenders can impose penalties on borrowers who sell a property before the mortgage term expires. Also, lenders may restrict prepayments that reduce the outstanding principal.

While lenders are usually focused on imposing penalties or restrictions on prepayments, a 2012 paper in the journal *Real Estate Economics* noted that they should also recognize their benefits: namely that attractive prepayment options can attract "more creditworthy borrowers."[102]

By default, fixed-rate mortgages are more expensive. The longer the fixed-rate term, the higher the interest rate. Thus, if borrowers were to ask for longer renewal terms, lenders might charge even higher interest rates to account for the interest rate differential. A borrower's risk appetite matters as well. Risk-averse borrowers tend to prefer the stability and certainty of fixed-rate mortgages while the risk-loving would weigh the risk and reward of adjustable rates that could fall further (or rise) in the future.

The choice of a mortgage has broader impacts on labour market efficiency, as well. A 2018 paper in the *Journal of Money, Credit and Banking* explains that fixed-rate mortgage borrowers impose a negative externality such mortgages may "discourage borrowers from moving to other regions despite better employment opportunities."[103]

In Canada, the amortization period for a mortgage is usually 25 or 30 years, at which point the principal amount owed is reduced to zero. However, the maturity date of fixed-rate mortgages is often not greater than five years

---

[101] Blatchford, A. (2019, May 6). Bank of Canada's Poloz: There are 'good reasons' to encourage mortgage terms longer than 5 years. *The Canadian Press*. Retrieved from https://globalnews.ca/news/5245517/bank-of-canada-poloz-mortgage-backed-securities-longer-terms/

[102] Daglish, T., & Patel, N. (2012). Fixed Come Hell or High Water? Selection and Prepayment of Fixed-Rate Mortgages Outside the United States. In *Real Estate Economics* (Vol. 40, Issue 4, pp. 709–743). https://doi.org/10.1111/j.1540-6229.2012.00334.x

[103] Lee, K. (2018). Fixed-Rate Mortgages, Labor Markets, and Efficiency. *Journal of Money, Credit, and Banking, 50*(5), 1033–1072. https://onlinelibrary.wiley.com/doi/abs/10.1111/jmcb.12516?casa_token=mxBEU7Vzhio AAAAA:EwQyJL2XK7KpbfRU2W1qqeL5Pm6UFKiF4Tv9GmlwPfq34nUxnx1OckuPU7h KAvk_LUbKOs3XRiRbTovJ

and most likely not greater than 10 years. At that point, the mortgage is fully due and payable. Thus, the mortgage must be refinanced for the outstanding balance at each maturity date.

This raises an interesting question. Why does the mismatch between the amortization period and mortgage term exist in the first place? Why aren't lenders offering maturity terms that are the same as the amortization period? For the answer, one must consult Section 10 of the Interest Act, which dates to 1880. The Act imposes certain restrictions on a lender's ability to impose penalties on borrowers should they chose to prepay or redeem a mortgage after the expiration of five years.

In a 2018 paper by the C.D. Howe Institute, Michael K. Feldman explains that Section 10 was enacted to protect farmers from "being locked into long-term mortgages at high interest rates and subjected to large penalties when they sought to pre-pay."[104] Feldman explains that exemptions were introduced to Section 10 later. However, the constraints still impede residential mortgages from having maturity dates that match their amortization periods. For this to happen, Feldman recommends an amendment to the Act that would afford a residential mortgage borrower "the right to redeem the mortgage at least every five years, regardless of the term of the mortgage, with a penalty capped at three months' interest."

Poloz also suggested that there may be an interest in developing a private market for mortgage-backed securities in Canada. However, Feldman says that the mismatch between the amortization period and maturity terms would expose security investors "to the risk that the mortgage might not be refinanced at maturity, leading to the need to liquidate the mortgage." Thus, the mismatch between maturity and amortization acts as a structural constraint.

However, an even bigger constraint is that the returns on prime residential mortgages are not attractive to large investors given other comparable investment opportunities. There is clearly a need to innovate in real estate markets, including in mortgage finance. However, if the constraints highlighted in the C.D. Howe study are valid, innovation might have to wait for legislation.

Our discussion of public policy and housing concludes by considering whether municipal services and revenues would change if property taxes were imposed separately on land and the improvements built upon it.

---

[104] Feldman, M. (2018). *The Case for Longer Mortgages: Addressing the Mismatch between Term and Amortization.* https://doi.org/10.2139/ssrn.3136493

WHY IT'S TIME TO RETHINK OUR PROPERTY TAX REGIMES

Owners of more expensive homes pay higher property taxes. But in return, those paying higher property taxes do not necessarily receive more or better local services than those neighbours who pay less. That is one of several shortcomings in the way property taxes are devised, imposed and collected that contribute to a frequent sense of discontent among taxpayers.

Property taxes are usually levied to support local services and to create a direct link between where tax revenues are raised and spent. Services like public transit, policing, snow or waste removal and education are often paid for, in full or partially, by residents through property taxes and user fees. However, unlike user fees, there is not always a direct link between the amount, frequency, and quality of service received by an individual homeowner and the property taxes they pay.

A comparative analysis of property tax regimes by two leading Canadian urban economists, Enid Slack and Richard Bird at the University of Toronto, reveal a variety of norms around the world, including some regions, such as Ireland, where households self-assess their own property values.[105]

Professors Bird and Slack highlight several general shortcomings in property tax regimes. Property taxes, they argue, are "unrelated" to the ability of the homeowner to pay. They are also "unsuitable," because the revenue raised supports services that have nothing to do with property, per se. Finally, they are "inadequate," as they fail to fully provide the financial means needed to support local services. The huge bureaucracies set up to assess property values also impose large costs on taxpayers, and the debate over who should assess land and property values and set tax rates is far from settled.

Property taxes can be contentious especially when owners disagree with the assessed values. An example of an exponential increase in commercial property taxes was observed in Toronto when some downtown retailers saw their property tax bills skyrocket after the Municipal Property Assessment Corporation (MPAC) assessed the retail properties for the highest possible land use, i.e., condominiums.[106] Only when the retailers appeared set for a tax revolt did the MPAC retreat and reassess the values.

---

[105] Slack, E., & Bird, R. M. (2015). *How to Reform the Property Tax: Lessons from Around the World*. https://play.google.com/store/books/details?id=moCMzQEACAAJ
[106] Yazdani, T. (2019, December 13). 'Don't tax the heart out of Toronto:' Independent businesses struggle to survive as taxes skyrocket. *CityNews*. Retrieved from https://toronto.citynews.ca/2019/12/13/buisness-property-taxes-skyrocket-toronto/

LOWER HOUSING PRICES, HIGHER PROPERTY TAX RATES

RESIDENTIAL PROPERTY TAX BY CITY
IN DOLLARS PER $1,000 OF ASSESSED VALUE

Winnipeg	$12.5
Halifax	$12.1
Ottawa	$10.9
Montreal	$10.4
Regina	$9.8
Saskatoon	$9.1
Edmonton	$7.8
Toronto	$7.1
Calgary	$5.8
Vancouver	$3.5

SOURCE: CSCA, RYERSON UNIVERSITY
SPATIAL IMPLICATIONS OF THE RESIDENTIAL PROPERTY TAX

NATIONAL POST

Figure 5.5 – Residential Property Tax in Canadian Cities

Part of the disconnect over property taxes arises because both land and the structure built on it (so-called "improvements") are taxed together. Since the same tax rate, known as the Millage rate, applies to all residential properties in a municipality, owners of high valued dwellings end up paying more.

Some will argue that the owners of expensive homes are likely to be well off and hence can pay higher property taxes. But wealth and income taxes are separate from taxes on real property. If one insists on levying higher taxes on the well-off, we must then call the property tax what it really is: an indirect wealth or income tax.

At the same time, owners of larger or more expensive homes pay proportionately for their consumption of water, hydro, or gas. The size of the dwelling is not a factor in what a household receives in municipal services, but it impacts the cost of utilities they consume.

How would municipal revenue and services change if "property taxes" were split and levied separately on the land itself and the value of the structure built upon it? In a 2016 paper published by the Centre for the Study of Commercial Activity at Ryerson University, Maurice Yeates, Tony Hernandez, and Matthew Emmons offer a comprehensive review of property tax rates across Canada.[107]

Among their key observations, they describe a potential regime that separates the unimproved capital value (land value) from the improved

---

[107] Yeates, M., Hernandez, T., & Emmons, M. (2016). *Spatial implications of the residential property tax.* Centre for the Study of Commercial Activity.

capital value (structure) and that taxes the unimproved value more aggressively than the improved value. Such a regime would encourage owners to improve the built component when they realize that the bulk of the property tax is based on land value. Separating unimproved land value from the property value and taxing it more aggressively would make urban land more expensive to hold, but cheaper to build upon. That could help address the housing supply challenges exacerbating housing affordability challenges in urban Canada.

SUMMARY

Real estate markets, especially housing, are governed by diverse regulations enacted by the three tiers of government. Essentially, local or municipal governments enact laws that govern the use of land. However, senior tiers of government also enable or restrict land and property use. Chapter 5 built on the dialogue on regulatory issues discussed earlier in Chapter 2 and focused on government regulations that impact home buying and selling. For instance, mortgage stress tests introduced in January 2018 raised the conditions for obtaining a mortgage by requiring borrowers to qualify for a mortgage at a rate approximately 2% higher than the contracted rate with the lender. The chapter reviewed changes in regulations such as the stress test or a land transfer tax imposed on foreign homebuyers and their impact on housing markets.

6 REAL ESTATE INVESTMENTS

Economic theory and empirical analysis suggest that housing affordability improves with the supply of new housing. Yet, the "supply skeptics" believe that not to be the case. What gives? For decades, urban economists and housing advocates have debated the solutions for worsening housing affordability in large cities. Economists mention the age-old axiom of supply and demand. If the price of a good (demand) increases, the supply of the same good must increase to moderate its price.

Not so fast, say the skeptics. "Affordable housing does not come from more supply, if demand grows even faster," wrote Jennifer Keesmaat , Toronto's former chief planner and a mayoral candidate. She believed the demand for housing was "insatiable," requiring a policy response.

Urban economists believe that the required policy response is to increase the supply of new housing to meet the demand, rather than choking the supply with restrictive land-use regulations. Affordable housing has been a major concern for cities that have seen their populations and economies grow rapidly. The abundance of employment opportunities in a city attracts workers from other cities and countries resulting in an increase in the demand for housing. Thus, a common thread that runs through many vibrant cities, such as London, New York, San Francisco, Toronto and Vancouver is a lack of affordable housing. And whereas Canadian cities have encountered housing affordability challenges, other cities have grappled with these challenges for much longer and with limited success.

In a recently published article in the journal *Housing Policy Debate*, Vicki Been and co-authors analyze why supply skepticism exists and how to respond to it. They review a huge amount of existing research to determine whether new housing construction helps address housing affordability. The conclusion drawn from a review of almost 100 research publications was an unequivocal 'yes.' "We ultimately conclude, from both theory and empirical evidence, that adding new homes moderates price increases and therefore makes housing more affordable to low-and moderate income families," wrote the authors.[108] But that's not all.

The authors also observed that the addition of new housing at market prices is a necessary but not a sufficient condition to improve housing affordability for all. Such an approach might miss meeting the shelter needs of those who have been priced out of the market. Thus, the authors advocated for government intervention "to ensure that supply is added at prices affordable to a range of incomes."

Even though their strongly held beliefs are inconsistent with the preponderance of economic evidence, the supply skeptics have often been successful in restricting the supply of new housing using land-use regulations. In the Greater Toronto Area for instance, where housing challenges have become acute, housing supply is constrained because of land-use regulations and Nimbyism. Residents of neighbourhoods that predominantly comprise single-family homes oppose any attempt to densify and hence restrict the supply of new housing.

On the other side are those trying to impose arbitrarily high development densities in the outer suburbs and beyond that are inconsistent with demand and land economics. The result is the same: a lack of sufficient housing supply.

The skeptics fail to recognize that even when housing prices do not moderate with new construction, it is additional evidence for more housing construction. Imagine the increase in housing prices in the absence of any new housing construction.

The challenge in housing affordability is to ensure new housing is built to meet the shelter needs across the income spectrum and not just for high-income earners. It is true that even housing built to draw market prices and rents over time, through market filtering, will improve affordability for low-income earners. However, the filtering process takes time.

Housing challenges prompted Microsoft to commit US$500 million to improve housing affordability in Seattle, where the software giant is headquartered.[109] The participation of the private sector in addressing housing challenges is welcome though not enough. Consider that of the US$500 million pledged by Microsoft , US$475 million is in "market-rate loans" for the construction of new affordable housing. Microsoft is donating

---

[108] Been, V., Ellen, I. G., & O'Regan, K. (2019). Supply Skepticism: Housing Supply and Affordability. In *Housing Policy Debate* (Vol. 29, Issue 1, pp. 25–40). https://doi.org/10.1080/10511482.2018.1476899

[109] Coleman, V., & Rosenberg, M. (2019, January 16). Microsoft pledges $500 million to tackle housing crisis in Seattle, Eastside. *The Seattle Times*. Retrieved from https://www.seattletimes.com/seattle-news/homeless/microsoft-pledges-500-million-to-help-develop-affordable-housing-in-seattle-and-on-eastside/

only US$25 million outright to address homelessness.

The federal government is understandably sensitive to housing challenges. In a 2019 speech, Bill Morneau, Canada's finance minister, announced the government was exploring ways to improve housing affordability for millennials. The 10-year $40-billion national housing strategy announced in fall 2017 to improve social and rental housing apparently has not made a noticeable difference in housing affordability. The government is ready to make yet another housing pledge.

To make a noticeable and meaningful difference, all tiers of government and the private sector must come together to leverage all available resources to improve housing affordability for the working classes which are as vital for sustained economic progress as the high-tech, high-earning workers. Increasing supply needs to be a big part of that solution.

SUPPLY-SIDE CONSTRAINTS NEED A NEW APPROACH

Housing and land prices in urban Ontario experienced a dramatic increase between 2013 and 2018. The Liberal government responded in April 2017 by imposing new transfer taxes on foreign homebuyers and legislating additional restraints on landlords.

The changes arrested the increase in housing prices but caused a huge decline in the number of housing transactions. By June 2017, for instance, housing sales were down by 38 per cent year-over-year.

Housing prices in large urban markets in Ontario, including the Greater Toronto Area (GTA), appear to be rising again. As housing markets recover from the regulatory shocks and uncertainty, as they did in British Columbia, the Ontario electorate is keen to determine whether the political parties competing for their votes have any plans or insights to improve affordability for new homebuyers and renters.

Two competing schools of thought have emerged on what is behind the eroding housing affordability in urban Ontario. One blames the demand-side factors, such as historically low mortgage rates and foreign homebuyers, among others, for housing price escalation. The same group also accuses builders and developers of hoarding land to create an artificial shortage of land that can be developed, though offers no proof in support.

The other group blames excessive regulations that restrict the supply of developable land, which raises land prices leading to even higher housing prices. This group calls for releasing more land for development and advocates less-stringent development regulations.

While housing prices were fluctuating in Ontario, the provincial government in May 2017 released its revised and updated long-term Growth Plan for the Greater Golden Horseshoe that stipulates expected population and employment growth targets for the region, designates developable land, and stipulates minimum density thresholds for future development.

The Growth Plan is explicit about certain provisions. It designates 800,000 hectares of ecologically sensitive land as greenbelt on which any future development is prohibited.[110] It also stipulates that most new development should occur in already-designated, built-up areas with minimum population density threshold of 50 persons plus jobs per hectare that will be raised to 80 in the future.

A contentious debate continues about how much developable greenfield land is in the greater Toronto and Hamilton area (GTHA). Neptis Foundation, a Toronto urban research group, claims that enough gross land - 56,200 hectares - has been earmarked to absorb all types of development targets by 2031.[111] On the other hand, development consultants Malone Given Parsons (MGP) estimates that a mere 17,200 hectares is available for residential development after one excludes non-developable land (marshes, wetlands, cemeteries, etc.), land designated for commercial uses and land already under development.[112] MGP further questions whether the minimum density threshold of 80 persons plus jobs per hectare is even possible in (or feasible for) remote suburban communities.

Whereas consensus evades the land-supply question, all concerned agree that the supply of single-family housing units has not kept pace in the region. Consider the City of Toronto where 83 per cent of the 84,343 residential units completed between 2012 and 2016 were condominium apartments. And while the housing prices rapidly escalated in the GTA, housing starts declined by 8.6 per cent between 2015 and 2016.

Such lopsided housing development patterns worsen affordability because they create a mismatch between what consumers want and what markets are supplying. 2018 surveys revealed that whereas 65 per cent of Canadian homebuyers preferred single-family homes, 82.5 per cent of the homes supplied were multi-family (condominiums).

That excessive land development regulations constrain the supply of new housing is also a consensus argument. Research by leading urban economists demonstrates that excessive development regulations are correlated with lower housing supply and higher prices.

It didn't help the region when a 2016 Fraser Institute report revealed that

---

[110] The Canadian Press. (2016, May 11). Ontario's Greenbelt lands could grow by 9,000 hectares. *CBC News*. Retrieved from https://www.cbc.ca/news/canada/toronto/ontario-greenbelt-plan-1.3576619

[111] Neptis Foundation. (2016). No shortage of land for homes in the Greater Toronto and Hamilton Area. Retrieved from https://www.neptis.org/publications/no-shortage-land-homes-greater-toronto-and-hamilton-area

[112] Malone Given Parsons Ltd. (2017, April 4). Getting the Growth Plan Right. Retrieved from https://www.mgp.ca/news/title-of-article-goes-here-g4ddd-95zg9-aslhr-n4y6n-56kj3

Toronto was the most regulated city in Canada where approval times for land development were two-times higher than in other urban centres.[113]

There is a unique opportunity to rethink the housing puzzle in urban Ontario where the challenges are acute in the Toronto region. The supply-side of the housing equation is not working. This does not imply that one paves over the ecologically sensitive lands. Such a knee-jerk reaction will be highly irresponsible and short-sighted.

A change in direction and thinking is due. It is therefore imperative that political leaders vying for the support must share their visions about land and housing challenges.

A viable strategy for increasing housing supply in Canadian cities is to repurpose underused land. Bombardier's exit from Downsview Airport presents a world-class redevelopment opportunity for Toronto.

375 ACRES IN TORONTO TAKE OFF

The trouble with land is that they're not making it anymore. The time-tested adage seems particularly relevant in Canada's biggest real estate markets, where many an expert believes the scarcity of developable land is the primary contributor to housing affordability challenges.

Even when land is available for development, parcels are not usually large enough to develop a mix of housing. Thus, high-rise condominiums dominate new housing construction in Vancouver and Toronto, and most new developments have been of single land use, i.e., either exclusively residential or commercial. Mixed-use developments have surprisingly been rare.

Toronto, however, may soon get some reprieve for land scarcity: Transportation giant Bombardier Inc. intends to vacate the massive Downsview site in the city's north end, which houses an aircraft assembly facility and a sparingly used airstrip. At 375 acres, the site has the potential to vastly outstrip many other large, well known urban renewal projects.

The Hudson Yards project in Manhattan, for instance, is considered one of the largest private development projects in recent memory. The project was motivated by similar concerns as the Downsview site, i.e., to use newly expanded transit to the fullest and to redevelop underused lands.

At its completion, Hudson Yards redevelopment will boast 18 million square feet of new residential and commercial space including 100 new shops and restaurants and 5,000 residential units. A luxury hotel and a public school

---

[113] Green, K. P., Filipowicz, J., Lafleur, S., & Herzog, I. (2016). *The impact of land-use regulation on housing supply in Canada.* Fraser Institute Vancouver, Canada. https://www.fraserinstitute.org/sites/default/files/impact-of-land-use-regulation-on-housing-supply-in-canada-exec-summary.pdf

will also be constructed at the site. Compared to the potential of the Downsview site, the Hudson Yards development is tiny, covering 24 acres of which 14 have been dedicated as open space.[114]

Canary Wharf in London, England, developed initially by Canadian builders Olympia and York, is another relevant example of redevelopment, though it is primarily commercial. The 97-acre site has a working population of 120,000 individuals housed in 37 office buildings.[115] The site also supports over 300 restaurants. With 16 million square feet of office, retail, and leisure space, Canary Wharf is one of the most sought-after business locations in Europe. The intense development is supported by a London Underground station that happens to be one of the busiest stations that serves only a single (Jubilee) line.

Both offer lessons and hope for the Toronto site, which is a good candidate for mixed-use redevelopment. The proximity to three subway and one GO stations will facilitate transit-oriented development with a significant potential for intensification near the existing and newly built transit stations. Furthermore, relocation of nonconforming land use, e.g., an airport, is likely to improve the value of existing properties that are often depressed because of noise pollution and visual encumbrance.

The adverse impact of proximity to an airport extends even further because height restrictions near airports limit the floor area ratio for land in the vicinity. Once the airport is relocated, the neighbouring land can also be redeveloped at a higher intensity.

The stated planning objectives of the City of Toronto and the province, such as the updated growth plan for the Greater Golden Horseshoe, recommends new mixed-use developments at higher density. The specified minimum density target for urban growth centres in the City of Toronto is 400 residents and jobs combined per hectare (2.5 acres).[116]

The Downsview site is not among the designated urban growth centres. The site is currently zoned for commercial uses. If the site is rezoned for mixed-use development resulting in a mix of diverse housing types, office, hotels, and other conforming land use, the planning objectives of high-density development at or above the density thresholds can easily be realized. At the same time, redevelopment of Downsview site can help rejuvenate surrounding neighbourhoods some of which have long battled blight and

---

[114] Hudson Yards New York. (n.d.). About Hudson Yards. Retrieved from https://www.hudsonyardsnewyork.com/sites/default/files/2019-03/HY_PressKit_NEW_031219_web_final.pdf

[115] Canary Wharf Group PLC. (n.d.). The Height of Success – Canary Wharf. Retrieved from https://group.canarywharf.com/portfolio/canary-wharf/

[116] City of Toronto. (2019, September 30). Growth Plan (2019) and Municipal Comprehensive Review/Conformity Exercise Requirements Report. Retrieved from https://www.toronto.ca/legdocs/mmis/2019/ph/bgrd/backgroundfile-138428.pdf

crime.

The redevelopment of the Downsview site will also improve the intensity of transit use at Sheppard West (formerly Downsview) and the newly launched Downsview Park subway stations. If the status quo maintains and the site remains underutilized, these stations are likely to starve for ridership because of the launch of a subway station at York University that has, in the past, generated most of the transit demand at the former Downsview station.

The mixed-use development has the potential to increase transit ridership by new residents in peak direction and by new workers heading to work at offices or similar establishments in the reverse commute direction. The Downsview site offers the opportunity to build a city within a city.

They are not making land anymore. But with a little imagination and initiative - and collaboration between governments and communities - we can make the most of what is already there.

While redeveloping underutilized sites is one strategy that can help increase housing supply, investing in infrastructure can also unlock housing supply and moderate housing prices. However, infrastructure spending by the federal and provincial governments has not kept pace with promised amounts.

INFRASTRUCTURE GRIDLOCK CRIMPS HOUSING SUPPLY

Investing in infrastructure is a requirement for sustained economic growth. Housing affordability also depends on infrastructure development because extending the spatial reach of infrastructure makes more land developable, which facilitates new housing construction.

Despite its critical role in economic development, Canada continues to face an underfunding of infrastructure. In Ontario alone, investment in infrastructure relative to GDP declined in 2018-19.

The estimate for the size of the urban (municipal) infrastructure deficit in Canada reaches well into the billions of dollars. Despite the willingness of the federal and provincial governments to make infrastructure investments a budgetary priority, actual spending has not kept pace with the promised amounts.

A report by the Parliamentary Budget Office (PBO) in March 2019 exposed the gap between the promised and invested funds in infrastructure. The report highlighted that the Investing in Canada Plan (IICP) earmarked $187.8 billion for infrastructure investments for the 2016-17 to 2027-28 period.[117]

---

[117] The Parliamentary Budget Officer. (2020, June 17). Update on the Investing in Canada

Federal government spending on infrastructure is based on cost-sharing with provincial and municipal governments. The PBO report found that IICP helped "increase municipal capital spending, but not provincial capital spending." The provinces spent $3.8-billion to $5.4-billion less than what they would have in the absence of federal investments. By contrast, municipal governments spent a billion dollars more on infrastructure in 2017-18 than they would have in the absence of the federally matched funds.

The displaced funds have an adverse economic impact on the economy. Had the provincial spending matched the PBO's projected spending, real GDP in 2016-17 would have increased by 0.15 per cent, thus growing jobs in the "range of 7,550 to 8,100."

The point being made is not that the provinces reduced spending on infrastructure in absolute terms. They in fact increased infrastructure spending. The fine point is that the federal funds ended up displacing some of the planned provincial expenditures on infrastructure.

Whereas the PBO report does not highlight any deficiencies in federal spending on infrastructure, the stats reported suggest that of the $188 billion in planned spending between 2016 and 2028, the feds were only able to transfer less than $6 billion to the provinces for the 2016-17 and 2017-18 periods.

Another way of looking at the underspending by the provinces is to realize that of the planned $100 billion in infrastructure spending in 2016-17 and 2017-18, the provinces spent approximately $85 billion. The resulting gap is a considerable sum of $15 billion in forgone provincial infrastructure investments.

The Canadian Centre for Economic Analysis has produced several reports to analyze the underinvestment in infrastructure in Ontario. The Centre noted that "while the dollar value of infrastructure investment grew by 11 per cent between 2011 and 2018, investments as a percentage of Ontario's GDP decreased from 3.25 per cent to 2.79 per cent - a 14.2-per-cent drop in this key measure."[118]

What these numbers imply is that the spending in infrastructure is "not keeping pace with economic growth." The Centre estimated that Ontario must increase investments in infrastructure to at least 5.4 per cent of GDP to maximize the real GDP growth.

Inadequate infrastructure spending is not necessarily a result of missing political will. Michael Fenn and co-authors of a 2019 discussion paper

---

Plan. Retrieved from https://www.pbo-dpb.gc.ca/en/blog/news/RP-2021-008-S--update-investing-in-canada-plan--point-plan-investir-dans-canada

[118] Gismondi, A. (2019, June 6). Budgets still under investing in infrastructure: CANCEA. Retrieved from https://canada.constructconnect.com/dcn/news/economic/2019/06/budgets-still-investing-infrastructure-cancea

published by the Lawrence National Centre for Policy and Management at Western University identified six categories of risk that concern infrastructure development.[119] Among the identified risks is the industry capacity risk that arises when sufficient engineering and construction expertise, machinery, and trades are not available to meet the growing demand for infrastructure construction. Also, regulatory and governance risks could contribute to delays in project identification and approval; and failure in consensus-building between public and private sector entities.

A lack of adequate spending on infrastructure affects the livability of large and small towns. It also exposes existing communities to increasing risks. The flooding in Eastern Canada in 2019 and the 2013 floods in Calgary are examples of how vulnerable cities are to extreme weather events.

Inadequate spending on infrastructure limits future growth. A lack of adequate storm sewer capacity in central Toronto acts as a constraint to further densify the urban core. At the same time, greenfield developments in the outer suburbs could also be constrained by the limited capacity of sewers, water mains, roads, and public transit.

Municipalities are required to maintain an inventory of developable land to meet short-term development needs. Investing in infrastructure will result in a larger supply of developable land in desirable locations, which is likely to reduce land prices and increase the pace of construction.

Research has shown that housing affordability challenges are best met by an increase in the supply of housing, which depends upon developable land. That investing in infrastructure can help moderate housing prices is yet another reason to focus on strategic investments in infrastructure.

Increasing the supply of rental housing is another key to the housing affordability challenge. Rental condominium units, though much maligned in real estate discussions, provide tens of thousands of rental units in large Canadian cities. Without these rental condominium units, rents would increase significantly.

REAL ESTATE MARKET NEEDS CONDO INVESTORS

Many real estate market commentaries have been critical of privately owned housing, especially condominiums, being a major source of new rental supply. Implicit in this criticism is the call for more purpose-built rentals.

---

[119] Fenn, M., Nanji, M., Rolfe, J., & Sussman, A. (2019). Moving Canada's Economic Infrastructure Forward: Addressing Six Risks to Timely, Economical and Prudent Project Selection and Delivery. Retrieved from https://publicsectornetwork.co/insight/moving-canadas-economic-infrastructure-forward-addressing-six-risks-to-timely-economical-and-prudent-project-selection-and-delivery/

A whole host of factors determine the channels through which new rental housing is supplied. Some of the reasons why the supply is likely to come in the form of small-sized condominiums, instead of purpose-built, multi-family rental buildings, include lenders requiring developers to presell a significant portion of the planned dwellings, the youthification of urban demographics, capital gains taxes, rent control regulations and high land prices.

The growing housing affordability challenges in urban Canada have led many to search for the causes behind rapidly escalating house prices. Some said foreign homebuyers were primarily responsible for the sudden spike.

Provincial governments, starting with British Columbia in 2016 and Ontario in 2017, responded with a series of interventions, including targeted transfer taxes on foreign homebuyers. The tightening of mortgage regulations, especially the stress test, by federal regulators was another moderating factor.

These interventions were followed by an immediate slowdown in rising housing prices. In some jurisdictions, prices even started to decline. A concomitant decline in the number of housing transactions (that is, sales) meant that some potential buyers ended up renting longer than expected. The outcome was higher-than-usual demand for rental units, characterized by a steady increase in rents, despite tightening rent control regulations, and record low rental vacancy rates in populous urban housing markets.

In the absence of a sizable resurgence in purpose-built rentals, most new rental housing supply has been in the form of condominiums owned by private households whose investments in real estate expanded the available rental stock.

Surprisingly, real estate investors have been blamed for an increase in rents. Some believe that an increase in condominium prices contributed to an increase in rents in places such as Toronto. A 2019 report by the Canadian Centre for Economic Analysis - commissioned by the City of Toronto - revealed that condominium rents from 2006 to 2018 increased by 30 per cent in the city.[120]

The June 2019 release of Statistics Canada's Canadian Housing Statistics Program (CHSP) revealed that 45.7 per cent of the condominiums in the City of Vancouver and 37.9 per cent in Toronto were not occupied by owners, which suggests that these units were either vacant, rented or maintained as a second residence.[121]

---

[120] Canadian Centre of Economic Analysis & Canadian Urban Institute for the Affordable Housing Office of the City of Toronto. (2019). Toronto Housing Market Analysis – From Insight to Action. Retrieved from
https://www.toronto.ca/legdocs/mmis/2019/ph/bgrd/backgroundfile-124480.pdf
[121] Government of Canada, Statistics Canada. (2019, June 11). Canadian Housing Statistics Program, 2018. Retrieved from https://www150.statcan.gc.ca/n1/daily-quotidien/190611/dq190611a-eng.htm

OWNER-OCCUPIED RESIDENTIAL PROPERTIES

■ Ontario ■ British Columbia ■ Nova Scotia

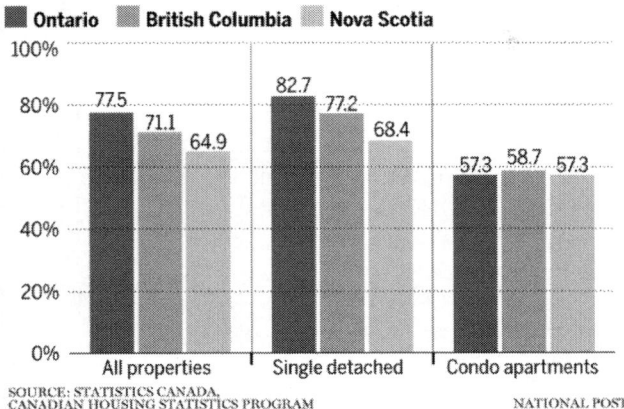

SOURCE: STATISTICS CANADA,
CANADIAN HOUSING STATISTICS PROGRAM   NATIONAL POST

Figure 6.1 – Percentage of Owner-Occupied Residential Properties in Ontario, British Columbia and Nova Scotia

Unlike the condo critics, Canada Mortgage and Housing Corp. views condominium rentals as a positive, with a recent housing market analysis noting that "rental condominiums continue to provide relief to a supply-strapped primary rental market."[122]

The critics of investor-driven supplies of rental housing seldom entertain the obvious counterfactual: what would be the average rent if condominium rentals disappeared from the market? In the absence of tens of thousands of rental condominium units, rents would be much higher than current levels.

The investor-driven supply of condominium rentals serves two important purposes: they provide an alternative channel for the supply of rental housing in the absence of needed new purpose-built rentals to keep pace with the growing population; and, secondly, they deliver a high-quality living space with amenities that are often missing in aging and fatigued purpose-built rentals buildings. Those critical of investors who buy condominiums and subsequently rent them also ignore one obvious fact: private investors finance the rental supply, even purpose-built rentals.

Multi-family purpose-built rental dwellings are needed. For one thing, they offer the security of tenure, unlike condominiums, which can be withdrawn from the market at short notice. Also, such units usually offer no-frills housing, which is often less expensive to rent than condominiums.

---

[122] Canada Mortgage and Housing Corporation. (2018). Rental Market Report – Greater Toronto Area. Retrieved from
https://www.realestateforums.com/content/dam/Informa/realestateforums/2019/portal/Reports/rental-market-reports-toronto.pdf

The revival of purpose-built rentals in Canada in the late 2010s, though small in magnitude, broke new ground in providing high-quality accommodation. These units increase the rental stock, but will unlikely be deemed affordable by the marketplace.

The supply of new affordable rental units will require incentives by government and changes to existing regulations that hinder the supply of purpose-built rentals. Governments could help expand the rental supply by reviewing the provisions for capital gains and rent control that the housing industry has identified as impediments to rental construction.

While real estate investors play an important role in increasing rental supply, they are often portrayed simply as speculators. As the following section will discuss, distinguishing between investment and speculation in real estate is not a straightforward exercise.

THE LINE BETWEEN SPECULATION & INVESTMENT

The escalation in urban housing prices has raised concerns about "speculation," with some regulators and market watchers pointing the finger of blame specifically at foreign buyers.

The Ontario government, for example, bought the speculation narrative and introduced a new 15 per cent tax that is called the "Non-Resident Speculation Tax" in April 2017. Other regulators, including the Bank of Canada, also observed in May 2017 that rising housing prices in Toronto were being driven by "speculation."

When it comes to real estate, however, drawing the line between investment and speculation is not as clear cut as it may sound. If you argue that expecting capital gains in return for an investment in an asset does not necessarily make it speculation, then the distinction becomes even more difficult.

Benjamin Graham, the author of famed investing books including *Security Analysis* (first published in the 1930s), made one of the most frequently referenced distinctions between investment and speculation. Graham and his co-author observed that an "investment operation is one which, upon thorough analysis, promises safety of principal and an adequate return. Operations not meeting these requirements are speculative."

Unlike investing in stocks, however, in most cases investing in real assets does not carry the risk of losing the principal in its entirety, especially in the long-run. And even if property values plunge, the rental income stream generated by investment properties largely holds steady.

Another feature usually attributed to speculation is the shorter investment time horizon. Those active in flipping condos, i.e., investing in pre-or under-construction condominiums and later assigning the rights to another investor in a short-period at a higher price could be labelled as speculators, by this measure. But flippers do serve a productive purpose as they are inherently different from households that acquire housing with the intent to occupy it. Condo flippers are often the ones who offer the much-needed risk capital in the approval (pre-construction) phase of a project to builders and developers, thus helping them satisfy the pre-requisites set by the banks for larger construction loans.

If the risk investors (condo flippers) leave the market, where will the risk capital come from? When one acquires the rights to an unbuilt or a recently built unit from a flipper, one is expected to pay more for acquiring a less risky asset. The initial investors (call them speculators if you must) invested earlier not in a house but in an idea or a plan that would take years to complete with uncertainties (risk) abound for the completion date. The risk in investing in a yet-to-be-built condo is much higher than walking into an open house and making an offer. While there are, no doubt, some people buying existing condominiums who are out to make a quick buck, a large percentage of short-term holders are buying at this pre-construction phase.

The term "speculator" has also been used loosely to refer to private investors who acquire housing and rent it out, but this, we feel, is yet another misappropriation of the term. Those who invest in housing and then make it available to renters, though being driven by expectations of capital gains in future, are serving an important economic purpose. They are the primary suppliers of new rental housing in large urban centres.

And since the current rents are not sufficient to cover the mortgage, taxes, and other costs associated with owning an investment property, private investors are essentially subsidizing renters, in the hopes that future capital gains will offset the lack of adequate cash flow now.

Professors J. R. Markusen and D. T. Scheffman analyzed the sudden escalation in housing prices in the early seventies in Canada and the impact of a similar "land speculation tax" in Ontario.[123] They noted that then, too, speculators were being blamed for price escalation without anyone first defining the difference between investors and speculators. Their solution was to define a speculator as one who buys and sells land (or housing) "without the intention of affecting improvements, or using the land as an input in a production process."

By that definition, neither condo flipping nor investor owned rental housing qualifies as speculation: Investors provide housing that generates a stream of rental services, and flippers provide risk capital for new housing development when no one else steps up. Invoking the "speculator" bogeyman may be good politics, but economically speaking it doesn't tell the

---

[123] Scheffman, D. T., & Markusen, J. R. (1977). *Speculation and Monopoly in Urban Development.* University of Toronto Press, Scholarly Publishing Division.

whole story. In fact, there are historical examples of speculation improving declining housing markets. One such case occurred in Paris in the late 19th century where speculators played a critical role in erecting thousands of residential buildings.

IN ASSESSING THE VALUE OF SPECULATION, REMEMBER PARIS

Canadians often hold a pejorative view of speculation in property markets. Foreign and local investors are dubbed as speculators and are held partially or wholly responsible for the worsening of affordability, especially in and around Vancouver and Toronto. Even governments are convinced of speculation is bad. Ontario, for instance, introduced a tax in 2017 and branded it as the Non-Resident Speculation Tax.

At the same time, Canadian urbanists never tire of singing the praises of all things Paris. They are not alone. We are all in awe of the boulevards, the courtyards, the facades, the monuments and the parks. Nous sommes tous amoureux de Paris - and that's an understatement.

But while Paris' built form is there for all to admire, what is not at all apparent is the critical role played by investors and speculators in erecting thousands of residential buildings a little over a century ago, when Paris grew by a million residents in a matter of decades. If it were not for the ingenuity of architects turned financiers, Paris would have been much smaller in size and possibly grandeur.

The city builders in late nineteenth century Paris realized that the demand for urban housing far exceeded the supply and the only way to catch up was to create new financial channels to funnel money into the new housing projects.

In a meticulous study of the city builders of the late 19th-century Paris, Alexia Yates, a professor of economic history at the University of Manchester and a native of Pouch Cove, Newfoundland and Labrador, reveals the financial underpinnings of a building boom that was unprecedented at the time and has few parallels in modern day Europe. Her book, *Selling Paris: Property and Commercial Culture in the Fin-de-siècle Capital*, broadens the conversation from the city's urban design to the financing tools and institutions that helped make Paris what it is today.[124]

While Haussmann dominates the usual discourse about the City of Light, Professor Yates introduces us to others whose buildings are scattered across the city, but whose names have "not come down to posterity." In 1875, just

---

[124] Yates, A. M. (2015). *Selling Paris*. Harvard University Press. https://play.google.com/store/books/details?id=tCqoCgAAQBAJ

past the site of the under-construction Sacré-Coeur Basilica, the Montmartre Real Estate Company had established the largest work site in Paris where hundreds of workers were busy erecting new roads and 88 apartment buildings on a 32,000 square meter site. Between 1879 and 1885, no fewer than 13,500 buildings were erected across Paris, which increased the rental value of the housing stock by at least a quarter.

Most new housing in late 19th-century Paris was built for renters. Hence most of those who invested in construction had no plans to live in the buildings they helped finance. The new rental stock had become part of investment portfolios. Between 1870 and 1900, 253 real estate companies were established in Paris to fund real estate development.

As is the case today in Canada, there were detractors who found everything wrong with the credit-financed construction on the industrial footing. What they couldn't foresee was the adverse impact of not being able to house the ever-increasing number of new urban residents who were moving to Paris from all over.

Parisian architects and engineers embraced not just finance, but also "big data," analytics, marketing and media to prepare the ground for a boom in housing construction. The architects became newspaper columnists in Le Figaro with weekly columns on marché immobilier starting as early as in 1881. The engineers published comprehensive stats on property transactions and generated choropleth maps to demonstrate trends in property markets and demographics.

In Canada, city building remains a conflicted affair. Construction depends upon risk capital that investors bring at the early planning stages when buildings and neighbourhoods are nothing more than sketches on a piece of paper. They invest - call it speculation - in the idea of future buildings and neighbourhoods. Investors, foreign and local, can end up financing great cities. Just look at Paris if you are not convinced.

We continue our discussion by taking a closer look at Toronto housing data and challenging the notion that real estate investors are to blame for rental market downturns.

DON'T BLAME REAL ESTATE INVESTORS FOR MARKET WOES

Unlike owner-occupied housing, our understanding of rental housing is inadequate at best. Even basic information on the rental market, such as the type and size of housing across neighbourhoods, is not readily available. This leaves landlords, investors, and renters make do with incomplete and, at times, dated information. A straightforward question about what percentage of the dwellings in an urban market are rented out by private households requires a serious exercise in data mining.

For improved rental market outcomes and decision-making, the information gaps must be filled post-haste. The housing stock in a city could be segmented as owner-occupied housing and rental housing. The latter, however, could be further segmented as rental housing in purpose-built rental units, publicly owned subsidized rental units and rental housing held by private households that may include condominiums and other low-rise dwelling types.

Let's take the City of Toronto as an example. The 2016 census reported Toronto was home to 2.7 million people living in 1.1 million dwelling units. One oft-cited statistic suggests that 47 per cent of the dwellings in the city are rental units, with owner-occupied housing at 53 per cent constituting a small majority. While this figure tells us that owners inhabit 53 per cent of the dwellings in the city, it says nothing of how much housing owned by private households is rented out.

RENTAL HOUSING BREAKDOWN

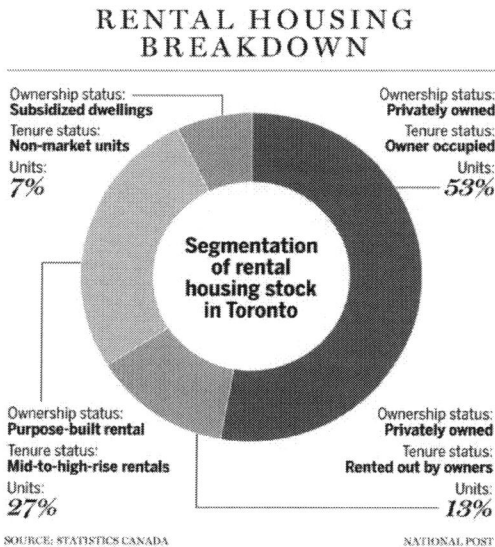

Ownership status:
Subsidized dwellings
Tenure status:
Non-market units
Units:
7%

Ownership status:
Privately owned
Tenure status:
Owner occupied
Units:
53%

Segmentation of rental housing stock in Toronto

Ownership status:
Purpose-built rental
Tenure status:
Mid-to-high-rise rentals
Units:
27%

Ownership status:
Privately owned
Tenure status:
Rented out by owners
Units:
13%

SOURCE: STATISTICS CANADA   NATIONAL POST

Figure 6.2 – Toronto Rental Housing Ownership and Tenure Status

Intrigued by the lack of information, we took a deep dive into the census with the help of Statistics Canada. We continue with the City of Toronto as the test case. The first step involves identifying condominiums in the rental housing stock. Of the 525,835 rental dwellings, condominiums accounted for 96,870 units, representing almost one in five units.

The next few steps involve a series of assumptions. We assume that all non-condominium apartment buildings are purpose-built rental buildings, which accounted for 367,000 dwelling units. We further assumed that private households owned the remaining low-rise rental stock comprising single-detached and other attached dwellings representing another 62,000 dwelling units. Thus, the combined size of privately owned rented stock can be estimated by adding condominiums and low-rise rentals resulting in almost 160,000 units in the City of Toronto.

The previous estimate is somewhat inflated because it also includes the non-market subsidized dwellings, which are more frequently found in mid- to high-rise apartment units. Once we account for the 77,560 subsidized dwelling units, a more realistic picture emerges of housing segmentation in Toronto with the privately owned rented dwellings estimated at 150,000 units (including condominiums) and nearly 300,000 purpose-built mid- to high-rise rental apartments.

We can now see that the oft-cited metric that 53 per cent of the dwellings in Toronto are owner-occupied under-represents the housing stock owned by private households. The privately owned dwellings rented out by households, estimated at 13 per cent of the total housing stock (150,000 units), raise the privately held housing stock estimate to 66 per cent.

The household investors, who are often pejoratively referred to as speculators, account for one in three market rental units (excluding subsidized housing). These numbers should dispel some of the myths that have fuelled disdain for the investors who make renting possible for a large segment of the population, even as a report by CIBC and Urbanation that showed many were experiencing negative cash flow on their rental properties.[125]

They should also serve as a reminder for Ontario's government - and others provincial governments across Canada - to dig deeper into the data when formulating housing policy.

Tighter rental regulations that crack down on investment do not incent the supply of new rental housing. Rather, policies that strive to increase the supply of rental stock while improving housing affordability should be pursued.

We move on from our discussion of rental housing to consider the role that pre-build homes play in housing markets.

PRE-BUILD BUYS ARE NOT FOR THE FAINT OF HEART

For most homebuyers or sellers, real estate transactions are unique in the way they are structured. For many families, buying a home also involves selling one. And the time when a sale is contracted and when it finally closes can

---

[125] Hildebrand, S., & Tal, B. (2018, April 6). A Window Into the World of Condo Investors. *Urbanation*. Retrieved from https://www.urbanation.ca/sites/default/files/Urbanation-CIBC%20Condo%20Investor%20Report.pdf

vary from weeks to months for existing dwellings, to as long as several years for unbuilt dwellings.

A lot may change between registration of a sale and the final transaction. A slowdown in the housing market could have serious implications for those active in the housing market especially when the purchase of a dwelling is contingent upon the sale of an existing one.

Research has highlighted the plight of families that bought pre-build homes at the peak of the market. However, by the time the dwellings were ready to be occupied, housing markets experienced a slowdown in sales accompanied by a decline in values.

This could prove a double-edged sword for many. First, the mortgage loan for the newly built dwelling at the time of occupation ends up much higher relative to the reduced market value of the new dwelling. Second, a decline in the value of the family's existing home, which they must sell to pay for the new dwelling, will result in an unexpectedly large decrease in equity than was originally intended to be ported over to the new dwelling.

Declining home prices imply that buyers are neither able to finalize the purchase of the new dwelling - given the high loan-to-value ratio - or be able to sell the existing dwelling. Also, any change in regulations that makes borrowing more difficult will be an additional constraint.

The obvious motivation for buying pre-construction dwellings is to secure the purchase price today while expecting an increase in its value in the future. Furthermore, the sale is secured by a down payment and not the full purchase price.

Despite the expected benefits, for those interested in buying pre-construction dwellings some caveats are in order. The first consideration is the time it takes for a construction project to move from pre-sale to registration or occupancy. For condominiums, this could take as long as five years, which means that the market fundamentals and mortgage regulations could change drastically by the time one is expected to close on the sale.

A quick recap of the major changes in market regulations between 2013 and 2018 suggests that it was much harder to borrow in 2018 than it was in 2013. For example, the 30-plus-year mortgage was no longer readily available in 2018. Also, the stress test implemented in 2018 required borrowers to qualify at a higher mortgage rate than the actual rate. Depending upon the rate of increase over a five-year period and given one's inability to lock in mortgage terms, one could face much higher payments in the future under higher rates.

Even if the value of the dwelling unit increases over time, it will not help with higher-than-expected mortgage payments. Consider the following. A report by Urbanation in Toronto revealed that the average resale price per square foot (psf) of those condos that turned over in 2017 "was 51 per cent higher than their average pre-sale price" of $541 psf. That is, the average price of presale condos appreciated by 51 per cent in five years.[126]

For an investor, the appreciation in price is welcome news. However, for non-investors who intend to live in the condo, what matters is their ability to secure a mortgage at the time of occupancy at favourable terms. This challenge is illustrated with an example.

The expected payment at a discounted 5-year mortgage rate of 2.9 per cent on a $375,000 loan in 2012 was $1,750. This is what the household would have budgeted for five years before they would have moved in. The new stress test, however, would require the borrower to qualify at 4.9 per cent. At that rate, the same monthly mortgage payment of $1,750 would only support a loan of $305,000, leaving a shortfall of $70,000.

Buying a pre-construction unit is not for the fainthearted or for those who lack an appetite for risk. The known unknowns and the unknown-unknowns compound the inherent risks that may suit investors, but not those who intend to occupy the same units years later.

In the final section of this chapter, we will examine money laundering in the real estate sector in British Columbia and its potential impact on housing affordability.

MONEY LAUNDERING IN REAL ESTATE RIFE WITH UNCERTAINTY

In May 2019, a panel of three academics established by British Columbia's Minister of Finance released a report exploring the role that money laundering played the province's real estate market. The report found that money laundering had likely inflated B.C. housing prices by five per cent.[127]

The 184-page report details the methods and assumptions used to estimate the amount of money laundered in Canada and then further determines the amount laundered through real estate in B.C. In so doing, the report relies heavily on previous research on money laundering from other jurisdictions.

The report does not identify a single laundered dollar or an account with laundered money or even a single purchase of property purchased using ill-gotten wealth. So how did the report come up with $7.4 billion in laundered money in BC of which it estimated $5.3 billion made it into real estate? The report primarily relied on previous international estimates that stated that roughly two to five per cent of global GDP comprised laundered money. It

---

[126] Urbanation. (2019). Condo owners make big gains, but nearly half aren't making enough rent to cover costs. Retrieved from https://www.urbanation.ca/news/217-condo-owners-make-big-gains-nearly-half-arent-making-enough-rent-cover-costs

[127] Government of British Columbia. (n.d.). Combatting Money Laundering in B.C. Real Estate. Retrieved from https://www2.gov.bc.ca/gov/content/housing-tenancy/real-estate-bc/consultations/money-laundering

assumed that the flow of ill-gotten wealth to Canada from other countries depends upon the attractiveness of the host country and the cultural affinity it may have with a source country. Furthermore, the report relies on a global database of crimes per country and estimates of the "amount of money that needs to be laundered per crime" generated by an Australian expert in 1995 to come up with the $7.4 billion figure for laundered money in B.C. in 2018.

The report identified some unusual suspects for inflows of laundered money to Canada. The bulk of the estimated inflows to Canada originated in the U.S. followed by Northern Europe and Western Europe respectively. Estimates of inflows from Eastern Asia, including China, totalled only $0.8 billion in 2015.

Essentially, the amount of laundered money from foreign and domestic sources engaged in criminal activity ends up being roughly two per cent of Canada's or provincial GDP. Hence, estimates of money laundering are larger for more populous provinces with larger GDP. However, the estimate for Alberta was disproportionately higher and that for Ontario was lower as a fraction of their respective GDPs.

The relationship between laundered funds and real estate appears even more tenuous. The report assumes that if each dollar of the $7.4 billion estimated for money laundering is invested, as opposed to consumed for other purposes, and that 72 per cent of the portfolio is invested in real estate, the amount laundered through real estate would be $5.3 billion. Under revised assumptions, estimates for money laundered through real estate were as low as $0.8 billion. Thus, when the panel estimated that housing prices in B.C. were five per cent higher because of money laundering, the panel relied on the upper limit estimate of $5.3 billion. Had it used the lower limit of $0.8 billion, it would have found a much lower impact.

The report is not without caveats about the uncertainties in generating the reported estimates. It warns that "after making a large number of assumptions, the panel's best estimate is that the effect of money laundering is to make house prices in B.C. 3.7 per cent to 7.5 per cent higher than they would be in the absence of all money laundering."

The report carries an informative appendix by Professor Tsur Somerville of the University of British Columbia that offers evidence of suspected activities in the B.C. housing markets. He analyzed categories of suspect real estate transactions including those that involved ownership by "legal persons" (legal firms, businesses) as opposed to "natural persons," properties owned by foreign nationals or those owned without a mortgage or financed by unregulated lenders. Professor Somerville's tabulations revealed that the share of "suspicious" real estate transactions was much higher in Whistler, where a significant fraction of homes (especially condominiums) was owned by foreign nationals and legal persons.

The report also found that over 40 per cent of the residential properties in B.C. were owned without a mortgage. However, this is no different from other jurisdictions in Canada. Furthermore, the report noted that most owners of a principal residence without a mortgage were seniors, "suggesting a large number of downsizers purchasing with wealth" and hence not criminally motivated.

The report highlighted several indicators of suspicious transactions, such as mortgages from unregulated lenders being more common for high-value properties. Similarly, the share of suspicious transactions was higher for properties transacting in 2018 than before. But are these statistics sufficient proof of wrongdoing? The report warns against rushing to a conclusion. "The nature of money laundering is such that simple cross-tabulations cannot determine whether a property was purchased with dirty money or not," the report cautioned.

When it comes to money laundering, the known unknowns are many. "The proportion of funds from local sources and inflows is unknown. The behaviour of criminals in terms of choosing to use these flows for consumption and investment is unknown. To the extent that the funds are invested, the portfolio allocation behaviour of criminals is unknown and whether or not it is the same for two types of flows is unknown."

With such warnings about "considerable margins of errors" "where any effort to predict the volume of money laundering in real estate is compounding uncertainty with uncertainty," it will be prudent not to blame the affordability challenges solely on foreigners or money laundering.

Even if the report's findings that the estimated impact of money laundering "would be to increase housing prices by about five per cent," is taken at face value, it still does not explain the other factors that caused single-family houses in Vancouver to appreciate annually by 30 per cent.

The report's recommendations for greater transparency in property and land ownership and co-ordinated oversight of financial transactions by various governments are necessary to move from estimates to hard evidence of money laundering.

SUMMARY

The mechanics and entities necessary for the development of new real estate or to promote and facilitate transactions in real estate markets was the focus of this chapter. Construction of any real estate requires investments and investors. Investors are also risk-takers whose expectations of the future returns, pejoratively called speculation, is needed for new construction without which the initial mobility capital to advance these construction projects would be missing. At the same time, this book repeatedly makes a case for additional supply to counter the increase in housing prices resulting from an increase in demand for housing. Hence, investments in new housing construction by investors is seen as a pivotal driver to expand the real estate stock in Canada. Other issues, such as a lack of adequate public infrastructures, such as roads, water supply, or drainage, were discussed to illustrate the prerequisites for land development. A brief discussion of the alarm raised about the use of laundered money in real estate was also presented with the caveat that the hue and cry about laundered money being behind the increase in housing prices in British Columbia lacked hard evidence.

7 THE RENTAL MARKET

Housing stock is differentiated by tenure as owner-occupied and rental housing. Housing tenure has been an important consideration for housing policy and housing market strategy. A healthy mix of owner-occupied and rental housing is needed for a balanced housing market in diverse urban settings. Rental housing comprises a large segment of the housing stock in urban Canada. As part of the housing mix, rental housing is essential not just for affordability, but also for ensuring labour force mobility across competitive urban labour markets. With enough supply of rental housing near large urban labour markets, workers can relocate to different cities or part of the same city in pursuit of better employment opportunities. Rental housing therefore allows workers not to be tied down by the transaction costs and taxes involved in home purchasing and ownership.

As same time, rental housing is often less expensive than owner-occupied housing. The difference in shelter costs between rental housing (rents) and owner-occupied housing (ownership costs) is largely because of the differences in quality and location of housing. In housing markets with rapidly rising prices, rental housing provides flexibility to mid- to low-income households and protects them from excessive price shocks.

Rental housing has been the subject of tremendous government intervention over the years. Governments have tried to impose rent controls to protect renters from excessive increases in rents. At the same time, rent controls and other government measures may act as disincentives such that the landlords either fail to maintain the quality of existing rental units or not build new purpose-built rentals. This chapter takes a closer look at the issues related to rental housing. It presents a discussion of housing policies over the past five decades in Canada related to rental housing.

THE TROUBLE WITH RENT CONTROL

Rent controls and stabilization are supposed to improve the lives of renters. They seldom do. Still, from New York to Toronto, such restrictions are politicians' favoured response to housing shortages and affordability concerns.

The Ontario Liberals followed that mantra in April 2017 when they restricted the annual rent increases for existing tenants to a maximum of 2.5 per cent. The then Ontario Premier Kathleen Wynne claimed such measures were needed to cool rents and house prices.

Six months later, the unintended consequences of rent restrictions have started to appear. A report by Urbanation revealed that no fewer than 1,000 planned purpose-built rentals have been converted to condominiums in the GTA.[128] More are likely to follow, thus further restricting the supply of rental housing in Ontario.

Rarely is the chasm between political expedience and economic reality so wide. Writing in *The New York Times*, Nobel laureate Paul Krugman has noted that while economists may often find consensus elusive on matters of policy, rent control is an exception. According to Krugman, the "analysis of rent control is among the best-understood issues in all of economics, and - among economists, anyway - one of the least controversial." Krugman noted that 93 per cent of members of the American Economic Association believed that "a ceiling on rents reduces the quality and quantity of housing."[129]

It is not difficult to understand why and how rent control and rent stabilization measures hurt most renters in the long run. First, stringent rent control regulations discourage developers from building purpose-built rentals because such restrictions act as caps on future cash flows, making investments in rental properties less attractive.

Restrictions on rent increases adversely impact the value of investment properties, which will prompt some owners to sell their units before they lose even more value. In the end, the rental housing stock further shrinks. The scarcity hurts renters because a larger number of renters will compete for a shrinking supply of rental units.

---

[128] https://www.urbanation.ca/
[129] Krugman, P. (2000, June 7). Reckonings; A Rent Affair. *The New York Times*. Retrieved from https://www.nytimes.com/2000/06/07/opinion/reckonings-a-rent-affair.html

LAGGING RENTAL STARTS

In Ontario, rental starts as a percentage
of total housing starts have not kept pace
with the national average

RENTAL HOUSING STARTS

CANADA   ONTARIO   BRITISH COLUMBIA

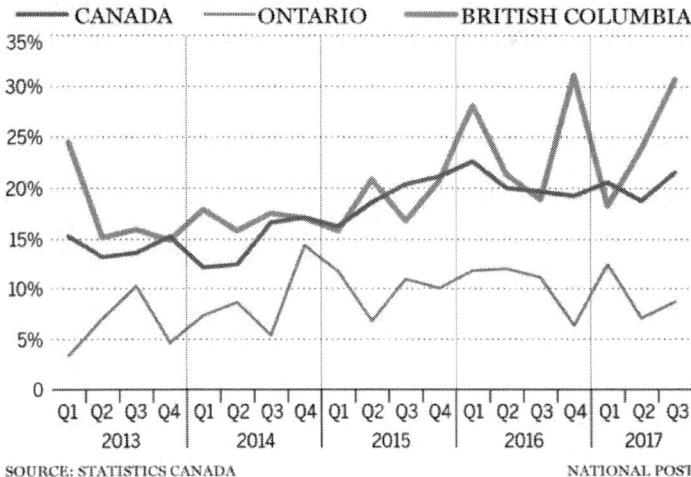

SOURCE: STATISTICS CANADA   NATIONAL POST

Figure 7.1 – Rental Starts as a Percentage of Total Housing Starts

Also note that when rent restrictions limit landlords' profits, they are less likely to keep rental stock in a state of good repair, as the profit margins squeeze periodic maintenance and upgrades become less frequent. This is also true for public landlords. All one needs is to look at the dilapidated housing units owned by municipal housing authorities in many cities.

In cases where landlords cannot recover even the operating costs or evict renters, rental units are left to rot. Once rental units are uninhabitable, landlords demolish them and build non rental residential or other real estate. This further shrinks the rental housing stock.

Supporters of rent control may contend that the above arguments are merely theoretical and lack empirical evidence. Fortunately, empirical evidence supports our contentions.

Consider Massachusetts, where rent controls were eliminated suddenly in 1995. There, the elimination of rent control "released a torrent of condominium conversions" such that the stock of condominiums increased by 32 per cent from 1994 to 2004 in Cambridge.[130] Decontrol even benefited

---

[130] Autor, D.H., Palmer, C.J., & Pathak, P.A. (2012). *Housing Market Spillovers: Evidence from the End of Rent Control in Cambridge Massachusetts* (No. WP12DA1). Retrieved from https://www.lincolninst.edu/sites/default/files/pubfiles/2163_1488_Autor_WP12DA1.pdf

the valuation of housing that had not been subject to controls: It appreciated on average by 12 per cent as a result.

Consider also the case of Nora Ephron, the famed filmmaker and screenwriter, who moved into a rent-controlled apartment in Manhattan in 1980. As she detailed in an article for *The New Yorker*, the rent for her luxuriously spacious five-bedroom unit was merely $1,500, and she lived in the apartment for years "in a state of giddy delirium." Ephron benefited from rent stabilization even when her rising income did not justify her staying in an apartment whose market rent was estimated at $12,000 per month. Ephron reluctantly left her rent controlled abode only after a new law allowed landlords to increase rents for tenants earning over $250,000.

So there you go. Rent control doesn't improve but exacerbates housing affordability. Rental construction rates in urban Ontario are already lagging those in British Columbia and the rest of Canada, and rent controls are likely to make the situation worse. The only solution: encourage the construction of new housing by easing restrictions on developable land and allowing greater flexibility in new housing types.

NO EASY ANSWERS IN RENT-OR-BUY DEBATE

To buy or not to buy, that is the question.

A report by National Bank of Canada suggests that it might be cheaper to rent than to own in some expensive real estate markets in Canada.[131] Many thus wonder whether they might be better off renting if the monthly rental payments are lower than the monthly mortgage payments.

There is no one right or wrong answer to the question of whether to rent or buy. In fact, the answer depends on individual circumstances, taste preferences and housing market conditions.

In the long run, though, homeowners often fare financially better than renters because home ownership enables forced savings that accumulate over the years, growing into a sizable nest egg.

The National Bank report revealed that the monthly mortgage payment on a median-priced condominium was higher than the average monthly rent for a similar unit in Toronto, Montreal, Vancouver, Victoria and Hamilton. At the same time, monthly mortgage payments were lower than rents in Calgary, Edmonton, Quebec City, Winnipeg and Ottawa.

The bank's report compared the total mortgage payment with rent. In so doing, the report unintentionally exaggerated ownership costs and understated rents.

The monthly mortgage payment comprises two parts: the mortgage interest and the principal amount. The principal being repaid each month is

[131] National Bank of Canada (2019). Housing Affordability Monitor. January 24, 2019.

a form of forced saving. A comparison of the net mortgage payment that excludes the principal is likely to change the calculus in ownership's favour.

In fact, a report comparing the ownership and rental costs by veteran housing economist Will Dunning revealed that when the principal repayment is netted out, the cost of ownership is less than renting in most combinations of housing types and locations. The report, published by Mortgage Professionals Canada, "compared the costs of renting five and ten years in the future. It finds that if mortgage rates remain at 3.25%, in 10 years the cost of ownership (on the net basis that takes out principal repayment) will be lower than the cost of renting for almost 98% of cases."[132]

RENT OR OWN?

Average monthly costs by city

■ Mortgage payment ■ Rent

City	Mortgage payment	Rent
Vancouver	$3,127	$1,913
Toronto	$2,624	$2,379
Victoria	$2,624	$1,573
Hamilton	$2,182	$1,521
Montreal	$1,355	$1,190
Calgary	$1,303	$1,524
Ottawa - Gatineau	$1,280	$1,586
Edmonton	$1,131	$1,355
Winnipeg	$1,095	$1,403
Quebec City	$1,037	$1,058

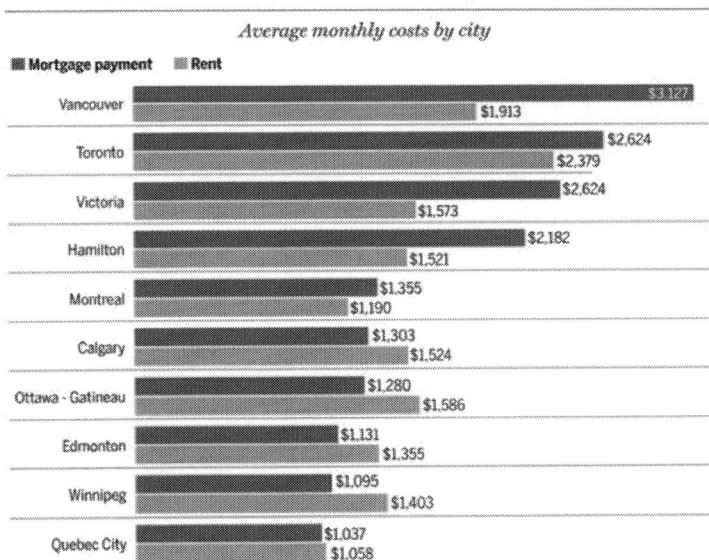

SOURCE: NATIONAL BANK OF CANADA, HOUSING AFFORDABILITY MONITOR, JANUARY 2019

NATIONAL POST

Figure 7.2 – Average Monthly Mortgage and Rent Costs for a two-bedroom *condominium*

Before the principal repayment is subtracted from the monthly mortgage payment, the author found that on average the "cost of owning exceeds the cost of renting an equivalent dwelling by $541 per month." After the principal is subtracted, however, the net ownership cost is $449 less than that of renting.

In markets with growing demographics and economies, housing prices

---

[132] Mortgage Professionals Canada. (2018, September 12). Consumer Report Finds Homeownership is the Affordable Alternative as Rent Costs Continue to Soar. Retrieved from https://www.newswire.ca/news-releases/consumer-report-finds-homeownership-is-the-affordable-alternative-as-rent-costs-continue-to-soar-693035391.html

often rise over time, resulting in even greater capital appreciation. Dunning's calculations though did not include price increases over time because of the uncertainty associated with the magnitude and timing of house price changes.

The long-term financial benefits of ownership are also well established. Dunning used data from Statistics Canada to compare the wealth status of renters and owners. As expected, he found that homeowners were "distinctly better off financially compared to tenants" with similar age and income profiles.

Rental units are often not of the same quality as owned units. The difference in structural quality, especially in purpose-built rentals, is part of the reason why rents on average are lower. A true comparison would require comparing the rents and ownership costs for the same units.

Even when one agrees with the numbers presented in the National Bank report, other challenges with renting remain. For instance, the cities with high housing prices and lower average rents might seem attractive to rent yet renting could prove challenging given the low rental vacancy rates.

In Toronto and Vancouver, the rental vacancy rates are down to around one per cent (RBC Economics, 2019).[133] Finding a rental unit in one's desired neighbourhood has become increasingly difficult because many households who would have changed tenure from renting to owning, couldn't do so anymore because of higher prices and stringent mortgage regulations. The result is an even higher demand for renting that is pushing rents higher and vacancy rates lower.

Statistics Canada's data on income dynamics show that the average household income of owner households is twice that of the renters. Whereas the renter households' incomes have grown faster than owner households from 2006 to 2016, the gulf between their incomes is too large to be narrowed considerably even in the long run.

Table 7-1: Average before-tax household income (owner and renter, 2016 constant dollars)

Year	Renter	Owner	All Households	Owner to renter income ratios
2006	47,800	96,500	81,200	2.02
2007	49,000	99,400	83,600	2.03
2008	50,900	101,600	84,900	2.00
2009	50,400	100,000	84,300	1.98
2010	50,000	100,700	84,500	2.01
2011	49,800	101,500	84,900	2.04

---

[133] RBC Economics. (2019). *Big city rental blues: a look at Canada's rental housing deficit*. Retrieved from http://www.rbc.com/economics/economic-reports/pdf/canadian-housing/housing_rental_sep2019.pdf

2012	50,900	103,600	86,900	2.04
2013	52,300	105,600	88,500	2.02
2014	53,700	106,000	89,400	1.97
2015	53,800	107,000	89,700	1.99
2016	54,700	105,900	89,000	1.94

Source: Statistics Canada

Higher household incomes not only facilitate the transition from renting to owning, they also enable households to select more desirable neighbourhoods, for example superior quality school districts, where rental units may be few or nonexistent.

Renting might still be preferred for younger cohorts, such as the millennials, whose careers might take them to different cities or countries. The fixed costs associated with home purchases in the form of transfer taxes and commissions could prove a deterrent to relocate for exciting opportunities elsewhere.

It makes sense to many in Montreal to rent and in Calgary to own. Thus, a prudent answer to the question of whether one should rent or buy is "it depends."

It is important to note that household income vary significant across cities. The difference in household incomes is also reflected in housing prices. Cities with higher household incomes also have high or higher housing prices.

Table 7-2: Average before-tax household income, all households, selected Metropolitan Areas, 2006 and 2016 (2016 constant dollars)

Year	2006	2016
St. John's	77,000	95,900
Halifax	77,600	85,000
Saint John	72,100	85,000
Saguenay	62,900	69,300
Québec	74,000	78,700
Sherbrooke	68,700	70,300
Trois-Rivières	58,400	66,500
Montréal	75,000	80,500
Ottawa - Gatineau	91,100	102,300
Ottawa - Gatineau (Ontario part)	94,200	108,200
Ottawa - Gatineau (Quebec part)	81,400	85,200
Kingston	77,100	88,900

Oshawa	94,600	101,500
Toronto	94,900	104,100
Hamilton	96,600	94,100
St. Catharines-Niagara	81,200	76,800
Kitchener-Cambridge-Waterloo	82,800	102,400
London	82,900	75,600
Windsor	83,400	90,500
Greater Sudbury/Grand Sudbury	78,500	83,000
Thunder Bay	86,000	86,300
Winnipeg	78,200	87,700
Regina	90,300	102,800
Saskatoon	73,800	96,000
Calgary	106,500	109,500
Edmonton	94,400	113,000
Abbotsford-Mission	79,800	85,500
Vancouver	86,900	92,300
Victoria	79,000	92,700

Source: Statistics Canada

WHAT KILLED RENTAL CONSTRUCTION IN CANADA?

One in three Canadian households lives in a rental unit. In populous municipalities, the fraction increases to one in two. Yet rental housing remains a sidebar in the housing narrative, which focuses overwhelmingly on home prices and mortgage rates. As homeownership continues to slip out of the hands of younger cohorts due to rising prices, renting remains the only viable alternative.

Households facing affordability challenges have consequently lengthened their rental tenures resulting in very low rental vacancy rates and rapidly rising rents. In Vancouver, Canada's third largest residential rental market, vacancy rates in October 2018 averaged around one per cent, whereas the increase in average rents equalled 6.8 per cent year-over-year (YOY). The rental situation was not much different in Toronto. However, in Montreal, Canada's largest residential rental market, vacancy rates in October 2018 declined by 33 per cent accompanied by a four-per-cent increase in average rents (YOY).

Low vacancy rates and rising rents define the rental housing markets in large cities across Canada. The average rent for a two-bedroom unit in

October last year was $1,467 in Toronto and $1,649 in Vancouver. While vacancy rates are higher in Calgary and Edmonton than in Toronto and Vancouver, Alberta is nevertheless seeing a trend toward lower vacancy rates and higher rents.

Insufficient rental housing supply seems to be the culprit. Many industry observers cite a four-decade-long drought in the supply of new purpose-built rental units. The investment in condominiums over the years, of which many units are acquired as an investment and rented out subsequently, to an extent compensated for lack of investment in purpose-built rentals.

However, purpose-built rentals offer tenure security that is missing in rented condominiums where a landlord can, at their discretion, withdraw the unit from the rental market.

Housing experts believe that the supply of rental units dried up in the seventies because of two changes in public policy. First, oft cited rent control (vacancy decontrol) regulations by various provincial governments, introduced initially in the early seventies, is believed to have dissuaded investors from rental markets.

The second public policy change involved the federal government introducing the capital gains tax, which was also applied to purpose-built rental properties. And since the tax is applied to nominal values, a landlord is expected to pay taxes on nominal and not a real increase in property values. In times of high inflation, the tax will have a significant adverse impact on profitability.

The Canadian Federation of Apartment Associations[134], an industry group representing the private residential landlords who own or manage approximately one million rental units, have put these concerns on the agenda for their next annual meeting to be held in May 2019 in Toronto.

John Dickie, the federation's president, believes that all tiers of government must make changes to ensure renting is a healthy and a viable housing alternative for Canadians. He believes that the feds must reform the tax policy for rental buildings so that the capital gains tax does not continue to be a deterrent for investment in rental housing. "The provinces and cities need to look hard at development charges, delays in planning approvals, and rent control restrictions. Those are the most important factors holding back much-needed purpose-built rental supply," Dickie said.

There is some good news on the rental front. The past few years have seen the beginnings of a resurgence in rental housing construction such that rental starts are closing the gap with condominium and owner-occupied starts.

---

[134] https://www.cfaa-fcapi.org/

ANNUAL HOUSING STARTS

Dwelling units by tenure and market type

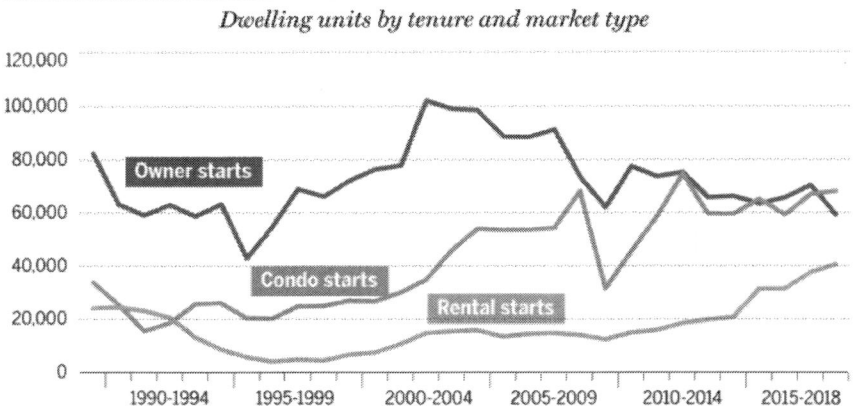

SOURCE: STATISTICS CANADA   GIGI SUHANIC / NATIONAL POST

Figure 7.3 – Canadian Annual Housing Starts

Low rental vacancy rates and rising rents in the recent past have started to attract new investment in rental housing construction. However, waiting for rents to rise to send a signal to investors might not be the best public policy.

Higher rents disproportionately affect housing affordability for those who struggle with securing adequate shelter for their families.

Thus, a preferred public policy response for affordable rental housing should not be a reliance on the market forces that will require the rents to rise before investment pours in.

Instead, public policy interventions, such as reviewing capital gains for rental housing, streamlined municipal approval processes and eliminating rent control regulations that discourage new rental construction can help ensure a steady and sufficient rental supply for a balanced housing market in Canada.

Increasing the rental housing stock in Canadian cities is an important policy objective. To improve housing affordability and an increase the supply of rental construction should Canada be looking at the German example of partnering and incentivizing the private sector for supplying purpose-built rentals.

GERMAN HOUSING MODEL

Is an increase in the number of renter households the answer to Canada's housing affordability challenges? Academic and professional commentaries have suggested that if Canada were to follow the example of certain European countries, where renting is more common than it is here, perhaps

Canada would be able to better cope with its housing affordability challenges.[135]

Implicit in such suggestions are several assumptions, including that housing affordability is a Canada-wide challenge. The RBC Housing Affordability Index in 2019, however, revealed that while home ownership costs relative to income have increased over time, the significant increases are confined to a select few cities in British Columbia and Ontario.[136] At the same time, Canadian cities with worsening housing affordability are also the ones where renting is more pronounced.

If renting were to be the answer to housing affordability, then Montreal should be more affordable for home buying than, let's say, Calgary or Edmonton. Unlike the two most populous cities in Alberta, renters far outnumber owners in Montreal. Yet, the share of median pre-tax household income in 2018/19 needed to cover home ownership costs in Montreal at 44.5 per cent is higher than Calgary at 40.3 per cent and Edmonton at 34.8 per cent (RBC Economics Research, March 2019).

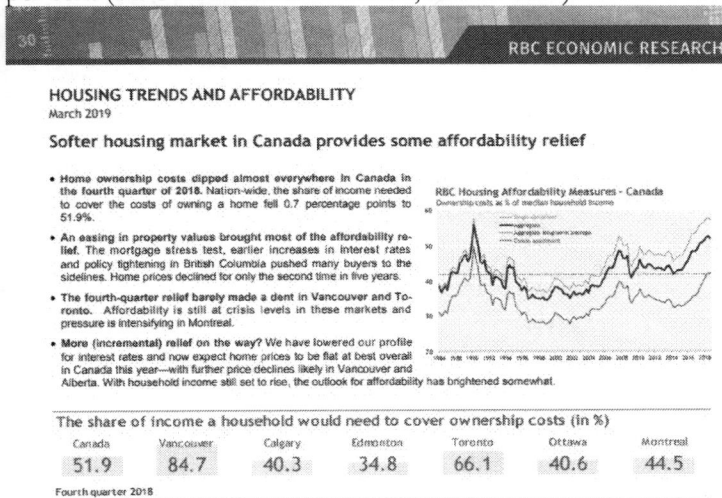

RBC ECONOMIC RESEARCH

HOUSING TRENDS AND AFFORDABILITY
March 2019

Softer housing market in Canada provides some affordability relief

- Home ownership costs dipped almost everywhere in Canada in the fourth quarter of 2018. Nation-wide, the share of income needed to cover the costs of owning a home fell 0.7 percentage points to 51.9%.

- An easing in property values brought most of the affordability relief. The mortgage stress test, earlier increases in interest rates and policy tightening in British Columbia pushed many buyers to the sidelines. Home prices declined for only the second time in five years.

- The fourth-quarter relief barely made a dent in Vancouver and Toronto. Affordability is still at crisis levels in these markets and pressure is intensifying in Montreal.

- More (incremental) relief on the way? We have lowered our profile for interest rates and now expect home prices to be flat at best overall in Canada this year—with further price declines likely in Vancouver and Alberta. With household income still set to rise, the outlook for affordability has brightened somewhat.

RBC Housing Affordability Measures - Canada
Ownership costs as % of median household income

The share of income a household would need to cover ownership costs (in %)

Canada	Vancouver	Calgary	Edmonton	Toronto	Ottawa	Montreal
51.9	84.7	40.3	34.8	66.1	40.6	44.5

Fourth quarter 2018

Figure 7.4 – Share of income needed to cover shelter costs (RBC Economics Research)

If there is an implied correlation between the overall prevalence of renting and affordability, the evidence is missing in Canada.

But what about the European fascination with renting? Is renting that much more pronounced in Europe than in North America? The answer is

---

[135] Keesmaat, J. (2019, July 26). To create affordable housing, let's banish the hoary myths of home ownership. *The Globe and Mail*. Retrieved from https://www.theglobeandmail.com/opinion/article-to-create-affordable-housing-lets-banish-the-hoary-myths-of-home/
[136] RBC Economics. (2019). RBC Housing Affordability Report. Retrieved from http://www.rbc.com/newsroom/reports/rbc-housing-affordability.html

no. Most Europeans own their homes. The highest home ownership rates (more than 70 per cent) are found in Spain, Ireland, Greece and Romania.

Even in Germany, which has one of the lowest home ownership rates in Europe, 51.4 per cent of the population lives in housing they own. Germany sometimes is cited as an example for Canada to follow. What is often missing in such comparisons is a full recognition of the unique historical circumstances that led to the present-day makeup of the German housing market.

RENTING AND AFFORDABILITY

There is no definitive relationship between affordability and the prevalence of renting

■ Share of income to cover ownership costs ■ Renters %

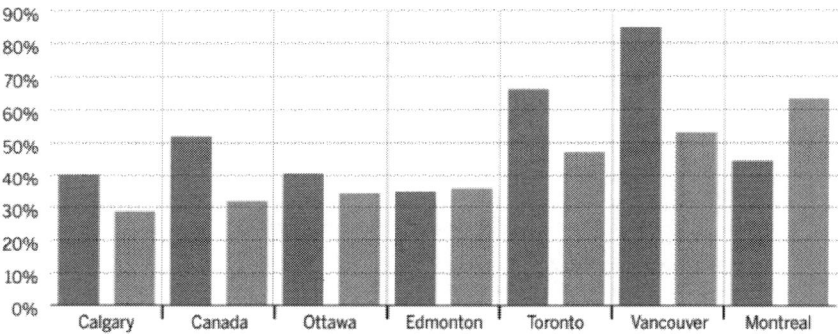

SOURCE: RBC ECONOMICS, STATISTICS CANADA   NATIONAL POST

Figure 7.5 – Relationship Between Housing Affordability and Prevalence of Renting in Canadian Cities

Writing in the journal *Housing Studies*, Professor Michael Voigtländer of the German Economic Institute explained why home ownership has been lower in Germany.[137] The Second World War left the former West Germany with a severe housing crisis. The war destroyed 2.25 million homes (20 per cent of the housing stock) and damaged another 2.5 million. An influx of 12.3 million refugees further exacerbated the housing shortage, which was estimated at 4.5 million dwellings in 1950.

What is worthy of learning from the German experience in housing is not just the outcome of lower home ownership, but the mechanisms introduced by the German government to address housing shortages. Contrary to what the supply skeptics in Canada believe, the German government dealt with the housing crisis by building more housing.

The government encouraged the private sector to partner with the state agencies to supply millions of new homes that "marked the beginning of

---

[137] Voigtländer, M. (2009). Why is the German Homeownership Rate so Low? *Housing Studies, 24*(3), 355–372. https://doi.org/10.1080/02673030902875011

'social' or subsidized assisted housing in Germany." The supply-side solutions worked. By 1962, the housing shortfall was down to 658,000 units.

Also important to note is that unlike the United Kingdom, where the government subsidies for rental housing were targeted only at public sector initiatives, the German government encouraged the private sector to build and maintain social housing by offering extensive tax incentives in return for keeping rents at affordable levels for 15 to 30 years.

The post-war credit crunch left Germany with a struggling financial system. As a result, mortgage markets did not develop as extensively in Germany as they did elsewhere. That homebuyers were expected to put down 30 per cent or more in equity further subdued the demand for owner-occupied housing. On top of that, subsequent German governments chose not to subsidize home ownership, something that was common in other countries, especially the United States.

It is also important to note that Germans have increasingly embraced home ownership in recent years. In 1993, 38.8 per cent of Germans lived in owner-occupied housing. By 2002, the share of owner-occupied households had increased to 42.6 per cent. The latest estimate is more than 51 per cent.

The increase in home ownership happened even though housing prices have remained flat or fallen in Germany. Rising housing prices provide an impetus for households to buy to hedge against future increases in housing costs. Falling prices usually have the opposite effect.

The 1990 reunification is another distinguishing feature of Germany's housing market. Housing in East Germany was dominated by prefabricated apartment blocks, a hallmark of Communist architecture. But the East Germans turned their backs not just on the ideology, but on the housing structures that came with it. In 2000, the former East Germany had almost one million vacant apartments - meaning there was an oversupply in one half of the country and an undersupply in the other.[138]

Another aspect of the German experience was its liberal approach to rent controls. Unlike in the U.K., where stringent rent-control policies caused a gradual deterioration and the subsequent decline of the rental stock, German rental policies were flexible, such that rents in subsidized housing, though lower, were not utterly out-of-step with market rates. Landlords in Germany could also pass on reasonable costs of property improvements to tenants.

In Canada, meanwhile, purpose-built rental construction has declined since the seventies. The Canadian Federation of Apartment Associations, an industry group representing the owners and managers of rental properties, identifies changes in tax regulations (capital gains tax) and rent control (vacancy decontrol) as factors that have adversely affected the profitability of

---

[138] Kim, L. (2000, November 9). Germany struggles to revive shrinking city centers. *The Christian Science Monitor.*

constructing new purpose-built rentals, thereby choking the supply of new rental units.

If the German housing model is to be emulated in Canada, the private sector must be incentivized to produce new purpose-built rentals and reverse the decline in rental construction. Germany was able to build millions of rental units by partnering with, and incentivizing, the private sector - not the other way around.

Another purported solution to the affordable housing problem is rent-to-own housing. However, as detailed in the following section, renting to own is not the housing affordability panacea that many proponents would have you believe it is.

RENTING TO OWN NO SILVER BULLET IN TODAY'S MARKET

When it comes to affordable housing, there are no silver bullets. Still, election campaigns deliver catchy slogans for stubborn housing problems, which at times defy economic fundamentals and common sense. The rent-to-own housing option, which surfaced as an electoral promise in the mayoral race in Toronto in 2018, is one such idea - is likely to limit housing and career choices of struggling households than expanding them.

Many supporters of rent-to-own (RTO) housing naively believe that it offers an affordable and viable alternative to mortgage finance for home ownership. The proponents argue that households who could not save for a down payment or are deemed uncreditworthy by mainstream lenders could rely on RTO for home ownership.

The reality is far more complex, and, in many circumstances, RTO programs can hurt the long-term financial prospects of struggling households. Before one signs off on an RTO housing contract, some basic facts must be understood.

An RTO contract enables a household to rent a dwelling that the household may buy in the future at a predetermined price. The RTO thus enables households to select a neighbourhood and dwelling of their choice. In instances where the household may not have enough for a down payment to secure a mortgage, the RTO might put such households on the path to home ownership.

At a predetermined date in the future, the transfer takes place from the landlord to the renter. The prearranged price offers protection to renters against unexpected housing price inflation.

What could possibly be wrong with such a benevolent arrangement? The answer is a lot. The devil, as always, is in the detail. To begin with, a typical RTO client is one with a down payment that is not adequate to qualify for a mortgage from mainstream lenders, who charge lower interest rates than the lenders who lend to highly leveraged borrowers. As the loan-to-value increases, so does the charged interest rate.

Given the way RTO contracts are structured, they may hurt the financial interest of a struggling household. For starters, a renter household cannot avoid a down payment, which is called the option money and is likely to be less than 20 per cent but is still required. The one-time, often non-refundable, payment at the initiation of an RTO contract buys renters the option to purchase the dwelling in the future.

The predetermined future purchase price serves as a hedge against rapidly increasing housing prices. Yet, if housing prices were to decline in the future, the renter must pay the higher agreed upon price. Equally important is the realization that the rent in RTO contracts is usually higher than the rent for a comparable property because part of the rent is credited towards the purchase price. So, from a cash flow perspective, an RTO contract carries a higher burden than a comparable rental unit.

While an RTO dwelling is not technically owned by the renter, it is still the renter's responsibility to maintain the property. Thus, if the furnace blows out during the renting phase, the renter might be on the hook for it, depending on the terms of the agreement. When the renting period ends, the renter has the option to purchase the dwelling. During the renting period, part of the rent accrues towards the purchase price, which is akin to building equity. However, the renter must borrow the balance from a lender. At this point, depending upon changes to interest rates, a mortgage could be cheaper or more expensive than when the RTO contract was signed.

RTO contracts are predicated on the assumption that the renters' finances in the future will improve in terms of creditworthiness. Should that fail to happen, the renter will have to walk away, leaving the equity built over the years behind. Furthermore, such contracts restrict one to the same location, making it expensive to relocate to more lucrative job markets in other cities.

Sanjiv Jaggia and Pratish Patel in the *Journal of Derivatives* analyzed RTO contracts in the U.S. after the Great Recession when many homes faced foreclosure.[139] Their analysis concluded that RTO contracts were no silver bullet. They found that lenders could benefit from entering into an RTO contract when a borrower was about to default on a mortgage. If the borrower faced severe financial constraints, the option to buy the dwelling in the future was essentially "worthless."

RTO contracts have existed with limited success in certain niche markets. But without subsidies, market-based RTO solutions to promote housing affordability are unlikely to succeed.

---

[139] Jaggia, S., & Patel, P. (2017). Rent-to-Own Housing Contracts under Financial Constraints. *The Journal of Derivatives*, 25(2), 62–78. https://doi.org/10.3905/jod.2017.25.2.062

A preferred option to improve housing affordability is to increase the supply of new housing by aggressively releasing land suitable for development and streamlining the development approval processes.

In addition to RTO housing, another strategy advanced by policymakers to improve housing affordability is purpose-built rentals. As detailed in the next section, purpose-built rentals come with their own set of challenges that limit their ability to provide affordable shelter for many Canadians.

PURPOSE-BUILT RENTALS MAY NOT OFFER RELIEF EITHER

Purpose-built rentals are considered an essential ingredient in the housing mix because they provide affordable shelter for those who are priced out of the ownership market or prefer to rent than own. Such rental stock is also usually cheaper than renting a unit in a condo building, which are often newer and offer better amenities.

But data from Toronto revealed rents in purpose-built rentals (PBR) were climbing at a faster rate and narrowing the gap with rental condominiums, so the assumption that they will remain cheaper than condos might need re-examining.

The rental dynamics in populous cities across Canada are characterized by low vacancy rates and rising rents. Why rental markets are becoming relatively more expensive and what can be done to address it are important considerations for maintaining balanced housing markets.

Analysis of listings on Rentals.ca[140] by Bullpen Consulting revealed that average monthly condominium rents in the central parts of Toronto were stable at approximately $2,600 between October 2018 and June 2019. But average rents for rental apartments increased to more than $2,100 from less than $2,000.

An increase in the demand for rental units is the apparent cause of rising rents. Stricter mortgage regulations along with higher housing prices, among other reasons, have kept a segment of renters, who would have otherwise transitioned to home ownership, in rental units longer than usual. Rental vacancy rates have, therefore, declined to result in a large number of new renters competing for shrinking available rental stock.

---

[140] Myers, B. (2020). Rentals.ca August 2020 Rent Report. Retrieved from https://rentals.ca/national-rent-report

RENTAL GAP

Ontario housing starts in centres of 50,000 and over

──── HOMEOWNER ──── RENTAL ──── CONDOMINIUM

Figure 7.6 – Ontario Housing Starts in Population Centres of 50,000 and over

The logical response to low vacancy rates and escalating rents is to increase the supply of rental units, either as condominiums or PBR. The primary advantage of PBR is the tenure security for long-term renters. Condo renters are always at risk of being forced to move should the landlord require the unit for personal use.

However, PBR construction faces more challenges than other residential types. Market fundamentals and construction finance, among other reasons, do not entice builders to choose PBR over condominiums or homeowner units. Often, lenders feel more comfortable financing condominium construction since they require developers to have pre-sold a sizable chunk of the planned development.

Thus, there is certainty in condominium lending, because the developer leverages the commitment to purchase pre-built units and deposits from prospective buyers. PBR construction, by comparison, carries uncertainty. The developer or the owner must complete the construction before leasing the units. The uncertainty about future rent structures and the ability to fully lease the building makes PBR construction financing more challenging.

Those reasons have helped condominium construction in Ontario dominate the residential construction sector in communities of at least 50,000 inhabitants. From January 2018 to June 2019, Ontario recorded 48,934 condominium starts compared to 42,370 homeowner and 12,412 rental starts, according to Statistics Canada.

Yet rental units dominate residential construction in Quebec. From

January 2018 to June 2019, there were 31,538 rental starts, more than the homeowner and condo starts put together.

The diversity in housing market outcomes, as is evidenced by the difference in tenure of new construction between Ontario and Quebec, requires housing policy and strategy to align with local dynamics.

Better city building paradigms adopted by PBR developers are contributing to the improved lending environment for rental apartment construction. Some developers are constructing mixed-use rental buildings with retail or offices at grade, and residential units above grade to build socially cohesive communities.

Jonathan Gitlin, president and chief operating officer of RioCan Real Estate Investment Trust[141], believes that mixed-use developments make better planning sense because they create balanced communities that are "animated throughout the day" and provide amenities for the community at large.

He also believes that the increase in construction financing support by Canada Mortgage and Housing Corp., the federal housing agency, has also helped PBR development.

The federal Liberals have invested more than $13 billion to support housing in Canada. The 2019 federal budget introduced provisions to support the construction of 42,500 new dwellings in markets with limited rental supply.[142] The government supplemented the Rental Construction Financing Initiative with "an additional $10 billion in financing over nine years."

If left to their own devices, urban land markets will select the highest and best use for development, even if it might not be socially optimal. Hence, governments have a role in promoting stability and diversity in housing markets.

Governments must, therefore, consider additional measures to incentivize the construction of rental apartments in populous cities where market fundamentals might favour the construction of other housing types.

The impact of rent control on rental housing supply in previous decades was discussed earlier in this chapter. The following section takes a closer look at how rent control may influence rental housing supply and affordability in the near future.

---

[141] https://riocan.com/
[142] Department of Finance Canada. (n.d.). An Affordable Place to Call Home. Retrieved from https://www.budget.gc.ca/2019/docs/themes/housing-logement-en.pdf

DOES RENT CONTROL STIFLE NEW BUILDS?

In 2018, Ontario did yet another somersault on rent control regulations. Premier Doug Ford's government reversed the stringent rent control regulations that were enforced earlier by the provincial Liberals. Under the revised regulations, new or previously unoccupied rental units will no longer be subject to rent control.

Existing tenants in purpose-built or private rentals will continue to be protected. The change in regulation applies to newly built or previously unrented units in existing buildings.

Since the Liberal government instituted stringent regulations in April 2017, that included price controls, rental vacancy rates have barely budged from levels of less than 2 per cent and rents have continued to rise. Evidence has mounted that such demand-side measures were ineffective.

Supply-side solutions, i.e., building more purpose-built rental units to ease the pressure, require incentives and rent control does not qualify as one.

The debate about rent control is far from over. Geordie Dent of the Federation of Metro Tenant's Association and Andrea Horwath, leader of the Ontario NDP, say that removing rent control in 1987 did not encourage new purpose-built rental construction in Ontario.

But the data suggest otherwise. Rental starts in Ontario were in free-fall from a high of more than 5,000 units in the third quarter of 1991, to fewer than a hundred units in the first quarter of 1997.

Rental starts in Ontario started to rise in 1999 and grew steadily until 2004, averaging around 1,000 starts each quarter. For the next 10 years, that number was relatively constant, while construction of condominium buildings accelerated in urban Ontario. Many new condominiums were made available to the rental market, thus growing the overall supply of rental units in purpose-built and private buildings.

Purpose-built rental starts in Ontario started to increase again, beginning in 2014, and reaching a high of 1,664 units in the first quarter of 2018. The question to ask is would the rental starts have reached these numbers, modest as they may be, had rent control regulations remained in place since the late eighties.

Voters in California have struggled with similar questions. For decades, housing prices and rents in urban areas have risen at rates that far outpaced the appreciation in average incomes. The desirability of the place for its natural endowments and as the hub of innovation in the United States has meant that the demand for all types of housing outpaced the supply.

In November 2018, California voters defeated Proposition 10, which would have allowed local governments to impose rent controls. In a fiercely contested ballot initiative that attracted more than US$100 million in campaign spending, voters rejected a move to repeal the Costa-Hawkins

Rental Housing Act. Among other provisions, the law allowed landlords to charge market rents when a rent-control unit is vacated.

RENT CONTROL SOMERSAULT

ONTARIO RENTALS STARTS QUARTERLY

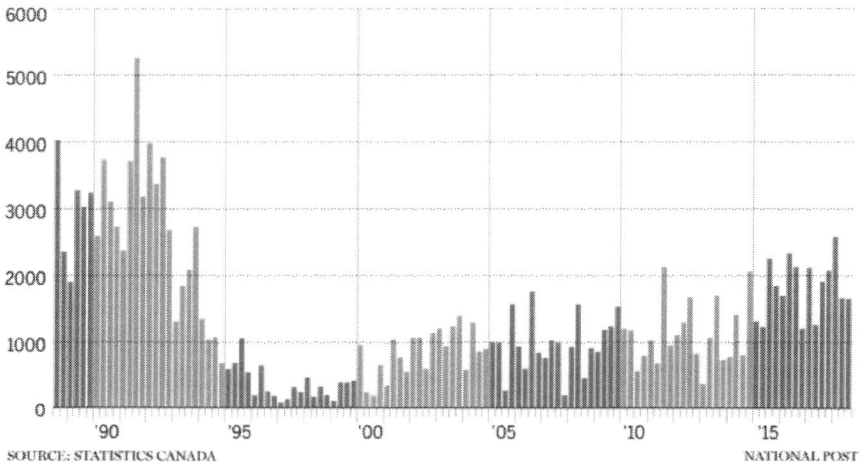

SOURCE: STATISTICS CANADA   NATIONAL POST

Figure 7.7 – Quarterly Ontario Rental Starts

Kenneth Rosen, a renowned urban economics professor with UC Berkeley, argued that rent controls shrink the supply of new rental units, expedite structural deterioration of rent controlled units, and encourage landlords to switch rental buildings to other residential or commercial uses.[143]

An overwhelming majority of economists agree with Rosen, that rental housing affordability will improve with an increase in the supply of rental units and not necessarily because of rent controls.

Whereas Proposition 10 lost at the state level, it did win the majority votes in urban counties where the housing affordability crisis is most acute. This suggests that many, if not the majority, of residents in tight market conditions believe in the efficacy of rent controls.

The debate about rent control efficacy in Canada can certainly use some hard empirical evidence. Some important questions demand answers. Is it indeed true that eliminating rent controls does not increase the supply of rental units? Do rents grow slower in rent-controlled markets in Canada? The available evidence can be stretched to support the arguments for and against rent control. However, a closer look at the research suggests that, in general,

---

[143] Rosen, K. T. (2018). *The Case for Preserving Costa-Hawkins: Three Ways Rent Control Reduces the Supply of Rental Housing.* Retrieved from https://mma.prnewswire.com/media/739365/Case_for_Preserving_Costa_Hawkins__Three_Ways_Rent_Control_Reduces_the_Supply.pdf?p=pdf

rent control decreases housing affordability.

RENT CONTROL HAS NOT BEEN EFFECTIVE

Do stricter rent control laws slow the increase in residential rents? Housing advocates and left-leaning governments believe they do. However, recent data from Ontario appears to offer further proof that this is not the case.

In April 2017, Ontario's then-Liberal government introduced the Rental Fairness Act, which expanded rent control to all private rental units. The Act restricted rent increases to 1.5 per cent in 2017 and introduced additional provisions to protect tenants from being evicted.

The Act was enacted to protect against "dramatic rent increases." Chris Ballard, then the Minister of Housing and Poverty Reduction, claimed that the Act would ensure that Ontarians "have an affordable place to call home."

The Toronto Real Estate Board's (TREB) Rental Market Report for the second quarter of 2018 revealed that the Rental Fairness Act has had no observable impact on market-based rents, which grew at similar rates from 2017 to 2018 as they did from 2016 to 2017. In fact, three-bedroom apartments experienced a significant increase in average rents in 2018.

TORONTO'S RISING RENTS

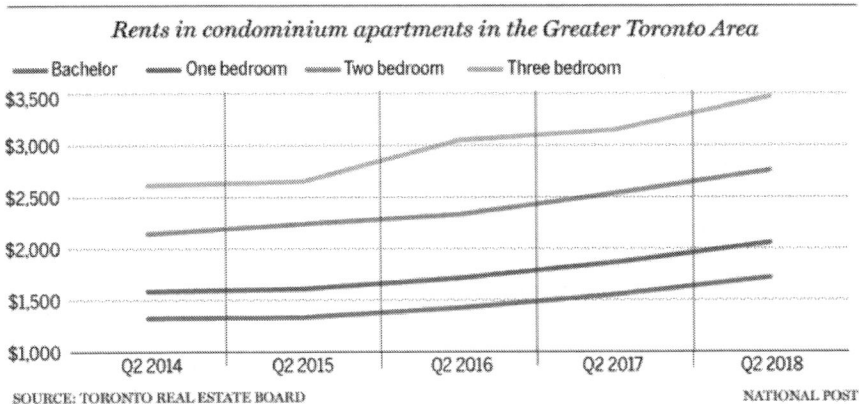

Rents in condominium apartments in the Greater Toronto Area

Figure 7.8 – Condominium Apartment Rents in the Greater Toronto Area

TREB's data is based on its rental listing service for the Greater Toronto and surrounding areas. From April to June 2018, almost 12,000 apartments were listed while 8,497 were leased. One and two-bedroom apartments constituted the largest segments of rental units. Also, almost a thousand townhouses were listed and 665 leased for the same period.

TREB data provides more of a market-based view of the rental market than what has been reported by the CMHC. Unlike TREB, which lists market-based units (condominiums and townhouses) that are primarily owned by private investors, CMHC's reporting of rental markets is largely for, but not restricted to, purpose-built apartment rentals.

Despite the differences in rental stock between CMHC and TREB, even CMHC's data reveals that instead of a break, rental rates accelerated in 2017. For instance, rents for two-bedroom units increased by 3.3 and 3.2 per cent in 2015 and 2016 respectively but jumped 4.2 per cent in 2017. If proponents of stringent rent controls were hoping for a decline in rent acceleration, it didn't happen.

The purpose-built rental universe has remained steady across most of Canada. In the Greater Toronto Area (GTA), the number of purpose-built rentals has remained around 330,000 units for more than a decade. During the same time, the number of rental condominiums in the GTA increased from under 50,000 to more than 100,000 units.

CMHC data for October 2017 reported average rents for two-bedroom units at $1,392 and $2,263 in purpose-built rental buildings and condominium apartments respectively. In comparison, TREB reported the average rent for two-bedroom condominium apartments in the fourth quarter of 2017 to be $2,627. Even for the condominium apartments, TREB reports higher rents attributed most likely to the higher quality of the underlying stock.

CMHC reported rents for purpose-built rental buildings are significantly lower because of their less than ideal location and dilapidated condition, a result of age and deferred maintenance. These buildings have remained under rent control for decades, and their owners are disincentivized to improve the quality of the rental stock. TREB data, by contrast, is based on privately owned rental condominiums whose owners, until recently, were incentivized to maintain their units in a state of good repair.

Since April 2017, condominium rentals and other dwelling types have also come under the rent control regime, thus creating the same disincentives for structural improvements of units as the ones observed for the purpose-built rentals.

The CMHC data reveals that, as expected, average rents in older buildings were lower than rents in newer buildings. Furthermore, rents on average are higher in the high-density urban core than the low-density suburbs, making suburbs significantly more affordable to rent than in or near the downtowns.

With high turnover rates where new tenants are not subjected to rent restrictions, rent controls are ineffective tools for addressing rapid rent increases. The average rent for units in purpose-built rentals and condominium apartments has risen far above the stipulated rate since the Rental Fairness Act was enacted. In the long run, rent controls reduce the growth in available rental stock, which further accelerates the increase in rents.

Rent stability is achievable primarily by increasing the supply of the rental stock. This requires changes in regulations to facilitate, instead of hindering, new residential development.

Another factor influencing the decision to rent or own for many Canadians, often unknowingly, is the lower levels of purpose-built rental construction compared to other residential starts. Innovative approaches from investors, developers and policymakers to encourage increased rental starts will be discussed in the following section.

RENTAL APARTMENTS SECTOR NEEDS INNOVATIVE IDEAS

Rental vacancy rates in Canada's biggest cities may be at record lows, but so far that high demand has yet to trigger an increase in purpose-built rental construction.

In fact, rental units have constituted only a small fraction of new construction since the early seventies, when rent control laws were first introduced in Ontario and British Columbia.

Real estate experts believe that the decades-long slump in rental construction will continue unless investors embrace innovative solutions, such as ones that facilitate joint ventures between entrepreneurial developers, who are looking for short-term returns, and institutional investors, who are in it for the long haul.

An NDP government in B.C. introduced rent control regulations in 1972. A Progressive Conservative government followed suit in Ontario in 1975. Over the next 42 years in Ontario, successive governments have subsequently extended the reach of the rent control regulations.

In 2017, the Ontario Liberals extended regulations to all rental units, including those that have come into use since November 1991 and which had previously been exempted. As it stands today, Ontario landlords can increase rents on existing tenants at a government prescribed rate, which was set at 1.8 per cent for 2018.

FALLING BEHIND

*While condo starts have skyrocketed in the
Toronto CMA, rental starts continue to lag*

RENTAL VS. CONDO STARTS
TORONTO CENSUS METROPOLITAN AREA, 1988 – 2018

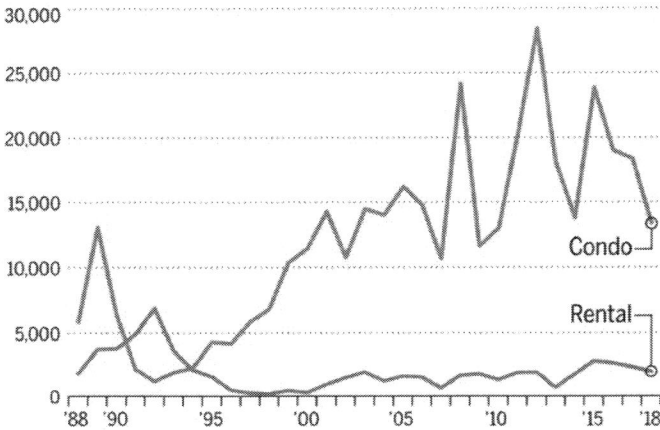

Figure 7.9 – Rental versus Condominium Starts in the Toronto Census Metropolitan Area. 1988-2018

Landlords may apply to the Landlord and Tenant Board for a higher increase in rent to offset necessary capital expenditures or other costs. However, such requests are often met with renters' anger and refusal to oblige.

Whereas renters have successfully lobbied governments to implement and tighten rent control regulations, it has not necessarily worked in their favour. Rent control regulations have turned the investors and builders away from purpose-built rentals to constructing condominiums while the demand for rental units has increased over time.

The Wellesley Institute, for instance, estimated that between 2011 and 2016, the number of renter households increased by 85,000 in the Toronto Census Metropolitan Area.[144] In comparison, Toronto registered only 10,000 rental starts during the same interval. With the shift from rental to condominium construction, renter households are thus being increasingly absorbed in condominiums owned by individual investors.

The fix, though, comes with uncertainty for renters, since the owner could

[144] Suttor, G., & Leon, S. (2017, October 27). 6 Toronto Rental Housing Highlights in the 2016 Census. Retrieved from https://www.wellesleyinstitute.com/housing/6-toronto-rental-housing-highlights-in-the-2016-census/

take the unit out of the rental stock, requiring the tenant to relocate. And with record low vacancy rates in purpose-built rental buildings, the odds of finding a long-term rental unit remain equally low. Furthermore, starting a new lease is likely to be more expensive since vacant rentals are not subject to rent controls.

That regulations hurt renters has been known for decades. Still, governments enforce such regulations to appease the renters, even though they are the ones who end up being worse off. Walter Block, writing in the *Mid-Atlantic Journal of Business* in 1989, noted that rental vacancy rates in Vancouver increased after B.C. abolished rent control in 1984, thus giving renters some breathing space.[145]

In comparison, the vacancy rate remained stubbornly low in Toronto where rent control regulations were even further tightened. If the status quo prevails, vacancy rates will remain low offering renters few long-term rental opportunities in well-maintained buildings. This could change if new purpose-built rental construction were to resume.

Derek Lobo, a real estate expert and the CEO of SVN Canada Inc., has structured innovative joint ventures between merchant apartment builders and institutional investors.[146] He insists that rental construction is profitable because of the sustained demand from millennials, who are mostly priced out of the ownership market, and seniors who would like to maintain a quality of life without the hassles of ownership.

However, the new demand can't be served by the existing rental units that have become functionally obsolescent. Mr. Lobo believes that the two-bedroom, one-washroom, eight-foot ceiling unit with no air conditioning does not attract the new renters who can afford to rent, if not own, quality abodes. A new class of high-end rentals could match the quality of condominiums while offering the security of tenure. See for example Aura at College Park, arguably Canada's tallest residential tower in 2019, building in Toronto that offers both rentals and condominiums and is in downtown Toronto.[147]

To achieve this goal, the builders' preference for short-term gains must be matched in joint ventures with the long-term investment needs and financing capacity of institutional investors, such as pension funds, whose preferences are for wealth generation and long-term cash flows.

New rental buildings could be placed near existing ones that have both surplus land and underground parking to be shared with the new buildings. In return, investors could assist with structural improvements to the neighbouring older buildings resulting in an increase in the supply of rental

---

[145] Block, Walter E., Rent Control: A Tale of Two Canadian Cities (July 21, 2011). *The Mid-Atlantic Journal of Business*, Vol. 25, No. 7, May 1989. https://ssrn.com/abstract=1892363
[146] https://svnrock.ca/company/cv-derek-lobo/
[147] https://www.canderelresidential.com/projects/aura-at-college-park/

units and an improvement in the quality of existing ones.

Without innovative approaches such as these, purpose-built rental construction will continue to languish.

Let's look at additional public policy strategies to increase rental housing supply, including streamlined municipal approval processes and eliminating rent control regulations.

SUMMARY

There is no one size fits all solution for rental housing challenges. Rent control, essentially the vacancy decontrol in Canada, and application of capital gains tax to purpose-built rental housing have not necessarily helped with the supply of dedicated rental units in Canada. At the same time, the emergence of condominiums since the 1970s has acted as surrogates to purpose-built rentals in large urban markets.

A healthy urban housing market requires a mix of housing by tenure, size, location, and type to meet the diverse housing needs of families who also are differentiated by size, type, and affordability. For growing cities like Toronto, Montréal, and Vancouver, the increase in population generates additional demand for new housing. Policies that encouraged builders and developers to increase the supply of housing, both owner-occupied and rental, are more likely to succeed in supporting balanced housing markets that must also be affordable than policies that limit entrepreneurship or put curbs on market agents responsible for building new space. At the same time, public-sector authorities must be cognizant of their responsibilities to ensuring provision of shelter space for those who are priced out of the housing markets by providing housing where rents are geared to income.

8 CITIES AS REAL ESTATE

More people on this planet (55%) live in urban areas than otherwise.[148] In Canada, the urbanized population is over 80%. By that account, more than 80% of the nation's real assets will also be in the cities. The physical core of the city is essentially a portfolio of real assets. From housing to office towers and warehouses, urban centres are characterized by an ubiquitous supply of real assets. Cities also compete for residents. Their attraction is economic activity and jobs. Workers from rural areas move to cities in search of jobs. Cities with fast growing economies attract workers from other countries where a surplus of skilled workers is searching for opportunities.

Successful cities attract workers who increase the demand for housing and services. If the construction of new housing does not keep pace with the increase in demand, housing prices start rising rapidly. Suburbs can ease pressure on housing prices when workers can relocate to suburbs and still be able to commute to work spending a reasonable amount of time and effort. This of course requires efficient transportation system that relies on public transit for higher throughput capacities.

This chapter discusses urban real estate. It tells the story of the transformation of suburbs from being undesirable, yet unavoidable, extension to cities to desirable places where families live in relatively affordable homes and raise kids near soccer fields, ice rinks, and baseball diamonds. The death and life of North American cities has been a focus of scholarship in the past.[149]. This chapter presents a few new stories that we

---

[148] United Nations Department of Economic and Social Affairs. (2018, May 16). 68% of the world population projected to live in urban areas by 2050, says UN. Retrieved from https://www.un.org/development/desa/en/news/population/2018-revision-of-world-urbanization-prospects.html.

[149] Jacobs, J. (1992). The death and life of great American cities. *New York: Vintage.*

have picked along the way.

THE SUBURBS NOW COMMAND RESPECT

Suburbs are the cradle of civilization, proclaimed Harold Spence-Sales who founded Canada's first urban planning program at McGill University in 1947. Suburbs are also the engine of demographic growth. A report by Professor David Gordon and others at Queen's University revealed that metropolitan areas accommodated an additional 3.2 million residents between 2006 and 2016, with suburbs accounting for 85 per cent of that growth. During that time frame, the number of dwellings in metropolitan areas increased by 1.46 million. Again, the suburbs and beyond accommodated 78 per cent of the growth in dwelling units.[150]

More than two out of three Canadians now live in a suburb, making Canada a suburban nation. But while Canadian households and builders have overwhelmingly favoured suburbs over neighbourhoods in the urban core, the suburbs don't seem to get any respect. Discussions about growth and planning in the popular press and on social media have a near-exclusive focus on high-density downtowns.

The Queen's report divided metropolitan areas into four mutually exclusive typologies. 'Active core' represented mostly inner-city urban neighbourhoods with a higher proportion of workers commuting by walk or cycle. 'Transit suburbs' represented neighbourhoods with a higher share of commutes by public transit. 'Auto suburbs' represented areas where workers commuted mostly by cars. Lastly, 'Exurbs' represented low-density rural areas included in the Census Metropolitan Areas. Suburban populations across Canada grew five times faster than the populations in urban cores and transit-centric suburbs. Yet planning professionals, including the authors of the report, see that as a problem that needs fixing. The authors offer recipes to target more growth to the urban core and transit-centric neighbourhoods.

The interventions intended to reverse suburbanization ignore the fundamentals of land economics and demographics and hence are unlikely to succeed. Land is cheaper in the suburbs and so is housing because suburbs are land rich. The neighbourhoods in the urban core are mostly built up with little, if any, developable land, which is reflected in higher land and housing prices. Since suburbs have excess land, development is more likely to occur there than places where land is scarce.

---

[150] Craig, A. (2018, September 6). Canada is a more suburban nation. *Queen's Gazette*. Retrieved from https://www.queensu.ca/gazette/stories/canada-more-suburban-nation

WHERE GROWTH LIVES

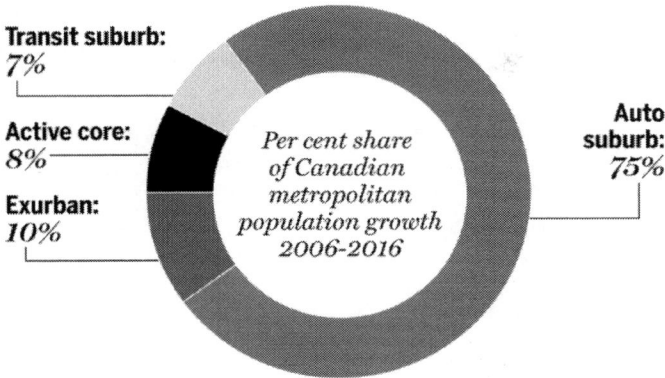

Transit suburb:
7%

Active core:
8%

Exurban:
10%

*Per cent share
of Canadian
metropolitan
population growth
2006-2016*

**Auto
suburb:**
75%

SOURCE: STILL SUBURBAN? GROWTH IN CANADIAN SUBURBS, 2006-2016.
QUEEN'S UNIVERSITY, AUG. 2018

NATIONAL POST

Figure 8.1 – Percent Share of Canadian Metropolitan Population Growth (2006-2016)

Even more significant is the heterogeneity in household sizes, composition and preferences. Large households need more shelter space, something that cannot be supplied at affordable prices in the urban core where dwellings are smaller. It is, therefore, no surprise that between "2012 and 2016, 83% of the 84,343 residential units completed in Toronto were condominium apartments," which are hardly suited for growing families, who increasingly turned to the suburbs.[151]

Urban planning literature, such as the Queen's University report, views suburbs with a narrow lens of population density and automobile-based mobility, while ignoring all other suburban manifestations including the most obvious one being affordability. If it were not for the suburbs, the housing affordability crisis would be even worse in fast-growing cities. New housing developments in the suburbs help ease population pressures on inner cities and thus provide an affordability cushion. In cities where new developments are increasingly targeted at the urban core and transit-oriented suburbs, such as Vancouver, housing affordability worsened even more.

But are suburbs without problems? Suburban living is associated with higher incidence of obesity, the report's authors remind us. However, researchers at the University of Toronto who tracked individuals over time, found "no evidence that urban sprawl causes obesity."[152] Previous findings

---

[151] City of Toronto. (2017). *Living in the City Survey 2016*. Retrieved from
https://www.toronto.ca/legdocs/mmis/2018/pg/bgrd/backgroundfile-110520.pdf
[152] Eid, J., Overman, H. G., Puga, D., & Turner, M. A. (2008). Fat city: Questioning the relationship between urban sprawl and obesity. *Journal of Urban Economics, 63*(2), 385–404.

of a relationship between suburban living and obesity failed to control for the fact that "the individuals who are more likely to be obese choose to live in more sprawling neighbourhoods."

Critics blame suburbs for auto-dependent lifestyles causing greater pollution and higher fossil fuel consumption. This is true. However, suburban demographics such as larger household size and the presence of children necessitate the use of the private automobile. Also, suburban residents do not necessarily work in transit accessible downtowns. Over time, as gasoline-powered vehicles are phased out, concerns over GHG emissions and fossil fuel dependence will likely lessen.

The future of growth cities will be even more concentrated in the suburbs. It is merely an outcome of land economics and demographics. Suburbs could be designed better with mixed-land uses and greater diversity in housing typologies. The following section considers potential repercussions if Toronto had been awarded Amazon's second headquarters.

AMAZON HQ2 IS A DOUBLE-EDGED SWORD

Amazon.com Inc. turned the search for a home for its second headquarters (HQ2) into an episode of The Bachelorette, with cities across North America trying to woo the online retailer. The Seattle-based tech giant narrowed down the choice to 20 cities, with Toronto being the only Canadian location in the running.[153]

While many in Toronto, including its mayor, were hoping to be the ideal suitor for Amazon HQ2, one must be mindful of the challenges such a union may pose.

Amazon announced in September 2017 that its second headquarters would employ 50,000 high-earners with an average salary of US$100,000. It would also require 8 million square feet of office and commercial space.

A capacity-constrained city with a perennial shortage of affordable housing and limited transport capacity, Toronto may be courting trouble by pursuing thousands of additional highly paid workers. If you think housing prices and rents are unaffordable, wait until the Amazon code warriors land to fight you for housing or a subway seat.

The tech giants do command a much more favourable view in North America than they do in Europe. Still, their reception varies, especially in the cities where these firms are domiciled. Consider San Francisco, which is home to not one but many tech giants and ever mushrooming startups. The

---

https://doi.org/10.1016/j.jue.2007.12.002
[153] Griswold, A. (2018, January 18). Amazon is thinking about putting HQ2 just about everywhere except Silicon Valley. *Quartz*. Retrieved from https://qz.com/1182913/amazon-amzn-hq2-shortlist-20-cities-that-made-the-headquarters-cut/

city attracts high-earning tech talent from across the globe to staff innovative labs and R&D departments.

These highly paid workers routinely outbid locals and other workers in housing and other markets. No longer can one ask for a conditional sale offer that is subject to financing because a twenty-something whiz kid will readily pay cash to push other bidders aside.

One wonders whether Toronto's residents, or those of whichever city ultimately wins Amazon's heart, will face the same competition from Amazon employees as do the residents of Seattle? The answer lies in the relative affordability gap.

Amazon employees with an average income of US$100,000 will compete against Toronto residents whose individual median income in 2015 was just $30,089.[154] It is quite likely the bidding wars that high-earning tech workers have won hands down in other cities will end in their favour in the city chosen for Amazon HQ2.

While I am mindful of the challenges that Amazon HQ2 may pose for a capacity constrained Toronto, I am also alive to the opportunities it will present. For starters, Toronto can use 50,000 high-paying jobs. The emergence of the gig economy has had an adverse impact in the City of Toronto, where employment growth has largely concentrated in the part-time category. Between 2006 and 2016, full-time jobs grew by a mere 8.7 per cent in Toronto, while the number of part-time jobs grew at four times that rate.[155]

While being the largest employment hub in Canada, with an inventory of roughly 180 million square feet, an influx of 8 million square feet of first-rate office space will improve the overall quality of commercial real estate in Toronto. It could also be a boon for office construction and a significant source of new property tax revenue for the city.

But those hoping the city itself might make money should seriously consider the fate of cities lucky enough to host the Olympics, which more often than not end up costing cities billions more than they budgeted for.

---

[154] City of Toronto. (2017). *2016 Census Backgrounder Income 2017 09 14*. Retrieved from https://www.toronto.ca/wp-content/uploads/2017/10/8f41-2016-Census-Backgrounder-Income.pdf

[155] City of Toronto. (2016). *Toronto Employment Survey 2016*. Retrieved from https://www.toronto.ca/legdocs/mmis/2017/pg/bgrd/backgroundfile-99543.pdf

COMPETING ON PRICE

The price of real estate varies widely in the 20 cities vying for HQ2

AVERAGE ANNUAL RENT FOR 75,000 SQ. FT. OFFICE, IN US$

New York City	$5,709,750
Washington D.C.	$2,793,000
Los Angeles	$2,738,431
Miami	$2,733,000
Boston	$2,693,250
Austin	$2,541,750
Chicago	$2,226,000
Philadelphia	$1,995,000
Denver	$1,973,250
Newark	$1,930,500
Toronto	$1,913,318
Nashville	$1,869,750
Raleigh	$1,854,750
Atlanta	$1,828,500
Dallas	$1,796,250
Pittsburgh	$1,634,250
Columbus	$1,442,250
Indianapolis	$1,407,000

SOURCE: HTTPS://WWW.RECODE.NET   NATIONAL POST

Figure 8.2 – Average Annual Rent for 75,000 Square Feet of Office Space in American Cities

Toronto may still pursue Amazon HQ2, but it should do so with the full knowledge of its strengths and vulnerabilities. At the very least, it should create contingency plans to address the resulting infrastructure deficit (not just public transit) and housing affordability issues before it throws open its doors for Amazon.

In November 2018, Amazon's second headquarters was awarded to Arlington, Virginia and Long Island City - a suburban neighbourhood in Queens, New York City. These two suburban locations were chosen as viable alternatives to the congested and expensive urban cores of nearby Washington D.C. and Manhattan. Subsequently, the deal with Long Island City fell apart.

AMAZON GOES TO THE SUBURBS

It's a huge win for the suburbs. In November 2018, Amazon.com Inc. confirmed that it had picked not one but two locations for its planned second headquarters, which it has dubbed HQ2. And instead of choosing downtown-centric locations in either New York (Manhattan) or Washington, D.C., Amazon picked suburban neighbourhoods in Queens and Arlington, Va.[156]

---

[156] Weise, K. (2018, October 23). Sorry Toronto: For Amazon HQ2 watchers, it's Northern Virginia that checks the most boxes. *Financial Post*. Retrieved from

The world's largest e-commerce and cloud computing company had launched the competition to host HQ2 in 2017, inviting bids from cities across North America. Amazon dangled the prospect of 50,000 high-paying jobs and billions in construction spending as bait. No fewer than 238 cities joined the bidding frenzy. Many offered huge tax breaks running into the billions of dollars and other incentives. In early 2018, Amazon announced a shortlist of 20 cities. Toronto was the only Canadian city to make that list.

In the end, the high-stakes real estate dating game ended with the suitor choosing two sites for its second home. While many pundits were surprised by the fact that the HQ2 will be split between two sites, even a bigger surprise must be the suburban locations.

The proposed locations mark a high point in the coming-of-age story of the suburbs, which were once viewed as nothing more than bedroom communities for workers who would leave every morning for work in the urban core. The suburbs of the past were single-purpose residential communities peppered lightly with small-scale office and some retail space.

Big city suburbs are often vibrant communities in which people can live, work, relax, and play. Clusters of high-rise buildings, which were once an exclusive hallmark of downtowns, are now just as readily spotted in communities far from the core.

The rise of suburban office real estate was popularized in Joel Garreau's 1991 book, *Edge City: Life on the New Frontier*. Garreau defined Edge Cities as suburban places with new developments of five million square feet or more of office space, 600,000 square feet or more of retail space, and a total number of jobs that exceeds the number of bedrooms.[157]

Robert Lang, a professor of public policy at the University of Nevada, expanded the definition of suburban office markets. First in Edgeless Cities and later in *Beyond Edgeless Cities*, Lang focused on the large swaths of rental office space located outside of primary and secondary downtowns.[158]

Lang's analysis of 13 large U.S. commercial real estate markets revealed that the suburban Edgeless City contained 40 per cent of the office space in the surveyed cities, including New York and Washington. However, the average across 13 markets hid some of the diversity - whereas 57 per cent of the regional office space in New York was in the primary downtown area,

https://business.financialpost.com/technology/sorry-toronto-for-amazon-hq2-watchers-its-northern-virginia-that-checks-the-most-boxes

[157] Garreau, J. (1992). *Edge City : Life on the New Frontier: Life on the New Frontier* (Vol. 1, pp. 1–548). Doubleday & Company, Incorporated.

[158] Lang, R. E., Sanchez, T., & LeFurgy, J. (2006). Beyond edgeless cities: Office geography in the new metropolis. *National Center for Real Estate Research, National Association of Realtors*. Retrieved from https://www.researchgate.net/profile/Thomas_Sanchez/publication/230820735_Beyond_e dgeless_cities_office_geography_in_the_new_metropolis/links/0fcfd50b5a04e9de6c000000 /Beyond-edgeless-cities-office-geography-in-the-new-metropolis.pdf

only 29 per cent of the office space in Washington was similarly situated.

Suburban office markets have matured even further since the publication of Edgeless Cities. That Amazon has selected two suburbs (albeit of relatively high density when compared with other cities) for its HQ2 offers further evidence in support of a growing future for suburban office real estate.

A study by CMHC suggests the benefits of moving to the suburbs for affordable housing options are offset by high commuting costs.[159] That might be true for those who must commute back to the urban core every day for work. But when employers also move to the suburbs, the commute distance and time for suburban residents can decline significantly. Mississauga, Ontario serves a good example of a balanced suburb, with fewer than 27 per cent of the residents commuting to a different city to work.

By choosing suburban locations for HQ2, Amazon has recognized that the suburbs may not be just bedroom communities. The suburbs, with abundant and less expensive land, are a viable alternative to the congested and expensive urban cores.

Not only can workers find relatively inexpensive housing, but suburban work locations also offer the opportunity for reverse commuting - going against the primary direction of traffic - in peak hours of travel. This transportation capacity will remain underutilized unless high-density suburban employment locations, such as the ones proposed by Amazon, are developed.

Next, we will discuss tax increment financing as a development tool for funding transit and other infrastructure by considering the proposed mixed use waterfront neighbourhood in Toronto.

TAX INCREMENT FINANCING HAS ITS PITFALLS

Sidewalk Labs, a subsidiary of Alphabet Inc. - the parent company of Google - has proposed to develop a smart mixed-use waterfront neighbourhood in Toronto. As part of its plan, Sidewalk has revealed that it is considering investing in new transit infrastructure and has proposed using future property-tax revenues to recoup such investments.[160]

The company's plans have met with reservations: The idea of a large corporation, or its subsidiary, laying claim to a share of tax dollars has alarmed many. These concerns come on top of earlier questions about who will own

---

[159] CBC News. (2018, November 13). CMHC finds Toronto commuting costs can outweigh cheaper suburban house prices. Retrieved from https://www.cbc.ca/news/business/cmhc-commuting-costs-housing-1.4903862

[160] Robson, W. (2019, July 18). Sidewalk Labs' proposed transit financing plan worth embracing. *The Toronto Star*. Retrieved from https://www.thestar.com/opinion/contributors/2019/07/18/sidewalk-labs-proposed-transit-financing-plan-worth-embracing.html

the data that Sidewalk Labs plans to collect about the people who will live, work, or pass through its planned waterfront development.

The company's plan to use what is known as Tax Increment Financing (TIF) is contributing to the public anguish, in part because the concept is not widely understood. Sidewalk Labs would like to build Light Rail Transit (LRT) using TIF. It doesn't help that, at least in Toronto, the previous election promises to build public transit (Smart Track) using TIF met with little success.

Understanding just what TIF is and how it works is key to assessing whether it is an appropriate tool for funding an LRT and other infrastructure along Toronto's eastern waterfront. Let's assume that the public sector invests in improving infrastructure at a particular place. As a result, the land and property values appreciate. Subsequently, the area attracts additional investments from the private sector, which further increases the appreciation in land values.

The government designates the place as a TIF District and freezes the property taxes at the assessed values before the investments took place. Over time, the municipal governments continue to receive the fixed property tax revenue using the base period assessed value. Any incremental increase in property tax revenue over time, say 30 years, accrues to the TIF Authority that applies the receipts to service bonds and debentures issued earlier to build the infrastructure. Once the TIF designation is over, the property tax revenue based on current market valuation reverts in entirety to the municipal governments. If all goes according to the plan, TIF works out. But in many other cases, TIF has run into trouble.

A 2016 paper (co-authored by Murtaza Haider) published by the Institute for Municipal Finance and Governance (IMFG) at the Munk School at the University of Toronto, explained the workings of TIF. It showed that TIF largely works for small projects under specific economic conditions. The paper reviewed dozens of TIF implementations in the U.S. and found three enabling conditions.[161] First, mixed land use developments were more successful in achieving marginal increases in property tax revenue than single-purpose land uses. Second, the timing mattered: TIF projects initiated during recessions were less likely to be successful. And finally, smaller TIF projects that intended to generate under $500 million in TIF revenue were more likely to succeed. Examples of multibillion-dollar TIF projects were few and far between and often met with significant challenges in generating sufficient cash flow, as economic conditions could change drastically over 30 years.

The IMFG paper "found only two examples of TIF where the amount of

---

[161] Haider, M., & Donaldson, L. (2016). *Can Tax Increment Financing Support Transportation Infrastructure Investment?* Retrieved from https://tspace.library.utoronto.ca/handle/1807/81215

debt raised was in excess of $1 billion. In both instances, TIF revenue fell short of the forecasted amounts because of the prevailing market conditions, which affected property values." There were no precedents on the scale of the $6 billion Sidewalk Labs has indicated it intends to raise through TIFs.

While this doesn't mean Sidewalk's proposal can't work, it does suggest governments are in uncharted territory when dealing with a project of such scope and should proceed cautiously. If service delivery costs over time increase at rates higher than the inflation rate, municipal governments could face challenges delivering the same level of services with restricted budgets.

In addition to TIF, Sidewalk Labs is also proposing to use another method to raise funds: land-value capture, which would allow it to charge other developers and landowners a share of the increase in land values resulting from its investments. While it will be a challenge for the company to establish that it "caused" the land values to rise beyond the level to which they would have otherwise risen, the setting of such a precedent could have unintended consequences, if other developers sought the same right.

The Sidewalk Labs proposal offers possibilities to reimagine the urban space and try innovative financing tools. It is the job of the governments to do due diligence to ensure that public interest is guarded along the way.

In the next section we will consider if it is still cheaper to live in the suburbs than urban areas when accounting for the cost of commuting.

DON'T LET COMMUTE 'COSTS' FROM SUBURBS FOOL YOU

Relative to the urban core, housing is less expensive in the suburbs. But do the savings get eaten up by increased commuting costs? That was one of the findings of a study by Canada Mortgage and Housing Corp. (CMHC), which claimed that - at least in the Greater Toronto Area (GTA) - "the cost of longer commutes can completely offset the savings from moving to more affordable municipalities."[162,163]

While the CMHC study alerted households to the hidden costs of suburbanization, Canadian census data nevertheless reveal most of the recent population growth in metropolitan areas has taken place in the suburbs.

But why are Canadian moving to the suburbs en masse, if affordability gains are not necessarily as advertised? The answer lies in the assumptions that drive the conclusions in the CMHC study, among them that dwelling

[162] CBC News. (2018, November 13). CMHC finds Toronto commuting costs can outweigh cheaper suburban house prices. Retrieved from https://www.cbc.ca/news/business/cmhc-commuting-costs-housing-1.4903862
[163] Canada Mortgage and Housing Corporation. (2018, November 13). Drive until you qualify: is the commute worth it? Retrieved from https://www.cmhc-schl.gc.ca/en/housing-observer-online/2018-housing-observer/drive-until-you-qualify-is-commute-worth-it

units and household sizes are the same across the urban landscape.

Furthermore, the study estimates commuting costs using median distances and does not factor travel times directly into the calculation. It further estimates suburban transit trip costs by regional train service (in this case, GO Transit) "for each municipality as the monthly fare (40 one-way trips) to commute to Union Station" in downtown Toronto.

Challenging these assumptions reveals that the suburban savings remain intact. First and foremost is the fact that dwelling units differ in sizes. According to the 2016 census, the average number of rooms in a dwelling in the City of Toronto was five. In the neighbouring suburb of Vaughan, the average number of rooms was 7.2.

Not only is the size of low-rise housing itself larger in the suburbs, but the lot sizes tend to be much larger, too, owing to the lower land prices. It is only by ignoring the huge difference in dwelling sizes that the mortgage carrying costs of smaller sized detached units in the City of Toronto can be equated to their much larger counterparts in the suburbs.

Census data from 2016 reveals that suburbs have larger homes because they shelter larger families. The average household size is 33-per-cent larger in Markham and 25-per-cent higher in Mississauga than the average household size in the City of Toronto. The smaller-sized households, i.e., singles and couples without children, need much less space than larger-sized families and therefore, on a per-square foot basis, smaller households outbid larger-sized households for housing in the urban core.

Another unstated assumption in the CMHC study is about the false choice between the suburbs and the central city for larger-sized households. The urban core offers fewer affordable choices for larger sized families. Even if the commuting costs were higher, which we will show is not necessarily the case, large families do not have a real choice between the suburbs and the core.

The CMHC study also bases its commuting costs on median distances. This favours the urban areas for two reasons. First, for the 12 per cent who walk or bike to work, the study assumes zero commuting costs. Second, since the study estimates costs based on distance and not time, it underestimates the duration of short-distance commutes in the congested urban core. Thus, the monthly commuting cost for the City of Toronto is estimated at a mere $115, even less than the cost of a monthly transit pass. In comparison, workers living in Georgina, 80 kilometres north of the city, are estimated to incur a cost of $1,079 for driving to work locations.

The 2016 census, though, presents a more nuanced picture. For starters, one in five residents of the City of Toronto commutes to a work location in the suburbs. Most of the suburb-bound Toronto residents, i.e., 83 per cent, commute by car. Almost 44 per cent of those who live and work in the City of Toronto commute by public transit and another 40 per cent commute by car on a very congested road network. At the same time, transit-based commutes on average are much longer in duration than those by automobile. By estimating commuting costs as a function of distance and not time unduly favours Toronto in this comparison.

The number of suburban workers who commute to the central city is small in the GTA. In Georgina's case, that number is 2,655. As for Oshawa, a suburb with an abundance of affordable low-rise housing, only 10,750 residents commute (largely by regional train service) to the City of Toronto.

While some suburban residents incur longer commutes, many more don't. The suburban commuting advantage is obvious when one considers shorter commutes of fewer than 15 minutes duration. According to the 2016 Census data, only 13 per cent of Toronto residents enjoyed commutes of shorter than 15 minutes duration. In suburban Oshawa, 28 per cent of commutes were less than 15 minutes long.

After stripping away the assumptions, the locational advantage of suburbs is obvious: cheaper housing with sufficient shelter space for families and commutes comparable to those of central city dwellers. Most of the population growth in Canada's metropolitan areas between 2006 and 2016 occurred in suburbs and building better public transit to link urban and suburban areas would do more to solve the housing affordability problem in the most expensive Canadian cities than building more units.

PUBLIC TRANSIT IS KEY TO HOUSING

Two contrasting pictures of Toronto's housing market emerged in August 2018. One showed the market is recovering from the previous year's slump when prices and sales fell. The other showed the market becoming increasingly unaffordable, prompting one mayoral hopeful to make affordable housing a central plank of her campaign. This housing market seesaw suggests the balancing act of maintaining healthy returns in housing while keeping the city affordable is becoming increasingly difficult.

July 2018 housing sales data in Toronto paints a picture of a recovering market with both sales and prices higher than a year earlier. After months of falling prices and sales, news of a recovery has elated homeowners, but not so much others who feel left out by the housing market.

Jennifer Keesmaat, Toronto's former chief planner who ran for mayor, promised to build 100,000 affordable units over the 10 years. Details of her plan are not known, and 100,000 may seem like a large number, but for a growing city, these units, even if built, are unlikely to have a large impact on improving affordability.

Such public-sector interventions seldom make a huge difference in housing markets. Even falling housing sales and prices do not necessarily improve affordability. Indeed, such developments can hurt those who were supposed to be the intended beneficiaries.

For example, falling Toronto housing prices and sales in 2017 did not make housing more affordable for low-income households because the prices of starter homes, favoured by first-time homebuyers, had little fat to lose.

Some first-time homebuyers who put money down on under-construction units in Barrie, Ont., a remote suburb of Toronto, struggled to come up with additional funds because the price they agreed to in 2017 was significantly more than the assessed value in 2018, resulting in a large difference between the mortgage amount and the price they must pay.

At the same time, falling prices do not imply that rents will follow suit. Rents are less volatile than home prices and are slow to adjust to housing market fluctuations. Thus, a short-term decline in housing prices does not necessarily result in more affordable rental units.

And then there are the unintended consequences of policies directed at improving housing affordability. For example, the Ontario government in 2017 imposed regulations that further restricted a landlord's ability to set rents. Yet a city staff report in 2018 stated that rents in purpose-built rentals in Toronto "have soared to a 15-year high, while vacancy rates are now the lowest they've been in 16 years."

PRICES ARE CHEAPER IN THE SUBURBS THAN IN TORONTO

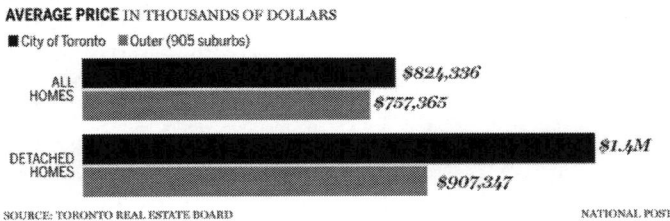

AVERAGE PRICE IN THOUSANDS OF DOLLARS

■ City of Toronto ▨ Outer (905 suburbs)

ALL HOMES: $824,336 / $757,365

DETACHED HOMES: $1.4M / $907,347

SOURCE: TORONTO REAL ESTATE BOARD   NATIONAL POST

Figure 8.3 – Average Home Prices in Toronto and its Suburbs

This housing market dilemma is not unique to Toronto. Other successful growing cities such as London, New York and Vancouver have faced the same conundrum for decades, if not longer. In Vancouver, many wonder if the city can still attract school teachers, municipal workers and others whose skills are essential, but whose wages are not sufficient to own or rent enough shelter space to meet their family's needs.

The solution to these issues could be to improve transportation infrastructure, which has played a key role in creating affordable housing within a reasonable commute of large urban employment centres. For instance, the commuter rail and subway systems in New York and London have stretched the boundaries of those cities farther out so that low-and middle-income workers can work in more central areas while still being able to afford the housing their families need without spending excessive time commuting back and forth to work.

The GO Transit system in Toronto and the Exo rail network in Montreal are examples of how public transportation infrastructure has improved accessibility and affordability for those who cannot afford market rents in the central city but still need to work there.

Publicly owned land in high-demand central areas could be used to build housing in partnership with the private sector, but a better approach would be to use the land in these areas for the best use - commercial/office development - and invest in rail-based transit to expand the housing boundaries of the city and its suburbs. And while building more high order transit is key to solving the housing affordability crisis, the importance of improving automobile access between suburban and urban areas cannot be underestimated.

HOUSING'S CAR VS. BUS EQUATION

Despite the early 2019 slowdown in home prices, housing affordability did not improve much in tight urban markets where prices and rents, relative to incomes, were still considerably high and rental vacancy rates were at record lows. As a result, pundits expected housing affordability and mortgage stress tests to figure prominently as the political parties geared up for the October 2019 federal election.

Though it might be tempting to focus just on the housing part of the equation, the other part - that is, affordability, which is tied to incomes and access to employment - also needs attention. Access to employment opportunities that pay living wages is an important determinant of housing affordability. But with jobs scattered all over the urban landscape, accessing them by public transit remains, and will continue to be, a formidable challenge.

The private automobile offers better accessibility to jobs in North America than public transit. Research shows that those who rely on public transit to access jobs face a severely constrained set of choices that could adversely impact their ability to earn enough to pay for shelter.

Indeed, almost everywhere in every city, job accessibility by cars is "an order of magnitude" higher, according to Jeff Allen and Steven Farber, geographers at the University of Toronto , who analyzed accessibility to jobs in Canada's eight most populous city regions in a paper published in January in *Transport Policy*.[164]

---

[164] Allen, J., & Farber, S. (2019). Sizing up transport poverty: A national scale accounting of low-income households suffering from inaccessibility in Canada, and what to do about it.

Yet despite the contradicting evidence, most planning authorities prescribe even more transit investments to help low-income earners get to jobs. The planners assume, rather naively, that low income workers would be better off commuting by transit than by car, given the high cost of car ownership.

AVERAGE ACCESSIBILITY TO JOBS BY CAR AND PUBLIC TRANSIT

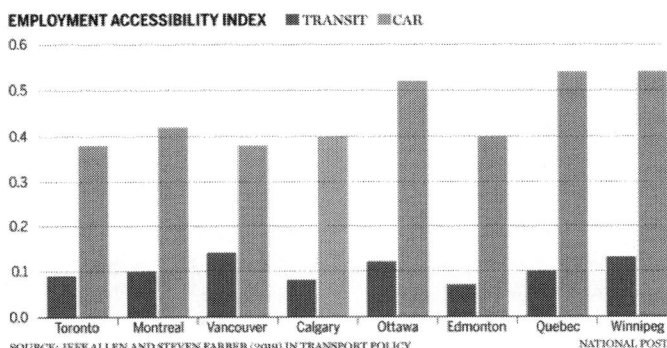

SOURCE: JEFF ALLEN AND STEVEN FARBER (2019) IN TRANSPORT POLICY   NATIONAL POST

Figure 8.4 – Employment Accessibility Index for Canadian Cities

This assumption was tested by David King, a professor at Arizona State University, and others in an article that appeared in the January 2019 issue of the *Journal of Planning Education and Research*. King and colleagues showed low-income households with cars improved their financial lot, whereas those without cars saw their finances worsen over time, despite automobile ownership costs.[165] Carless households were "falling further behind households with vehicles" and were "poorer in absolute terms today than they were 60 years ago," they observed. This led the authors to conclude that "for most people in most places - the high cost of owning a vehicle is probably lower than the cost of living without one."

This is not to suggest that improving accessibility by transit does not have merit. It certainly does. Where demand exists, transit offers higher efficiencies, fewer emissions and greater throughput capacities, as congestion on city roads would be worse without it. However, for accessing jobs, public transit serves downtowns better than other places. And as jobs have suburbanized, reaching them by transit is a formidable challenge for most workers. Equally important is that commutes by public transit are much slower.

Transport Policy, *74*, 214–223. https://doi.org/10.1016/j.tranpol.2018.11.018
165 King, D. A., Smart, M. J., & Manville, M. (2019). The Poverty of the Carless: Toward Universal Auto Access. *Journal of Planning Education and Research*, 0739456X18823252. https://doi.org/10.1177/0739456X18823252

Housing affordability challenges arise when shelter costs increase out of step with incomes. The sharp increase in housing prices from 2015 to the first quarter of 2017 exacerbated affordability challenges, but so did the stagnant, inflation-adjusted wages of mid-to low-income earners during that period. Whereas housing might be new to the federal election agenda, jobs and wages aren't. That's why government ministers boasted about the 800,000 jobs created between when the Liberals took control in November 2015 and February 2019.

If public policy to improve housing affordability were to follow empirical evidence, recent research unreservedly shows that the journey is easier by car than by public transit. Investing in public transit is important to support sustainable mobility in urban centres. However, this does not imply that the government should ignore the importance of maintaining and expanding the road networks that allow an overwhelming majority of workers to access jobs, earn a living and provide shelter for their families.

How workers reach the 800,000 new and millions of older jobs is part of the solution to the housing crisis. As the government contemplates ways to improve housing affordability, it will serve Canadians better by improving access to jobs that pay living wages. And in the coming decades, access will be influenced by new technologies, such as autonomous vehicles, that will reshape cities and real estate markets.

AUTONOMOUS VEHICLES WILL TRANSFORM MOBILITY AND REAL ESTATE

The March 2018 death of a pedestrian in a collision with a self-driven autonomous vehicle (AV) in Arizona raised concerns about the safety of such vehicles. Despite the tragic incident, research shows that advances in autonomous vehicle technology are soon going to transform the way we travel.

But AVs will not just affect transportation. They will also influence the shape and size of cities and, along with them, of real estate markets. The dimensions of cities have long been defined by the transportation technology of the time. As new modes of transportation allowed people to reach greater distances in less time, towns and cities expanded.

"For thousands of years, no matter what the transportation technology, the maximum desirable commute has been forty-five minutes," wrote journalist and author Joel Garreau in his book Edge City: Life on the New Frontier. Sixteenth-century Istanbul, he notes, "was never six miles across."[166]

---

[166] Garreau, J. (1992). *Edge City: Life on the New Frontier: Life on the New Frontier* (Vol. 1, pp. 1–548). Doubleday & Company, Incorporated.

Advances in motorized transportation and the emergence of mass transit in the past two hundred years have accelerated the pace of transformation in mobility and pushed the city limits outward. Rail-based mass transit and, later, the private automobile were the dominant forces in expanding city limits, making new parcels of land profitable to develop.

Transportation technologies did not alter just the size of the real estate markets, but also their structure by influencing the spatial distribution of prices and rents for housing and commercial real estate. Commercial real estate is much more expensive in and near downtowns. Similarly, housing within walking distance of a subway or a regional rail station is often more expensive than a comparable unit located further away.

Whereas some uncertainty remains about when fully (or less-than-fully) autonomous self-driving vehicles will become the norm, it is quite evident that the age of AVs will soon be upon us. While a sizable body of research on the mobility and safety aspects of AVs is already available, their effect on real estate markets has generated little scholarship. Some notable exceptions exist.

Writing in *Regional Science and Urban Economics*, the Russian economist Roman Zakharenko explains the likely impact of AVs on a city's size and shape.[167] Zakharenko notes that AVs will shift parking space from the urban core to the periphery because self-driving vehicles, after dropping their occupants in the urban core, will park themselves at a cheaper location away from the city centre. The demand for parking spaces in the urban core will decline, which will permit the further densification of economic activity in core areas, thus resulting in even higher rents. Concomitantly, AVs will lower the overall transportation costs and "will cause a city sprawl and rent decline outside of the city centre." Zakharenko estimates that land rents in the urban core may increase from 30 to 40 per cent whereas land rents may decline by the same amount in the periphery. AVs are likely to introduce a new type of land-use or real-estate class: the dedicated parking belt, where prices would be significantly lower than in the core itself and the distance more convenient than returning home.

While the AV-driven evolution in mobility requires preparation and planning, many cities have yet to get started. Erick Guerra, an assistant professor of city and regional planning at the University of Pennsylvania, noted in the *Journal of Planning Education and Research* that a survey of long-range regional transportation plans of the 25 most populous metropolitan areas, home to 40 per cent of the U.S. population, revealed barely any mention of AVs.[168]

[167] Zakharenko, R. (2016). Self-driving cars will change cities. *Regional Science and Urban Economics*, *61*, 26–37. https://doi.org/10.1016/j.regsciurbeco.2016.09.003

[168] Guerra, E. (2016). Planning for Cars That Drive Themselves: Metropolitan Planning Organizations, Regional Transportation Plans, and Autonomous Vehicles. *Journal of Planning*

Real estate asset managers also need to keep a close watch on how AVs are likely to transform mobility and urban built form. A note in the *Appraisal Journal* warns that AVs will "impact residential and commercial real estate. The confusion lies in knowing the degree of the impact, the timing of the impact, and how various sectors of the real estate market will change."[169]

The likely relocation of parking space from the urban core to relatively cheaper land nearby alone is going to create new challenges and opportunities for owners of commercial real estate. The task for real estate managers, city builders and urban planners is now to collaborate to improve mobility and real estate outcomes for citizens before autonomous vehicles make such decisions - autonomously.

In an age of self-driving cars, demand for parking spaces in the urban core will decline which will fuel the densification of downtowns and increase rents. Autonomous vehicles will also reshape parking structure design as self-parking vehicles will take up less parking space than traditional vehicles.

SELF-PARKING VEHICLES WILL CHANGE BUILDING DESIGN

Advances in transportation technology are transforming the way we travel. App-based ride-hailing and car-sharing are just a few examples. In the future, autonomous vehicles (AVs) will revolutionize the very contours of mobility. Not only will AVs be able to drive by themselves, they will also be able to park themselves.

Self-parking vehicles are expected to transform the architectural and structural designs of high-rise buildings. The cumulative effect of mobility innovations will reduce the demand for parking. Hence, if parking standards for new high-rise buildings are not revised, we might end up with surplus underground parking, which may be difficult to repurpose.

A 2019 report by Ryerson University's Urban Analytics Institute (of which Murtaza Haider was a co-author) explored the impact of innovations in transportation technology on the future demand for parking. The report observed that the current practice of requiring a fixed minimum number of parking spots in underground lots is likely to result in an eventual oversupply of parking.[170] Furthermore, minimum parking standards may also be

Education and Research, 36(2), 210–224. https://doi.org/10.1177/0739456X15613591

[169] Levine, M. L., Segev, L. L., & Thode, S. F. (2017). A Largely Unnoticed Impact on Real Estate--Self-Driven Vehicles. *The Appraisal Journal, 85*(1). Retrieved from http://search.ebscohost.com/login.aspx?direct=true&profile=ehost&scope=site&authtype=crawler&jrnl=00037087&asa=Y&AN=122227555&h=bqgV0m2r8ejmfIZoGzCdVNyZVl fgN6SfByDvZcHPnm5RAusU3LZ3xGb3ukxTEef5YwS0Bv97K4dQ%2BmqtHR1Tsg%3D %3D&crl=c

[170] Adediji, Y., Donaldson, L., & Haider, M. (2019). *How Parking Regulations Need to Evolve for*

contributing to housing affordability challenges because the cost of an underground parking spot varies between $50,000 and $100,000 in places where land values are high.

Parking studies have shown that automobile ownership is lower in high-rise buildings that facilitate car-sharing. Furthermore, younger cohorts have readily adopted ride-hailing while exhibiting a lower proclivity for car ownership than older cohorts. A decline in car ownership implies a decline in the demand for traditional parking spaces.

Whereas parking demand is likely to decline in the future, the demand for travel is expected to increase. The counterintuitive assertion stems from the way AVs are likely to operate. AVs may try to avoid expensive parking costs by deadheading back to the origin of the trip or another location offering inexpensive parking. This will result in additional zero occupancy trips that will be an additional contribution to traffic volumes.

Also, AVs will spend more time travelling while they serve the mobility needs of passengers whose trip origins, destinations, and trip times vary. Thus, mobility patterns of AVs will have more in common with taxi cabs than the private automobiles that are parked most of the time.

However, that's not all. Because AVs could communicate with each other, they may be parked in tandem in several rows. When required, AVs will move by themselves to allow other vehicles to leave. Thus, they will require a reduced amount of space for parking.

The construction industry has long been advocating for flexibility in minimum parking standards. The industry contends that providing underground parking is an expensive proposition that raises the price of dwellings in multi-residential buildings. With large cities struggling with housing affordability, the provision of underground parking could impede achieving the affordability goals.

The Ryerson University report recommends that cities consider revising the minimum parking standards in light of the expected decline in the demand for parking space. It also suggests building above grade parking in multi-residential buildings instead of underground parking. "Provision of above-grade parking is less expensive and at the same time allows for the repurposing of parking spaces if space becomes redundant in the future," the report argued.

The report listed examples of above-grade parking structures repurposed after space was no longer required for parking. In Cincinnati, Ohio, a parking garage was converted to a hotel featuring 239 rooms, an art gallery, and several other amenities. The adaptive reuse of the garage was financially more feasible than a complete teardown. Similarly, Northwestern University in

---

High-Rise Buildings -- A New Approach for Emerging Trends in Transportation, Housing, and the Environment. Urban Analytics Institute, Ryerson University.

Evanston, Ill., retrofitted a parking garage to develop an entrepreneurial innovation centre equipped with classrooms and shared meeting spaces. Because these parking structures were above-ground, it was possible to find alternative uses for them. Had this space been underground, repurposing alternatives would have been seriously limited.

Parking structures must be designed to allow for alternative uses in the future. Higher ceilings, gentler sloping slabs, and placement of elevator banks and staircases are some of the design considerations needed for the future transformation of parking spaces.

The skyline in large Canadian cities will showcase many more high-rise buildings in the future. Adjusting parking standards will help future-proof buildings by embracing flexibility in design to facilitate flexibility in future uses.

The final section in this chapter will examine how lessons from American rustbelt cities like Detroit can help revitalization efforts in the wake of the GM shutdown in Oshawa, Ontario.

GM'S EXIT DOESN'T MEAN OSHAWA BECOMES A DETROIT

When a large company shuts down in a small town, the entire local economy feels the impact. GM's decision to close its Oshawa car assembly plant in 2019 was no different. As thousands of gainfully employed workers anticipated layoffs, the effects spilled beyond the labour market into other economic sectors, including real estate.

While the number of workers projected to lose jobs at the GM's Oshawa assembly line was around 2,500, the number of those directly and indirectly affected was several times larger.[171] The integrated supply chains for large-scale manufacturing implies that many more workers employed elsewhere were affected when the products they produce were not needed at the assembly line in Oshawa.

The decline in manufacturing has contributed to the emergence of rust belts across America. Large and small towns, like Detroit and Flint in Michigan, became ghost towns as the manufacturing base eroded and well-paying jobs moved away.

Real estate markets also collapsed as a result, depriving municipal governments of essential tax revenue. The City of Detroit, for instance, ended up filing for Chapter 9 bankruptcy in 2013, the largest municipal

---

[171] Alini, E. (2018, November 26). GM Oshawa plant closing could affect nearly 15 per cent of auto industry jobs. *Global News*. Retrieved from https://globalnews.ca/news/4698395/gm-oshawa-plant-closing-job-losses/

bankruptcy in U.S. history.[172]

Just like Detroit, Oshawa is also a town known for automotive manufacturing. But that's where the similarities end. Oshawa's economic base is diverse and its proximity to Canada's largest employment hub in Toronto will give it the opportunity to reinvent itself if it embraces cultural diversity and retrains its resident labour force.

Statistics Canada reveals that of the 200,000 adult residents in Oshawa Census Metropolitan Area (CMA) in 2018, only nine per cent were employed in the manufacturing sector. A third of Oshawa residents were employed in retail, education services, health care and social assistance.

Oshawa's more affordable real estate also offered a cure for Toronto's growing housing pains. The average price of a detached house in Oshawa in 2018 was just $529,000, a fraction of the $1.3 million average in Toronto. Even when compared with the eastern neighbourhoods in the City of Toronto, detached homes in Oshawa cost 41-per-cent less. Where else can one find a waterfront property with pristine views of Lake Ontario and steps from Lakewoods Park listed under $800,000? That housing could come with a commuting tradeoff, especially if the loss of a major employer means residents must look elsewhere for work. Oshawa, though, enjoys fast and frequent public transit access to Toronto's downtown, with almost half-a-million people already working there.

With GO Transit running multiple trains from Oshawa each hour and reaching Toronto's downtown in an hour or less, a housing-commuting balance could be attractive for those who have not given up on owning a detached house. The growing numbers of commuting suburbanites are likely to stabilize housing markets in and around Oshawa, but large chunks of industrial and commercial real estate may soon become redundant.

A 2017 report by the Lincoln Institute of Land Policy focused on strategies to revitalize America's "smaller legacy cities" that suffered from losing their manufacturing bases.[173] The report listed eight strategies that helped these cities revive. Some of those strategies are relevant to Oshawa. The report encouraged a shared vision for prosperity between public and private sectors, encouraging private sector leaders to "also own the problem" and not leave remedial efforts to the government. A strong sense of place and a vibrant downtown also helped many cities to initiate the recovery, starting from those downtowns and stretching outward.

---

[172] Davey, M., & Walsh, M. W. (2013, July 18). Billions in Debt, Detroit Tumbles Into Insolvency. *The New York Times.* Retrieved from
https://www.nytimes.com/2013/07/19/us/detroit-files-for-bankruptcy.html
[173] Hollingsworth, T., & Goebel, A. (2017). *Revitalizing America's Smaller Legacy Cities -- Strategies for Postindustrial Success from Gary to Lowell.* Retrieved from
https://www.lincolninst.edu/publications/policy-focus-reports/revitalizing-americas-smaller-legacy-cities

The report further stressed that recovery efforts should focus on all workers who were affected and not just the ones with high-paying jobs. This observation is especially pertinent for Oshawa, where the percentage of adults with a bachelor's degree or higher checks in at just 22 per cent, half the rate of Toronto. With workplaces becoming increasingly knowledge-based, Oshawa will have to improve on the education and skills of its residents.

At the same time, Oshawa may also want to embrace diversity. While being just an hour from Toronto, Oshawa's ethnic diversity is starkly different. Whereas 47 per cent of people in the City of Toronto are immigrants, in Oshawa that figure is just 18 per cent.

A diverse and highly educated workforce has helped Toronto become an economic powerhouse and the hub for service sector employment in Canada. Oshawa can follow suit by improving its diversity, education, and skill credentials.

SUMMARY

What are cities if not real estate. The famed skylines of New York and Chicago, the tree-lined boulevards abutted by low-rise buildings on each side in Paris, the collage of formal and informal settlements in the modern-day Mumbai are examples of real estate that define the character of world's large and small cities. Where people live, work, study, shop or congregate becomes possible because of the structures located at such destinations. Our understanding of real estate will improve if we contextualize individual pieces of real estate in the larger urban context. Consider that two identically structured homes on identically sized lots will fetch different prices when be located in different cities. The urban part carries an intrinsic locational value that capitalizes uniquely in property values.

9 REAL ESTATE AND BEHAVIORAL SCIENCE

They are under 35, heavily indebted and own homes with relatively large mortgages and longer amortization periods. Also, they are readily found in Toronto or Vancouver.

Bank of Canada identifies the at-risk borrowers who are more vulnerable to economic shocks, such as a sudden loss in income or a rapid increase in mortgage rates. The highly indebted young borrowers have low-ratio mortgages, which are usually uninsured and have loan-to-value ratios below the 80 per cent threshold. But that's of little comfort: Their mortgage credit is large relative to their incomes, with loan-to-income ratios more than 450 per cent.

On January 1, 2018, the minimum qualifying rate for uninsured mortgages increased by the greater of the Bank of Canada's five-year benchmark rate or 200 basis points (two per cent) above the contractual mortgage rate. Realizing the large increase in uninsured mortgages in Toronto and Vancouver, OSFI, the federal regulator, tightened regulations for uninsured mortgages bringing them in line with insured mortgages.[174]

Given the limited success of previous interventions in arresting the sustained increase in housing prices and household debt, did the new measures achieve the intended objectives? A series of regulatory changes to arrest climbing housing prices had the expected result of a moderate to severe reduction in sales and prices in some large urban markets. Still, concerns about the rising household debt in Canada persisted with Canadian households being the most indebted among the OECD countries such that the average Canadian household debt is more than 100 per cent of per-capita

---

[174] Evans, P. (2017, October 17). OSFI sets new mortgage rules, including stress test for uninsured borrowers. *CBC News*. Retrieved from https://www.cbc.ca/news/business/osfi-mortgage-rules-1.4358048

GDP.[175]

The higher qualifying rate is likely to lower the size of mortgage loans that will be approved for most borrowers. As a result, some borrowers might postpone purchasing a house. At the same time, some potential sellers might delist their properties if they see prices dropping. A report by the Fraser Institute warned of negative impacts on mortgage markets "including higher loan pricing and reduced loan access for some consumers."[176]

HIGH LTI RATIOS ON THE RISE

Share of low-ratio mortgages
with LTI greater than
450 per cent

	2014	2016
Toronto	25	34
Vancouver	33	38
Calgary	16	21
Halifax	6	7
Montreal	13	13
Ottawa-Gatineau	8	10

SOURCE: BANK OF CANADA
FINANCIAL SYSTEM
REVIEW, NOVEMBER 2017

NATIONAL POST

Figure 9.1 – Percentage of Low-Ratio Mortgages with Loan-to-Income Ratios greater than 450 percent in Canadian Cities (2017)

The more stringent mortgage regulations announced by OSFI applied to federally regulated financial institutions that also included all major banks in Canada. OSFI further required lenders to adhere to stipulations for loan-to-value ratios intended to limit the size of loans relative to the value of the property.

Despite the tightening of regulations by federal and provincial governments, housing markets and borrowers in Canada refused to budge and were still eager to enter the marketplace. The 15 per cent tax on foreign buyers in British Columbia and Ontario had an initial impact on housing sales

---

[175] Evans, P. (2017, November 23). Canadian households lead the world in terms of debt: OECD. *CBC News*. Retrieved from https://www.cbc.ca/news/business/oecd-debt-1.4415860

[176] Mohindra, N. (2017, October 11). Uninsured Mortgage Regulation: From Corporate Governance to Prescription. Retrieved from https://www.fraserinstitute.org/studies/uninsured-mortgage-regulation-from-corporate-governance-to-prescription

and prices in the Greater Vancouver and Greater Toronto markets. However, markets are rebounding in Vancouver, and early signs of a recovery can be seen in Toronto.

Higher household debt in Canada was likely a result of historically low-interest rates that lasted over a long period of time. Given favourable interest rates, even Canadian governments could not resist the temptation to borrow. The billions of dollars being spent on infrastructure construction and renewal across Canada are financed by debt.

The question is how big a challenge does rising household debt in the short run (and the public debt in the long run) pose to the financial stability of Canadian markets. Prior attempts to limit household borrowing have met with little success. Regulators had previously tightened rules for insured residential mortgages, which accounted for 54 per cent of the $1.46 trillion mortgage credit. Similar stringent regulations were extended to uninsured mortgages, which were estimated at $666 billion.

Some housing market specialists pointed out the gaps in the planned regulatory changes, which applied only to federally regulated lenders. Exempted are the provincially regulated lenders including credit unions and caisses populaires who are also active in the mortgage market and account for 17 per cent of the mortgage lending in the uninsured segment.

It is likely that the regulations shifted some mortgage lending from federally regulated institutions to others. The Bank of Canada continued to list elevated levels of household debt and imbalances in housing markets among the top sources of vulnerability. An effective response to vulnerabilities must not be compromised by jurisdictional gaps.

In the next section we will discuss whether real estate agents work as hard to sell a client's home as they do to sell their own. Some research has suggested that agents push their clients to sell homes cheaply and quickly while other studies have offered a different perspective.

THE PRINCIPAL-AGENT PROBLEM IS NOT SO SIMPLE

Do real estate agents work as hard at selling their clients' homes as they do when they sell their own? Studies have suggested that agents push their clients to sell their homes cheaply and quickly. Research published in the journal *Real Estate Economics*, however, shows that the previous findings of real estate agents selling their own comparable homes for higher prices and keeping them longer on the market missed an obvious determinant for the difference: motivation heterogeneity.[177] Some sellers, especially institutional sellers, are

---

[177] Xie, J. (2018). Who Is "Misleading" Whom in Real Estate Transactions? *Real Estate Economics*, *46*(3), 527–558. https://doi.org/10.1111/1540-6229.12196

much more motivated to sell and could be driving the difference between sale prices of homes owned by clients and those owned by agents.

The economics literature has for long discussed the implications of the principal-agent problem, in which agents are motivated to act in their own interest and not necessarily in the interest of their clients. It took the bestselling book, Freakonomics, to popularize this problem as it pertains to real estate markets. Prof. Steven Levitt, one of the coauthors of Freakonomics, revealed the findings from a paper he later published in 2008.[178] His research found that "a real-estate agent keeps her own home on the market an average of 10 days longer and sells it for an extra 3-plus per cent, or $10,000 on a $300,000 house."

Levitt's findings generated significant backlash from the real estate industry. Essentially, his research was accusing real estate agents of depriving their clients of roughly 3.7 per cent of the homes' value by allowing clients to accept an offer instead of waiting for a better one. It didn't really help when Levitt later equated the services provided by realtors with those of pimps. "A realtor and a pimp perform the same primary service: marketing your product to potential customers," he wrote in the sequel, SuperFreakonomics.

While there is no love lost between the real estate industry and Levitt, he was not alone in questioning the utility of real estate agents. For instance, B. Douglas Bernheim and Jonathan Meer, writing in the journal *Economic Inquiry* in 2013, questioned whether real estate agents add any value to the sale price. They observed that if brokers' services were unbundled from listing on the Multiple Listing Service (MLS), the sale price for homes that used a broker was less than the price of homes sold directly by the owner.[179]

The decoupling of broker services from MLS listings has been a bone of contention in the real estate industry. For decades, the industry has resisted - in some cases using litigation - the attempts by some agents to offer discount brokerage services ranging from simple listings on the MLS to full service offerings including staging, marketing, promotion and running open houses.

Using a unique, though very small, data set of housing sales on Stanford University land where housing is exclusively listed by the university's housing office and could only be bought by the faculty or senior staff members, Bernheim and Meer showed that "when listings are not tied to brokerage services, a seller's use of a broker reduces the selling price of the typical home by 5.9 per cent to 7.7 per cent."

Obviously, housing on land owned by a university and sales restricted to

---

[178] Levitt, S. D., & Syverson, C. (2008). Market Distortions When Agents Are Better Informed: The Value of Information in Real Estate Transactions. *The Review of Economics and Statistics, 90*(4), 599–611. https://doi.org/10.1162/rest.90.4.599

[179] Bernheim, B. D., & Meer, J. (2013). Do Real Estate Brokers Add Value When Listing Services Are Unbundled? *Economic Inquiry, 51*(2), 1166–1182. https://doi.org/10.1111/j.1465-7295.2012.00473.x

faculty and staff members do not make a representative and compelling argument against the use of broker services. However, this study was unique because it was able to demonstrate the outcome when the listing is de-coupled from broker services, which is hard to demonstrate in the open market where the units for sale by owners may be inherently different from those listed on the MLS.

Prof. Jia Xie found a way to work around the limitations of earlier research that many believed was unfairly critical of the real estate industry. Using housing sales data from Indiana, Xie showed that whereas the average sale price of agents' homes was higher than that of their clients, the difference was primarily driven by inexperienced real estate agents and institutional clients, such as relocation companies and mortgage lenders who are "very motivated to sell even at substantially lower prices." Households thinking of selling their homes using a real estate agent should take comfort in Xie's research where he found "economically negligible" or "statistically insignificant" difference between the sale price of homes owned by agents and that of their clients.

We continue our evaluation of real estate and behavioral science by discussing Nimbyism, which has been a significant barrier to high-density housing development, especially in large Canadian cities.

NIMBYISM IS IMPOSING IN THE QUEST FOR AFFORDABILITY

Most people agree that new housing construction is key to addressing housing affordability challenges. Most people are also opposed to any high-density development within a kilometre of their homes.

That was one of the seemingly contradictory findings from an Ipsos Poll conducted on behalf of the Toronto Real Estate Board and Building Industry and Land Development Association into the attitudes of Torontonians toward new development. While the survey respondents opposed all types of residential development near their homes, the degree of opposition depended on the intensity of development, with a larger proportion opposing high-intensity, high-rise condominium and apartment projects.

The survey revealed that no fewer than 45 per cent of the respondents opposed the construction of new single-family detached residential development near their homes. Yet, the share of opponents increased gradually with the height of the proposed new construction, reaching 76 per cent for new high-rise condominiums.

Nimbyism (from Not In My Backyard) is known to have successfully prevented high-density residential infill across Canada, and is one of the many factors responsible for the gap between housing supply and demand in fast growing cities in Canada. NIMBYs are often affluent residents of established neighbourhoods who resist any attempt to intensify the built form near their homes. The idea of sharing nearby parks, ravines, roads and schools with newcomers has never been an attractive thought for the most. That the new residents of high-rise buildings might be able to see into in the backyards of established residents has also been a frequent concern.

One could sympathize with the current residents if they were opposing non-conforming land uses or noxious facilities. Consider the prospect of setting up a new landfill or an incinerator within a few hundred meters of a subdivision - the residents would be justified to oppose such construction because it is likely to affect their quality of life and adversely impact property values.

But the same is not necessarily true for conforming land uses, such as the construction of new residential units. Yet, it is quite common to see residents opposing new residential construction, citing increased traffic, crowding in schools, or environmental harm as the reasons for their discontent.

Nimbyism is also an example of cognitive dissonance: the residents agree that housing affordability will improve with the construction of new housing, yet the same residents oppose any new construction near their homes. Hence even when an overwhelming majority of the residents favour new construction to address worsening housing affordability - 87 per cent in the Ipsos poll - most residents oppose new construction near their homes.

OPPOSITION TO NEW DEVELOPMENT WITHIN 100 METRES OF HOME

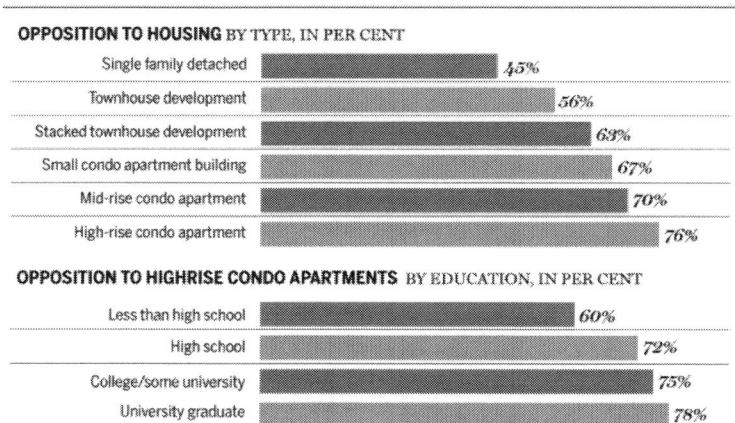

OPPOSITION TO HOUSING BY TYPE, IN PER CENT

Single family detached	45%
Townhouse development	56%
Stacked townhouse development	63%
Small condo apartment building	67%
Mid-rise condo apartment	70%
High-rise condo apartment	76%

OPPOSITION TO HIGHRISE CONDO APARTMENTS BY EDUCATION, IN PER CENT

Less than high school	60%
High school	72%
College/some university	75%
University graduate	78%

SOURCE: IPSOS   NATIONAL POST

Figure 9.2 – Toronto residents' opposition to new development within 100 metres of their home

New residents, however, do not just increase the use of existing municipal services; they also help build the municipal tax base, spreading costs over more taxpayers. In the absence of new residents, municipal service delivery costs continue to increase resulting in higher property taxes.

Despite the obvious benefits, Nimbyism often remains an insurmountable hurdle for developers. The degree of opposition differs by location and demographics. For instance, 28 per cent of the respondents from the City of Toronto did not oppose construction of high-rise apartment buildings near their homes. In comparison, only 22 per cent of the respondents in the 905 suburbs around Toronto were OK with nearby high-rise construction. The Ipsos poll further revealed that households without children were less likely to oppose high-rise apartment construction than those with children. Similarly, the opposition to nearby high-rise construction increased with education - a proxy for higher income - where less educated respondents were less likely to oppose than highly educated (high-income) respondents.

Andrew Whittemore and Todd BenDor in a paper in the *Journal of Urban Affairs* analyzed the motivations behind Nimbyism in the U.S. They revealed a range of motivations behind opposing high-density residential infill.[180] Whereas some respondents were motivated by "economic, esthetic, or lifestyle concerns" and the impacts on public services, others were influenced by "the prejudices that have historically informed the exclusionary zoning practices that other scholars have linked to segregation."

Those who oppose neighbourhood change might be motivated by altruistic reasons or prejudice. Their resistance to new residential development is partially the reason why housing is becoming increasingly unaffordable for younger cohorts and new residents.

Cities must grow and change to remain vibrant places of commerce and culture. Those who resist change risk the long-term viability of the very cities they adore.

The following section will consider rising home prices have resulted in many homebuyers exaggerating their incomes on mortgage applications.

MORTGAGE APPLICANTS ARE FLUFFING INCOME CLAIMS

Are Canadian homebuyers overstating their income on mortgage loan applications? A study of CMHC-insured mortgages seems to suggest the answer is yes. The study revealed that incomes reported on mortgage loan applications were systematically higher than those reported to the Canada Revenue Agency (CRA).

---

[180] Whittemore, A. H., & BenDor, T. K. (2019). Reassessing NIMBY: The demographics, politics, and geography of opposition to high-density residential infill. *Journal of Urban Affairs*, *41*(4), 423–442. https://doi.org/10.1080/07352166.2018.1484255

Since the subprime crisis, mortgage fraud became a subject of several inquiries in the U.S. The same has not been true north of the border, where not much has been known about the extent of mortgage fraud, or he degree to which misstatements on mortgage applications affects mortgage default rates.

A recent paper by CMHC researchers, however, explored those very subjects. Kiana Basiri and Babak Mahmoudi, in a paper presented at the American Real Estate and Urban Economics Association conference in Washington, D.C., found that an increase in housing prices increased the incidence of homebuyers exaggerating their incomes on loan applications.[181]

Drs. Basiri and Mahmoudi analyzed the possible income misstatement (PIM) by first time home buyers (FTHB) by comparing the incomes reported on mortgage applications and the ones reported on tax files from 2004 to 2014. They defined PIM as the difference over time between the growth in income reported to CMHC and the growth in taxable income filed with the CRA at the Forward Sortation Area (FSA) level. FSAs are the areas representing the first three characters of a six-digit postal code. A positive PIM would suggest that incomes stated on mortgage loan applications by FTHB have grown faster than the incomes reported to the CRA. Thus, it serves as a proxy for the extent that incomes are artificially being inflated to secure loans. The study reached two interesting conclusions. First, FTHB are more likely to misstate income in real estate markets with affordability challenges. Second, they found a correlation between higher default rates and the incidence of income misstatement.

Unlike repeat homebuyers who often have access to equity from the sale of the existing dwelling unit, FTHB rely on savings, loans and gifts to put together a minimum down payment for a mortgage. Hence, they are more stressed to accumulate sufficient collateral to qualify for a desirable loan amount. Commercial banks usually require 20 per cent down payment for residential mortgage loans. CMHC provides mortgage insurance in instances where down payment is at least 5 per cent but less than 20 per cent of the loan amount. During 2004 and 2014, CMHC covered 60 to 80 per cent of the insured mortgage loan market.

---

[181] Basiri, K., & Mahmoudi, B. (2018). Possible income misstatement on mortgage loan applications: Evidence from the Canadian housing market. *Real Estate Economics.* https://onlinelibrary.wiley.com/doi/abs/10.1111/1540-6229.12310?casa_token=mIVYc7Xe5NwAAAAA:nBzrda0SnRI0odj6Sk2Z5wR4dnY3G_D QYmaZewDnHL1yt0A8gsmWEOFZnr4tfBChKSOMWhqVhOIy4Mnw

BEHIND ON THE MORTGAGE

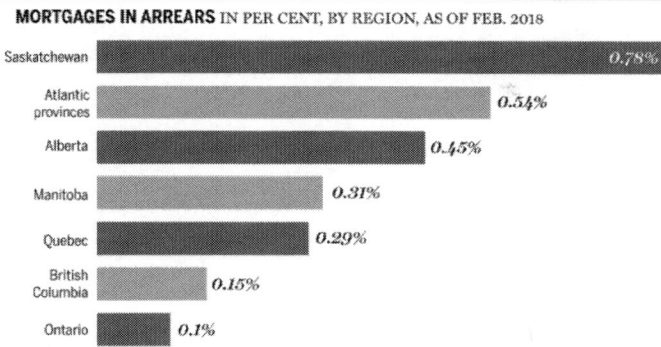

MORTGAGES IN ARREARS IN PER CENT, BY REGION, AS OF FEB. 2018

Region	Percent
Saskatchewan	0.78%
Atlantic provinces	0.54%
Alberta	0.45%
Manitoba	0.31%
Quebec	0.29%
British Columbia	0.15%
Ontario	0.1%

SOURCE: CANADIAN BANKERS ASSOCIATION   NATIONAL POST

Figure 9.3 – Percent of Mortgages that are in Arrears for Canadian Regions

The study revealed PIM was correlated with a higher rate of mortgage arrears, which represented mortgages that are 90 days or more past due within five years of loan origination. Furthermore, the study also found that an increase in PIM was correlated with an increase in insurance claims that are made once a mortgage has foreclosed.

The correlation between income exaggeration and mortgage default should not raise alarms about the state of mortgage finance in Canada. The Canadian Bankers Association reports a very low incidence of residential mortgages in arrears. At the end of February 2018, only 11,520 residential mortgages were in arrears in Canada representing a mere 0.24 per cent of all mortgages. In comparison, at the peak of the housing crisis in the U.S., the foreclosure rate was over 2.2 per cent.

Whereas housing price escalation was more pronounced in Ontario and British Columbia, their share of mortgages in arrears was lower at 0.1 and 0.15 per cent respectively. In comparison, the share of mortgages in arrears was significantly higher in Saskatchewan and other provinces where housing affordability challenges were not been as severe.

Another interesting finding was a lack of evidence for lax lending standards by mortgage finance companies (mortgage brokers), which the study defined as non-depository financial institutions. Many believe that unlike the regulated banks and other large lenders, mortgage brokers might be taking on high-risk mortgages with little due diligence on the creditworthiness of the borrowers. The study though found no evidence that suggested a higher incidence of PIM for broker-originated mortgages.

While mortgage fraud sounds alarming, the study also reported two positive outcomes in mortgage lending. First, the study did not discover a sizable difference in income growth between CMHC and CRA data. Second, income exaggeration did not escalate over the study period even when one observed a noticeable increase in housing prices across Canada.

This chapter will conclude by examining reasons why selling your house in May could result in less time on the market and a higher sales price.

IS MAY THE BEST TIME TO SELL YOUR HOUSE?

Real estate is not just about location, location, location. It's also about timing, timing, timing. Whereas location matters in real estate outcomes, the fact remains that a seller can do nothing to improve the location of an existing property. The same is not true for timing. Research has shown that sellers can optimize their returns on housing sales by picking the most opportune time to list and sell a property. And the best time to sell, for many jurisdictions across North America, is May. As temperatures in many parts of Canada start to rise, enthusiasm and hope also rise among real estate buyers and sellers.

The research arm of Zillow.com crunched large amounts of data in the U.S. and found that the "first half of May is the best time to list a home for sale to maximize sale price and minimize time on the market." How big is the payoff? Selling in May gets sellers approximately US$2,400 more than listing the property at other times.[182] Furthermore, houses sell two weeks sooner in early May on average than at other times. There is, of course, variance in the timing premium, which ranges from a high of US$15,300 in San Francisco (for late April sales) to a low of US$1,700 in Pittsburgh (in late March). While the timing payoff might be small in Pittsburgh, the speed of sales there serves as compensation: homes listed in late March, on average, sold 19.3 days sooner than at other times.

If early May is, in general, the best time to list your house, is there a best day to list? Across the U.S., Zillow found the best day to list was Saturday. For large local markets in the U.S., other "best days" included Friday and Sunday.

---

[182] Zillow. (n.d.). When Is the Best Time to Sell Your House? Retrieved from https://www.zillow.com/sellers-guide/best-time-to-sell/

SELL IN MAY

The average sale premium for U.S. cities where May was found to be the best time to list a house.

PREMIUM IN U.S. DOLLARS

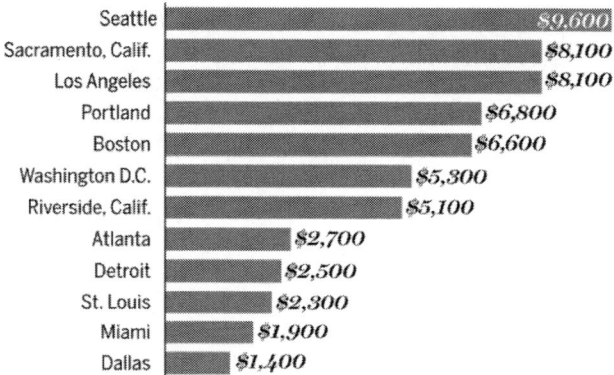

City	Premium
Seattle	$9,600
Sacramento, Calif.	$8,100
Los Angeles	$8,100
Portland	$6,800
Boston	$6,600
Washington D.C.	$5,300
Riverside, Calif.	$5,100
Atlanta	$2,700
Detroit	$2,500
St. Louis	$2,300
Miami	$1,900
Dallas	$1,400

SOURCE: ZILLOW.COM   NATIONAL POST

Figure 9.4 – Average May Sales Premium in Select U.S. Cities

Research from ATTOM Data Solutions, a firm specializing in real estate analytics, also found May to be the best month to sell. However, the best single day of the year to sell a house in the U.S. was June 28. ATTOM analyzed 14.7 million sales from 2011 to 2017 in the U.S. to conclude that May resulted in the highest premium of 5.9-percent above the estimated market value.[183] However, the average premium jumped to 9.1 per cent above the estimated market value on June 28.

Weather and consumer sentiment have a lot to do with housing sales volumes. Cold and wet weather is correlated with slower housing sales. The presence of seasonality in real estate markets, with sales rising in summer months and falling in winter months, is a well-established fact in Canada.

Anomalous weather, for example, an unexpected cold or wet spell, could also spill water on housing markets, as it did it in May 2017 in Toronto. While the housing markets were shaken up by new tax regulations announced in April 2017 and the turbulence at Home Capital, a large mortgage broker, heavy rains and flooding across the region made matters worse. Toronto received 157 mm of precipitation last May compared to just 25 mm in May 2016, and housing sales fell by 23 per cent year-over-year.

Housing experts cite several reasons why sales and prices are higher in early summer than in other months. The cold winter months, when snow

---

[183] Blomquist, D. (2018, April 25). May is the Best Month to Sell a Home Nationwide. Here's the Best Month to Sell in Your Local Market. Retrieved from https://www.attomdata.com/news/market-trends/home-sales-prices/best-time-to-sell-a-home/

piles up in curb lanes and in front of houses, are not ideal for visiting or inspecting properties. If roofs and alleyways are also covered with snow, home inspectors may be unable to vouch for a home's structural integrity. As the snow melts away and buyers shake off the winter blues, the pent-up demand for housing purchases is realized in early summer. Furthermore, houses show better with leaves on trees and green grass spread across the lawns.

Smart sellers must, therefore, add timing to the location mantra. Whereas sellers cannot pick a better location for their homes, they may pick a better time to sell.

SUMMARY

Real estate transactions are partially a result of the emotional highs and lows individuals experience as they evaluate and decide upon what real estate to buy or rent. At the same time, real estate agents, also humans, also respond to behavioural stimuli and incentives. Chapter 9 briefly discussed the behavioural underpinnings of real estate markets by looking at what motivates real estate agents, homebuyers and sellers. It looks at the thorny issues involving motivations and biases in the real estate industry, income falsification by homebuyers, and behavioural responses of buyers who might be willing to pay more for a property in a particular month of the year.

10 EMERGING TRENDS IN REAL ESTATE

When it comes to emerging trends in real estate, the focus shifts quickly to *proptech*, i.e., the use of technology in property markets. Companies bringing in technology to replace or complement the services by real estate agents, using blockchain to add additional layers of transparency, and bots to offer real time interactive advice are examples of innovation in real estate. WE recognize these trends and discuss them elsewhere in this book.

Here, instead, we review the non-tech based emerging trends. The legalization of marijuana and its impact on the demand for commercial real estate and values of nearby housing is one such example of emerging trends discussed in this chapter. Airbnb and its impact on rental housing affordability is another emerging trend in the real estate markets. Lastly, we discuss how creative developers are providing incentives to the owners of contiguous properties to sell so that the land can be developed at much higher intensities. Real markets have always been opened to embracing change and innovation. Here are some emerging trends.

THE GREEN RUSH BODES WELL FOR REAL ESTATE

They are calling it the green rush. Some are invoking comparisons with the Wild West. The legalization of recreational marijuana has generated tremendous interest and investment from all quarters, and the world of real estate has been no exception.

Millions of square feet of commercial real estate are in play. The marijuana industry in Canada requires warehouse, greenhouse and retail space to meet the demand of a growing market. While the growth presents exciting opportunities, the tremendous hype and uncertainty about how big the market will be poses real risks for investors in the real estate space.

Nevertheless, many in the commercial real estate industry believe that marijuana legalization couldn't have come at a better time, when industrial and retail rents were already showing signs of weakness owing to shrinking demand. This problem has been more acute for the retail sector, which has seen online sales compete aggressively with traditional brick-and-mortar outlets.

The experience in Colorado, the first U.S. state that legalized the recreational use of marijuana, is indicative of strong growth in demand for warehouse space for marijuana grow-ops and retail stores for distribution and sales. But how large is the demand for commercial real estate tied to marijuana production? According to the Altus Group, a large Canadian real estate firm, marijuana growing facilities have consumed 8.7 million square feet in the first nine months of 2018.[184]

The demand for real estate was more pronounced in B.C. and Ontario as marijuana grow-ops gobbled up space for warehouses, greenhouses and retail stores. Kelowna alone identified several hundred zoned sites for marijuana-oriented commerce. Logistics and distribution will generate even more demand for space.

Going forward, Alberta will see likely see significant demand for marijuana related real estate. Unlike other provinces that have restricted distribution through provincial liquor control boards, authorities in Alberta have licensed private operators for marijuana sales, opening up the possibility of innovative retail offerings. The Second Cup, for example, announced plans to convert some of their struggling locations to marijuana dispensaries.[185]

Retailers and mall operators are also pursuing marijuana businesses. Canada's largest privately-owned liquor retailer, Alcanna Inc., secured dozens of locations in Alberta to operate marijuana dispensaries.[186] In August 2018, RioCan REIT reportedly signed 18 cannabis dispensary leases in Alberta, B.C. and Ontario. High-end cannabis stores will soon be visible in malls across Canada where cannistas, like baristas before them, will help shoppers find products that suit their tastes.

In 2017, Health Canada revealed that 210,000 Canadians were licensed to use medical marijuana. Almost 11,000 individuals could grow marijuana for personal use while the rest bought it from government approved growers.[187]

---

[184] Wong, N. (2018, October 18). Demand for marijuana real estate "astronomical" as Canada legalizes. *Financial Post*. Retrieved from https://business.financialpost.com/real-estate/property-post/demand-for-pot-grow-ops-is-astronomical-as-canada-legalizes

[185] The Canadian Press. (2018, November 5). Second Cup converting 2 Alberta cafés to cannabis dispensaries, will review rest of chain. *CBC News*. Retrieved from https://www.cbc.ca/news/business/second-cup-earnings-1.4892915

[186] https://www.newcannabisventures.com/tag/alcanna/

[187] Rollason, K. (2017, October 23). Legal pot plants a growing worry. *Winnipeg Free Press*. Retrieved from https://www.winnipegfreepress.com/arts-and-life/life/cannabis/legal-pot-

With marijuana becoming available for recreational use, the number of users is likely to grow dramatically.

Statistics Canada estimated that Canadians spent almost $6 billion on marijuana in 2017. Most of the estimated five million users bought marijuana illegally for non-medical purposes. At the same time, the legal sale of alcohol reached $22 billion.[188]

The expected size of the retail marijuana market in Canada was not known for sure. Whereas the estimated sales were about $6 billion, it is not apparent how much of the demand will convert to legal channels through licensed dispensaries. Early reports from Alberta revealed that the sales from licensed stores in the first five days of legalized operations were in the millions. Nova Cannabis, owned by Alcanna Inc., reported that its five stores in Alberta registered $1.3 million in sales in the first five days alone.[189]

While the novelty of buying legal cannabis was certainly a factor, the demand bodes well for cannabis retailers, and for the owners and operators of commercial real estate in Canada.

The green rush will affect not only the commercial real estate market in Canada but residential markets as well. Pot shops will impact residential property values in surrounding neighbourhoods, and if Colorado is any indication, it might be for the better.

HOW POT SHOPS CAN DRIVE UP HOUSE PRICES

As Canada moved closer to legalizing the recreational use of marijuana, many speculated how the decision would affect society and the economy. While some were concerned about health and safety effects, others were optimistic about potential new tax revenues and the prospect of bringing the sale and distribution of marijuana out of the criminal sphere.

One area that few were talking about, however, is how legal marijuana would affect residential property markets. Writing in the prestigious journal *Real Estate Economics,* James Conklin and coauthors studied how the conversion of medical marijuana stores to recreational marijuana stores affected housing prices in Denver, Colorado where the recreational sale of marijuana was legalized in January 2014.

Their research provided strong evidence that homes located near such

---

plants-a-growing-worry-452395603.html
[188] Evans, P. (2018, January 25). Canadians spent $5.7B on marijuana last year, StatsCan estimates. *CBC News*. Retrieved from https://www.cbc.ca/news/business/marijuana-industry-1.4503152
[189] Alcanna Inc. (2018, October 23). Alcanna Provides First Results from Nova Cannabis. Retrieved from http://www.globenewswire.com/news-release/2018/10/23/1625371/0/en/Alcanna-Provides-First-Results-from-Nova-Cannabis.html

converted stores experienced a much higher increase in value than houses located farther away - as much as 8 per cent more.[190] Conklin and his co-authors were meticulous in their research. They implemented several robustness checks and falsification tests to avoid undue influence of spurious correlation. Their results remained consistent and stable and withstood the scrutiny of all tests.

Their results showed that single-family residences situated within 0.1 mile (528 feet) of a medical marijuana store that became a recreational marijuana store experienced an increase of 8 per cent relative to homes sold farther away. However, dwellings located between 0.1 mile and 0.25 mile from a converted store did not experience any proximity premium. The authors, therefore, concluded that the proximity premium was highly localized.

This finding raises several questions. For instance, why would housing prices report a proximity premium within such a small buffer zone around the converted stores? What possible benefits could a homeowner expect to derive from being that close to a marijuana dispensary, other than ease of access? Alternatively, why would a homebuyer not buy a structurally similar house that is a little further away, that was not rising in price so quickly? Equally relevant is the question of whether homebuyers who purchased homes near a marijuana store were even aware of the store's presence.

While Conklin and his coauthors were mindful of these limitations and "agnostic as to the underlying cause of our results," it is possible to speculate about some potential explanations. One possibility not raised in the study is that homes around marijuana dispensaries had been subject to a discount prior to legalization, but that legalization lifted the stigma around such homes. Another is that the stores had knock-on economic effects that were highly localized and boosted the economic profiles of their specific neighbourhoods.

While those are only guesses, theirs is not the only research demonstrating a strong linkage between the legalization of marijuana and higher housing prices.

In a paper in Economic Inquiry, Cheng Cheng and co-authors found almost similar results suggesting a 6 per cent premium in prices for homes sold in municipalities that legalized retail sales of marijuana, versus those that didn't.[191] Cheng and co-authors found that by August 2015, 46 out of the 271 incorporated municipalities in Colorado had passed laws enabling retail marijuana sales. Using even a more rigorous approach by restricting their

[190] Conklin, J., Diop, M., & Li, H. (2017). Contact High: The External Effects of Retail Marijuana Establishments on House Prices: Effects of Retail Marijuana on House Prices. *Real Estate Economics, 56*, 333. https://doi.org/10.1111/1540-6229.12220
[191] Cheng, C., Mayer, W. J., & Mayer, Y. (2018). The Effect of Legalizing Retail Marijuana On Housing Values: Evidence From Colorado. *Economic Inquiry, 56*(3), 1585–1601. https://doi.org/10.1111/ecin.12556

analysis to dwellings that sold multiple times during the study period they found similar results as Conklin and his co-authors.

The Canadian government expects annual recreational marijuana sales to be around $4 billion, which will be subject to a 10 per cent excise tax and additional provincial sales taxes. These taxes are expected to raise net new revenue mostly for provinces. Whether homeowners also see a high remains to be seen.

Airbnb is another emerging real estate trend that many housing advocates believe reduces available rental stock therefore increasing rents. However, studies have shown that, in Toronto, it is mainly mid-scale hotels that are most affected by Airbnb.

AIRBNB VS. RENTAL STOCK

Has Airbnb worsened the housing affordability for renters in large Canadian cities? Housing advocates believe that short-term rentals reduce the available rental stock thus contributing to the increase in rents. A review of the studies on Airbnb's impact on rental markets in Toronto and Vancouver suggests that there is some truth to these claims.

The short-term rental business - which operates through what are known in the industry as Online Vacation Rental Platforms (OVRP) - is one of the hallmarks of the sharing economy, allowing for peer-to-peer renting. The leading player, Airbnb, has grown from a modest rental with three airbeds in San Francisco in 2008 to a market valuation greater than that of hospitality giants like Hilton and Marriott.[192]

While short-term rentals have had a modest impact on hotels, restricted primarily to those considered budget or economy, many believe that short-term rentals have reduced the number of units that would have otherwise be available for long-term rental contracts, thus contributing to record-low rental vacancy rates and higher rents.

Despite the widespread concerns about the impact of OVRPs on long-term rental affordability, few systematic analyses of their impact on local housing markets are available. But that hasn't stopped large urban centres in Canada from implementing restrictions on the availability of short-term rentals.

Starting in September 2018, Vancouver restricted short-term rentals to primary residences. This implied that secondary suites in primary residences could be made available for short term rentals - or an entire primary residence

---

[192] Shieber, J. (2018, August 12). How Airbnb went from renting air beds for 10 to a 30 billion hospitality behemoth. *TechCrunch*. Retrieved from http://social.techcrunch.com/2018/08/12/how-airbnb-went-from-renting-air-beds-for-10-to-a-30-billion-hospitality-behemoth/

when the owner is away - but that investment properties, frequently condominiums, are ineligible.

City staff in Vancouver reported that the number of Airbnb listings fell considerably in the months after the new regulations went into force. Whereas 6,600 units were listed in April 2018, the number dropped to 3,742 units in September 2018. Media reports suggested that rents also stabilized in Vancouver.

While the correlation between new regulations and rent stability in Vancouver is apparent, one cannot imply causation because in addition to rents, housing prices and sales, which are largely not influenced by short-term rentals, also demonstrated significant weakness during that time.

Toronto city council also approved restrictions to limit the conversion of longer-term rentals to short-term. Yet an appeal to the Local Planning Appeal Tribunal pre-empted their implementation.

Meanwhile, research by Tyler Horton at the University of Ottawa found Airbnb had a small effect on rental housing.[193] He analyzed Airbnb listings in Toronto for October 2015. The study restricted the analysis to entire houses being available. Of the 4,270 Airbnb listings, many were available only on a limited basis, leaving only 2,690 listings with year-round availability. The study observed that the short-term rental units were concentrated in high-density neighbourhoods near tourist attractions. If all Airbnb units in the city's core neighbourhoods were returned to the long-term rental segment, the study found, the rental vacancy rate would increase by 3.98 per cent. For the rest of the city, if Airbnb disappeared, the vacancy rate would improve by a mere 0.2 per cent.

Similar research from the MIT's Centre for Real Estate explored the impact of Airbnb on hotels in Toronto.[194] The study found "a statistically positive impact on the change in the number of hotel room nights sold in the overall Toronto market." When the study categorized hotels into six classes based on quality, it found only the mid-scale hotels were negatively affected while the luxury and upscale hotels experienced no impact.

The regulations for short term rentals must consider both concerns over housing affordability and the need to sustain vibrant tourism in cities that attract millions of visitors each year. Various studies have shown that the impact of Airbnb and similar platforms is only modest on hotels. At the same time, research has shown that only a small fraction of the rental units viable for long-term renting is lost to short-term renting. Moreover, such units are in areas that are likely to attract tourists.

---

[193] Horton, T. (2016). *Reducing Affordability: AirBNB`s affect the Vacancy Rate and Affordability of the Toronto Rental Market* (MA, University of Ottawa). Retrieved from https://ruor.uottawa.ca/bitstream/10393/35791/1/Horton_Tyler_2016_researchpaper.pdf
[194] Mohamad, H. (2016). *Estimating the Impact of Airbnb on Hotels in Toronto* (Master of Science in Real Estate Development). Massachusetts Institute of Technology.

Stringent regulations might improve long-term rental vacancy rates but adversely affect tourism industry. A prudent approach will be to strive for a balance.

This chapter concludes with a discussion of land assembly – where adjacent homes sold together can fetch more money than if they were sold separately.

WHEN 2 + 2 IS MORE THAN 4 WITH 'LAND ASSEMBLY'

Two plus two is four, but not necessarily in land assembly. In the land-starved housing market in Vancouver, developers are incentivizing owners of contiguous homes to sell so that three or more lots can be assembled to build new condominiums. If sold individually, these homes would fetch much less. When sold together, they become more than the sum of their parts.

Plottage and plattage are essential to land development. When assembling contiguous parcels into a larger one carries more value, it's called plottage. When there is value in splitting a larger parcel into smaller units, it's called plattage.

Plattage is common in low-density greenfield developments where owners of large swaths of land sell smaller chunks for new development. In built-up areas where large empty lots are scarce, plottage is the name of the game - and Vancouver is the field where it's being played.

A 2018 trip to Vancouver revealed that developers were aggressively pursuing plottage to increase housing density and supply. In choice neighbourhoods such as Dunbar-Southlands, where single-family homes were the dominant type, and empty lots are even harder to spot than rarely seen owls on the nearby Jericho Beach, neighbours deliberated how to respond to the soft buy offers from developers.

Michelle Yu is a Vancouver-based realtor who specializes in land assembly sales. She has successfully sold 17 assembled lots. The task involves convincing owners of neighbouring lots to simultaneously put their properties up for sale.[195] The For Sale sign hanging outside the properties promptly displays "Assembly Lots," signalling to the developers the opportunity to buy the contiguous lots to redevelop as condos or townhouses.

For homeowners, the plottage dividends could be huge. In one instance, three homes built in 1979 near the Little Mountain social housing complex on Main Street were assessed for $1.4 million each. Once assembled, the

---

[195] Cheung, C. (2018). Meet the realtor transforming Vancouver one block at a time. *Vancouver Courier*. Retrieved from
https://www.vancouverisawesome.com/2018/02/21/michelle-yu-vancouver-realtor/

three units sold for more than $10 million.[196]

It's not just the developers instigating land assembly in Vancouver. In some places, such as East Broadway between Nanaimo and Rupert streets, homeowners got on with land assembly after realizing that their otherwise less glamorous 33-foot lots could fetch as high as $3.4 million in a land assembly sale.[197]

For many homeowners, receiving an offer that is significantly more than the assessed value is an attractive proposition. Being offered a multiple of the assessed value would certainly be tempting. Still, land assembly is not as common as the exorbitant buy offers would suggest. Several market and planning impediments make land assembly a tough sell.

Zoning bylaws are the obvious first hurdle. If densification is not on the cards and on the land use maps, land assembly for high density development will not be possible. While the tall residential towers near downtown Vancouver might give the impression of high density living, Greater Vancouver, as proxied by the Vancouver Census Metropolitan Area (CMA), is comprised essentially of low-to medium-density neighbourhoods.

Our research, using the 2016 Census data, shows that of the 480-odd census tracts (neighbourhoods) that make up the Vancouver CMA, fewer than one fifth of the neighbourhoods boast a population density of 6,400 persons per square kilometre or higher. In fact, several choice neighbourhoods along commercial streets have residential population densities between 1,500 and 6,000 persons per sq. km.

These neighbourhoods can certainly use some density when older and less attractive units are replaced by modern-looking higher density developments that need not be high-rises. Some of the medium-density neighbourhoods in Vancouver have not seen an increase in population and are therefore stuck with a stagnant or shrinking property tax base. In fact, certain parts of neighbourhoods such as Dunbar-Southlands and Arbutus Ridge reported a population loss between 2011 and 2016.

[196] ibid
[197] Slattery, J. (2017, January 8). Attempted land assembly deal has 33-foot East Vancouver lots listed for $3.4 million. *Global News*. Retrieved from https://globalnews.ca/news/3168279/attempted-land-assembly-deal-has-33-foot-east-vancouver-lots-listed-for-3-4-million/

NOT TOO DENSE

Most neighbourhoods in Vancouver show low-to-medium population density

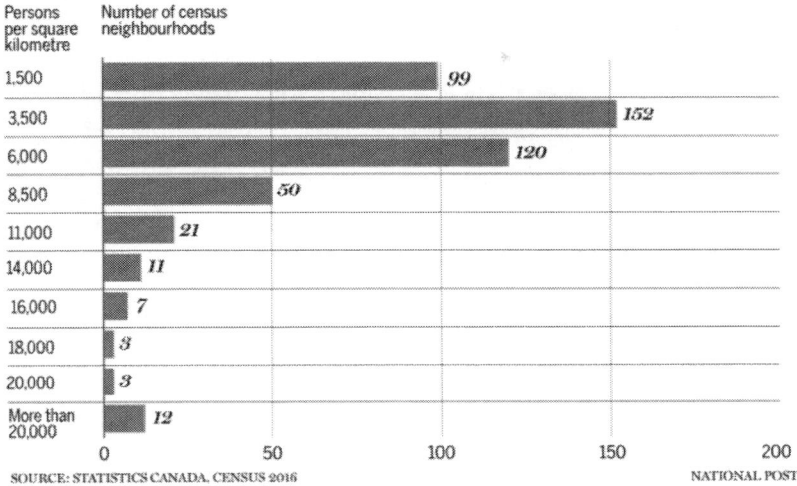

Persons per square kilometre	Number of census neighbourhoods
1,500	99
3,500	152
6,000	120
8,500	50
11,000	21
14,000	11
16,000	7
18,000	3
20,000	3
More than 20,000	12

SOURCE: STATISTICS CANADA, CENSUS 2016   NATIONAL POST

Figure 10.1 – Population Density of Neighbourhoods in the Vancouver Census Metropolitan Area

The other impediment is Vancouver's high housing prices that could still be too high for some as they try to re-enter the housing market after selling their smaller house in a land-assembly deal. And of course, the NIMBYs are always omnipresent trying to block any change on their block.

Despite claims by some academics, Vancouver, just like Toronto, has a housing supply problem. When prices escalate rapidly, it is mostly because not enough new housing of the right type at the right location at the right time is entering the market.

New residential developments of modest scale and density when done by professional developers, and not by homeowners masquerading as builders, can help replace dilapidated housing stock with newer, attractive units that will bring new neighbours who will also help expand the local property tax base.

SUMMARY

Lifestyles are not constant over time. Taste preferences change and new trends emerge. Real estate is not immune to such shifts in tastes and styles. Consumption of marijuana for recreational use was, until recently, illegal in Canada. It is now legal for adults to consumer marijuana for recreational uses under some limitations. The cultural and legal shift has implications for real estate markets. The aforementioned discussion shows how the demand for warehouses space might be affected by the legalization of marijuana.

Furthermore, the proximate location to a marijuana dispensary might have an impact on property values.

As taste parameters and the resulting socio-economic realities shift, it creates room for innovation and emergence of new trends. How space is being used today and how it may be used I the future will rely on how societal needs and preferences change. There will always be emerging trends in real estate.

11 THE FINTECH & HIGH-TECH OF REAL ESTATE

For a potential buyer, a house's list price conveys only partial information. What the house sold for in the past and the sold price of recent comparables are equally desirable for a smart consumer.

Potential homebuyers in Canada can search the MLS database online and explore structural details of housing units down to pictures of toilet bowls and shower stalls. They also have access to the asking prices. What the houses sold for in the past is the forbidden fruit hidden behind the MLS firewall.

That information was also the subject of a long and contentious legal battle between the Competition Bureau and the Toronto Real Estate Board, with the former hoping to make that data more accessible to the public, and the latter arguing it should be tightly held due to privacy issues. The Federal Court of Appeal confirmed a ruling in favour of the Competition Bureau.

In a world where digitization of the economy has added unprecedented economic value, is it wise to argue against liberating data or restricting its dissemination by fax, phone, or hard copy? Real-time dissemination of housing sales data with a fuller set of information will open housing markets to innovative products and services. It will increase the size and scope of real estate markets for the benefit of realtors and consumers alike.

Timely and complete information leads to better decisions. A simple thought experiment can establish this fact. Let's assume, as a prospective homebuyer, you have shortlisted two houses in different neighbourhoods. Both houses are priced at $995,000. You visit both houses and learn from listing agents that the recent comparable sales averaged at $800,000 for one house and $650,000 for the other. Will learning about the difference between a house's list price and the average sale price of recent comparables change your perspective? One house is listed for 24-percent more than comparables versus the other for 53-percent more. If you had known the sale price of the comparables in advance of the visit, which required investing time and effort, would you have shortlisted the same two houses for a visit? Latent in the sold price data are clues for homebuyers that influence their decision-making. As it stands, homebuyers must obtain this information from real estate agents. This adds a lag in information dissemination that could affect expectations and perspectives.

HOUSE HUNTING
IN THE DIGITAL AGE

Where homebuyers in the U.S. found their homes in 2016

Directly from sellers/Knew the sellers	1%
Print newspaper advertisement	1%
Directly from sellers/Knew the sellers	1%
Print newspaper advertisement	1%
Home builder or their agent	2%
Friend, relative or neighbor	4%
Yard sign/open house sign	8%
Real estate agent	34%
Internet	51%

SOURCE: 2016 NATIONAL ASSOCIATION OF REALTORS' PROFILE OF HOME BUYERS AND SELLERS

NATIONAL POST

Figure 11.1 Where U.S Homebuyers Found Their Homes (2016)

The longer it takes to learn about the difference in a house's asking price and the sold price of comparables, the more likely one is to develop preferences with incomplete information. This is not to suggest that consumers are incapable of revising their preferences when more information becomes available at a later stage. Nevertheless, it stands to reason that consumers are more likely to make informed choices at the very beginning of a search conducted with full information as opposed to at even later stages of one in which information is released over time or with restrictions on the way it is disseminated.

The case for keeping the sales price data out of the public's direct reach is often made for privacy reasons. It has been argued that buyers and sellers would prefer sold prices to be kept off-line. This is nothing more than a red herring.

Housing sales details, including sold price, are a matter of public record and are available, albeit not readily, from municipal and other registries. To argue that sold price should only be revealed to customers by a real estate agent is akin to arguing that a legal verdict should only be shared via lawyers because of confidentiality reasons. But that's not the case. One can readily access case history in Canada online with financial details of the litigants.

Equally relevant to the debate is the fate of pending sales data. Before a sale closes (and is officially registered by the authorities), it stays in a real estate purgatory often for a time varying between less than a week to many months. This implies that while a sale has been contracted, it hasn't closed. For the timeliness of data, the pending sales price is the most relevant piece of information for future and impending sales and consumer decision-making.

If pending sales data and earlier sold prices were made available online, which many innovative brokers desire, it opens the door to innovative products. For instance, automated valuation models could be implemented to offer statistically robust estimates of housing values using real-time data to benefit buyers and sellers alike.

Bourses have been providing real-time data for stocks, bonds and other financial products for decades. The innovative financial products and services that resulted from real-time disclosure of financial data should be a cause of optimism for those opposing the liberation of real estate data.

Millennials will soon be the largest cohort of first-time homebuyers, and they will be seeking real estate advice through advanced online platforms. Technology-based solutions, such as those offered by Nobul, will provide a digital marketplace where real estate agents will seek out buyers and sellers and are rated for the quality of their services muck like Uber drivers.

THE UBER OF REAL ESTATE IS COMING

Matches are made in heaven, or so we are told. But in today's hyper-connected world, matches are increasingly made in cyberspace, and real estate is increasingly no exception.

Before buyers and sellers are matched for sale, they need to be matched to real estate agents. Those interested in selling a property need an agent to list the property on the Multiple Listing Service. In the past, it was either word of mouth, a chance flyer from a realtor in your mailbox, or a billboard that would bring an agent and a prospective client together.

In the future, real estate, as it embraces technology, will empower consumers through more efficient and transparent marketplaces. Already, the industry is seeking to update the legal framework that governs it in order to promote transparency, especially as it applies to situations such as bidding wars, when buyers are left in the dark as to the bids of others.

As for technology, instead of buyers and sellers searching for an agent, the agents will be competing for their business. Canadian entrepreneurs have already started to implement technology-based solutions. Some of these platforms are nascent yet present a picture of marketplaces that will soon become the norm.

Nobul.com is one example of a digital marketplace that helps agents, buyers, and sellers find products and services efficiently. The digital marketplace is designed for agents to compete for business thus providing buyers and sellers with the opportunity to compare services and choose an agent whose offerings they like the most.

Nobul.com's model can be explained with an example. Let's say you are interested in selling your home. You would like to know what services agents offer and how much commission they will charge in return. You create an account on Nobul.com at no cost and provide details of your property. Soon, you will start receiving proposals from agents who would list the services they offer and the commission they charge.

Now, imagine such a platform to have been running for years and has thousands of real estate agents actively assisting the customers who in turn rate the agents for the quality of their service. Agents with higher ratings for quality and competitiveness will have an edge in the digital marketplace. A seller who is approached by numerous agents could choose one with a competitive bid and higher rating.

Digital matchmaking is certainly not a new idea. Computer-assisted matchmaking services were first introduced in the late 1950s. However, for such services to have a mass appeal required a massive networking platform, the internet. But that took some time and innovation. Internet-based dating services, such as Match.com, were finally up and running by the mid-nineties. Numerous others followed. Tinder, a popular location aware social media app, was launched in 2012, bringing the practice of swiping left or right to prominence.

The adoption of technology has never been uniform across all cohorts. A Pew Research Centre Survey revealed that in 2015, almost 15 per cent of the American adults have tried online dating.[198] A 2017 survey of the newly married revealed that 19 per cent of the brides had met their spouses online. The adoption of digital platforms, however, is more pervasive among younger cohorts. The Pew survey found that young adults, between the ages of 18 and 24, were more likely to use online dating services with more than one in four reported to have tried the online platforms. With millennials and Generation Z growing in numbers and economic clout over time, digital solutions and marketplaces will likely see greater acceptance and use.

Millennials are also going to be the largest cohort of first-time homebuyers. They would have no previous relationship with real estate agents and hence would need referrals. Parents and friends could be the ones referring agents to them. However, given their proclivity for all things digital,

---

[198] Smith, A. (2016, February 11). 15% of American Adults Have Used Online Dating Sites or Mobile Dating Apps. *Pew Research Center*. Retrieved from https://www.pewresearch.org/internet/2016/02/11/15-percent-of-american-adults-have-used-online-dating-sites-or-mobile-dating-apps/

millennials and even younger cohorts are likely to search for solutions online.

Digital matchmaking services have disrupted or interrupted several industries. Uber and other online ride-sharing apps have disrupted the taxi service business model by matching riders with drivers. Airbnb and other online hospitality services have interrupted (i.e., not yet disrupted) the hospitality and tourism business by matching short-term guests with those offering lodging. In both instances, younger cohorts have rushed to adopt the new digital platforms.

Given favourable demographics, digital matchmaking in the real estate vertical is likely to grow. The key to success is not just technology but also service. These platforms will have to be more than a matchmaker. Quality control and responsiveness to customer needs will be the key as the business grows from being a niche to becoming mainstream.

Along with digital matchmaking, computational advances in blockchain and artificial intelligence will also reshape the real estate sector. One possible application is in the mass appraisal market that involves determining the value of groups of properties at a given time.

BLOCKCHAIN AND AI WILL RESHAPE REAL ESTATE

Innovations in computing and information technologies are transforming businesses at an unprecedented pace. The real estate sector will not be spared, and that's good news. Advances in artificial intelligence, analytics and blockchain will improve the real estate industry by achieving greater efficiencies and identifying and mitigating risks.

While real estate will remain true to its traditional brick-and-mortar roots, technological innovations will transform the way the sector operates. Consider blockchain, which offers great promise for transparency, data accuracy, and data aggregation. Essentially, a blockchain is a "distributed database that maintains a growing list of data items and that is hardened against manipulation and counterfeiting," explained Jan Veuger in the journal *Facilities* in 2017.[199]

Once a block is added, it acts as a "building passport." It allows one to aggregate all relevant information about a building in one place from ownership records to structural details down to the latest renovations. Such information can be made readily available to those interested.

---

[199] Veuger, J. (2017). Attention to disruption and blockchain creates a viable real estate economy. *Journal of US-China Public Administration*, *14*(5), 263–285.
https://www.researchgate.net/profile/Jan_Veuger/publication/322392878_Attention_to_Disruption_and_Blockchain_Creates_a_Viable_Real_Estate_Economy/links/5b7c2e61299bf1d5a719de02/Attention-to-Disruption-and-Blockchain-Creates-a-Viable-Real-Estate-Economy.pdf

Another example of technological innovation is valuation models. For centuries, the value of a real estate asset was determined by expert opinion that involved examining earlier comparable sales, applying some judgments and coming up with an estimate. The process was error- and bias-prone.

The practice was transformed in the past few decades when statistical models effectively replaced the expert estimates. The use of computer algorithms in valuation became the norm. Advances in data storage and computing powers meant that statistical models improved in predictive accuracy.

Advances in analytics imply that even more sophisticated computing algorithms will be the norm in the valuation space. Whereas statistical models of the regression type are common today, the future will see a wider application of machine learning algorithms including Artificial Neural Networks (ANN) and Support Vector Machines (SVM).

Computational advances are likely to transform the mass appraisal market that involves determining the values of groups of properties at a given time.

Big users of mass valuation models are public sector entities responsible for property taxation. The property tax is calculated for all properties at a given date, which requires estimating the value of each property in the tax roll. Not getting the valuation right could lead to expensive litigation costing millions.

The other big users of mass valuation are mortgage lenders who would like to ascertain the value of a property before extending the loan. Again, getting the value wrong could expose the lender to greater risk.

Research shows that machine learning algorithms offer improved performance for predictive analytics. The gains over the traditional regression type models are even higher when data depict non-linearities.

Numerous startups have emerged in the U.S. and Canada trying to get a piece of the automated valuation business in real estate. The startups have met with varying degrees of success in securing venture capital. The real success though is their ability to deliver an accurate valuation of real properties. For this, they must rely on not just the best algorithms but also the best data.

Garbage in, garbage out applies to the AI world as well. An AI or machine learning model learns from the data we feed to train the algorithm. Poor quality data means poor training and inferior forecasts. Thus, the future success of predictive modelling is incumbent on improving techniques to weed out outliers and erroneous data.

AI, therefore, needs blockchain to access high-quality property data. Advances in AI models are focused on replicating the workings of a human brain. It is rather odd that computer-based models were introduced earlier to replace human decision-making with algorithm-based tools.

The future is far from certain. If computers can think like humans, will they make the same cognitive mistakes that humans make? Or being artificially intelligent, will computers be able to mimic human decision-making without being swayed by emotions? Real estate transactions, especially housing, may never be devoid of emotions.

If AI implies intelligence without emotions, valuation models may depict a greater variance between estimates generated by humans and computers. It's free will and the readiness to be swayed by emotions that separates humans from robots. AI-driven automated valuation models are fast improving in statistical intelligence. Emotional intelligence, though, is hard to machine learn.

Real estate industry players that fail to innovate risk being left behind. Case in point is the Toronto Real Estate Board's (TREB) unwillingness to share detailed home sales data online which restricts consumer choice. However, there is an opportunity for TREB to adapt by embracing analytics and becoming not just a data vendor but a purveyor of property market insight.

LET THE REAL ESTATE INDUSTRY INNOVATE

In August 2018, the Supreme Court dismissed the Toronto Real Estate Board's (TREB) application seeking leave to appeal an earlier federal court decision in which the Competition Bureau had accused TREB of anti-competitive practices. The decision paved the way for property (especially housing) sales data to be made readily available to buyers and sellers.[200]

However, TREB's response to the ruling suggested that it would be some time before consumers benefit from the innovations in big data, Artificial Intelligence (AI), and analytics, which have transformed many industries in the past, but have largely bypassed the real estate industry in Canada.

TREB is the largest real estate board in Canada with over 50,000 members. The Board resisted past attempts to launch discount brokerages and prevented Board members from listing detailed home sales data, especially sale prices, online. This has created an information asymmetry between listing agents and prospective buyers, as the only way to get sale price information was to approach a real estate agent.

The Supreme Court order changed all that. According to a statement by the Competition Bureau, TREB had to remove "restrictions on the display of historical listings and sale prices online through virtual office websites" (VOW).[201]

---

[200] Kalinowski, T. (2018, August 23). Supreme Court dismisses real estate board's appeal application on sold data. *The Toronto Star*. Retrieved from https://www.thestar.com/business/real_estate/2018/08/23/supreme-court-dismisses-real-estate-boards-appeal-application-on-sold-data.html

[201] Noakes, S. (2018, August 23). TREB loses Supreme Court bid to appeal release of real estate sold figures. *CBC News*. Retrieved from https://www.cbc.ca/news/business/treb-real-

TREB, in an advisory to its members, appeared to be complying with the court order. However, TREB warned that those members who would like to make "sold, withdrawn, expired, suspended or terminated listing information available" must do so "in compliance with the VOW Agreement", which allows access to data through a password-protected VOW "operated by a TREB Member for informational purposes in the context of residential real estate transactions."[202]

TREB lists residential and nonresidential properties for sale and rent. The above suggests that TREB allowed only residential property data to be made available through VOW. It's not explicitly stated but can be assumed that residential rental transactions could also be listed on VOWs.

However, TREB, even after the Supreme Court order, refused to let its members derive or share any insights from the real estate transaction data. It cautioned the members that the "data cannot be scraped, mined, sold, resold, licensed, reorganized or monetized in any way, including through the sale of derivative products or marketing reports."

In a world awash with data and analytics, TREB decided to join the ranks of digital-age Luddites. For decades the real estate boards in Canada have been data rich and insight poor. The wealth of information TREB holds cannot be subject to datamining for the benefit of Board members or the consumers.

Recent advances in analytics, AI, and data science have transformed entire economies where data-driven intelligence has led to greater profits, larger markets and reduced inherent risks. This became possible because smart businesses used data to generate insights for evidence-based decision-making.

At the same time, businesses let their data be used in innovative ways by others for the larger benefit of the industry. Just look at the airline industry, which opened the doors to its data so that innovative entrepreneurs could generate online solutions that helped grow the airline business.

Even traditional businesses, such as Walmart, transformed their core by using data as a competitive advantage. Walmart's agile supply chain is an excellent example of how data-driven business models reduce overheads and inventory sizes for greater profits.

Smart businesses do not rely just on in-house capabilities to analyze data for better insights. They are making proprietary data available for hackathons where data scientists compete to develop improved predictive analytics.

Netflix is just one example of a company that crowd-sourced algorithms for better client services. Alphabet (Google's parent company), Facebook and

estate-sale-prices-1.4795903
[202] Dingman, S. (2018, September 3). TREB presses brokers on data protection. *The Globe and Mail.* Retrieved from https://www.theglobeandmail.com/real-estate/article-treb-presses-brokers-on-data-protection/

Twitter are among the largest businesses in the world, and their raisons d'être are nothing but data and analytics.

TREB and other boards generate data and content that drive millions to their websites - they are content and data rich. The natural next step in TREB's evolution is to embrace analytics and become not just a data vendor but a purveyor of property market insight. But instead of encouraging and facilitating that transition, TREB tried to restrict it. It imposed unproductive constraints on the use of data by limiting its use to providing "residential real estate brokerage services between a Realtor and a client or customer."
TREB's lack of imagination and initiative are preventing innovation and restricting consumer choices. Ignorance is not bliss. And it's not folly to be wise. Why TREB believes so remains a puzzle.

In the following section we will consider the fate of real estate agents and the traditional brick-and-mortar brokerage model as technology continues to evolve.

AGENTS WILL SURVIVE THE ONLINE BROKERAGE ERA

When it comes to technology, the choice is between disrupting and being disrupted. Real estate brokerages are no exception. Adapting to the times and technology is the key not only to success but to survival.

In June 2018, TheRedPin, a real estate tech startup in Toronto, called it quits and entered receivership. TheRedPin was one of the early adopters of technology in the sector, and tried to harness the value latent in real estate transaction data with artificial intelligence and deep learning. Yet the journey from a promising start to receivership lasted just seven years. Traditional brokerages, in comparison, last for decades if not longer.

Data and knowledge-based industries are in a state of disequilibrium. Since they rely heavily on technology, which is evolving rapidly, getting the right model is proving hard for many. Thus, laggards and leaders both share unique risks and vulnerabilities.

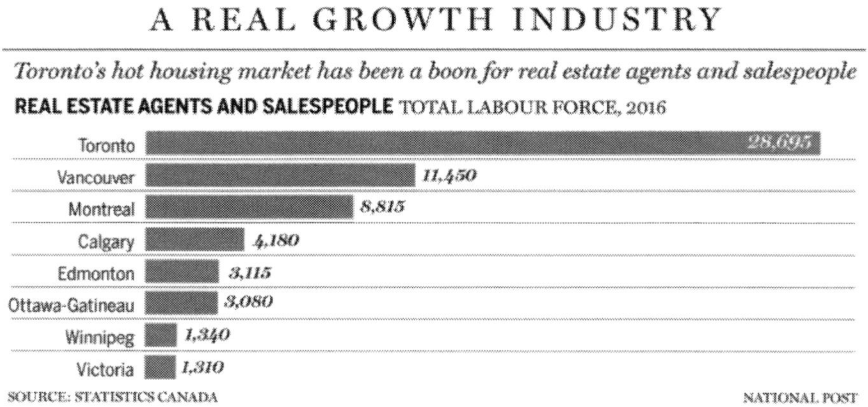

A REAL GROWTH INDUSTRY

Toronto's hot housing market has been a boon for real estate agents and salespeople

REAL ESTATE AGENTS AND SALESPEOPLE TOTAL LABOUR FORCE, 2016

Toronto	28,695
Vancouver	11,450
Montreal	8,815
Calgary	4,180
Edmonton	3,115
Ottawa-Gatineau	3,080
Winnipeg	1,340
Victoria	1,310

SOURCE: STATISTICS CANADA   NATIONAL POST

Figure 11.2 – Number of Real Estate Agents and Salespeople in Canadian Cities (2016)

As the real estate industry transforms, brokerages and agents strive to adopt. Some are predicting a demise of the traditional brick-and-mortar brokerage model. Others suggest that the days of real estate agents are numbered.

Voxel Worlds is a tech company in the U.S. that aims to complement the real estate industry with virtual reality tools. Max Agrad, its president, argues that "the internet has solved the information asymmetry problem faced by homebuyers." Thus, he predicts "real estate agents will be obsolete in a few years."[203] Agrad's conviction is perhaps rooted in a $2-million first-round funding from investors who share his enthusiasm about technology replacing agents in the real estate industry.

Yet, the frequent demise of similar tech startups and the longevity of the established brokerages raises doubts about such unbridled enthusiasm for change. Technology will continue to transform the real estate industry. Brick-and-mortar brokerages are likely to adapt click-and-order paradigms. Still, real estate agents remain at the heart of buying and selling real estate. Better technology will improve the way people search for information about the real property. But helping during the search is only one aspect of what a real estate agent can bring to the table.

Even contemplating a world where offers are made, negotiated and ultimately accepted digitally, there are still many ways an agent can provide value. For one, real estate agents calm anxious buyers and sellers. As soon as a binding offer is accepted, buyers wonder if they have paid too much while sellers wonder if they have sold it too quickly and a better offer might still be out there. Providing perspective on the wider market and understanding

---

[203] Randall, S. (2018, June 19). "Real estate agents will be obsolete in a few years." claims tech chief. Retrieved from https://www.canadianrealestatemagazine.ca/market-update/real-estate-agents-will-be-obsolete-in-a-few-years--claims-tech-chief-244089.aspx

trends are not easy skills to replicate.

It is for this kind of reason that eXp Realty, a U.S.-based brokerage that uses a virtual office environment, continues to add agents to its roster.[204] The company announced this week that it has doubled the number of real estate agents to 12,000 in a matter of months. The company trades on NASDAQ and reached a market cap of one billion dollars in 2018. It even expanded into British Columbia.

At the same time, traditional brokerages such as Long & Foster continue to survive and expand. Cofounded by Wes Foster in 1968 and staffed with 11,000 agents, the Virginia-based realtor was the largest independent real estate brokerage by sales volume in the United States in 2018. They have seen and embraced change over the past 50 years.

Ignoring the forecasts of doom and gloom, Home Services of America, an affiliate of Warren Buffett's Berkshire Hathaway, acquired Long & Foster in September 2017.[205] Also, it doesn't have to be an either-or choice between brick-and-mortar and click-and-order. There is room for fusion between the two models. Consider that the U.S.-based Zillow Group Inc., a real estate information company with a market cap of over US$12 billion, partnered with Century 21, a traditional real estate brokerage in Canada to display Century 21's listings on Zillow's web portals.[206] In June 2018, Zillow carried detailed information on more than 110 million homes in the U.S.

While real estate businesses will adapt to survive, and some may disappear making room for new innovative ones, real estate agents are likely to stay for a longer time. Their utility will not diminish in a tech-centric environment. That's the reason why Wes Foster believes "good agents will always be needed."[207]

The next section will discuss why Canadian governments need more up-to-date data on mortgage fraud given that more Canadians are exaggerating earnings and understating liabilities on loan applications due to rising home prices, high debt, and regulatory changes.

---

[204] https://www.exprealty.com/

[205] McCallister, D. (2017, September 8). Long & Foster Sold To Warren Buffett's HomeServices Of America. Retrieved from https://www.npr.org/sections/thetwo-way/2017/09/08/549359615/long-foster-sold-to-warren-buffetts-homesevices-of-america

[206] Zillow. (2018, June 6). Zillow Partners with CENTURY 21 Canada; Will Feature Canadian Listings on Zillow This Year. Retrieved from http://zillow.mediaroom.com/2018-06-06-Zillow-Partners-with-CENTURY-21-Canada-Will-Feature-Canadian-Listings-on-Zillow-This-Year

[207] Haider, M., & Moranis, S. (2018, June 21). Don't expect real estate agents to disappear any time soon. *Financial Post*. Retrieved from https://financialpost.com/real-estate/dont-expect-real-estate-agents-to-disappear-any-time-soon

WHY CANADA NEEDS MORE DATA ON MORTGAGE FRAUD

People looking to buy homes in the red-hot early 2018 Toronto housing market received something of a reprieve, as sales and prices both declined, though the latter only modestly. But while prices fell relative to the peak in early 2017, they remained significantly elevated relative to household income levels.

At the same time, household debt in Canada continued to grow, hitting $1.8 trillion if you include mortgage debt. Once all types of debt are considered, Canadian households owed $1.71 for every dollar of disposable income. Excluding mortgages, the average debt per person was $22,837.[208]

The combination of prices growing faster than incomes, high debt, and regulatory changes - such as stress tests requiring households to qualify at a significantly higher interest rate - put households in a difficult financial bind. Even law-abiding individuals could find themselves tempted to embellish their earnings or understate their liabilities in the bid to secure a mortgage for their family's dream home.

The prospect of a spike in mortgage fraud in Canada was raised in February 2018, when the ratings agency S&P Global Ratings warned that it expected the phenomenon to increase, and potentially even pose a risk to the big banks.[209] With memories of subprime mortgages triggering the Great Recession still fresh, any suggestion of an elevated risk of mortgage fraud was bound to raise concerns among regulators and lenders.

So was Canada heading towards a subprime-like crisis? Something that extreme seemed highly unlikely, but there was a need for a greater understanding of the dynamics of the Canadian market. The data on mortgage fraud was slightly dated. Equifax Canada in January 2017 reported that suspected fraudulent mortgage applications had risen by 52 per cent since 2013.[210] Equifax noted that falsified account statements were the most common indicators of possible mortgage fraud.

Did this mean that prospective buyers were lying on their mortgage applications by either embellishing their incomes or understating their liabilities? Equifax couldn't say for certain as it could not entirely attribute the

---

[208] Evans, P. (2017, December 14). Canadians owe $1.71 for every dollar of disposable income they have — a new record high. *CBC News*. Retrieved from https://www.cbc.ca/news/business/debt-income-1.4448098

[209] McNeely, A. (2018, February 26). S&P warns more mortgage fraud could emerge at Canadian banks. *Bloomberg News*. Retrieved from https://www.bnnbloomberg.ca/mortgage-fraud-prompts-s-p-to-lower-canada-bank-risk-metric-1.1009395

[210] Equifax Canada. (2017, January 11). Equifax Canada: Mortgage Fraud on the Rise. Retrieved from https://www.consumer.equifax.ca/about-equifax/press-releases/-/blogs/equifax-canada-mortgage-fraud-on-the-rise/

increase in suspicious applications to "consumers overstating personal income or falsifying applications."

Since subprime mortgage lending had a large role in instigating the Great Recession, mortgage lending came under greater scrutiny in the U.S. where information about the prevalence and scope of mortgage fraud was more readily available.

The U.S. experience revealed that whereas households may be guilty of indulging in "little white lies" in their applications, the real harm to financial systems came from organized mortgage fraud perpetrated by industry insiders or organized criminals. Lax standards set by unscrupulous lenders or brokers, who are motivated by commissions tied to the underwriting volumes, hold a greater responsibility than individual households whose primary motivation is to become a homeowner.

An article in *Real Estate Issues* in 2012 noted that the FBI categorizes mortgage fraud as "a material misstatement, misrepresentation, or omission relied on by an underwriter or lender to fund, purchase, or insure a loan." The Bureau estimated annual losses from mortgage fraud to be in the range of US$4 billion to US$6 billion in 2012.[211]

FBI collects mortgage fraud data from Suspicious Activity Reports (SARs) filed by the federally insured financial institutions. The number of SARs increased from 26,000 in 2005 to 92,000 in 2011. In March 2018, Barclays Bank was fined US$2 billion in the U.S. to settle claims by investors who purchased toxic mortgage-backed securities from the bank back in 2007.[212]

Unlike U.S. mortgage fraud data, estimates for Canada are hard to come by. Apart from the infrequent press releases by rating agencies and credit monitoring firms, hard evidence for the extent and scope of mortgage fraud and default is missing in Canada.

Canadian regulators and lenders must collaborate to monitor, identify and prosecute mortgage fraud in Canada. Despite higher levels of household debt, Canadian household finances were stable with consumer bankruptcies down by 1.7 per cent and 90-day plus delinquency rates falling by 6.4 per cent yea-rover-year in April 2018.

This was, however, no reason to be complacent. Economic conditions and household fortunes may change fast and unexpectedly. There is an urgent need to understand the economics of mortgage fraud in Canada. Vigilant and

[211] Stowell, N. F., Barker-Cagwin, K., & Fellows, J. (2012). Mortgage fraud: Current trends and issues. *Real Estate Issues*, 37(2), 42–51. https://www.cre.org/wp-content/uploads/2017/04/37_2_3_Mortgage_Fraud.pdf

[212] Morris, S., & Finch, G. (2018, March 29). Barclays Wins Its DOJ Gamble With $2 Billion Mortgage Settlement. *Bloomberg News*. Retrieved from https://www.bloomberg.com/news/articles/2018-03-29/barclays-agrees-to-pay-2-billion-to-settle-u-s-rmbs-suit

transparent monitoring of mortgage finance will build confidence in Canadian financial institutions.

The final section of this chapter will consider how the facility management industry should adopt smart technologies and training programs to build and maintain more energy-efficient green structures.

SMART BUILDINGS ARE GETTING SMARTER, BUT CAN MANAGERS KEEP UP?

With trillions of dollars in commercial real estate assets, building and facility managers are searching for innovative ways to maintain structures in a state of good repair while reducing operating costs by cutting waste and energy consumption.

In the United States alone, buildings account for 40 per cent of the total energy consumed in 2019, which outpaces energy used up by any other sector.

Developments in communication and information technology, advanced computing, and smart algorithms in a hyper-connected world present new opportunities for managing buildings and structures. Enabled by technology, smart buildings have the potential to consume less energy, generate less waste, and provide better quality spaces to inhabitants.

While the concept of energy-efficient green buildings is appealing, its implementation relies on a smart workforce to join the ranks of building and facility managers. A trade show focusing on building and facility management revealed that the shortage of skilled professionals could be the Achilles heel for the energy-efficient future. A series of expert panels at the REMI Show '19 in Toronto discussed how the Internet of Things, which enables an extensive network of interconnected computers, sensors and objects combined with smart algorithms driven by deep learning and artificial intelligence, has the potential to transform building and facility management.[213]

Whereas 2019 estimates of the market for smart technology in facility management stand at around US$15 billion, that figure was expected to soon grow to $137 billion.

The use of data in building management reveals performance indicators that remain hidden otherwise. A 2015 article in the journal *Sustainable Cities and Society* reported water use from 2,046 multi-residential buildings in New York City.[214] The buildings had a minimum size of 50,000 square feet. The

---

[213] https://www.remishow.com/rapidly-evolving-real-estate-ind

[214] Kontokosta, C. E., & Jain, R. K. (2015). Modeling the determinants of large-scale building water use: Implications for data-driven urban sustainability policy. *Sustainable Cities and Society*, *18*, 44–55. https://doi.org/10.1016/j.scs.2015.05.007

research found that buildings "in neighbourhoods with a greater proportion of renter-occupied units have far higher water use intensity than similar-owner occupied structures." At the same time, water use was found to be lower in co-op buildings. Without data, it would not be possible to know what type of neighbourhoods or buildings have higher or lower water consumption.

While data enables the facility management industry to make smart decisions, the industry faces labour force challenges. The aging workforce implies that many front-line workers will soon be retiring. The industry is struggling with attracting younger cohorts. Careers in facility management are not high on the list of professional pursuits of Millennials and Generation Z. Furthermore, the opportunities to train building managers in analytics are also limited.

The nature of work in the future is somewhat uncertain. Advances in automation and artificial intelligence are likely to disrupt the work being done by humans. Many jobs will disappear when autonomous machines replace human labour. However, evolving technologies are giving birth to new opportunities and careers. Facility management is one such field that is about to transform from being hardware focused to software enabled.

Modern buildings are equipped with thousands of sensors recording air quality, humidity, motion, temperature and the presence of noxious gases. The sensors continuously record energy consumption and waste. Smart algorithms running on networked computers analyze sensor-generated data in real time.

The advanced instrumentation generates sophisticated building performance statistics that are displayed on information dashboards. The workforce needed to make informed and smart decisions from the treasure trove of sensor-generated data needs to be both building-science and data-science savvy. Such workers are in very short supply.

Research by Stanford University's Professor Rishee K Jain, which was published in the journal *Building and Environment*, also observed that those responsible for building energy management "lack the background and experience in data analytics and/or resources to create, interpret and translate results of complex simulations into actionable insights."[215] Their research concluded that "professionals need more and improved training, especially for simulation tools."

The facility management industry will be one of the largest sources of instrument-generated data. Most colleges and universities in Canada do not offer degrees in analytics applied to building energy management.

[215] Srivastava, C., Yang, Z., & Jain, R. K. (2019). Understanding the adoption and usage of data analytics and simulation among building energy management professionals: A nationwide survey. *Building and Environment*, *157*, 139–164. https://doi.org/10.1016/j.buildenv.2019.04.016

Educational programs to train workers in building informatics, a cross between building science and data science, is an example of a forward-thinking curriculum that will prepare the workforce for the fast-evolving field of building and energy management.

SUMMARY

The advances in computer and information technology have impacted all sectors of the economy and are now increasingly impacting the real estate industry. Chapter 11 identified how ubiquitous computing and information technology are creating new ways to bring buyers and sellers together. The real estate brokerage industry is set for a reset with technology ready to redefine the transactional landscape but also providing ways and avenues to expand the scope of businesses possible in the real estate sector. At the same time, upcoming technologies, such as blockchain and artificial intelligence, are also going to influence how real estate is bought and sold. The chapter also discussed the importance of ready availability of real estate transaction data for innovators to create new products and services to benefit the industry and other stakeholders. The reluctance to release data or to limit its use for the benefit of the real estate industry was also discussed. Lastly, the chapter illustrated how building management is likely to change and evolve by embracing technology for sustainable and profitable operations of large and small real estate.

.

REFERENCES

Adediji, Y., Donaldson, L., & Haider, M. (2019). How Parking Regulations Need to Evolve for High-Rise Buildings -- A New Approach for Emerging Trends in Transportation, Housing, and the Environment. Urban Analytics Institute, Ryerson University.

Agarwal, S., Amromin, G., Ben-David, I., Chomsisengphet, S., Piskorski, T., & Seru, A. (2017). Policy Intervention in Debt Renegotiation: Evidence from the Home Affordable Modification Program. The Journal of Political Economy, 125(3), 654–712. https://doi.org/10.1086/691701

Akbari, A. H., & Aydede, Y. (2012). Effects of immigration on house prices in Canada. Applied Economics, 44(13), 1645–1658. https://doi.org/10.1080/00036846.2010.548788

Alcanna Inc. (2018, October 23). Alcanna Provides First Results from Nova Cannabis. Retrieved from http://www.globenewswire.com/news-release/2018/10/23/1625371/0/en/Alcanna-Provides-First-Results-from-Nova-Cannabis.html

Alini, E. (2018, November 26). GM Oshawa plant closing could affect nearly 15 per cent of auto industry jobs. Global News. Retrieved from https://globalnews.ca/news/4698395/gm-oshawa-plant-closing-job-losses/

Allen, J., & Farber, S. (2019). Sizing up transport poverty: A national scale accounting of low-income households suffering from inaccessibility in Canada, and what to do about it. Transport Policy, 74, 214–223. https://doi.org/10.1016/j.tranpol.2018.11.018

Allen, M. T., Cadena, A., Rutherford, J., & Rutherford, R. C. (2015). Effects of real estate brokers' marketing strategies: Public open houses, broker open houses, MLS virtual tours, and MLS photographs. Journal of Real Estate Research, 37(3), 343–369. Retrieved from http://aresjournals.org/doi/abs/10.5555/0896-5803.37.3.343

Allen, M. T., Dare, W. H., & Li, L. (2018). MLS Information Sharing Intensity and Housing Market Outcomes. Journal of Real Estate Finance and Economics, 57(2), 297–313. https://doi.org/10.1007/s11146-017-9612-5

Autor, D.H., Palmer, C.J., & Pathak, P.A. (2012). Housing Market Spillovers: Evidence from the End of Rent Control in Cambridge Massachusetts (No. WP12DA1). Retrieved from https://www.lincolninst.edu/sites/default/files/pubfiles/2163_1488_Autor_WP12DA1.pdf

Baiceanu, R. (2016, September 12). The Profile of the Canadian Home Buyer. Retrieved from https://www.point2homes.com/news/canada-real-estate/profile-of-canadian-home-buyer.html

Bains, J. (2019, February 5). Watchdog stands by controversial mortgage stress test. Retrieved from https://ca.finance.yahoo.com/news/watchdog-stands-controversial-mortgage-stress-test-191901661.html

Basiri, K., & Mahmoudi, B. (2018). Possible income misstatement on mortgage loan applications: Evidence from the Canadian housing market. Real Estate Economics. https://onlinelibrary.wiley.com/doi/abs/10.1111/1540-6229.12310?casa_token=mIVYc7Xe5NwAAAAA:nBzrda0SnRI0odj6Sk2Z5wR4dnY3G_DQYmaZewDnHL1yt0A8gsmWEOFZnr4tfBChKSOMWhqVhOIy4Mnw

Been, V., Ellen, I. G., & O'Regan, K. (2019). Supply Skepticism: Housing Supply and Affordability. In Housing Policy Debate (Vol. 29, Issue 1, pp. 25–40). https://doi.org/10.1080/10511482.2018.1476899

Benetton, M., Bracke, P., Cocco, J. F., & Garbarino, N. (2019). Housing Consumption and Investment: Evidence from Shared Equity Mortgages. https://doi.org/10.2139/ssrn.3374421

Bernheim, B. D., & Meer, J. (2013). Do Real Estate Brokers Add Value When Listing Services Are Unbundled? Economic Inquiry, 51(2), 1166–1182. https://doi.org/10.1111/j.1465-7295.2012.00473.x

Bershidsky, L. (2019, March 27). Don't Expect Car Ownership to Become Obsolete. Bloomberg News. Retrieved from https://www.bloomberg.com/opinion/articles/2019-03-27/millennials-aren-t-making-car-ownership-obsolete

Bilyk, O., Ho, A.T.Y., Khan, M., & Vallée, G. (2020). Household indebtedness risks in the wake of COVID-19. Retrieved from https://www.bankofcanada.ca/2020/06/staff-analytical-note-2020-8/

Bilyk, O., & Nyenhuis, M. (2018). The Impact of Recent Policy Changes on the Canadian Mortgage Market (No. 2018-35). Retrieved from https://www.bankofcanada.ca/2018/11/staff-analytical-note-2018-35/

Blais, P. (2018). Planning the Next GGH. Retrieved from https://www.neptis.org/publications/planning-next-ggh

Blatchford, A. (2019, May 6). Bank of Canada's Poloz: There are 'good reasons' to encourage mortgage terms longer than 5 years. The Canadian Press. Retrieved from https://globalnews.ca/news/5245517/bank-of-canada-poloz-mortgage-backed-securities-longer-terms/

Block, Walter E., Rent Control: A Tale of Two Canadian Cities (July 21, 2011). The Mid-Atlantic Journal of Business, Vol. 25, No. 7, May 1989. https://ssrn.com/abstract=1892363

Blomquist, D. (2018, April 25). May is the Best Month to Sell a Home Nationwide. Here's the Best Month to Sell in Your Local Market. Retrieved from https://www.attomdata.com/news/market-trends/home-sales-prices/best-time-to-sell-a-home/

Bogin, A., Doerner, W., & Larson, W. (2019). Local House Price Dynamics: New Indices and Stylized Facts. Real Estate Economics, 47(2), 365–398. https://doi.org/10.1111/1540-6229.12233

Brown, S. (2017, November 6). Daily Poll: Is opposition to Marpole homeless shelter just NIMBYism? Vancouver Sun. Retrieved from https://vancouversun.com/news/local-news/daily-poll-is-opposition-to-marpole-homeless-shelter-just-nimbyism

Calanog, V., & Denham, B.B. (2017, February 15). The Shrinking Office Footprint. Retrieved from https://www.reis.com/the-shrinking-office-footprint/

Canada Mortgage and Housing Corporation. (2018, April 13). Homeowners income was about double that of renters in 2016. Retrieved from https://www.cmhc-schl.gc.ca/en/housing-observer-online/2018-housing-observer/homeowners-income-was-about-double-that-of-renters-2016

Canada Mortgage and Housing Corporation. (2018, February 6). Non-permanent residents: increasing influence on housing. Retrieved from https://www.cmhc-schl.gc.ca/en/housing-observer-online/2018-housing-observer/non-permanent-residents-increasing-influence-

housing#:~:text=Because%20of%20the%20way%20their,overall%20popul
ation%20numbers%20would%20suggest

Canada Mortgage and Housing Corporation. (2018, November 6). Housing Market Activity to Moderate in 2019 and 2020: CMHC Report. Retrieved from https://www.cmhc-schl.gc.ca/en/media-newsroom/news-releases/2018/housing-market-activity-moderate-2019-2020-cmhc-report

Canada Mortgage and Housing Corporation. (2018, November 13). Drive until you qualify: is the commute worth it? Retrieved from https://www.cmhc-schl.gc.ca/en/housing-observer-online/2018-housing-observer/drive-until-you-qualify-is-commute-worth-it

Canada Mortgage and Housing Corporation. (2018, December 13). Household Debt-to-Income Ratio Near Record High. Retrieved from https://www.cmhc-schl.gc.ca/en/housing-observer-online/2018-housing-observer/household-debt-income-ratio-near-record-high

Canada Mortgage and Housing Corporation. (2018). Rental Market Report – Greater Toronto Area. Retrieved from https://www.realestateforums.com/content/dam/Informa/realestateforums/2019/portal/Reports/rental-market-reports-toronto.pdf

Canada Mortgage and Housing Corporation. (2019). Residential Mortgage Industry Report. Retrieved from https://assets.cmhc-schl.gc.ca/sf/project/cmhc/pubsandreports/residential-mortgage-industry-report/residential-mortgage-industry-report-69589-2019-en.pdf?rev=b3a87353-b29f-4926-a460-572ef239dd41

Canada Mortgage and Housing Corporation. (2019, June 17). Federal Government Makes it Easier for Middle Class Canadians to Buy their First Home. Retrieved from https://www.cmhc-schl.gc.ca/en/media-newsroom/news-releases/2019/federal-government-makes-easier-for-middle-class-canadians-buy-first-home-toronto

Canadian Centre for Economic Analysis. (2015). Socio-Economic Analysis: Value of Toronto Community Housing's 10-Year Capital Investment Plan and Revitalization. Retrieved from https://www.torontohousing.ca/capital-initiatives/Documents/Third-party%20economic%20impact%20study.pdf

Canadian Centre of Economic Analysis & Canadian Urban Institute for the Affordable Housing Office of the City of Toronto. (2019). Toronto Housing Market Analysis – From Insight to Action. Retrieved from https://www.toronto.ca/legdocs/mmis/2019/ph/bgrd/backgroundfile-124480.pdf

The Canadian Press. (2016, May 11). Ontario's Greenbelt lands could grow by 9,000 hectares. CBC News. Retrieved from https://www.cbc.ca/news/canada/toronto/ontario-greenbelt-plan-1.3576619

The Canadian Press. (2018, November 5). Second Cup converting 2 Alberta cafés to cannabis dispensaries, will review rest of chain. CBC News. Retrieved from https://www.cbc.ca/news/business/second-cup-earnings-1.4892915

Canadian Real Estate Association. (n.d.) Housing Market Stats. Retrieved from https://www.crea.ca/housing-market-stats/

Canary Wharf Group PLC. (n.d.). The Height of Success – Canary Wharf. Retrieved from https://group.canarywharf.com/portfolio/canary-wharf/

CBC News. (2018, November 13). CMHC finds Toronto commuting costs can outweigh cheaper suburban house prices. Retrieved from https://www.cbc.ca/news/business/cmhc-commuting-costs-housing-1.4903862

Cheng, C., Mayer, W. J., & Mayer, Y. (2018). The Effect of Legalizing Retail Marijuana On Housing Values: Evidence From Colorado. Economic Inquiry, 56(3), 1585–1601. https://doi.org/10.1111/ecin.12556

Chernick, H., Reschovsky, A., & Newman, S. (2016). Effect of the Housing Crisis on the Finances of Central Cities. Retrieved from https://www.urban.org/sites/default/files/the_effect_of_the_housing_crisis_on_the_finances_of_central_cities.pdf

Cheung, C. (2018). Meet the realtor transforming Vancouver one block at a time. Vancouver Courier. Retrieved from https://www.vancouverisawesome.com/2018/02/21/michelle-yu-vancouver-realtor/

City of Toronto. (2016). Toronto Employment Survey 2016. Retrieved from https://www.toronto.ca/legdocs/mmis/2017/pg/bgrd/backgroundfile-99543.pdf

City of Toronto. (2017). Living in the City Survey 2016. Retrieved from https://www.toronto.ca/legdocs/mmis/2018/pg/bgrd/backgroundfile-110520.pdf

City of Toronto. (2017). 2016 Census Backgrounder Income 2017 09 14. Retrieved from https://www.toronto.ca/wp-content/uploads/2017/10/8f41-2016-Census-Backgrounder-Income.pdf

City of Toronto. (2019, September 30). Growth Plan (2019) and Municipal Comprehensive Review/Conformity Exercise Requirements Report. Retrieved from https://www.toronto.ca/legdocs/mmis/2019/ph/bgrd/backgroundfile-138428.pdf

Clayton, F., & Shi, H. Y. (2019). WOW! Toronto Was the Second Fastest Growing Metropolitan Area and the Top Growing City in All of the United States and Canada (No. Blog Entry 35). Retrieved from https://www.ryerson.ca/cur/Blog/blogentry35/

Coleman, V., & Rosenberg, M. (2019, January 16). Microsoft pledges $500 million to tackle housing crisis in Seattle, Eastside. The Seattle Times. Retrieved from https://www.seattletimes.com/seattle-news/homeless/microsoft-pledges-500-million-to-help-develop-affordable-housing-in-seattle-and-on-eastside/

Conklin, J., Diop, M., & Li, H. (2017). Contact High: The External Effects of Retail Marijuana Establishments on House Prices: Effects of Retail Marijuana on House Prices. Real Estate Economics, 56, 333. https://doi.org/10.1111/1540-6229.12220

Craig, A. (2018, September 6). Canada is a more suburban nation. Queen's Gazette. Retrieved from https://www.queensu.ca/gazette/stories/canada-more-suburban-nation

Cullinane, S. (2018, July 10). Up to 70 people dead after Quebec heat wave. CNN. Retrieved from https://www.cnn.com/2018/07/10/americas/quebec-heat-wave-deaths-wxc/index.html

Dachis, B., Duranton, G., & Turner, M. A. (2012). The effects of land transfer taxes on real estate markets: evidence from a natural experiment in Toronto. Journal of Economic Geography, 12(2), 327–354. https://doi.org/10.1093/jeg/lbr007

Daglish, T., & Patel, N. (2012). Fixed Come Hell or High Water? Selection and Prepayment of Fixed-Rate Mortgages Outside the United States. In Real Estate Economics (Vol. 40, Issue 4, pp. 709–743). https://doi.org/10.1111/j.1540-6229.2012.00334.x

Davey, M., & Walsh, M. W. (2013, July 18). Billions in Debt, Detroit Tumbles Into Insolvency. The New York Times. Retrieved from https://www.nytimes.com/2013/07/19/us/detroit-files-for-bankruptcy.html

Department of Finance Canada. (n.d.). An Affordable Place to Call Home. Retrieved from https://www.budget.gc.ca/2019/docs/themes/housing-logement-en.pdf

Dingman, S. (2018, September 3). TREB presses brokers on data protection. The Globe and Mail. Retrieved from https://www.theglobeandmail.com/real-estate/article-treb-presses-brokers-on-data-protection/

Dunning, W. (2017). Annual State of the Residential Mortgage Market in Canada. Mortgage Professionals Canada.

Dunning, W. (2018). Report on the Housing and Mortgage Market in Canada. Retrieved from https://mortgageproscan.ca/docs/default-source/consumer-reports/housing-and-mortgage-market-report_july2018.pdf

The Economist. (2018, May 10). Big investors are giving university digs an upgrade. Retrieved from https://www.economist.com/finance-and-economics/2018/05/10/big-investors-are-giving-university-digs-an-upgrade

Eid, J., Overman, H. G., Puga, D., & Turner, M. A. (2008). Fat city: Questioning the relationship between urban sprawl and obesity. Journal of Urban Economics, 63(2), 385–404. https://doi.org/10.1016/j.jue.2007.12.002

Eliot, L. (2019, August 4). The Reasons Why Millennials Aren't As Car Crazed As Baby Boomers, And How Self-Driving Cars Fit In. Forbes Magazine. Retrieved from https://www.forbes.com/sites/lanceeliot/2019/08/04/the-reasons-why-millennials-arent-as-car-crazed-as-baby-boomers-and-how-self-driving-cars-fit-in/

EMS delay caused by safety concerns, chief says. (2009, July 14). The Globe and Mail. Retrieved from https://www.theglobeandmail.com/news/national/ems-delay-caused-by-safety-concerns-chief-says/article4213179/

Equifax Canada. (2017, January 11). Equifax Canada: Mortgage Fraud on the Rise. Retrieved from https://www.consumer.equifax.ca/about-equifax/press-releases/-/blogs/equifax-canada-mortgage-fraud-on-the-rise/

Evans, P. (2017, October 17). OSFI sets new mortgage rules, including stress test for uninsured borrowers. CBC News. Retrieved from https://www.cbc.ca/news/business/osfi-mortgage-rules-1.4358048

Evans, P. (2017, November 23). Canadian households lead the world in terms of debt: OECD. CBC News. Retrieved from https://www.cbc.ca/news/business/oecd-debt-1.4415860

Evans, P. (2017, December 14). Canadians owe $1.71 for every dollar of disposable income they have — a new record high. CBC News. Retrieved from https://www.cbc.ca/news/business/debt-income-1.4448098

Evans, P. (2018, January 25). Canadians spent $5.7B on marijuana last year, StatsCan estimates. CBC News. Retrieved from https://www.cbc.ca/news/business/marijuana-industry-1.4503152

Feldman, M. (2018). The Case for Longer Mortgages: Addressing the Mismatch between Term and Amortization. https://doi.org/10.2139/ssrn.3136493

Fenn, M., Nanji, M., Rolfe, J., & Sussman, A. (2019). Moving Canada's Economic Infrastructure Forward: Addressing Six Risks to Timely, Economical and Prudent Project Selection and Delivery. Retrieved from https://publicsectornetwork.co/insight/moving-canadas-economic-infrastructure-forward-addressing-six-risks-to-timely-economical-and-prudent-project-selection-and-delivery/

France-Presse, A. (2019, September 8). Summer heatwaves in France killed 1,500, says health minister. The Guardian. Retrieved from http://www.theguardian.com/world/2019/sep/09/summer-heatwaves-in-france-killed-1500-says-health-minister

Fry, R. (2017, May 5). More young adults are living at home, and for longer stretches. Pew Research Center. Retrieved from https://www.pewresearch.org/fact-tank/2017/05/05/its-becoming-more-common-for-young-adults-to-live-at-home-and-for-longer-stretches/

Fry, R. (2016, May 24). For First Time in Modern Era, Living With Parents Edges Out Other Living Arrangements for 18- to 34-Year-Olds. Pew Research Center. Retrieved from https://www.pewsocialtrends.org/2016/05/24/for-first-time-in-modern-era-living-with-parents-edges-out-other-living-arrangements-for-18-to-34-year-olds/

Galbraith, N., Truong, J., & Tang, J. (2019, March 6). Living alone in Canada. Retrieved from https://www150.statcan.gc.ca/n1/pub/75-006-x/2019001/article/00003-eng.htm

Garreau, J. (1992). Edge City: Life on the New Frontier: Life on the New Frontier (Vol. 1, pp. 1–548). Doubleday & Company, Incorporated.

The General Social Survey: New Data Overview. (2008). Retrieved from https://www150.statcan.gc.ca/n1/pub/89-631-x/89-631-x2008001-eng.htm

Gismondi, A. (2019, June 6). Budgets still under investing in infrastructure: CANCEA. Retrieved from https://canada.constructconnect.com/dcn/news/economic/2019/06/budgets-still-investing-infrastructure-cancea

Gopinath, G. (2020, April 14). The Great Lockdown: Worst Economic Downturn Since the Great Depression. Retrieved from https://blogs.imf.org/2020/04/14/the-great-lockdown-worst-economic-downturn-since-the-great-depression/

Gordon, Josh. (2020, September 13). The 'supply crisis' in Canada's housing market isn't backed up by the evidence. *The Globe and Mail.* https://www.theglobeandmail.com/opinion/article-the-supply-crisis-in-canadas-housing-market-isnt-backed-up-by-the/.

Government of British Columbia. (n.d.). Combatting Money Laundering in B.C. Real Estate. Retrieved from https://www2.gov.bc.ca/gov/content/housing-tenancy/real-estate-bc/consultations/money-laundering

Government of Canada, Statistics Canada. (2017, August 2). Census in Brief: Young adults living with their parents in Canada in 2016. Retrieved from https://www12.statcan.gc.ca/census-recensement/2016/as-sa/98-200-x/2016008/98-200-x2016008-eng.cfm

Government of Canada, Statistics Canada. (2017, August 2). The Daily — Families, households and marital status: Key results from the 2016 Census. Retrieved from https://www150.statcan.gc.ca/n1/daily-quotidien/170802/dq170802a-eng.htm

Government of Canada, Statistics Canada. (2017, October 25). The Daily — Housing in Canada: Key results from the 2016 Census. Retrieved from https://www150.statcan.gc.ca/n1/daily-quotidien/171025/dq171025c-eng.htm

Government of Canada, Statistics Canada. (2017, November 29). The Daily — Education in Canada: Key results from the 2016 Census. Retrieved from https://www150.statcan.gc.ca/n1/daily-quotidien/171129/dq171129a-eng.htm

Government of Canada, Statistics Canada. (2018, April 26). Data tables, 2016 Census. Retrieved from https://www12.statcan.gc.ca/census-recensement/2016/dp-pd/dt-td/Index-eng.cfm

Government of Canada, Statistics Canada. (2018, November 28). Canadian postsecondary enrolments and graduates, 2016/2017. Retrieved from https://www150.statcan.gc.ca/n1/daily-quotidien/181128/dq181128c-eng.htm

Government of Canada, Statistics Canada. (2019, January 25). The Daily — Canada's population estimates: Age and sex, July 1, 2018. Retrieved from https://www150.statcan.gc.ca/n1/daily-quotidien/190125/dq190125a-eng.htm

Government of Canada, Statistics Canada. (2019, June 11). Canadian Housing Statistics Program, 2018. Retrieved from https://www150.statcan.gc.ca/n1/daily-quotidien/190611/dq190611a-eng.htm

Government of Canada, Statistics Canada. (2020, September 9). Postsecondary enrolments, by registration status, institution type, status of student in Canada and gender. Retrieved from https://www150.statcan.gc.ca/t1/tbl1/en/tv.action?pid=3710001801

Graham, S. (2014). Super-tall and Ultra-deep: The Cultural Politics of the Elevator. Theory, Culture & Society, 31(7-8), 239–265. https://doi.org/10.1177/0263276414554044

Green, K. P., Filipowicz, J., Lafleur, S., & Herzog, I. (2016). The impact of land-use regulation on housing supply in Canada. Fraser Institute Vancouver, Canada. https://www.fraserinstitute.org/sites/default/files/impact-of-land-use-regulation-on-housing-supply-in-canada-exec-summary.pdf

Grenier, É. (2017, May 7). Seniors now outnumber children in Canada, census figures show. CBC News. Retrieved from https://www.cbc.ca/news/politics/2016-census-age-gender-1.4095360

Griswold, A. (2018, January 18). Amazon is thinking about putting HQ2 just about everywhere except Silicon Valley. Quartz. Retrieved from https://qz.com/1182913/amazon-amzn-hq2-shortlist-20-cities-that-made-the-headquarters-cut/

Guerra, E. (2016). Planning for Cars That Drive Themselves: Metropolitan Planning Organizations, Regional Transportation Plans, and Autonomous Vehicles. Journal of Planning Education and Research, 36(2), 210–224. https://doi.org/10.1177/0739456X15613591

Haider, M., & Donaldson, L. (2016). Can Tax Increment Financing Support Transportation Infrastructure Investment? Retrieved from https://tspace.library.utoronto.ca/handle/1807/81215

Haider, M., & Miller, E. (2000). Effects of Transportation Infrastructure and Location on Residential Real Estate Values: Application of Spatial Autoregressive Techniques. Transportation Research Record: Journal of the Transportation Research Board, 1722, 1–8. https://doi.org/10.3141/1722-01

Haider, M., & Moranis, S. (2017, December 7). Don't get fooled by the "forward buy" in real estate data. Financial Post. Retrieved from https://business.financialpost.com/real-estate/the-haider-moranis-bulletin-dont-get-fooled-by-the-forward-buy-in-real-estate-data

Haider, M., & Moranis, S. (2018, June 21). Don't expect real estate agents to disappear any time soon. Financial Post. Retrieved from https://financialpost.com/real-estate/dont-expect-real-estate-agents-to-disappear-any-time-soon

Haider, M., & Moranis, S. (2020, June 4). Why office real estate landlords aren't panicking just yet. Financial Post. https://financialpost.com/real-estate/property-post/why-office-real-estate-landlords-arent-panicking-just-yet

Harapyn, L. (2019, February 8). Overheating housing market was 'terrifying.' Why Royal LePage's CEO is OK with the mortgage stress test. Financial Post. Retrieved from https://business.financialpost.com/real-estate/overheating-housing-market-was-terrifying-why-royal-lepages-ceo-is-ok-with-the-mortgage-stress-test

Harney, K.R. (2018, May 8). Single women account for more real estate purchases than single men. The Washington Post. Retrieved from https://www.washingtonpost.com/realestate/single-women-account-for-more-real-estate-purchases-than-single-men/2018/05/08/0f3cee66-521e-11e8-a551-5b648abe29ef_story.html

Harris, J. C. (1998). Survey Slams Door on Open Houses. Tierra Grande.

Heaps Estrin. (2019, July 30). BMW Canada and The Heaps Estrin Real Estate Team launch luxury real estate initiative. Retrieved from https://heapsestrin.com/bmw-canada-and-the-heaps-estrin-real-estate-team-launch-luxury-real-estate-initiative/

Heisz, A., & Richards, E. (2019, April 18). Economic Well-being Across Generations of Young Canadians: Are Millennials Better or Worse Off? Retrieved from https://www150.statcan.gc.ca/n1/pub/11-626-x/11-626-x2019006-eng.htm

Heller, M. (n.d.). The Tragedy of the Anticommons | The Wealth of the Commons. Retrieved from http://wealthofthecommons.org/essay/tragedy-anticommons

Hildebrand, S., & Tal, B. (2018, April 6). A Window Into the World of Condo Investors. Urbanation. Retrieved from https://www.urbanation.ca/sites/default/files/Urbanation-CIBC%20Condo%20Investor%20Report.pdf

Hollingsworth, T., & Goebel, A. (2017). Revitalizing America's Smaller Legacy Cities -- Strategies for Postindustrial Success from Gary to Lowell.

Retrieved from https://www.lincolninst.edu/publications/policy-focus-reports/revitalizing-americas-smaller-legacy-cities

Horton, T. (2016). Reducing Affordability: AirBNB`s affect the Vacancy Rate and Affordability of the Toronto Rental Market (MA, University of Ottawa). Retrieved from https://ruor.uottawa.ca/bitstream/10393/35791/1/Horton_Tyler_2016_r esearchpaper.pdf

Hudson Yards New York. (n.d.). About Hudson Yards. Retrieved from https://www.hudsonyardsnewyork.com/sites/default/files/2019-03/HY_PressKit_NEW_031219_web_final.pdf

Hunter, J. (2018, February 21). New B.C. housing measures are "bold steps," minister says. The Globe and Mail. Retrieved from https://www.theglobeandmail.com/news/british-columbia/canadians-with-bc-vacation-homes-to-be-hit-with-new-tax/article38061049/

International Monetary Fund. (2020, April 8). Latest Global Housing Watch Data. Retrieved from https://www.imf.org/external/research/housing/

Jaggia, S., & Patel, P. (2017). Rent-to-Own Housing Contracts under Financial Constraints. The Journal of Derivatives, 25(2), 62–78. https://doi.org/10.3905/jod.2017.25.2.062

Jacobs, J. (1992). The death and life of great American cities. New York: Vintage.

Kalinowski, T. (2018, August 23). Supreme Court dismisses real estate board's appeal application on sold data. The Toronto Star. Retrieved from https://www.thestar.com/business/real_estate/2018/08/23/supreme-court-dismisses-real-estate-boards-appeal-application-on-sold-data.html

Keesmaat, J. (2019, July 26). To create affordable housing, let's banish the hoary myths of home ownership. The Globe and Mail. Retrieved from https://www.theglobeandmail.com/opinion/article-to-create-affordable-housing-lets-banish-the-hoary-myths-of-home/

Kim, L. (2000, November 9). Germany struggles to revive shrinking city centers. The Christian Science Monitor.

King, D. A., Smart, M. J., & Manville, M. (2019). The Poverty of the Carless: Toward Universal Auto Access. Journal of Planning Education and

Research, 0739456X18823252.
https://doi.org/10.1177/0739456X18823252

Kontokosta, C. E., & Jain, R. K. (2015). Modeling the determinants of large-scale building water use: Implications for data-driven urban sustainability policy. Sustainable Cities and Society, 18, 44–55. https://doi.org/10.1016/j.scs.2015.05.007

Krugman, P. (2000, June 7). Reckonings; A Rent Affair. The New York Times. Retrieved from https://www.nytimes.com/2000/06/07/opinion/reckonings-a-rent-affair.html

Kuligowski, E. D., Peacock, R. D., & Averill, J. D. (2013). Modeling the Evacuation of the World Trade Center Towers on September 11, 2001. In Fire Technology (Vol. 49, Issue 1, pp. 65–81). https://doi.org/10.1007/s10694-011-0240-y

Lane, M. A., Seiler, M. J., & Seiler, V. L. (2015). The Impact of Staging Conditions on Residential Real Estate Demand. Journal of Housing Research. Retrieved from http://aresjournals.org/doi/abs/10.5555/1052-7001.24.1.21

Lang, R. E., Sanchez, T., & LeFurgy, J. (2006). Beyond edgeless cities: Office geography in the new metropolis. National Center for Real Estate Research, National Association of Realtors. Retrieved from https://www.researchgate.net/profile/Thomas_Sanchez/publication/2308 20735_Beyond_edgeless_cities_office_geography_in_the_new_metropolis/ links/0fcfd50b5a04e9de6c000000/Beyond-edgeless-cities-office-geography-in-the-new-metropolis.pdf

Latif, E. (2015). Immigration and Housing Rents in Canada: A Panel Data Analysis. Economic Issues, 20(1).

Lee, K. (2018). Fixed-Rate Mortgages, Labor Markets, and Efficiency. Journal of Money, Credit, and Banking, 50(5), 1033–1072. https://onlinelibrary.wiley.com/doi/abs/10.1111/jmcb.12516?casa_token =mxBEU7VzhioAAAAA:EwQyJL2XK7KpbfRU2W1qqeL5Pm6UFKiF4 Tv9GmlwPfq34nUxnx1OckuPU7hKAvk_LUbKOs3XRiRbTovJ

Levine, M. L., Segev, L. L., & Thode, S. F. (2017). A Largely Unnoticed Impact on Real Estate--Self-Driven Vehicles. The Appraisal Journal, 85(1). Retrieved from http://search.ebscohost.com/login.aspx?direct=true&profile=ehost&scope=site&authtype=crawler&jrnl=00037087&asa=Y&AN=122227555&h=bqgV0m2r8ejmfIZoGzCdVNyZVlfgN6SfByDvZcHPnm5RAusU3LZ3xGb3ukxTEef5YwS0Bv97K4dQ%2BmqtHR1Tsg%3D%3D&crl=c

Levitt, S. D., & Syverson, C. (2008). Market Distortions When Agents Are Better Informed: The Value of Information in Real Estate Transactions. The Review of Economics and Statistics, 90(4), 599–611. https://doi.org/10.1162/rest.90.4.599

Malone Given Parsons Ltd. (2017, April 4). Getting the Growth Plan Right. Retrieved from https://www.mgp.ca/news/title-of-article-goes-here-g4ddd-95zg9-aslhr-n4y6n-56kj3

Mathieu, E., & Rider, D. (2019, April 5). Ottawa pledges $1.3 billion for Toronto Community Housing repairs. The Toronto Star. Retrieved from https://thestar.com/news/city_hall/2019/04/05/ottawa-pledges-13-billion-for-toronto-community-housing-repairs.html

McCallister, D. (2017, September 8). Long & Foster Sold To Warren Buffett's HomeServices Of America. Retrieved from https://www.npr.org/sections/thetwo-way/2017/09/08/549359615/long-foster-sold-to-warren-buffetts-homesevices-of-america

McCarthy Tétrault LLP. (2018, March 8). 2018 B.C. Budget: What It Means for B.C. Real Estate. Retrieved from https://www.mccarthy.ca/en/insights/blogs/lay-land/2018-bc-budget-what-it-means-bc-real-estate

McNeely, A. (2018, February 26). S&P warns more mortgage fraud could emerge at Canadian banks. Bloomberg News. Retrieved from https://www.bnnbloomberg.ca/mortgage-fraud-prompts-s-p-to-lower-canada-bank-risk-metric-1.1009395

McNutt, L. (2019, May 2). Best Places to Live: Canada Liveability Report. Retrieved from https://blog.remax.ca/canada-liveability-report/

Mendes, S. (2018, April 2). Understanding the Millennial Workforce. Restaurants Canada. Retrieved from https://blog.restaurantscanada.org/index.php/2018/04/02/understanding-the-millennial-workforce/

Mian, A., Rao, K., & Sufi, A. (2013). Household balance sheets, consumption, and the economic slump. The Quarterly Journal of Economics, 128(4), 1687–1726. Retrieved from https://academic.oup.com/qje/article-abstract/128/4/1687/1849337

Mian, A., & Sufi, A. (2012). The Effects of Fiscal Stimulus: Evidence from the 2009 Cash for Clunkers Program*. The Quarterly Journal of Economics, 127(3), 1107–1142. https://doi.org/10.1093/qje/qjs024

Mohamad, H. (2016). Estimating the Impact of Airbnb on Hotels in Toronto (Master of Science in Real Estate Development). Massachusetts Institute of Technology.

Mohindra, N. (2017, October 11). Uninsured Mortgage Regulation: From Corporate Governance to Prescription. Retrieved from https://www.fraserinstitute.org/studies/uninsured-mortgage-regulation-from-corporate-governance-to-prescription

Morris, S., & Finch, G. (2018, March 29). Barclays Wins Its DOJ Gamble With $2 Billion Mortgage Settlement. Bloomberg News. Retrieved from https://www.bloomberg.com/news/articles/2018-03-29/barclays-agrees-to-pay-2-billion-to-settle-u-s-rmbs-suit

Morissette, R. (2019, April 16). The Wealth of Immigrant Families in Canada. Retrieved from https://www150.statcan.gc.ca/n1/pub/11f0019m/11f0019m2019010-eng.htm

Mortgage Professionals Canada. (n.d.). A Profile of Home Buying in Canada. Retrieved from https://mortgageproscan.ca/docs/default-source/default-document-library/infographic2.pdf?sfvrsn=ab289ea_0

Mortgage Professionals Canada. (2018, September 12). Consumer Report Finds Homeownership is the Affordable Alternative as Rent Costs Continue to Soar. Retrieved from https://www.newswire.ca/news-releases/consumer-report-finds-homeownership-is-the-affordable-alternative-as-rent-costs-continue-to-soar-693035391.html

Myers, B. (2020). Rentals.ca August 2020 Rent Report. Retrieved from https://rentals.ca/national-rent-report

Naidu-Ghelani, R. (2019, January 5). Home ownership costs to rise in 2019 even as housing market cools: RBC. CBC News. Retrieved from https://www.cbc.ca/news/business/house-prices-affordability-income-

1.4966211

National Association of Realtors. (2017). 2017-Profile-of-International-Activity-in-US-Residential-Real-Estate.pdf. Retrieved from https://www.nar.realtor/sites/default/files/documents/2017-Profile-of-International-Activity-in-US-Residential-Real-Estate.pdf

National Association of Realtors. (n.d.). Home Buyer and Seller Generational Trends Report 2017. Retrieved from https://www.nar.realtor/sites/default/files/reports/2017/2017-home-buyer-and-seller-generational-trends-03-07-2017.pdf

National Association of Realtors Research Department. (2017). 2017 profile of home staging. Retrieved from https://www.nar.realtor/sites/default/files/migration_files/reports/2017/2017-profile-of-home-staging-07-06-2017.pdf

Neptis Foundation. (2016). No shortage of land for homes in the Greater Toronto and Hamilton Area. Retrieved from https://www.neptis.org/publications/no-shortage-land-homes-greater-toronto-and-hamilton-area

Newinhomes.com. (2019, April 4). Greater Toronto Area resale housing market remains steady through first quarter of 2019. Retrieved from https://www.newinhomes.com/blog/greater-toronto-area-resale-housing-market-remains-steady-through-first-quarter-of-2019

Noakes, S. (2018, August 23). TREB loses Supreme Court bid to appeal release of real estate sold figures. CBC News. Retrieved from https://www.cbc.ca/news/business/treb-real-estate-sale-prices-1.4795903

Ontario Securities Commission. (2017). Missing Out: Millennials and the Markets. Retrieved from https://www.osc.gov.on.ca/documents/en/Investors/inv_research_20171127_missing-out-report.PDF

Pagliaro, J. (2018, March 12). Toronto facing a massive $1.42-billion budget gap in five years. The Toronto Star. Retrieved from https://thestar.com/news/gta/2018/03/12/toronto-facing-a-massive-142-billion-budget-gap-in-five-years.html

The Parliamentary Budget Officer. (2020, June 17). Update on the Investing in Canada Plan. Retrieved from https://www.pbo-

dpb.gc.ca/en/blog/news/RP-2021-008-S--update-investing-in-canada-plan-
-point-plan-investir-dans-canada

Pavlov, A., & Somerville, T. (2018). Immigration, Capital Flows and
Housing Prices. Real Estate Economics, 41, 221.
https://doi.org/10.1111/1540-6229.12267

Peltier, E. (2019, July 26). As Extreme Heat Becomes New Normal in
Europe, Governments Scramble to Respond. The New York Times.
Retrieved from
https://www.nytimes.com/2019/07/26/world/europe/france-europe-
extreme-heat.html

Petramala, D., & Clayton, F. (2018). Millennials in the Greater Toronto and
Hamilton Area: A Generation Stuck in Apartments? Retrieved from
https://www.ryerson.ca/content/dam/cur/pdfs/policycommentaries/CU
R_Research_Report_Millennial_Housing_GTHA_May_22.pdf

Poloz, S. S. (2018, April 23). Opening Statement before the House of
Commons Standing Committee on Finance. Retrieved from
https://www.bankofcanada.ca/2018/04/opening-statement-april-23-2018/

Poloz, S. S. (2018, May 1). Canada's Economy and Household Debt: How
Big Is the Problem? Retrieved from
https://www.bankofcanada.ca/2018/05/canada-economy-household-debt-
how-big-the-problem/

Quora. (2017, October 16). Why Millennials Are Buying Fewer Cars Than
Older Generations. Forbes Magazine. Retrieved from
https://www.forbes.com/sites/quora/2017/10/16/why-millennials-are-
buying-fewer-cars-than-older-generations/

Randall, S. (2018, June 19). "Real estate agents will be obsolete in a few
years." claims tech chief. Retrieved from
https://www.canadianrealestatemagazine.ca/market-update/real-estate-
agents-will-be-obsolete-in-a-few-years--claims-tech-chief-244089.aspx

RBC Economic Research. (2018). Housing trends and affordability.
Retrieved from http://www.rbc.com/economics/economic-
reports/pdf/canadian-housing/house-sep2018.pdf

RBC Economics. (2019). Big city rental blues: a look at Canada's rental
housing deficit. Retrieved from

http://www.rbc.com/economics/economic-reports/pdf/canadian-housing/housing_rental_sep2019.pdf

RBC Economics. (2019). RBC Housing Affordability Report. Retrieved from http://www.rbc.com/newsroom/reports/rbc-housing-affordability.html

Robson, W. (2019, July 18). Sidewalk Labs' proposed transit financing plan worth embracing. The Toronto Star. Retrieved from https://www.thestar.com/opinion/contributors/2019/07/18/sidewalk-labs-proposed-transit-financing-plan-worth-embracing.html

Rollason, K. (2017, October 23). Legal pot plants a growing worry. Winnipeg Free Press. Retrieved from https://www.winnipegfreepress.com/arts-and-life/life/cannabis/legal-pot-plants-a-growing-worry-452395603.html

Rosen, K. T. (2018). The Case for Preserving Costa-Hawkins: Three Ways Rent Control Reduces the Supply of Rental Housing. Retrieved from https://mma.prnewswire.com/media/739365/Case_for_Preserving_Costa_Hawkins__Three_Ways_Rent_Control_Reduces_the_Supply.pdf?p=pdf

Royal LePage. (2017, August 17). Largest Cohort of Millennials Changing Canadian Real Estate, Despite Constraints of Affordability and Mortgage Regulation. Retrieved from https://www.royallepage.ca/en/realestate/news/largest-cohort-of-millennials-changing-canadian-real-estate-despite-constraints-of-affordability-and-mortgage-regulation/

SaveSmallBusiness.ca. (n.d.) Debt won't save our small businesses. Retrieved from https://savesmallbusiness.ca/

Savills UK. (2017, October 6). Global Student Housing Investment Breaks Records. Retrieved from https://www.savills.co.uk/insight-and-opinion/savills-news/156478-1

Scheffman, D. T., & Markusen, J. R. (1977). Speculation and Monopoly in Urban Development. University of Toronto Press, Scholarly Publishing Division.

Sen, C. (2019, April 25). Young People Can't Buy Homes Until Older Owners … Move On. Bloomberg News. Retrieved from https://www.bnnbloomberg.ca/young-people-can-t-buy-homes-until-older-owners-move-on-1.1249312

Shieber, J. (2018, August 12). How Airbnb went from renting air beds for 10 to a 30 billion hospitality behemoth. TechCrunch. Retrieved from http://social.techcrunch.com/2018/08/12/how-airbnb-went-from-renting-air-beds-for-10-to-a-30-billion-hospitality-behemoth/

Siddall, E. (2019, March 5). Are current mortgage rules too strict? No. The Toronto Star. Retrieved from https://thestar.com/opinion/contributors/thebigdebate/2019/03/05/are-current-mortgage-rules-too-strict-no.html

Slack, E., & Bird, R. M. (2015). How to Reform the Property Tax: Lessons from Around the World. https://play.google.com/store/books/details?id=moCMzQEACAAJ

Slattery, J. (2017, January 8). Attempted land assembly deal has 33-foot East Vancouver lots listed for $3.4 million. Global News. Retrieved from https://globalnews.ca/news/3168279/attempted-land-assembly-deal-has-33-foot-east-vancouver-lots-listed-for-3-4-million/

Smith, A. (2016, February 11). 15% of American Adults Have Used Online Dating Sites or Mobile Dating Apps. Pew Research Center. Retrieved from https://www.pewresearch.org/internet/2016/02/11/15-percent-of-american-adults-have-used-online-dating-sites-or-mobile-dating-apps/

Smith, C. (2019, April 2). Real Estate Board of Greater Vancouver reports brutally slow sales in March. The Georgia Straight. Retrieved from https://www.straight.com/news/1222321/real-estate-board-greater-vancouver-reports-brutally-slow-sales-march

Srivastava, C., Yang, Z., & Jain, R. K. (2019). Understanding the adoption and usage of data analytics and simulation among building energy management professionals: A nationwide survey. Building and Environment, 157, 139–164. https://doi.org/10.1016/j.buildenv.2019.04.016

Stowell, N. F., Barker-Cagwin, K., & Fellows, J. (2012). Mortgage fraud: Current trends and issues. Real Estate Issues, 37(2), 42–51. https://www.cre.org/wp-content/uploads/2017/04/37_2_3_Mortgage_Fraud.pdf

Student Dwell Toronto. (2019). About. Retrieved from https://studentdwellto.ca/About-Main

Suttor, G., & Leon, S. (2017, October 27). 6 Toronto Rental Housing Highlights in the 2016 Census. Retrieved from https://www.wellesleyinstitute.com/housing/6-toronto-rental-housing-highlights-in-the-2016-census/

SVN Rock Advisors Inc. (n.d.). Canadian Purpose Built Student Accommodation Advisors. Retrieved from https://svnrock.ca/national-student-housing-group/

United Nations Department of Economic and Social Affairs. (2018, May 16). 68% of the world population projected to live in urban areas by 2050, says UN. Retrieved from https://www.un.org/development/desa/en/news/population/2018-revision-of-world-urbanization-prospects.html.

Urbanation. (2019). Condo owners make big gains, but nearly half aren't making enough rent to cover costs. Retrieved from https://www.urbanation.ca/news/217-condo-owners-make-big-gains-nearly-half-arent-making-enough-rent-cover-costs

Veuger, J. (2017). Attention to disruption and blockchain creates a viable real estate economy. Journal of US-China Public Administration, 14(5), 263–285. https://www.researchgate.net/profile/Jan_Veuger/publication/322392878_Attention_to_Disruption_and_Blockchain_Creates_a_Viable_Real_Estate_Economy/links/5b7c2e61299bf1d5a719de02/Attention-to-Disruption-and-Blockchain-Creates-a-Viable-Real-Estate-Economy.pdf

Voigtländer, M. (2009). Why is the German Homeownership Rate so Low? Housing Studies, 24(3), 355–372. https://doi.org/10.1080/02673030902875011

Weise, K. (2018, October 23). Sorry Toronto: For Amazon HQ2 watchers, it's Northern Virginia that checks the most boxes. Financial Post. Retrieved from https://business.financialpost.com/technology/sorry-toronto-for-amazon-hq2-watchers-its-northern-virginia-that-checks-the-most-boxes

Whittemore, A. H., & BenDor, T. K. (2019). Reassessing NIMBY: The demographics, politics, and geography of opposition to high-density residential infill. Journal of Urban Affairs, 41(4), 423–442. https://doi.org/10.1080/07352166.2018.1484255

Wikipedia. (2020, September 8). All models are wrong. Retrieved from https://en.wikipedia.org/wiki/All_models_are_wrong

Wong, G. (2008). Has SARS infected the property market? Evidence from Hong Kong. Journal of Urban Economics, 63(1), 74–95. https://doi.org/10.1016/j.jue.2006.12.007

Wong, N. (2018, October 18). Demand for marijuana real estate "astronomical" as Canada legalizes. Financial Post. Retrieved from https://business.financialpost.com/real-estate/property-post/demand-for-pot-grow-ops-is-astronomical-as-canada-legalizes

Xie, J. (2018). Who Is "Misleading" Whom in Real Estate Transactions? Real Estate Economics, 46(3), 527–558. https://doi.org/10.1111/1540-6229.12196

Yates, A. M. (2015). Selling Paris. Harvard University Press. https://play.google.com/store/books/details?id=tCqoCgAAQBAJ

Yazdani, T. (2019, December 13). 'Don't tax the heart out of Toronto:' Independent businesses struggle to survive as taxes skyrocket. CityNews. Retrieved from https://toronto.citynews.ca/2019/12/13/buisness-property-taxes-skyrocket-toronto/

Yeates, M., Hernandez, T., & Emmons, M. (2016). Spatial implications of the residential property tax. Centre for the Study of Commercial Activity.

Zakharenko, R. (2016). Self-driving cars will change cities. Regional Science and Urban Economics, 61, 26–37. https://doi.org/10.1016/j.regsciurbeco.2016.09.003

Zillow. (2018, June 6). Zillow Partners with CENTURY 21 Canada; Will Feature Canadian Listings on Zillow This Year. Retrieved from http://zillow.mediaroom.com/2018-06-06-Zillow-Partners-with-CENTURY-21-Canada-Will-Feature-Canadian-Listings-on-Zillow-This-Year

Zillow. (n.d.). When Is the Best Time to Sell Your House? Retrieved from https://www.zillow.com/sellers-guide/best-time-to-sell/

INDEX

223, 224, 226, 229
Housing Studies, 172
housing supply, 25, 31, 43, 101, 111,
112, 117, 118, 137, 140, 142, 143,
145, 148, 169, 178, 186, 213, 229
Howard Chernick, 116
HPI, 40, 41, 44, 45
HQ2. *See* Amazon
Hudson Yards, 143, 144
HVAC, 90
ICT, 87
IMF, 31, 76, 80
immigrants, 1, 13, 14, 15, 17, 20, 30,
63, 208
Immigrants, 13, 14
immigration, 1, 13, 14, 15, 18, 37, 51,
63, 101, 129
Immigration, 13, 14, 15
India, 29, 30
Indiana, 213
Innovation, Science and Economic
Development Canada, 81
Investing in Canada Plan, 145, 146
investors, 6, 35, 37, 42, 55, 75, 119,
127, 134, 147, 148, 149, 150, 151,
152, 153, 155, 157, 169, 170, 181,
183, 184, 185, 222, 240, 243
Ipsos, 213, 214, 215
Ireland, 135, 172
J. R. Markusen, 151
James Conklin, 223
Japan, 92
Jeff Allen, 200
Jennifer Keesmaat, 139, 198
Jesse Elders, 92
Jia Xie, 213
Joel Garreau, 193, 202
John Dickie, 169
Jon Shell, 81
Jonathan Gitlin, 178
Jonathan Meer, 212
Journal of Derivatives, 175
Journal of Housing Research, 69, 70
Journal of Money, Credit and Banking,
133
*Journal of Planning Education and
Research*, 201, 203, 204

Journal of Real Estate Research, 71, 72
Journal of Urban Affairs, 215
Journal of Urban Economics, 74, 189
*Journal Real Estate Finance and
Economics*, 72
Kastner Lam LLP, 92
Kenneth Rosen, 180
Key Home Inspections, 83
Kiana Basiri, 216
Kitchener, 36, 168
Kone Corp., 92
Konfidis Brokerage, 82
labour force, 9, 11, 45, 81, 161, 207,
245
land speculation tax, 151
Land Transfer Tax, 50, 58
Lawrence National Centre for Policy
and Management, 147
Liberal government, 32, 33, 119,
120, 141, 179, 181
life expectancy, 23
Light Rail Transit, 195
Lincoln Institute of Land Policy, 207
London, 120, 121, 139, 144, 168, 199
Long & Foster, 241
low-income, 2, 10, 13, 29, 111, 140,
161, 199, 200, 201, 202
low-rise housing, 100, 103, 132, 197,
198
Malone Given Parsons, 142
Manhattan, 86, 115, 143, 164, 192
Marcus T. Allen, 71
marijuana, 221, 222, 223, 224, 225,
229
Marissa Mayer, 85
Mark Lane, 69
Mark Weisleder, 79
Markham, 19, 197
Massachusetts, 163, 226
Matteo Benetton, 120
Matthew Emmons, 136
Maurice Yeates, 136
Median, 16, 95, 131
Melbourne, 76
MERV-13, 93
Mexico, 29, 30
Michael Fenn, 146

ABOUT THE AUTHOR

Murtaza Haider is a professor of Data Science and Real Estate Management at Ryerson University. He also serves as the research director of the Urban Analytics Institute. Professor Haider holds an adjunct professorship of Engineering at McGill University in Montreal. From 2011 to 2014, Professor Haider served as the Associate Dean of Research and Graduate Programs at the Ted Rogers School of Management.

Dr. Haider is the author of Getting Started with Data Science: Making Sense of Data with Analytics, which was published by the IBM Press/Pearson in 2016. Professor Haider's research interests include business analytics, data science, forecasting housing market dynamics, transport/ infrastructure/ urban planning, and human development in Canada and South Asia.

Professor Haider is a syndicated columnist with Post Media. His weekly column on real estate markets appears nationally in *The Financial Post* and local newspapers including *Ottawa Citizen*, *Vancouver Sun*, *Calgary Herald*, *Edmonton Sun*, and *Montreal Gazette*. He also writes occasionally on urban development challenges for *The Globe and Mail* and *The Toronto Star*.

Murtaza Haider holds a Masters in transport engineering and planning and a Ph.D. in Civil Engineering (Urban Systems Analysis) from the University of Toronto.

Manufactured by Amazon.ca
Bolton, ON